ACCLAIM FOR RICHARD HOLMES'
## Sidetracks

"Holmes is quite simply the best literary biographer now active in English." —*The New Criterion*

"More than anyone else in our time, Holmes has stressed the *art* of biography. . . . Holmes' prose is lyrical, ingratiating, romantic." —*The Washington Post*

"Now and again a biographer comes along who transmits in-depth scholarship through an ingratiating style, who approaches the writing of a life as an opportunity for self-expression, even for literary distinction. Don't we return to James Boswell and Lytton Strachey largely for the urbane pleasure of their company? Certainly I do, just as I eagerly pick up anything by Holmes. . . . When he starts to write, the sentences are those of an artist rather than an academic." —Michael Dirda, *The Wilson Quarterly*

"These pieces undeniably confirm why Holmes has been setting new and challenging standards for how biographers approach their subjects, and they make for glorious reading indeed." —*Publishers Weekly* (starred review)

"Wonderful. . . . It is fascinating to watch Mr. Holmes' interest develop as his life changes, from the intense youth to the contented, mature biographer." —*The Washington Times*

## ALSO BY RICHARD HOLMES

*One for Sorrow*
(poems)

*Shelley: The Pursuit*

*Gautier: My Fantoms*
(translations)

*Shelley on Love*

*Coleridge*

*Footsteps: Adventures of a Romantic Biographer*

*Nerval: The Chimeras*
(with Peter Jay)

*Mary Wollstonecraft and William Godwin:*
*A Short Residence in Sweden* and *Memoirs*

*Kipling: Something of Myself*
(with Robert Hampson)

*De Feministe en de Filosoof*

*Coleridge: Early Visions, 1772–1804*

*Dr. Johnson & Mr. Savage*

*Coleridge: Selected Poems*

*The Romantic Poets and Their Circle*

*Coleridge: Darker Reflections, 1804–1834*

RICHARD HOLMES

# Sidetracks

Richard Holmes is the author of *Shelley: The Pursuit,* for which he won the Somerset Maugham Award; *Footsteps: Adventures of a Romantic Biographer,* which Michael Holroyd described as "a modern masterpiece"; and *Coleridge: Early Visions,* the highly acclaimed winner of the 1989 Whitbread Book of the Year Prize. *Dr. Johnson & Mr. Savage* received the James Tait Black Award and *Coleridge: Darker Reflections* was a National Book Critics Circle Award finalist. Holmes is a Fellow of the Royal Society of Literature and was made an OBE in 1992. In 2001 he was appointed the first Professor of Biographical Studies at the University of East Anglia. He lives in London and Norfolk, with novelist Rose Tremain.

# SIDETRACKS

*Explorations of a Romantic Biographer*

# RICHARD HOLMES

VINTAGE BOOKS
A DIVISION OF RANDOM HOUSE, INC.
NEW YORK

To my old friend and advisor
Peter Janson-Smith
through thick and *beastly thin*

FIRST VINTAGE BOOKS EDITION, DECEMBER 2001

*Copyright © 2000 by Richard Holmes*

The Library of Congress has cataloged the Pantheon edition as follows:
Holmes, Richard, 1945–
Sidetracks : explorations of a romantic biographer / Richard Holmes.
p.     cm.
Includes index.
ISBN: 0-679-43846-7
1. Holmes, Richard, 1945– .   2. Authors, English—Biography—History
and criticism.   3. Authors—Biography—History and criticism.
4. Biographers—Great Britain—Biography.   5. Biography as a
literary form.   6. Romanticism.   I. Title.
PR6058.0455 Z464 2000   820.9—dc21   00-033984

**Vintage ISBN: 0-679-75771-6**

www.vintagebooks.com

Printed in the United States of America
10   9   8   7   6   5   4   3   2   1

# Contents

*Prologue*

WE WERE AT a café table, under the plane trees, far in the south, with the evening light flowing away down the river. I was asking the beloved novelist those old, fascinating questions: How do you find your stories? Where do your ideas come from? When she said, with that sudden challenging smile of hers: 'But how do you find *your* subjects; where do *they* come from?' And I answered almost without thinking, between two mouthfuls of the cold white wine: 'Down many sidetracks.' She laughed and looked out into the gathering dark. 'I think you'd better explain that,' she said. So I have tried.

This book is my attempt to explore – as well as to explain – something of these mysterious biographical pathways. (I love the French word *sentier* for a track, because it also hints at the notion of a line of smell or perfume, as in 'on the scent'.) It is a biographer's collection of short pieces, rather like a novelist's collection of short stories, but it has a theme and purpose. It is the fragmented tale of a single biographical quest, a thirty-year journey in search of the perfect Romantic subject, and the form to fit it. It is my personal casebook.

For me biography has always been a personal adventure of exploration and pursuit, a tracking. It is uncertain in its beginning, when even the first outline of a glimpsed subject may change into someone else, or become a minor role in another life, or simply fade away into the historical undergrowth. It is tantalizing in its final destination, when a completed biography invariably leaves so much else to be discovered, sometimes by other means. It is often surprising in retrospect, when previously hidden perspectives and retrospectives emerge. I conclude that no biography is ever definitive, because that is not the nature of such journeys, nor of the human heart which is their territory. Sometimes all one achieves is another point of departure. Such are the shifting themes of this collection.

Looking back I see, rather to my surprise, that I have written (or failed to write) one biography about every three or four years. This seems to be a languid, circadian rhythm that comes quite naturally to me. But during that slow, ruminative period of researching, travelling, dreaming and writing (which go on simultaneously), the journey also spreads out in many unexpected directions. It produces a great deal of material that, for one reason or another, never gets into the final book; or else erupts later as a kind of after-shock or aftermath. I suspect many biographers experience this.

Yet these wanderings from the main path, these seductive sidetracks over another part of the hill, are often the places where I have learned most about my subjects and have felt most free in their company. They also tell something about how a particular biography was brought to life. As Shakespeare's Polonius put it (a very fond and foolish old fellow), 'by indirections find directions out'.

So this book is organized, like a series of traveller's tales or informal route-maps, around the main biographical voyages I have taken over the last thirty years. All of them concern more or less Romantic themes; some of them actually produced books; others signally failed to do so – and these I am particularly attached to. I think it is sometimes supposed that biographers advance steadily and relentlessly from publication to publication, along a kind of well-signed literary motorway. Perhaps some of them do; but I am more of a rambler and botanizer myself. As a matter of record, here is a list of my major biographical subjects, with their results in brackets.

1969–70: Chatterton (an essay, no biography)
1971–74: Shelley (a biography, *Shelley: The Pursuit*)
1973–79: A Gothic Victorian (many sketches, no biography)
1975–79: Gautier and Nerval (sketches, translations, unpublished biography)
1979–80: Scott and Zelda Fitzgerald (a single sketch)
1980–85: A Romantic Traveller (sketches, finally *Footsteps*)
1986–87: William Godwin and Mary Wollstonecraft (an essay, no biography)
1982–89: Coleridge (half a biography, *Coleridge: Early Visions*)

1990–94: Johnson (a fragment of biography, *Dr Johnson &
        Mr Savage*)
1994–98: Coleridge (second half of a biography, *Coleridge:
        Darker Reflections*)
1999 . . . A Runaway Life (but that could go anywhere)

The sidetracks that arose from these main expeditions take
several, perhaps surprising forms. For I am fascinated by the many
different ways in which a 'true story' can be told. Why should the
biographer be limited to one kind of narrative voice, one kind of
discursive prose? So they include two radio-plays, several travel
pieces, a large number of character-sketches, some autobiographical fragments, some formal essays, and a very informal short story
for BBC Radio Four's 'Book at Bedtime'. All of them were written
as different ways of investigating biographical material: to see how
far certain hints and possibilities could be taken down the path,
explored and relished.

It is this love of imaginative displacement, of seeking and *snuffling* on the trail of another life, so essential to literary biography,
which I hope also unites this collection. It is the history of a
self-education, a sentimental education perhaps. It aims to record
whatever I have learned about the peculiar magic, and haunting
life-music, of this most contemporary, most lovable and perhaps
most ephemeral of forms.

To be sidetracked is, after all, to be led astray by a path or an
idea, a scent or a tune, and maybe lost for ever. But no true
biographer would mind that, if he can take a few readers with
him. To find your subject, you must in some sense lose yourself
along the way. This is my record of such departures from the
straight and narrow. I hope it will encourage others to turn aside,
to *reconnaître*, to stray purposefully into the vast geography of the
human heart by which we come to know ourselves.

# I

# A Romantic
# Premonition

# INTRODUCTION

LOOK BACK, and the past becomes a story. The fixed shadowy shapes begin to move again, and make new patterns in the memory, some familiar, some strange. I now see that this early essay strongly reflects my own first three years in London, where I arrived from Cambridge in summer 1967, aged twenty-one. Prospects were fair, work was easy to find in those days, and I had a good circle of friends. Yet the truth was that I felt suicidally lonely and depressed for much of the time. This was not particularly unusual for a young man coming to the big city. But I was mad to write, I felt I was nothing unless I could write. The inky demon drove me night and day, and I simply could not see how he (or she) could be appeased. I am not sure that this feeling has ever left me. I think all writers, of whatever kind, must have such a demon. I believe the demon follows them in the street and ends up sitting on their graves.

I started, by luck, with a little freelance journalism. As this was the late Sixties, I was soon commissioned to write a book called 'Prodigy'. I think it was meant to be about poets, film stars and pop stars who died young. (It was the John Keats – James Dean – Janis Joplin thing.) Instead I became fascinated by the eighteenth-century poet Thomas Chatterton, and he led me back into the world of English Romanticism, and in a sense saved my life by giving it a new dimension. I took my first deliberate 'footstepping' trip down to Bristol, where he was born, and for the first time examined original manuscripts in London, where he died. I discovered the peculiar magic of historical research, and experienced that sense of imaginative displacement which intoxicates all writers. I began to live what is, I suppose, the conscious double-life of the biographer, with one foot in the present and the other continually in the past. Suddenly I had found that space in which it became possible to write: my own version of Virginia Woolf's 'room of one's own'. The essay that emerged was taken by my friend Peter Janson-Smith to the publisher Jock Murray, who astonished me by giving up half an entire issue of the *Cornhill Magazine* to it. (The magazine closed shortly thereafter.)

One of the strangest things about the essay is that it contains – in walk-on parts – almost everybody that I have subsequently written about over the next thirty years. So I now see it, in a way, as a kind of audition for my vocation as a biographer. Not me auditioning them, but vice versa: my waiting subjects checking me out. The illogical feeling that *your subjects somehow choose you* is common to many biographers.

It contains many other premonitions too, some of which I am still discovering. The path to my book on Shelley, though then invisible, has now become obvious to me. The emphasis on solitude, the extreme sense of dislocation and isolation from a normal social world, which is one enduring version of the Romantic sensibility (though capable of both comic and tragic expression), was strongly in the ascendant, and would remain with me for a long time to come. I can clearly catch a young man's voice, impatient and unreasonable with the adult world (Walpole, Johnson) that holds back a fuller understanding. But whose is the voice? Empathy is the most powerful, the most necessary, and the most deceptive, of all biographical emotions. It is instructive to look back on it, subtly at work, throwing both light and shadow into city streets which were already for me partly real, and partly imagined. The insistent rhythm of the opening paragraph was repeated, unconsciously, fifteen years later in the opening paragraph of *Footsteps*. Both end with the keyword 'eighteen', a retrospective declaration of Romantic youth. But above all in 'Chatterton', so much concerned with the dead, I first glimpsed the people and the period in history which were to become most dazzlingly alive for me.

# THOMAS CHATTERTON

## The Case Reopened

> *'For had I never known the antique lore*
> *I ne'er had ventur'd from my peaceful shore,*
> *To be the wreck of promises and hopes,*
> *A Boy of Learning, and a Bard of Tropes . . .'*
>
> CHATTERTON

> *'Oh thou, or what remains of thee,*
> *Ælla, the darlynge of futurity,*
> *Lett this mie songe bolde as thy courage be,*
> *As everlastynge to posteritie.'*
>
> ROWLEY

## 1 *'The brazen slippers alone remain'*

IN THE HIGH SUMMER of 1770, while most of genteel and literary London was refreshing itself at continental spas, picnicking on country house lawns or promenading at the seaside resorts, in an angular third-floor attic above a Holborn side-street, in a locked room littered with minutely shredded pieces of manuscript, Thomas Chatterton died in acute pain from arsenic poisoning. He did not appear to have eaten for several days, but there were traces of opium in his mouth and between his teeth. He was not yet eighteen.

In his short lifetime Chatterton had written some six hundred pages of verse, one finished and one unfinished tragedy, a burletta, and so much freelance satirical journalism that it was still being published by London editors a year after his death. His name became the centre of the most fashionable literary controversy of the decade, in which many eminent scholars, writers and littérateurs fought tempestuously to establish that Chatterton was either a prodigy of poetical genius or a cheap, adolescent forger with the habits of a delinquent. When the immediate heat of this discussion had died down, it emerged that Chatterton's achievement had been compared by many critics as second only to Shakespeare's. Coleridge drafted a long Monody to him at the age of sixteen, and spent another thirty years of his life adding to it and making corrections. The Victorians went on to dedicate wildly partisan poetry and criticism on both sides of his reputation. David Masson published a warm melodramatic novel based on his life in 1874, and Rossetti became deeply obsessed with the figure of Chatterton in the closing years of his old age. The young Meredith posed as the model of Chatterton in puce silk pantaloons for the famous painting by Henry Wallis and while the work was being executed in Chatterton's original attic room (later destroyed by fire) Meredith took the opportunity to open an affair with the painter's wife. In France Alfred de Vigny produced a High Romantic play; and this in turn became a bad Italian opera by Leoncavallo. Chatterton's works were translated into French and German, while new English editions followed each other steadily: in 1803, 1810, 1842, 1871, 1885, 1906 and 1911.

Then suddenly after the First World War the flow stopped. There have been no new editions; and with the exception of one faithful scholar, E. H. Meyerstein, there has been, until very recently indeed, almost no further critical interest. Even the *Penguin Book of English Verse* does not now acknowledge the existence of Chatterton, Thomas, in its index. Perhaps only a few lines of his remain current, with their curious haunting bitterness and their unstable dying rhythms:

> Come, with acorne-cuppe and thorne
> Drain my hertes blood away;
> Lyfe and all its good I scorn
> Daunce by night, or feast by day.
> My love is dead
> Gone to his death-bed
> All under the wyllow-tree

In all this, in the mixture of strange, contradictory, challenging and sometimes oddly depressing circumstances, Chatterton is the great example of the prodigy-figure in English poetry. Prodigy has as its root meaning something out of the run of natural affairs and occurrences, something directly counter to natural processes themselves – a wonder, an exhilaration of the spirit. There is something particularly valuable about such a figure. He is like a precedent. He is like a guarantee for the wildest human hopes, and at the same time a talisman against failure or limitation or the pressures of mediocrity. He is an outpost of the imagination. With Chatterton, it has always tended to be the completed gesture of life which produced the writing, and not the writing alone, that has exercised the deepest fascination and influence on others. Only one generation after Chatterton's death, this was already clear to William Hazlitt who gave his opinion in a long aside during his public lectures at the Surrey Institute on 'The English Poets'(1818).

'As to those who are really capable of admiring Chatterton's genius,' said Hazlitt, who knew very well that Keats was in his audience, 'I would only say that I never heard anyone speak of any of his works as if it were an old well-known favourite, and had become a faith and a religion in his mind. It is his name, his youth, and what he might have lived to have done, that excite our wonder and admiration. He has the same sort of posthumous fame that an actor of the last age has – an abstracted reputation which is independent of anything we know of his works' (Lecture VII). The comparison with the actor is good, although with fifty years of film behind us now it loses some of its force. It is also rather an intriguing comparison. Hazlitt had no illusions about the true nature of Chatterton's 'forgeries', but he still appears to have thought, unconsciously at least, in terms of the young prodigy playing out *someone else's* part. In a literary and in a psychological sense this has a deep relevance to the life that Chatterton lived, and perhaps also to the death that he is reputed to have died.

Keats, incidentally, was disappointed with Hazlitt's views, although it was almost certainly a previous lecture which kindled some real resentment against Hazlitt's treatment of the poet to whom Keats had dedicated *Endymion*. The passage was probably this one, the closing peroration from Lecture VI; it is an important attitude and seems to express an element of jealousy, that essential but honest jealousy of the critic for the poet:

> I cannot find in Chatterton's works anything so extra-
> ordinary as the age at which they were written. They
> have a facility, vigour, and knowledge, which were pro-
> digious in a boy of sixteen, but which would not have
> been so in a man of twenty. He did not show extraord-
> inary powers of genius, but extraordinary precocity. Nor
> do I believe he would have written better, had he lived.
> Great geniuses, like great kings, have too much to think
> of to kill themselves; for their mind to them also 'a
> kingdom is'. With an unaccountable power coming over
> him at an unusual age, and with the youthful confi-
> dence it inspired, he performed wonders, and was will-
> ing to set a seal on his reputation by a tragic
> catastrophe. He had done his best; and, like another
> Empedocles, threw himself into Aetna, to ensure
> immortality. The brazen slippers alone remain!

It is curious how the flourish, the joy with which Hazlitt the great Romantic critic flings off that last magnificent image to his Surrey Institute audience, effectively undermines his own case. He is responding, in spite of himself, in spite of his rational and de-liberated critical strictures, to the quality of magnificence, of exhil-aration, achieved by Chatterton's life and work as a complete entity.

But by Lecture VII Hazlitt had altered his position, or at least his tone. 'I am sorry that what I said in conclusion of the last Lecture respecting Chatterton, should have given dissatisfaction to some persons, with whom I would willingly agree on all such matters. What I meant was less to call in question Chatterton's genius, than to object to the common mode of estimating its magnitude by prematureness.' He then delicately delivers one of those republican bombshells that delighted Keats. 'Had Chatter-ton really done more, we should have thought less of him . . . who knows but he might have lived to be poet-laureate?' Yet overall his attitude remains the same, and his judgement on the prodigy-figure has a lasting and representative force, many times repeated, and especially sympathetic to the more sceptical and technical quality of appreciation almost universal today.

There is an anecdote retold in the diaries of the poet W. S. Blunt which may help to suggest the pitch, the emotional frequency, which the phenomenon of the youthful prodigy, in this case of Chatterton, is capable of reaching in the minds and imaginations of other men, and especially writers, irrespective of the lapse of time or the fluctuations of critical assessment. It concerns the Victorian lyric poet Francis Thompson. Blunt had the story in 1907 from Wilfred Meynell, who had become a close friend and mentor of Thompson's before his death in the November of that year. 'He – Thompson – used, before I knew him, to sleep at night under the Arches of Covent Garden where every quarter of an hour he was liable to be kicked awake by the police and told to move on. It was in an empty space of ground behind the Market where the gardeners threw their rubbish, that, just before, he had resolved on suicide. He then spent all his remaining pence on laudanum, one large dose, and he went there one night to take it. He had swallowed half when he felt an arm laid on his wrist, and looking up he saw Chatterton standing over him and forbidding him to drink the other half. I asked him when he had told me of it how he had known that it was Chatterton. He said "I recognised him from the pictures of him – besides, I knew that it was he before I saw him" – and I remembered at once the story of the money which arrived for Chatterton the day after his suicide' (*My Diaries*, Vol. 2, p. 191).

An illusion. A drug-induced hallucination. After all, no authentic picture of Chatterton was ever made. Yes, but it is an interesting and powerful kind of illusion, that prevents a man from taking his own life; and incidentally correctly forecasts the arrival of help – Meynell's letter to Thompson reached him the next day. Chatterton is one of those very few artistic figures – there are many more in religion and politics – who seem at times to have taken command of certain areas of the psychic landscape. Their image has been conjured up, and their presence has produced a palpable effect. It can only be described delicately, tentatively. One is not talking about ghosts, although Chatterton with his marvellous instinct for the Gothic would undoubtedly have provided a classic specimen. Shelley, in his long poem *Adonais* on the death of Keats, wrote this:

> When lofty thought
> Lifts a young heart above its mortal lair
> And love and life contend in it, for what
> Shall be its earthly doom, the dead live there
> And move like winds of light on dark and stormy air.

It is informative to read this without preconceptions about High Romantic eulogizing, but as a straight description in slightly old-fashioned language of an unusual condition of mind. The dead live there and move like winds of light on dark and stormy air. (Shelley's quality of verbal helium, the absolute clarity with which it renders and uplifts mental processes, has long required calm reassessment.)

The point is important for two reasons. First, because it suggests how the subject of Chatterton has always appealed to responses and judgements far deeper than mere literary taste. We encounter this again and again. To put it more sharply, it appeals to the recurrent need to idealize the image of others, and to interpret historical events and artistic achievements as the expression of something, by definition inexplicable, called 'genius'. It appeals to our need to reassure ourselves with the past, and to see our own desires, and perhaps even our own faces, somehow magically canonized in the pale indistinct features of the wonderfully – but safely – dead. One has to be aware of that from the outset.

Second, it is – like Hazlitt's actor comparison – suggestive of something that happened most powerfully and dramatically in Chatterton's own mind.

## 2   'To the Garret quick he flies'

Chatterton was born in Bristol in November 1752 and he never seems to have got over it. He was never reconciled to his circumstances: always he was looking for some alternative place, or alternative age. Latterly, as for Rimbaud in Charleville, the capital city began to exercise an hypnotic attraction and he staked everything on getting there and taking it by storm.

> But bred in Bristol's mercenary cell
> Condemned with want and penury to dwell,
> What generous passion can refine my line?

Chatterton's home was the small schoolhouse in Pyle Street, directly opposite the marvellous looming Gothic buttresses and tracery of St Mary Redcliff church. St Mary Redcliff dominated Pyle Street with its massive shadowy presence; morning and evening St Mary Redcliff bells would fill the rooms of the house. Chatterton's father had been the schoolmaster of the Pyle Street free-school and also sexton of St Mary Redcliff. The schoolhouse and the church were both his territory, and they both became Chatterton's. The father was by all accounts a curious man. He was a singer, and had sung officially in the Bristol Cathedral choir; but he also sang unofficially to himself on the long walks that he was noted for taking, and talked to himself as well. He was a collector and something of an antiquarian. He collected old coins and books and manuscripts, and when he became sexton of St Mary Redcliff he found a rich source of material in the hitherto neglected Muniment Room, with its many boxes and chests of papers, whose long slit window looked out over the top of the North Porch. Many of these ancient papers were transferred from the Muniment Room to the schoolhouse, and in the course of time to the attic room which was Chatterton's. These papers were the only direct link that Chatterton had with his father, who died in the summer before he was born. Chatterton also had an elder sister, who had been born out of wedlock.

For a prodigy he was a solitary child and a slow one. At seven he was still unable to read. He dawdled about the schoolhouse, and about the aisles and tombs of St Mary Redcliff.

> Thys is the manne of menne, the vision spoke,
> Then belle for Evensonge my senses woke.

But there was already another side to his character. His sister, later Mrs Newton, recalled eight years after his death: 'My brother very early discovered a thirst for pre-eminence. I remember, before he was five years old, he would always preside over his playmates as their master, and they his hired servants.' The Victorian biographers tell the most winsome of the childhood anecdotes to illustrate that same 'thirst for pre-eminence'. At the age of five he was apparently offered a Delft cup as a present to be decorated with 'a lyon rampant'. But instead Chatterton asked that the picture should represent an angel with a trumpet. When asked why, he replied airily – 'to blow his name about'. The story is nice, but may be apocryphal; the temperament it illustrates is certainly authentic. In a fatherless household, one is not surprised. A Bristol friend remembered him at a later stage, as a schoolboy and legal apprentice: 'That vanity, and an inordinate thirst after praise, eminently distinguished Chatterton, all who knew him will readily admit. From a long and intimate acquaintance with him, I venture to assert, that from the date of his first poetical attempt, until the final period of his departure from Bristol, he never wrote any piece, however trifling in its nature, and even unworthy of himself, but he first committed it to every acquaintance he met, indiscriminately, as wishing to derive applause from productions which I am assured, were he now living, he would be heartily ashamed of . . .' (Letter from Mr Thistlethwaite to Dr Milles). There is a good deal of personal sourness and pique in this statement, and as to Chatterton communicating *all* his poems it is simply incorrect. But as a description of Chatterton's impression on friends and everyday acquaintances, the touchiness, the arrogance, the self-importance, the 'eagerness of applause even to an extreme', it has the ring of truth.

Perhaps the most convincing and also the most amusing evidence comes from a distant relative of Chatterton's, a certain Mrs Ballance, who was lodged in the same house as Chatterton when he first came to London. As a relation, she obviously tried to be neighbourly. She recalled with exasperation, 'he was as proud as Lucifer. He very soon quarrelled with her for calling him "Cousin Tommy", and asked her if she had ever heard of a poet's being called *Tommy*. But she assured him she knew nothing of poets and only wished he would not set up for a Gentleman.' Mrs Ballance added a pathetic and very human note: 'He frequently said he should settle the nation before he had done; but how could she think her poor cousin Tommy was so great a man as she now finds he was? His mother should have written word of his greatness, and then, to be sure, she would have humoured the gentleman accordingly.'

But if Chatterton's character was manifest from the start, his capabilities were not. The first important moment seems to have been when he began to read. The way any primary skill is first exercised – swimming, riding, reading – often has a decisive effect on its subsequent development. Chatterton began to read only very gradually, and then in a curious and highly significant fashion. Mrs Newton, his sister, again recalled: 'He was dull in learning, not knowing many letters at four years old, and always objected to read in a small book. He learnt the alphabet from an old Folio music-book of my father's, my mother was then tearing up for waste paper: the capitals at the beginning of the verses, I assisted in teaching him.' The importance of this earliest reading material has never been fully realized.

From the very start, literature and the medieval legacy of the St Mary Redcliff papers were identified in Chatterton's mind. And not only at an intellectual level. For Chatterton's contact with this special past, so inextricably involved with both his dead father and the earlier inhabitants, writers and artists of St Mary Redcliff, had from the beginning a solid material presence of vellum and parchment scraps which filled the little schoolhouse with their dust and oily odour and resilient crackling touch. They were a vivid familiar presence, totally uninvested with the sacred and scholarly aura which museums, glass cases, and academic pince-nez normally impart to such things. The Chatterton family were at times almost literally ankle-deep in the medieval past. We know that the mother quite casually used them for knitting patterns, or for 'waste paper' torn up presumably for fires or cleaning; and that many of the schoolhouse books were actually covered by these papers in the form of makeshift dust jackets. It was the large illuminated capitals on some of these sheets which first caught the young Chatterton's eye. Gothic and medieval scripts were his earliest acquaintance. He read the tomb inscriptions and brasses as another child reads specially edited fairy tales. His first solid piece of reading was the bristling Germanic-Gothic pages of the family's Black Letter Bible. In short, Chatterton came to literary consciousness in another world. It was Bristol, but it was late-medieval Bristol. It was the Bristol of the men like William Canynges who helped to rebuild and restore St Mary Redcliff, and of the late-medieval scholar-poets whom great men such as Canynges befriended and patronized, acting almost as a father might have done. It was above all (as it turned out), the Bristol of a brilliant poet-monk whose first name was oddly enough the same as Chatterton's; an admirer of Chaucer, an admirer of St Mary Redcliff, an intimate friend of the fatherly William Canynges, the brilliant star of the whole company of talented poets. This poet-monk's name was Thomas Rowley. But Thomas Rowley never existed. Only in Thomas Chatterton's head. From a single inscription on a tomb, Chatterton was to create this man's life, his letters, his poems, his ballades, his Tragedies, his most intimate concerns with the problems of living and literature. Thomas Rowley was everything that Thomas Chatterton desired to be. And in the most real and most disturbing sense, Thomas Rowley *was* Thomas Chatterton.

At the age of seventeen, just before he left Bristol for London, Chatterton was to write one of his most outlandish and ambivalent documents, a Will. In it, he addressed his stupid and ungenerous patrons of reality, and to one of them wrote this:

> Thy friendship never could be dear to me;
> Since all I am is opposite to thee.
> If ever obligated to thy purse
> Rowley discharges all; my first chief curse!
> For had I never known the antique lore
> I ne'er had ventur'd from my peaceful shore,
> To be the wreck of promises and hopes,
> A Boy of Learning, and a Bard of Tropes;
> But happy in my humble sphere had mov'd
> Untroubled, unsuspected, unbelov'd.

Of course, it asserts nothing except Rowley's primary importance and responsibility. The whole piece is shot through with a bitter ironic flare characteristic of Chatterton. Those last three epithets are much more curious than they seem at first sight; and the idea that Chatterton would ever conceivably have been 'happy in his humble sphere' is laughable. Chatterton must have laughed as he wrote it. But if so, the laughter must have sounded harsh.

The creation of Rowley is one of the most extraordinary events in English literature. It is not easily accounted for. A body of scholars stood out against it for some thirty years after Chatterton's death. Chatterton's own acquaintances – who invariably and incorrectly thought that they were his *intimates*, a notable point – were adamant almost to a man. One Mr T. Cary writing in 1776: 'Not having any taste for ancient poetry, I do not recollect his ever having shewn them to me; but that he often mentioned them, at an age, when (great as his capacity was) I am convinced he was incapable of writing them himself, I am very clear in, and confess it to be astonishing, how any person, knowing these circumstances, can entertain even a shadow of a doubt of their being the works of Rowley.' (Interestingly, Cary then adds a sentence which reveals in a flash his deep but unconscious sense of the ambiguity of identity in Chatterton: 'Of this I am very certain, that if they are not Rowley's, they are not Chatterton's.') Even in this present age, when every sixth-former is drilled with Ezra Pound's idea of the poetic *persona* and T. S. Eliot's concept of impersonality and the 'objective correlative', the Rowley–Chatterton relationship remains as extraordinary and mysterious as ever. Though W. P. Ker in *The Cambridge History of English Literature* has a perceptive observation: 'Nothing in Chatterton's life is more wonderful than his impersonality; he does not make poetry out of his pains or sorrows, and when he is composing verse, he seems to have escaped from himself.' That last phrase can be taken more literally than Ker meant.

The crucial fact about the creation of Rowley is that Rowley grew as Chatterton grew. In 1760, when Chatterton was eight, he was sent to board at Colston Hall, a local charity school, and he remained there until he was fifteen. Colston served bad food and bad education. Its curriculum ran to the Three Rs only, with nothing remotely scientific or classical. It is said that owing to the combination of too much free time and too little free space, the pupils usually slept for ten or twelve hours a day, and this generally with two or three of them to a single bed. It makes one speculate on what strange world of half-waking companionship this unusual situation fostered. The single most suggestive fact, however, concerns a tiny detail of the Colston Hall uniform which went unnoticed for almost a century. The Colston Hall charity boys were required to wear a blue gowned overall belted at the waist, and to have their hair cut short and *tonsured*, like so many little novices in a monastery. The adolescent Chatterton must indeed have felt a curiously vivid and physical identity with his poet-monk

Thomas Rowley: a presence as yet unnamed, but nevertheless swiftly growing now from its childhood origins in the Muniment Room with its high slit windows above the North Porch of St Mary Redcliff.

One of Chatterton's earlier recorded poems has a striking bearing on the psychology of this long moment of wonderful but also sinister gestation. It was written in 1763 when he was eleven. It is not a so-called Rowley poem, but his first excursion into the snappy, efficient, satirical style currently fashionable: all couplets and nudges. From the start, Chatterton could turn this out effortlessly. The poem is called 'Sly Dick'. It purports to tell of someone who receives a visitation from the Devil during the night, which informs him how he may make his fortune – dishonestly of course. How conscious Chatterton was of the underlying drama of this little piece of doggerel – particularly in its terms of night-visitation, temptation, hidden location of fortune, and secretive manner of exploitation – the reader may judge for himself.

> Sharp was the frost, the wind was high
> And sparkling Stars bedeckt the Sky,
> Sly Dick in arts of cunning skill'd,
> Whose Rapine all his pockets fill'd,
> Had laid him down to take his rest
> And soothe with sleep his anxious breast.
> 'Twas thus a dark infernal sprite
> A native of the blackest Night,
> Portending mischief to devise
> Upon Sly Dick he cast his eyes;
> Then strait descends the infernal sprite,
> And in his chamber does alight:
> In vision he before him stands,
> And his attention he commands.
>
> Thus spake the sprite – Hearken my friend,
> And to my counsels now attend.
> Within the Garret's spacious dome
> There lies a well stor'd wealthy room.
> Well stor'd with cloth and stockings too,
> Which I suppose will do for you . . .
>
> When in the morn with thoughts erect
> Sly Dick did on his dream reflect,

> Why faith, thinks he, 'tis something too,
> It might – perhaps – it might – be true
> I'll go and see – away he hies,
> And to the Garret quick he flies,
> Enters the room, cuts up the clothes
> And after that reeves up the hose:
> Then of the cloth he purses made,
> Purses to hold his filching trade.

The true identity of the 'Garret's spacious dome', and the store of cloth which he 'cuts up' to make his fortune, flash up at one instantly. They are of course the Muniment Room and the ancient papers within it. Without leaning on this little piece too much, it seems likely that the eleven-year-old Chatterton at some level or other was powerfully aware of the peculiar forces now gathering in and around him ready for his disposal. They had not yet taken the shape of Rowley. But already he was deeply divided as to whether it would be for the best or for the worst. His second early poem, 'Apostate Will', about a Methodist preacher who turns High Anglican when a convenient place is offered, contains a similar sense of a 'filching trade', and also that characteristic feeling of ambivalent identity which is so marked in Chatterton and the nature of his creative gift. (Both poems also have strong elements of childish plagiarism, relating to fables by John Gay.)

Strictly speaking, this is to anticipate. The first piece of 'medieval' writing was not actually made public by Chatterton until he was fifteen and had left school; and then, in answer to inquiries, he was to say – defending his 'originals' from first to last – that he had only recently discovered such great treasures in his mother's house. But it seems unquestionable that Rowley and the world of Rowley's fifteenth-century Bristol had been maturing long and steadily in Chatterton's mind and imagination. Colston Hall, built on the site of the medieval Priory of St Augustine's Back, was always remembered favourably by him in this connection. In his 'Will' he adopts the satiric medieval practice, used notably by François Villon, of bequeathing his better qualities (such as Modesty) to the various public figures who are most in need of them. His 'disinterestedness' is bequeathed as follows, in a wry passage which connects Rowley and Colston Hall: 'Item ... To Bristol all my spirit and disinterestedness, parcels of goods unknown on her quay since the days of Canning and Rowley! 'Tis true a charitable Gentleman, one Mr Colston, smuggled a considerable quantity of it, but it being proved that he was Papist, the Worshipful Society of Aldermen endeavoured to throttle him with the Oath of Allegiance.' Chatterton rarely had anything good to say for a modern institution of Bristol, and when he does, it is remarkable.

Colston served him in two ways. First by providing an embryo group of friends, or at least acquaintances, in whom he could begin to satisfy his need for notice and applause. And second, in failing to weigh his mind down with any academic material of the depressing kind which such establishments are formally designed to provide, but rather allowing him freedom to pursue his own private and increasingly idiosyncratic reading and research. His sister, Mrs Newton: 'About his tenth year he began (with the trifle my mother allowed him for pocket-money) to hire books from the circulating library ... Between his eleventh and twelfth year, he wrote a catalogue of the books he had read, to the number of seventy: History and Divinity were the chief subjects. At twelve he was confirmed by the Bishop ... Soon after this, in the week he was door-keeper (at Colston), he made some verses on the last day, I think about eighteen lines; paraphrased the ninth chapter of Job; and not long after, some chapters in Isaiah. He had been gloomy from the time he began to learn, but we remarked he was more cheerful after he began to write poetry. Some satirical pieces we saw soon after.' Now he was started.

Chatterton left Colston some time in the winter of 1766, or the spring of 1767; at any rate when he had turned fourteen. Before that time had come, a number of events occurred whose significance was great but indirect. He formed a close friendship with a boy somewhat older than himself, Thomas Phillips. The relationship was to be tragically short, but Phillips was one of those invaluable personalities, a catalyst. A school-friend gave this typically portentous picture: 'The poetical attempts of Phillips had excited a kind of literary emulation amongst the elder classes of the scholars; the love of fame animated their bosoms, and a variety of competitors appeared to dispute the laurel with him.' This helped; it was the first materialization of Chatterton's company of poets. Related to it, the death of the brilliant contemporary satirist, Charles Churchill, who had gone to visit Wilkes (exiled in Boulogne on account of the notorious No. 45 of the *North Briton*), served to give the young writers both a literary and political martyr. Churchill died in 1764. In the following year there was a notable publishing event, the appearance in three duodecimo volumes of Percy's celebrated *Reliques of Ancient English Poetry*. These certainly came into Chatterton's hands, one of the primary texts of the Romantic revival. So the hidden medieval world was nourished as well.

When Chatterton left Colston, he was extremely lucky to be apprenticed to a Bristol attorney, John Lambert Esq. He took up the job in July 1767. It was a remarkable success for an ex-Colston boy; but in practice it involved mere clerical copying and drudgery, and Chatterton did not find himself occupied fully for more than two or three hours a day. He continued to haunt the circulating libraries; he took to walking certain young ladies on the green; and most important of all, he began to take old St Mary Redcliff papers and parchments with him to work. Friends referred to vague 'copying' and 'transcribing' processes. He covered many parchment scraps with his own version of medieval script. He became fascinated by architecture and heraldry and the business of family trees. These subjects also fascinated Thomas Rowley. For Rowley now existed.

After such a long gestation, things moved quickly. The main external events were as follows. In July 1768, the old bridge across the river Avon was replaced by a new one, and Chatterton, making his first of many bids for fame, sent a fictitious account of the opening of the original bridge, purporting to have been drawn from a medieval manuscript, to Felix Farley's *Journal*. The *Journal* was the local Bristol magazine and gossip column, and the publication of his contribution soon brought two Bristol littérateurs, George Catcott and William Barrett, snuffling on to the young man's trail. Catcott and Barrett are two wholly comic figures, part fools and part villains, who stumble through this period of Chatterton's career as if Laurel and Hardy had tried to organize the Fourth Act of *Hamlet*. For the next eighteen months they pose as Chatterton's patrons, lending him books and showing him off to their friends at numerous little soirées, while encouraging him to bring forth a stream of letters, ballads, elegies and dramatic poetry, all also purporting to be medieval: notably the work of the fifteenth-century writers who surrounded William Canynges in Bristol, and above all of the poet-monk and intimate of Canynges – Thomas Rowley. (Barrett was writing a History of Bristol, and for him Chatterton conveniently produced descriptions of medieval painting and architecture, grotesque family trees, and gorgeous examples of local heraldic devices – all spurious.)

One of the finest of the early Rowley productions was this fragment which praised St Mary Redcliff and its great restorer William Canynges. It is of particular interest in that it performs a strange transmutation of the 'Sly Dick' poem; it is a vision and a supernatural command, but this time the opposite of Satanic. Moreover, in using the same short four-stress line and rhyming couplets, it yet manages to produce a simplicity quite literally worlds away from 'Sly Dick's' satiric jingle. 'Onn Oure Ladies Chyrche' by Thomas Rowley –

> As on a hille one eve sittinge,
> At oure Ladies Chyrche muche wonderinge,
> The cunninge handieworke so fine
> Han well nighe dazzeled mine eyne.
> Quod I: some cunninge fairy hande
> Yreer'd this chapelle in this lande;
> Full well I wot, so fine a sighte
> Was n'ere yreer'd of mortal wighte.
> Quod Truth: thou lackest knowledgynge;
> Thou forsooth ne wotteth of the thinge.
> A Rev'rend Fadre, William Canynge hight [called]
> Yreered up this chapelle bright;
> And eke another in the Towne
> Where glassie bubblinge Trymme doth roun.
> Quod I: ne doubt for all he's given
> His soule will certes goe to heaven.
> Yea, quod Truth, then go thou home
> And see thou do as he hath done.
> Quod I: I doubte, that can ne be,
> I have ne gotten markes three.
> Quod Truth: as thou hast got, give almes-deeds so:
> Canynges and Gaunts could do ne moe.

This and many other small pieces, together with the brilliant narrative ballad 'The Death of Sir Charles Bawdin', the two poetic tragedies 'Godwyn' and especially 'Æella' (of which the famous and beautiful Minstrel's Song is a mere chorus), and numerous Epistles, Prologues and Songs, were all accepted blandly and beamingly by Catcott and Barrett who never dreamed of looking a gift-horse let alone a prodigy in the mouth; they calmly accepted everything as genuine curios and antiquities pouring forth in a gratuitous flood at their feet, as if young Chatterton were the keeper of some magic casket of inexhaustible delights. It never seemed to cross their minds that beauty is the most terrible and merciless of masters. Mrs Newton: 'He was introduced to Mr Barrett and Mr Catcott; his ambitions increased daily. His spirits were rather uneven, sometimes so gloom'd, that for many days together he would say but very little, and that by constraint. When in spirits, he would enjoy his rising fame; confident of advancements, he would promise my mother and me should be partakers of his success ... About this time he wrote several satirical poems, one in the papers, on Mr Catcott's putting the pewter plates in St Nicholas towers. He began to be universally known among the young men. He had many cap acquaintances, but I am confident few intimates.' 'Many cap acquaintances' is apt. The role of the satirical poetry was now becoming obvious; it kept him on balance in a situation fluctuating violently between tragedy and farce which only an English provincial city with its mixture of greed, pomposity and eloquent mediocrity could ever have provided.

When occasionally Chatterton was asked to exhibit his 'originals', he either prevaricated successfully or else forged with excruciating crudeness (forty-two scraps still survive in the British Museum) practically illegible parchments which he then aged with ochre, candle-flame, glue, varnish, or plain floor-dirt. Catcott and Barrett, the redoubtable double, stored them away without a murmur. At the same time they judiciously criticized his public forays into the local exchange of satirical verses. And had their noses, or rather their ears, nearly bitten off for it –

> No more, dear Smith, the hackney'd Tale renew:
> I own their censure, I approve it too.
> For how can Idiots, destitute of thought,
> Conceive, or estimate, but as they're taught?

> Say, can the satirising Pen of Shears,
> Exalt his name, or mutilate his ears?
> None, but a Lawrence, can adorn his Lays,
> Who in a quart of Claret drinks his praise.

This poisonous piece, which continues for some hundred lines
and is one among many, is gently accompanied by the following:
'Mr Catcott will be pleased to observe that I admire many things
in his learned Remarks. This poem is an innocent effort of poetical
vengeance, as Mr Catcott has done me the honour to criticise my
Trifles.'

At the same time, Chatterton was also writing this, for his own
private satisfaction:

> Since we can die but once, what matters it,
> If rope or garter, poison, pistol, sword,
> Slow-wasting sickness or the sudden burst
> Of valve arterial in the noble parts
> Curtail the miseries of human life?
> Tho' varied is the Cause, the Effect's the same:
> All to one common Dissolution tends.

And yet, all the while, the tonsured figure of Thomas Rowley
was walking through the streets of Bristol or brooding by the
apprentice's chair in the office of John Lambert. Through Rowley's eyes the scorn and enmity of authority, and the imminent
threat of death, were transmuted. They assumed a bold narrative
line which gloried in the simplicity of the issues at stake, and, as
in 'The Death of Sir Charles Bawdin', marched forward in that
hypnotic pageantry of primal emotions which the medieval ballad
traditionally invokes:

> King Edward's soule rush'd to his face,
> He turned his hedde away,
> And to his broder Gloucester
> He thus did speke and say:

> 'To him that so-much-dreaded Death
> Ne ghastlie terrors bringe,
> Behold the manne! He spake the truth
> He's greater thanne a Kinge!'

> 'So let him die!' Duke Richard sayde;
> 'And may echone our foes

Bend down they're neckes to bloudie axe
And feede the carrion crowes.'

And now the horses gentlie drewe
Sir Charles up the highe hille;
The axe did glyster in the sunne,
His precious bloode to spille.

It was Coleridge, the great admirer of Chatterton, who wrote *The Rime of the Ancient Mariner* some twenty years later.

Chatterton tried other outlets. He sent a copy of an 'original' piece of a medieval painting catalogue to Horace Walpole in London. After an exchange of correspondence, Walpole somewhat callously rebuffed the young poet on the grounds that his material seemed suspect. Walpole, who had recently achieved a *succès de scandale* with his faked *Castle of Otranto*, should have known better. He suffered for it later. Chatterton had more success with the London publisher Dodsley of Pall Mall; and in May of 1769 he even managed to place one of his 'medieval' Eclogues in the newly founded *Town and Country* magazine. It made him increasingly restless. He chafed at Lambert's office. He flung out extended satires with titles like 'The Whore of Babylon' and shocked many Bristol worthies by his bitter and scurrilous attacks. He took to producing execrable love-poetry, elephantine in its sub-Miltonic ornament, for his friends – his cap acquaintances – to give to their current amours. One can imagine how choicely it amused him. Possibly he had an affair himself. There was a certain Miss Ramsey. But time seemed to be running out. In the late summer of 1769, two of his intimates died. The first was Thomas Phillips, the extent of whose contribution and support we shall never know. Chatterton wrote a long elegy to him, but the pain was too close, and for the most part it is numb. There is one place, however, where a moment of intense atmospheric and visual sharpness breaks through, presaging Chatterton's final achievement in the amazing 'African Eclogues' he was to write in the last weeks in London. The passage describes the shuffling figure of Winter who carries the frozen landscape about his shoulders like a cloak; perhaps also it describes a final vision of Phillips; or even of that other, inward Thomas, Thomas Rowley who was so blasted by the chill reception of a modern and indifferent Bristol:

> Pale rugged Winter bending o'er his tread,
> His grizzled hair bedropt with icy dew;
> His eyes, a dusky light congeal'd and dead,
> His robe, a tinge of bright etherial blue.
>
> His train a motley'd sanguine sable cloud,
> He limps along the russet dreary moor,
> Whilst rising whirlwinds, blasting keen and loud,
> Roll the white surges to the sounding shore.

The other friend was Peter Smith. He committed suicide.

Chatterton sat out the winter of 1769–70. Now he was seventeen. In April he made his bid for London, propelled by a moment of crisis which seems to have been partly stage-managed and partly genuine. As ever, the ambivalent mixture. 'Between 11 and 2 o'clock' on the evening of Saturday April the 14th, 'in the utmost distress of mind' Chatterton dashed off his 'Will' containing both verse and prose, with the clear indication that he intended to commit suicide: 'If after my death which will happen tomorrow night before eight o'clock, being the Feast of the Resurrection, the Coroner and Jury bring it in Lunacy, I will and direct that Paul Farr Esq and Mr John Flower, at their joint expense, cause my body to be interred in the Tomb of my Father's . . .' This document was discovered by John Lambert on his clerk's desk, and Chatterton was hastily hunted out, appeased, and released from his articles with the attorney, thus freeing him from all obligations in Bristol. Neither Lambert nor anyone else appears to have picked up the element of angry satire and pure youthful outrage which so clearly motivated Chatterton's writing: 'This is the last Will and Testament of me Thomas Chatterton, of the city of Bristol; being sound in body, or it is the fault of my last Surgeon; the soundness of my mind, the Coroner and Jury are to be judges of, desiring them to take notice, that the most perfect Masters of Human Nature in Bristol distinguish me by the title of the Mad Genius; therefore, if I do a mad action, it is conformable to every action of my life, which savour'd of insanity.' Chatterton unfurls the idea of insanity like a battle flag: he shakes it under the nose of his elders, slyly mocking their own provincial limitations, their own humdrum eighteenth-century commercial notions of 'Human Nature'. One recognizes a quality of icily controlled desperation. 'Insanity' was also his flag of freedom. Released from Lambert's drudgery, his copy of 'Æella' sold to the obliging Cat-cott for a few paltry guineas, leave taken of his many cap acquaint-ances and firm promises of success made to his mother and sister, Chatterton caught the Bristol stage and journeyed up to the capi-tal in a snow-storm.

The last four months of Chatterton's life, those spent in London between the end of April and the end of August 1770, are the most closely documented of all, with some dozen extant letters of his to Bristol, and the material accumulated by Herbert Croft and published in *Love and Madness* (1780), from interviews with Chatterton's landladies and fellow lodgers. The many essays and quirky 'character' tales which he contributed at this time to London journals also throw a vivid though oblique light on his changing fortunes. His two extraordinary 'African Eclogues', with their unique sense of tropical sweltering claustrophobia and almost hallucinogenic visions of tribal violence, are dated in May and June. And the last and greatest Rowley poem, 'The Excelente Balade of Charitie', belongs with certainty to the very end. The picture forms a coherent dramatic whole, though with a number of poignant and tragic omissions. It is the eye of the myth inherited, and then misinterpreted, by the Romantics.

The remaining chronology is simple. Chatterton first stays near relations in Shoreditch (the helpful Mrs Ballance); later, in June, he moves to seedier lodgings in Brooke Street, Holborn. He sells a Burletta to the Marylebone Gardens for five guineas, but it is not performed. He catches a 'cold', then apparently gets better. He writes songs, more journalism, works all night but earns noth-ing. His landlady offers him meals. He writes to Barrett that he wants to become a ship's surgeon. He has conversations with Mr Cross, the corner chemist. He appears hungry; people see him less frequently. On the 25th of August 1770 his door is broken open and, in the words of the Coroner, he is found 'to have swallowed arsenic in water, on the 24th of August, and died in consequence thereof, the next day'. Barrett's account is as follows: 'He took a large dose of opium, some of which was picked out from between his teeth after death, and he was found the next morning, a most horrid spectacle, with limbs and features dis-torted as after convulsions, a frightful and ghastly corpse. Such was the horrible catastrophe of T. Chatterton, the producer of Rowley and his poems to the world.' At the end he even confused the surgeons.

## 3 *'The Muses have no Credit here'*

Yet that was nothing as compared with the confusion of the London literati. The first of 'Rowley's Poems' appeared in an anonymous pirated edition of 1772, price half-a-crown; and five years later in 1777 the first major and authoritative collection appeared with over 300 pages of poems and a scholarly Introduction by Mr Tyrwhitt: 'Poems, Supposed to have been written at Bristol, by Thomas Rowley'. Thereafter a steady flow of new editions, new Commentaries, new Appendices and Remarks and Observations set up something like a Chatterton Industry. (He even became voguish – 'Chatterton handkerchiefs' were sold in the street as ladies' favours.) The confusion arose initially because the literary detection and polemics on the 'Rowley or Chatterton' issue rapidly became the prime aspect of the Chatterton affair. Very few writers attempted to make any estimate of the value of the poems themselves; almost no one considered the impact of Chatterton's mixture of Gothic and simplistic styles and material on the hard, intricate, neo-classic sheen of contemporary verse; and no one at all realized the immense symbolic potential such a prodigy-poet, such a miracle of youth and 'inspiration' and inward, hidden creativity, would give to the later poets and theorists of the Romantic revolution. They were limited to their urbane and London-centred concepts of poetry, and they did not see what had happened. They did not see that already in Chatterton the eighteenth-century 'cool' intellect had been disestablished in favour of remote landscapes and distant provincial tones – the West Country, and shortly Cumberland, the Lowlands of Scotland, Northamptonshire (Coleridge, Wordsworth, Burns, Clare), and ultimately Italy and Greece (Keats, Shelley, Byron, Landor, Browning). This was later to be summed up in the feeling that went about among the poets that London, which had received and nourished Dryden, Pope and Johnson, had rejected and murdered

Chatterton. London had turned her face away. The poets never really trusted London again until the 1890s, when gangling and fragile men like Ernest Dowson and Lionel Johnson began to woo her once more in an effete but insistent manner, telling her that she was as beautiful and mysterious as Paris after all, and drinking themselves stupid in her dingier bars.

The greatest critics of the time were deeply perplexed. Chatterton had broken the rules. He was too young. He was dishonest. He was a provincial. Worst of all, he was 'uneducated', lower class, a charity-school boy and an attorney's clerk. The matter was impossible. In their judgements of his work, they found they were having to take into account both his circumstances and his youth, and this galled them because it was highly irregular and had nothing to do with the accepted neo-classical standards of aesthetic achievement. Indeed, their position is curiously close to the exclusive aesthetic orthodoxy of criticism today.

Thus Dr Johnson is recorded in 1776 by Anna Seward in one of his inimitable peremptory outbursts: 'Pho, child! Don't talk to me of the powers of a vulgar uneducated stripling. He may be another Stephen Duck. It may be extraordinary to do such things as he did, with means so slender; – but what did Stephen Duck do, what could Chatterton do, which, abstracted from the recollection of his situation, can be worth the attention of Learning and Taste? Neither of them had opportunities of enlarging their stock of ideas. No man can coin guineas, but in proportion as he has gold.' The last remark somehow makes one wince: it had a tragic and literal application to Chatterton's case, and the droptic Doctor – who had himself started out as a local schoolmaster – should have had more feeling than to use it. The ideals of 'Learning and Taste' take on a sharply elitist and self-complacent quality in this context; though they are powerful enough elsewhere. Most important, however, is the underlying argument: that something called 'genius' cannot be produced out of a hat – it requires a special *milieu* and a special training in which the 'stock of ideas' can be enlarged. These Chatterton did not, in the Doctor's opinion, have; and hence, gold could not be coined from air. Johnson did in fact visit Chatterton's birthplace, and it would be fascinating to know just how large a range of 'ideas' he imagined could be absorbed there, and just what his impressions of the *milieu* were.

At any rate, worthy of the attention of Learning and Taste it emphatically was *not*. Johnson's opinion is still a representative one.

The opinion of Thomas Warton, poet laureate and equally weighty judgement, also implicitly condemned Chatterton for his lack of maturity and of 'correct' training and situation. Nevertheless, Warton's attitude in the second edition of his monumental *History of English Poetry* (1776) is strikingly different to Johnson's in that he at least appreciated how remarkably Chatterton *had* broken the rules and dazzled normal expectation: 'Chatterton', he surmised, 'will appear to have been a singular instance of prematurity of abilities: to have acquired a store of general information far exceeding his years, and to have possessed that comprehension of mind, and activity of understanding, which predominated over his situation in life and his opportunities of instruction.' In fact this is a judgement of an altogether different calibre, for in that slightly nebulous phrase – 'the comprehension of mind, and activity of understanding' – Warton is genuinely trying to reach for some (ultimately Romantic) concept of *innate* imaginative ability by which Chatterton could have reached out beyond his immediate limitations. All the same, Warton was no Lakelander but had the moral bottom of his age. He disapproved. In his final summary, he says this: 'He was an adventurer, a professed hireling in the trade of literature, full of projects and inventions, artful, enterprising, unprincipled, indigent, and compelled to subsist by expedients.' This was the same Chatterton that Keats was to call a 'flow'ret', blasted by cruel winds.

But fundamentally these opinions lack any awareness of the extraordinary *dual relationship* that Chatterton developed and acted out with his surroundings and native city, Bristol. For Bristol, in the present, was the focus for all his outrage and contempt; while Bristol, in the late-medieval past, was the projection of everything he loved and desired and imagined.

Historically, Chatterton's Bristol of the 1760s was the second city in the kingdom, renowned – as say Birmingham is today – for its raw mercantile spirit, seething with new commercial enterprises; it was a city dominated by the power of local trading interests, and famed for its street riots, its civic pageants, its rowdy bought elections. There was a continuous cycle of demolition and new building, and the population was around 45,000 and increasing. The first recorded lock-out in England occurred in Bristol in 1762; and guild festivals, burnings in effigy of politicians and prize-fighting were all popular pastimes. Many of the streets were still unnavigably narrow, and goods traffic was often restricted to the same horse-drawn sleds which pulled Sir Charles Bawdin to his execution; now, however, they moved at high and unceremonious pace. Many shop doors and windows were hung with offensive advertisement sheets and boards; and one visitor complained that every single shop-boy seemed to be wearing silk stockings. Pope described it distastefully as 'if Wapping and Southwark were ten times as big, or all their people ran into London'. The poet Richard Savage – who died there in misery and penury – apotheosed it as a city of

> Upstarts and mushrooms, proud relentless hearts,
> Thou blank of Sciences, thou dearth of Arts!

Living in such a city, it seems even more remarkable that Chatterton should have spent his time engrossed in old documents, or mooning round the shadowy vaulted nave of St Mary Redcliff reading the brasses, or gazing vacantly at the then blunted spire from nearby Temple Meads. But that, we know, is what he did.

A particularly vivid account was taken by Dr Milles from William Smith, a Colston Hall friend, and brother of the Peter Smith who committed suicide. 'Chatterton was very fond of walking in the fields,' he recorded, 'and particularly in Redcliffe meadows; of talking with (Smith) about these MSS and reading them to him: "You and I" (says he) "will take a walk in Redcliff meadow, I have got the cleverest thing for you that ever was: it is worth half a crown to have a sight of it only, and to hear me read it to you." He would then produce and read the parchment. He used to fix his eyes in a kind of reverie on Redcliff church, and say "this steeple was once burnt by lightning; this was the place where they formerly acted plays"' (Dr Milles, *Rowley*, 1782). Chatterton's ability to bring to life and dramatize the inanimate remnants of the past, even to display them to his friends as something still magically active in the present, is an essential element in the imagination which dramatized itself as Thomas Rowley. In this, St Mary Redcliff is a central feature, a palpable proof of both historical and psychological continuity. In these last two stanzas of Rowley's second poem 'Onn Oure Ladies Chyrche', one can see exactly how Chatterton brings the stone to life:

> Thou seest this mastrie of a human hand,
> The pride of Bristowe and the Westerne lande,
> Yet is the Builders vertues much moe greate
> Greater than can by Rowlies pen be scande.
> Thou seest the saints and kinges in stonen state,
> That seemd with breath and human soule dispande:
> As pared to us enseem these men of slate,
> Such is great Conynge's minde when pared to God elate.
> [*dispande* – swelling, expanding
> *pared* – compared]

and then, his anger at the cheap mercantile and mediocre ambitions of his contemporary Bristolians rises also to Rowley's tongue and is there transformed:

> Well mayest thou be astounde, but viewe it well;
> Go not from hence before thou see thy fill
> And learn the Builders vertues and his name;
> Of this tall spire in every countye tell
> And with thy tale the lazing rich men shame.
> Showe how the glorious Canynge did excelle,
> How he good man a friend for kinges became
> And glorious paved at once the way to heaven and fame.

For this Chatterton has condensed a stanza from Spenser, but with a characteristic and brilliant addition of a final clarion alexandrine which gives a tone at once both proud and deeply nostalgic. It is interesting to note the word on which the last stress of the completed poem falls, and settles.

These qualities of pride, nostalgia and hard ambitious anger probably find their finest expression in Rowley's 'Ælla: A Tragycal Enterlude' with its high chivalric story-line and firmly localized Bristol setting. In the 'Song to Ælla' which forms a Prologue, Chatterton suddenly creates a beautiful and haunting melodic cadence of differing line-lengths, surging outwards and falling softly back, which is so far from the automated verse-movements of the eighteenth century, and so completely and richly Romantic in its uncircumscribed flux of emotions, that one begins to see why Keats and Rossetti held him in such special reverence. The bold Gothic effect of coloured violence is uniquely Chatterton's.

> Oh thou, or what remaines of thee,
> Ælla, the darlynge of futurity,
> Lett this mie songe bolde as thy courage be
> As everlastynge to posteritie.

> When Dacia's sons, whose haires of bloode redde hue
> Like kinge-cuppes brastinge withe the morning dew
> Arrang'd in dreare array
> Upon the lethale day
> Spred far and wide on Watchets shore;
> Then dydst thou furiouse stande
> And by thy valiante hande
> Beesprengedd all the mees withe gore.

The best comment ever made on Rowley's curious language and spelling is by the modernist Irish poet, Austin Clarke. How often only a poet understands how another poet has worked. Clarke said: 'To Chatterton, these bristling consonants and double vowels were like the harness and martial gear of medieval days. Plain words, mailed in strange spellings, might move like knights in full armour amid the resounding panoply of war.'

But for Chatterton in the other mercantile Bristol, the war was bitterly direct, and the weaponry of style was brittle and contemporary. There he did not summon up the gentle imaginative influence of Spenser, but instead he turned to radical political figures like Robert Wilkes and to Wilkes' comrade in letters, the coarse and fluent satirist, Charles Churchill. So it came about that the poet who could lie gazing in Redcliff meadows and produce the hymn to 'Oure Ladies Chyrche', could also within a few months produce 'The Whore of Babylon'. This is perhaps the liveliest of his many satirical sorties, clubbing right and left with his blunt-ended couplets. The formal subject is an attack on the Bishop of Bristol, on Lord Bute, and a good selection of King George III's more obnoxious ministers; it is packed with names and slanders and scurrilities, and lasts unflaggingly for 500 lines. Towards the end Chatterton makes a decisive attack on the attitudes he abhorred – (Rowley nodding appreciatively in the background):

> The Muses have no Credit here, and Fame
> Confines itself to the Mercantile Name;
> Then clip Imagination's wings, be wise,
> And great in Wealth, to real Greatness rise.
> Or if you must persist to sing and dream,
> Let only Panegyric be your theme:
> Make North a Chatham, cannonize his Grace,
> And get a Pension or procure a Place.
>
> Damn'd narrow Notions! tending to disgrace
> The boasted Reason of the Human Race.
> Bristol may keep her prudent Maxims still,
> But know, my saving Friends, I never will.
> The Composition of my Soul is made
> Too great for servile avaricious Trade –
> When raving in the Lunacy of Ink
> I catch the pen and publish what I think.

The final couplet gives a memorable picture, although the scholar E. H. Meyerstein discovered in 1930 how extremely closely Chatterton sometimes imitated Churchill, and that the couplet in question is a rather neat summary of three lines from Churchill's poem 'Gotham'. Just such a scholarly point brings us back to Dr Johnson's 'uneducated stripling'. It demonstrates that Chatterton had always been enlarging his stock of ideas on his own. Colston Hall or Lambert's attorney office did not really touch him. Instead, Chatterton performed his own intellectual odyssey in the circulating libraries of the town, and in the imaginative life of Thomas Rowley. 'The dead live there and move like winds of light on dark and stormy air.' His education was an intense and personal drama in which he entered as the major actor. Chatterton faced the idea of all passively received knowledge with gestures of derision that, from a sixteen-year-old, sting with a wholly modern arrogance:

> O Education, ever in the wrong,
> To thee the curses of mankind belong;
> Thou first great author of our future state,
> Chief source of our religion, passions, fate . . .
> Priestcraft, thou universal blind of all,
> Thou idol, at whose feet all nations fall,
> Father of misery, origin of sin,
> Whose first existence did with Fear begin . . .

That particular attack on priestcraft was probably picked up from the seventeenth-century radical political poet, Fulke Greville; another proof of Chatterton's range, for he must have read Greville's play *Mustapha*.

James Thistlethwaite, who has already had much to say on his school-friend's 'inordinate vanity', had even more to say on the fantastic range of Chatterton's obscure researches. (This was also to be an outstanding trait in Rimbaud, who turned to alchemy.)

> In the course of the year 1768 and 1769 – Chatterton being between 15 and 16 years old – wherein I frequently saw and conversed with C., the eccentricity of his mind, and the versatility of his disposition, seem to have been singularly displayed. One day he might be found busily employed in the study of Heraldry and English Antiquities, both of which are numbered amongst the most favourite of his pursuits; the next, discovered him deeply engaged, confounded, and perplexed, amidst the subtleties of metaphysical disquisition, or lost bewildered in the abstruse labyrinth of mathematical researches; and these in an instant again neglected and thrown aside to make room for astronomy and music, of both which sciences his knowledge was entirely confined to theory. Even physics was not without a charm to allure his imagination, and he would talk of Galen, Hippocrates, and Paracelsus, with all the confidence and familiarity of a modern empirick.

Thistlethwaite, it should be pointed out, considered himself to be something of a bard at this time, and was renowned for striding around Bristol with a pair of pistol-butts sticking out of his pockets. But allowing for his love of flourish – perfectly displayed in the peacock struttings of these sentences – the picture of Chatterton in his jackdaw enthusiasm, his frantic and undaunted explorations into whatever caught his fancy and then perhaps his imagination, is tremendously compelling. It is also recognizably provincial and oddly unbalanced. It is not what Matthew Arnold, a hundred years later, would confidently describe as 'of the centre'. It is peculiar. It contains the essential dissenting element, the waywardness, the impatience, the somehow attractive pigheadedness, of the radical innovator. It also contains the delinquent, the social outcast.

There would be something about the eyes; they would be over-bright, incalculable.

## 4 'This group of dirty-faced wits'

Chatterton was solitary in Bristol and in London, but he was never alone. In fact all his life he had the gift of striking up acquaintances; people were fascinated by him, although in the long run one gains the strong impression that most people were uneasy with him and disliked him. His letters from London to Bristol often include a positive confetti of greetings to old school-friends and ladies of the green. But they contain as well this telling aside: 'My youthful acquaintances will not take it in dudgeon that I do not write oftener to them, than I believe I shall: but as I had the happy art of pleasing in conversation, my company was often liked, where I did not like: and to continue a correspondence under such circumstances would be ridiculous.' What is telling is of course the *way* he says it.

Chatterton did not feel diffident about seeking help and interest from men of experience and influence either. When, in an ironic and somewhat posturing exchange of letters, Horace Walpole rebuffed him and his 'antiquities' in the spring of 1769, it seems clear that Walpole was considerably pinched by a sixteen-year-old addressing him as an equal, a presumption which he found 'singularly impertinent'. Chatterton later recounted the affair to an adult relation – Mr Stephens of Salisbury – in the very coolest and most casual of manners: 'Having some curious Anecdotes of Painting and Painters, I sent them to Mr Walpole, Author of "Anecdotes of Painting", "Historic Doubts" and other pieces, well known in the learned world. His answer I make bold to send you. Hence I began a Literary correspondence, which ended as most such do. I differed with him in the age of a MS. He insists on his superior talents, which is no proof of that superiority. We possibly may engage in one of the periodical publications; though I know not who will give the onset...' This was written when Chatterton was about sixteen and a half. What is quite breathtaking is the discipline and absolute outward control in retelling what had actually been his first major rejection by the London cognoscenti, a bitter blow. Most aspiring adolescents would have fallen into passionate recriminations. But Chatterton: 'which ended as most such do.'

This control, this inner hardness, is certainly paramount in his relations with his two redoubtable patrons, Catcott and Barrett; and he seems to have exercised it generally in his choice of friends and his maintenance of a deliberate distance between them and himself. A list of these friends, published in Robert Southey's edition of 1803, is particularly fascinating in that it shows their jobs and professions, giving a striking proof of Chatterton's intellectual isolation. Part of the list reads as follows: 'T. Skone, a surgeon; Thomas Cary, pipe maker; H. Kator, sugar baker; W. Smith, a player; M. Mease, vintner; Mr Clayfield, distiller; Mr William Barrett, surgeon; Mr George Catcott & Mr Burgum, pewterers and partners; The Rev. Alexander Catcott, antiquarian; John Rudhall, apothecary; Carty, woollen-draper; Hanmer, grocer; Capel, jeweller; James Thistlethwaite, stationer.' Altogether there are twenty-seven names. Further, it will be remembered that in their letters of reminiscences collected by Herbert Croft and Robert Southey, none of them – Thistlethwaite, Thomas Cary, Smith, John Rudhall – felt there was the least chance that Rowley and Chatterton could possibly have been the same.

Neither did Catcott and Barrett. But their position is a good deal more ambiguous.

> To Barrett next, he has my thanks sincere
> For all the little knowledge I had here.
> But what was knowledge? Could it here succeed?
> When scarcely twenty in the town can read.

With one exception (the Eclogue published in *The Town and Country* in May 1769), all the Rowley poems were first obtained direct from Chatterton by either Catcott or Barrett. (About the forgery aspect: only *two* of the forty-two 'original parchments' had by the British Museum after Barrett's death turned out to contain poetry; the rest were prose pieces, catalogues, heraldic designs and drawings. All the other poetry exists only in Chatterton's undisguised 'copies'.) The character and motives of these two men are intriguing. Barrett is faintly sinister. A retired surgeon living in a comfortable house on the banks of the Avon, he was immersed in local antiquarian studies for his proposed 'History of Bristol'. He thus had considerable personal interest in Chatterton's MSS, and published them in his 'History' several years after the poet's death as *bona fide* documents, although by then their validity was clearly very doubtful. It is ironic that Chatterton, and not he, should be called dishonest. There is something cold about the man, and one does not like to think of them together. 'Mr Barrett adds, that he often used to send for him from the Charity-School (which is close to his house) and differ from him on purpose to make him earnest, and to see how wonderfully his eye would strike fire, kindle, and blaze up . . .' There is also that curious reference in Chatterton's Will: 'Being sound in body, or it is the fault of my last Surgeon'. There is no proof whatsoever that this was a disguised reference to Barrett; but once it has been noticed, one cannot help wondering if it might have been. The significance is both comic and unpleasant.

Barrett's friend, George Catcott the pewterer – the only person in Bristol who ever paid Chatterton for his work – was altogether different. Chatterton called him 'Catgut'. He stammered and liked loud poetical recitation; he was impetuous and eccentric, partially humpbacked, totally unabashed. In his shop he once spat in the eye of a customer, 'because he had a propensity'. He had a mania for 'pre-eminence' and getting in the news that must have delighted Chatterton. He once transported himself across the skeleton of the new Bristol Bridge on a donkey because he desired to be recorded as the first man ever to cross over it. He also dragged himself up by a rope to the top of the new spire of St Nicholas, in order to have the honour of placing one of his pewter plates (commemorating the deed) in the unfinished stonework at the 200-foot summit. The story goes that when this had been achieved, the workmen removed the rope – 'the bargain being for going up only'. All these and many other glorious deeds, Chatterton recorded in a lively satiric poem entitled 'Happiness'. Catgut wore fistfuls of ostentatious rings, the largest being a carnelian representing the profile of Charles I. What grotesquely distorted reflections were he and Barrett of Rowley's fatherly, distinguished and beloved patron William Canynges:

Catcott is very fond of talk and fame;
His wish a perpetuity of name . . .
Incomparable Catcott, still pursue
The seeming Happiness thou hast in view;
Unfinish'd chimnies, gaping spires complete,
External fame on oval dishes beat;
Ride four-inch bridges, clouded turrets climb,
And bravely die – to live in after-time.
Horrid idea! if on rolls of fame
The twentieth century only find *thy* name . . .
On matrimonial pewter set thy hand,
Hammer with evr'y power thou canst command,
Stamp thy whole self, original as 'tis
To propagate thy whimsies, name and phyz –
Then, when the tottering spires or chimnies fall
A Catcott shall remain admir'd by all.

This sort of comic and occasional verse gives a clue to the sump of literary sub-life in which posturing poetasters like the stationer Thistlethwaite wallowed, and which Chatterton seems both to have arrogantly disdained and to have frequently utilized for his own purposes. In the June 1771 edition of *The Town and Country*, an anonymous correspondent – possibly Cary – gives a lively description of this local Bristol scene which was already coming into some national prominence as a result of Chatterton's death. (This was one of E. H. Meyerstein's most notable discoveries.) It is from this that Chatterton had made his bid to escape:

> Nor are we altogether without literary improvements, a fondness for which seems to be infused even in the lower classes of society; amongst other refinements, there is started up a set of geniuses, who call themselves a *Spouting Club* . . . These disciples of Melpomene choose to keep their scheme as private as the nature of the undertaking will admit, as many of the principal performers are still in their non-age, and servants by covenant for a certain term; but like lads of spirit, detest control, scorn the drudgery of dirty mechanics, and pant for fame in the more glorious fields of literature . . . In this group of dirty-faced wits, are three or four Authors and Poets, who have already composed, or at least *transposed*, more verses than Dryden or Pope ever

wrote, and with much more elegance and fire, as these prodigies of erudition, their fellow members, very confidently assert. The effusions of their brains are eclogues, elegies, epigrams, epitaphs, odes and satires, with the last of which they keep their neighbours in awe; for if a man by any transaction has rendered himself ridiculous, these wits immediately published his folly in a lampoon, by setting his name at the top of a halfpenny publication called A New Copy of Verses, to the great diversion of themselves and the public . . .

This is in many ways a *locus classicus*: a phenomenon like Chatterton is never isolated; however exceptional, he is the product of a definite social ambience. In the Spouting Club of 1771 one recognizes many of his characteristics continuing to exist in less extraordinary form. Moreover, it is fascinating to see that in another twenty years' time the situation in Bristol had been almost revolutionized from a literary point of view. For this became the city where Coleridge and Robert Southey planned the Pantisocratic society on the banks of the Susquehanna; and from where Southey wrote back to his London publishers – 'Bristol deserves panegyric instead of satire. I know of no mercantile place so literary.' It is bitterly ironic that Chatterton should be so largely responsible for Bristol's salvation in the eyes of the metropolis. He himself had written from London in May 1770: 'Bristol's mercenary walls were never destined to hold me – there, I was out of my element. Now I am in it – London! Good God! How superior is London to that despicable place Bristol – here is none of your little meannesses, none of your mercenary securities, which disgrace that miserable hamlet.'

Alone among Chatterton's Bristolians, perhaps one man perceived any of the poet's true qualities. We know little enough about him except that Chatterton thought him an irredeemable bigot. He was Catgut's elder brother, the Rev. Alexander Catcott. When the scholar-investigator, Michael Lort, first began to comb Bristol for evidence in the 1770s, the Rev. Catcott alone suspected the true authorship of Rowley. His penetrating comment is recorded by Lort: 'A. Catcott told me that, his suspicions being awakened, Chatterton was aware of this, and much on his guard; he had a large full grey eye, the most penetrating Mr (sic) Catcott had ever seen, and the eye of his understanding seemed no less penetrating. He would catch hints and intelligence from short conversations, which he would afterwards work up, and improve, and cover up in such a manner that an attentive and suspicious person only could trace them back to the source from whence he derived them.'

Later, Keats would call a process, very similar to this one, Negative Capability. The anvil and smithy of his brain.


## 5 'The pale children of the feeble sun'

In the only fragment of his last letter from London in August 1770 that has survived, Chatterton said: 'I am about to quit my ungrateful country. I shall exchange it for the deserts of Africa, where tigers are a thousand times more merciful than man' (quoted by Winslow, *The Anatomy of Suicide*, 1840). One thinks of Rimbaud.

Yet in these last four months, it becomes increasingly difficult to take any of Chatterton's own words literally. His letters home are full of successes that never materialized. The sweltering heat of the narrow streets in summer along which he plodded, from editor to editor, seems to have filled his head with strange delusions and tropical visions. Africa, its heat and violence and beauty, is a continual theme with him, and produces the two magnificent 'African Eclogues':

> On Tiber's banks where scarlet jasmines bloom
> And purple aloes shed a rich perfume;
> Where, when the sun is melting in his heat
> The reeking tygers find a cool retreat,
> Bask in the sedges, lose the sultry beam
> And wanton with their shadows in the stream.
> On Tiber's banks, by sacred priests rever'd
> Where in the days of old a god appear'd –
> 'Twas in the dead of night, at Chalma's feast
> The tribe of Alta slept around the priest . . .
>
> ('The Death of Nicou', June 1770)

Here, with phrases like 'reeking tygers' he reaches a new, exotic precision; one is tempted to call it a hallucinogenic power. It is probable that Chatterton began taking opium at this time, at first as an antidote to his 'Cold', and later perhaps as an antidote to reality. One of his last friends was Mr Cross, the chemist on the corner of Brooke Street; he once shared a barrel of oysters with him. Cross supplied him with a number of medicaments, and almost certainly opium. This is not in itself surprising. In the eighteenth century, and indeed well on into the nineteenth century, opium was used as a regular adult pain-killer and stimulant, usually taken in solution as laudanum. Toothaches, head-colds, stomach diseases, gout, rheumatism all yielded to the poppy; it was the exact equivalent of the modern barbiturate. Nevertheless, it seems as if Chatterton was in the end taking opium doses in direct powder or stick form – and that is hardly medicinal. A deep stain running through nineteen leaves of Chatterton's London notebook was finally analysed in 1947. Dr Walls of South-Western Forensic Laboratory reported conclusive evidence: 'I cut a piece out of the stain on the back page and tested this. It gives a positive reaction for opium alkaloid (i.e. morphine etc.).'

The relationship between drugs and artistic creativity is still obscure and has always been in dispute; the argument ranges from 'Kubla Khan' and 'The English Stage Coach' (De Quincey) to *The Naked Lunch* and Kerouac's peyote poems. In the 'Ode to a Nightingale', a classic Romantic text in this respect, Keats classes drugs – 'the dull opiates' – with alcohol – 'Bacchus and his pards' – and Poesy as one of the three primary mediums of fantasy. While Rimbaud, making a fierce literal reading of Baudelaire, classes drugs with alcohol and sexual experience (preferably perverse, or at least exotic) as one of the primary means of the poet's systematic and prolonged derangement of the senses. This is, however, literary and theoretical. In practice, drugs with their expense, their destruction of social relationships, their attendant physical diseases, and their inherent tendency to expand, distort and dissipate the senses into *passivity* of outlook (whereas all artistic effort requires concentration, sensual intensity and tremendous *activity*) – drugs make at best only a short-term partnership with creativity. Moreover they occupy the passive, or female, side of that partnership, providing relief rather than direct stimulus, providing the unconscious pool of images rather than the conscious netting and binding of images into actual artistic forms. (Some of these issues are discussed in Alethea Hayter's book, *Opium and the Romantic Imagination*, 1968.)

All the same, in poetry the drug-supported and drug-fed imagination does produce quite characteristic and brilliant effects. Most notably, there is a combination of very bright, very minute, high-definition images with a completely contrasting sense of entirely vague sweeping movements, undefined expanses and landscapes, and massive blurred shiftings of light and shade. In Chatterton's earliest 'African Eclogue', which is dated Shoreditch May 2nd 1770, about a week or ten days after he had arrived in London, these characteristics are already recognizable. The poem is called 'Narva and Mored', the names of two young African lovers. The central passage begins:

> Three times the virgin, swimming on the breeze,
> Danc'd in the shadow of the mystic trees:
> When, like a dark cloud spreading to the view
> The first-born sons of War and Blood pursue.
> Swift as the elk they pour along the plain
> Swift as the flying clouds distilling rain
> Swift as the boundings of the youthful roe
> They course around and lengthen as they go.
> Like the long chain of rocks, whose summits rise
> Far in the sacred regions of the skies
> Upon whose top the black'ning tempest lours,
> Whilst down its side the gushing torrent pours,
> Like the long cliffy mountains which extend
> From Lorbar's cave, to where the nations end,
> Which sink in darkness, thick'ning and obscure
> Impenetrable, mystic, and impure,
> The flying terrors of the war advance
> And round the sacred oak, repeat the dance.

The most extraordinary thing is the almost total dissolution of the formal eighteenth-century couplets into a rushing, shapeless, undirected torrent of images which gives free expression to the wildness and passion of the African tribal dance, as Chatterton understood and imagined it. The dance is both a dance of war by the tribesmen, and a dance of ecstatic sexual expectancy by the young virgin Mored ('Black was her face, as Togla's hidden cell, / Soft as the moss where hissing adders dwell'). It is so typical of Chatterton that Lorbar's cave is impenetrable, mystic and *im*pure. The love of Narva and Mored ends in simultaneous union and destruction: 'Lock'd in each other's arms, from Hyga's cave, / They plunged relentless to a wat'ry grave'. If the passage reminds one of something else, it will turn out to be the opening section of Coleridge's opium dream-poem 'Kubla Khan', written some thirty years later.

In these 'African Eclogues', as in the journalistic prose tales and articles Chatterton dashed off for money, and indeed in everything else he wrote during these last four months, one is continually coming across lines or whole passages which recall the reader – with a sudden frisson of horror and pity – to the situation Chatterton himself was in. The most terrible moment in 'Narva and Mored' is a single image which bubbles up in the seething flow of description for four lines, and then vanishes again without trace or explanation:

> . . . Where the pale children of the feeble sun
> In search of gold through every climate run,
> From burning heat to freezing torments go
> And live in all vicissitudes of woe . . .

But it is only in the last of the Rowley poems, 'The Excelente Balade of Charitie', that Chatterton seems to have produced a total equivalent of his condition, a complete symbolic enactment of his hopes and terrors. There is a superb equity in the fact that it was only Thomas Rowley, his double, his other self across three centuries, who could provide him with the material, the stance, and the final distancing to accomplish this most measured and beautiful and poignant of his works. The measuredness is particularly important. None of Chatterton's subsequent critics or biographers seems to have realized just how unbalanced, how thoroughly *peculiar* Chatterton became in those first few weeks alone. The first two letters home are amusingly carried off, and reveal exactly the pride and rather disarming boastfulness one might have expected from him. The note is aptly struck in: 'I get four guineas a month by one Magazine: shall engage to write a History of England, and other pieces, which will more than double that sum . . . I am quite familiar at the Chapter Coffee-House, and know all the geniuses there. A character is now unnecessary; an author carries his character in his pen.' (That last remark is an interesting side-light on his use of personae at Bristol.)

But by the letter of May 14th, a kind of glittering wildness is coming over him: 'Miss Rumsey, if she comes to London, would do well as an old acquaintance, to send me her address. – London is not Bristol. – We may patrole the town for a day, without raising one whisper, or nod of scandal. – If she refuses, the curse of all antiquated virgins light on her: may she be refused when she shall request! Miss Rumsey will tell Miss Baker, and Miss Baker will tell Miss Porter, that Miss Porter's favoured humble, though but a *young* man, is a very old lover; and in the eight-and-fiftieth year of his age: but that, as Lappet says, is the flower of a man's days; and when a lady can't get a young husband, she must put up with an old bedfellow. I left Miss Singer, I am sorry to say it, in a very bad way; that is, in a way to be married. – But mum – Ask Miss Suky Webb the rest; if she knows, she'll tell ye. – I beg her pardon for revealing the secret; but when the knot is fastened, she shall know how I came by it – Miss Thatcher may depend upon it, that, if I am not in love with her, I am in love with nobody else . . .' And so on for another page or so, with Miss Love, Miss Cotton, Miss Broughton and Miss Watkins. It is still amusing stuff, but his imagination seems over-stimulated, the jokes and innuendoes and declarations spin out with a sort of exalted panic. It is also clear that he is very lonely, and he desperately hopes that Miss Rumsey will be coming to the city. A paragraph in the next letter, to his sister dated May 30th, ends with: 'Humbly thanking Miss Rumsey for her complimentary expression, I cannot think it satisfactory. Does she, or does she not, intend coming to London? Mrs O'Coffin has not yet got a place; but there is not the least doubt but she will in a little time.' The letter finished with a scrawled PS: 'I am at this moment pierced through the heart by the black eye of a young lady, driving along in a hackney-coach – I am quite in love: If my love lasts 'till that time, you shall hear of it in my next.' It is throw-away, but rather revealing.

In these letters there is only one reference to Rowley (though several to St Mary Redcliff). It is an odd one. It shows that Rowley was on his mind, but it appears to be bidding him farewell as a companion. 'As to Mr Barrett, Mr Catcott, Mr Burgum, &c., they rate literary lumber so low, that I believe an author, in their estimation, must be poor indeed! But here matters are otherwise; had Rowley been a Londoner, instead of Bristowyan, I could have lived by copying his works.' In his characteristically ambiguous manner, Chatterton appears to be wondering if Rowley *could* in fact be turned into a Londoner: whether Rowley could survive outside the environment of medieval Bristol which created him, and could perhaps expand into more universal themes that would move far beyond the old localized settings. This is exactly what 'The Balade of Charitie' did do: there is no other Rowley poem with a more timeless setting and theme, and no other Rowley poem which has so finely absorbed the humane and observant style of Chaucer. The idea was to mature until July; a powerful island of calm amid Chatterton's turmoil and uncertainty and distress.

Some time in June Chatterton left Shoreditch, and moved to the cheaper and seedier area of Holborn. He took an attic room in the second house along Brooke Street from the High Holborn end. It was an area of disrepute. Labourers from Ireland, criminals and prostitutes lived there. It was the home of the Cato Street conspiracy. Clergymen when they visited their flock in these streets were accompanied by bodyguards. Chatterton's landlady was a Mrs Angel, a dressmaker. Dressmaking in that area was often synonymous with brothel keeping. Round the corner in Fox Court was where Richard Savage was born. Mr Cross kept his chemist shop on the corner. Even nowadays, with the pink neo-gothic edifice of the Prudential Insurance Building looming respectably along the right-hand side of the road, it is not a comforting street to be in. You cannot see enough sky.

In June the letters quickly began to get shorter. The one to his sister, dated June 19th, begins with a sudden sharpness. 'Dear Sister, I have a horrid cold. – The relation of the manner of my catching it may give you more pleasure than the circumstance itself.' His story tells of hanging out of his window in the middle of the night to listen to a drunken woman singing bawdy songs in the street below. It ends with a conclusion that seems, in the context, to have a fairly obvious double meaning. 'However, my entertainment, though sweet enough in itself, has a dish of sour sauce served up in it; for I have a most horrible wheezing in the throat; but I don't repent that I have this cold; for there are so many nostrums here, that 'tis worth a man's while to get a distemper, he can be cured so cheap.' The man's distemper referred to here is almost certainly some form of venereal disease.

Nineteenth-century scholarship has been prudishly silent on this point. As it was silent on Keats dosing himself with mercury for the same complaint. Not until Meyerstein's book of 1930 was there any consideration of the likelihood that Chatterton might have caught venereal disease; although it was a very common and rather unremarkable fact of a young man's life in the London of the time. Indeed, in the London of any young man's time since Shakespeare. The matter would be quite insignificant if it were not for the entirely different light that it throws on the development of Chatterton's drug-taking, and most important of all, in the actual circumstances of his death. There is only one authentic reference in this matter. It comes from Michael Lort, that shrewd scholar-investigator who had extracted a particularly interesting statement from the Reverend Catcott (see supra, p. 38), and whose manners were, according to Fanny Burney, 'somewhat blunt and odd'. Michael Lort's evidence is simply this: that he had cross-questioned the chemist Mr Cross, and 'Mr Cross says he (Chatterton) had the Foul Disease which he would cure himself and had calomel and vitriol of Cross for that purpose. Who cautioned him *against the too free use* of these.' It is tremendously significant. Chatterton 'would cure himself' – of course, that is in character. We know that Chatterton was fascinated by medical matters and had in the past borrowed many books on surgery from Barrett. He would look after himself; his pride, his hardness would demand it. Yet suppose things did not go quite according to plan? Suppose the disease, whatever its form, at first seemed merely to get worse; or suppose it disappeared and then recurred – which is often the case? Vitriol could be a long and very painful treatment, especially for someone of Chatterton's age and in his difficult circumstances.

The crucial fact is, then, this: arsenic, in small regulated doses, could also be used as a more drastic cure for venereal disease; and opium could – rashly but understandably – be used as a pain-killer. Arsenic and opium simultaneously. The Coroner reported arsenic poisoning; Barrett the surgeon recorded evidence of opium, he assumed an overdose. If all these facts are true, then an entirely different picture begins to emerge. One is led to ask, is the tradition of 200 years quite wrong? Is this a case of suicide at all? Why, come to think of it, should Chatterton have left no suicide note, no Villonesque Last Will and Testament? (The only extant 'Will', as we have seen, was made four months previously, a device for escaping from Lambert's.) Is it not possible, is it not really rather likely, that what happened on the night of the 24th of August was a tragic mistake, a terrible miscalculation? In fact did Chatterton ever surrender to his circumstances, to himself, to the soft Romantic gesture of Wallis's painting? Did his angry courage ever break at all? These are difficult questions to answer. We may never have the evidence to answer them satisfactorily. The ambivalence may have gone with him into oblivion. But I think his death was a mistake.

If the inner life is doubtful to the end, Herbert Croft, the author of *Love and Madness*, discovered some vivid external impressions from his interviews with Chatterton's last neighbours. The house where Chatterton lodged in Shoreditch was run by a plasterer and his wife, Mr and Mrs Walmsley. With them were two young relatives, a niece and a nephew. Also Mrs Ballance, whose acquaintance we have already made. After Mrs Ballance's *faux pas* over 'Tommy', little seems to have passed between them. But Mrs Ballance had something to say about that silence too. 'He would often look steadfastly in a person's face, without speaking, or seeming to see the person, for a quarter of an hour or more, till it was quite frightful; during all this time (she supposes, from what she has since heard), his thoughts were gone about something else.'

The master of the household, Mr Walmsley, was less forthcoming. Yet a perfectly ordinary artisan's opinion of a young poet who was to become the darling of the Romantics is not without what one might call sociological interest. 'Mr Walmsley saw nothing of him, but that there was something manly and pleasing about him, and that he did not dislike the wenches.' Chatterton would probably have been rather pleased with that description.

Mrs Walmsley, like all London landladies that ever were and ever will be, looked out for the more domestic virtues in her lodger; but was not without a streak of romance sweetly disguised in the depth of a doubtless ample bosom. She liked her young literary gentleman to have a bit of style. 'Mrs Walmsley's account is, that she never saw any harm of him – that he never *mislisted* her ["misled" her perhaps; or perhaps "mistressed" her?]; but was always very civil, whenever they met in the house by accident – that he would never suffer the room, in which he used to read and write, to be swept, because, he said, poets hated brooms.' That seems rather to have tickled Mrs Walmsley, but she was certainly not going to admit it: 'she told him she did not know any thing that *poet folks* were good for, but to sit in a dirty cap and gown in a garret, and at last to be starved.' Secretly she may have even approved. 'During the nine weeks he was at her house, he never stayed out after the family hours, except once, when he didn't come home all night and had been, she heard, *poeting* a song about the streets.' At which point Mrs Ballance rushes back into the breach to cover up for poor Tommy. 'This night, Mrs Ballance says, she knows he lodged at a relation's, because Mr W's house was shut up when he came home.'

But that is only what the adults saw. Mrs Walmsley's niece kept her eyes much wider open, and took something of a fancy to him; but she was puzzled by him, even slightly alarmed: 'For her part, she always took him more for a mad boy than anything else, he would have such flights and *vagaries* – that, but for his face and her knowledge of his age, she should never have thought him a boy, he was so manly, and *so much himself* – that no women came after him, nor did she know of any connexion; but still, that he was a sad rake, and terribly fond of women, and would sometimes be saucy to her.' His eating arrangements were peculiar too: 'he ate what he chose to have with his relation (Mrs B) who lodged in the same house, but he never touched meat, and drank only water, and seemed to live on air.' To that the nephew added: 'he lived chiefly on a bit of bread, or a tart, and some water.'

The nephew, whose name Herbert Croft does not record, was probably the youngest in the house, younger even than Chatterton. For the first six weeks of Chatterton's stay he shared a bed-room with him. 'He used to sit up almost all the night, reading and writing ... he (the nephew) was afraid to lie with him; for to be sure, he was a *spirit*, and never slept ... he never came to bed till very late, sometimes three or four o'clock, and was always awake when he (the nephew) waked; and got up at the same time, about five or six – that almost every morning the floor was covered with pieces of paper not so big as sixpences, into which he had torn what he had been writing before he came to bed.'

The detail of the torn paper is interesting. It harks back to the Pyle Street schoolhouse where papers and parchments were scattered on tables and floors; it carries forward to the final scene in Brooke Street where the shredded papers were wrongly taken as evidence of a fit of despair. And it suggests so strongly and simply the immense inwardness and privacy which the act of composition, divided between himself and Rowley, had always contained for Chatterton: something so secretive it made him cover his tracks instinctively.

He gave no reason for quitting Shoreditch. 'They found the floor of his rooms covered with little pieces of paper, the remains of his *poetings*, as they term it.'

In Brooke Street the track does run out. Croft never managed to trace Mrs Angel, his dress-making landlady. A certain Mrs Wolfe, a barber's wife, who lived a few doors down, remembered one detail. 'Mrs Angel told her, after his death, that, as she knew he had not eaten anything for two or three days, she begged he would take some dinner with her on the 24th of August; but he was offended at her expressions, which seemed to hint he was in want, and assured her he was not hungry.' Somehow it rings true – one imagines how he would take offence. The other stories sound a bit like ingenious apocrypha. He was seen in a tavern drinking Shakespeare's health in bad wine; he was seen in St Pancras churchyard reading the epitaphs; he was seen at the Brooke Street's bakers being refused bread on tick.

Yet there is a grim and miraculous concordance between these final marginalia of his outward life, and the last and loveliest of Rowley's visitations, 'The Excelente Balade of Charitie'. In thirteen vivid and melodic stanzas, it tells of a poor 'hapless pilgrim' who has fallen on bad times and is now sick, poverty-stricken and destitute, his clothes threadbare and his body ravaged. He stands alone in a wide unlocated landscape, with a dark ponderous storm moving over the horizon towards him. 'He had no housen theere, ne any convent nie.' He shelters under a holm-oak. The storm breaks.

Liste! now the thunder's rattling clymmynge sound
Cheves slowlie on, and then embollen clangs
Shakes the hie spyre, and losst, dispended, drown'd,
Still on the gallard eare of terrour hanges;
The windes are up; the lofty elmen swanges,
Agayn the levynne and the thunder poures,
And the full clouds are braste attenes in stonen showers.

By using the Rowley dialect and spelling with a wild freedom he
had never before achieved, Chatterton here brings off one of the
finest pieces of onomatopoeic poetry in the whole of English verse.
It is quite unnecessary to know semantically what 'clymmynge' or
'swangen' mean; the sound, even the very look of the words tell
you exactly what is happening, the power and terror of the storm.

The portrait of the pilgrim as he huddles under the oak is
superb. It glows with a kind of transcendental pity for all men
who are outcast or broken. It is almost as if Rowley were describing
Chatterton in a vision of his own; as if the roles had been reversed:

Look in his glommed face: his sprighte there scanne;
Howe woe-be-gone, howe withered, forwynd, deade!
Haste to thy church-glebe-house, ashrewd manne!
Haste to thy kiste, thy only dortoure bedde.
Cold, as the clay which will gre on thy hedde,
Is Charitie and Love among high elves:
Knightis and Barons live for pleasure and themselves.

[A few words are difficult here, but not very: 'forwynd' means
sapless; 'ashrewd' means cursed by fortune; 'kiste' is a coffin; and
'dortoure' is obviously a dormitory or bedroom.]

A figure now appears through the blasting storm, 'spurreynge
his palfry oer the watery plain'. It is an Abbott, and he is described
with Chaucerian accuracy and judgement: 'His cope was all of
Lincoln clothe so fine, with a gold button fastened neere his
chynne', and his horse's head has been plaited with roses. The
pilgrim begs for aid, the Abbott – with the solemn inevitability of
the medieval ballad – rudely refuses him. ('Varlet, replied the
Abbatte, cease your dinne; This is no season almes and prayers
to give; My porter never lets a faitour [tramp] in.') And he spurs
away.

The storm breaks out with renewed ferocity. But through the

downpour 'faste reyneynge oer the plain a priest was seen'. This man is a poor friar, 'Ne dighte full proude, ne buttoned up in golde; His cope and jape [gown] were gray, and eke were clene'. The pilgrim begs for alms; the friar immediately produces a silver groat from his pouch. 'The mister pilgrim did for halline [joy] shake.' Then with a marvellous unexpected gesture of generosity, the friar gives his cloak to the pilgrim. 'Here take my semicope, thou arte bare I see; Tis thyne, the Seynctes will give me my reward.' He disappears into the rain.

It is difficult to get out of one's head the impression that Chatterton is in some primary symbolic sense that 'unhailie pilgrim'; and the friar in grey who appears out of the storm and so freely gives aid is Thomas Rowley. Perhaps it makes no sense. But in this last known work, maybe precisely because it *is* the last known work, the figures move through the simple heraldic ritual of charity with a power much greater than their own individual humanity. The storm against them is all storms; it is the storm of circumstance, the storm of the mind, the storm of the body; it is the storm of passion, of creativity, of ambition, of loneliness. But there is no final despair; help comes, life is made out. There is no despair at Pyle Street, or at Colston Hall, or at Lambert's drudging office; there is no despair at Shoreditch, or at Brooke Street in the attic.

Above all, the poet did not despair in the attic.

# II

## Lost in France

# INTRODUCTION

So Chatterton gallantly passed me on to Shelley. For four years I was immersed in the travelling, dreaming and writing of his biography (as I have recounted in *Footsteps*). But once I had finished, or at least survived the book, every instinct told me to get away from London. I took the ferry to Calais in the winter of 1974. I remained in France on and off for two years, writing articles and reviews in a little attic room in the ninth arrondissement of Paris, at 9 rue Condorcet (not far from the boulevard Montmartre and the Marché Cadet) which is glimpsed in various disguises in the pieces of this section. I would walk down at night, in those pre-fax days, to mail my articles *express* (the magic dark blue sticker) back to London from the all-night Bureau de Poste near the Bourse. I was still lonely here, but I got to know Paris, the Île de France, and Normandy, and had my own romantic adventures which I now think left their shadow, or perfume, on these pieces.

But what I was looking for was the next subject, something which would take me directly into the heart of French Romanticism, among a later and very different group of artists and writers. Within a few months, I thought I had found it. What I had discovered was the great portrait collection of the nineteenth-century French photographer, Felix Nadar, in the Bibliothèque Nationale, which was then in the rue Richelieu, with its old penumbrous reading-room lit by green glass reading lamps at each desk. As I imply in this first piece, it seemed that Nadar would provide a wonderful opportunity for a biographic *ensemble*, the study of a whole Romantic generation, something extraverted and flashlit, full of melodrama and gaiety and humour.

But quite unexpectedly, my researches drew me in another

direction. I came across a series of striking studio portraits of two literary colleagues, the journalist Théophile Gautier and the poet Gérard de Nerval. These men had been friends since childhood, attending the Lycée Charlemagne together in the boulevard Saint-Antoine in the 1820s, growing up as youthful disciples of Victor Hugo, and both making brilliant but very different careers in the Paris of Louis-Philippe, the 1848 insurrection, and the Second Empire. Outwardly, Gautier's career was a triumph, ending as one of the great established Parisian men of letters: a poet, a highly paid columnist in the newspaper *La Presse*, an intimate of Flaubert, and patron to Baudelaire who dedicated *Les Fleurs du Mal* to him.

But Nerval's life appeared to be a disaster, increasingly rootless and poverty-stricken, ending in a series of internments in an asylum in Passy and eventual suicide in an alley leading down to the river Seine. The stark contrast in their destinies seemed to me to tell an essential story about Romanticism. So I felt my way along the interwoven paths of their biographies, beginning with a first journalistic sketch of Gautier, like a mirror image, visiting London. I then assembled and translated a collection of his autobiographical fantasy tales, *My Fantoms*, and out of this collection arose the story of 'Poor Pierrot'. Here was a haunting mythical figure from the Commedia dell' Arte, who came literally to life in the career of the mime artist Deburau. This Pierrot's biography had a sadness and sudden violence which foreshadowed Nerval's.

But when I came directly to Nerval himself, I found the path of traditional biography blocked, for the reasons I have explained in *Footsteps*. I wrote a 400-page biography of the two friends, 'Poets in Paris', but it never cohered and I felt gradually that I was lost in a maze of shifting journeys and identities. I was lost in France. When I came back to England in 1976, all that seemed to remain was a kind of echo-chamber of voices in my head, a kind of fragmented sound-track of their friendship.

As a last effort to record those voices, and at least mark the fading contours of my research before they disappeared entirely, I wrote a radio-play in that odd hybrid but fascinating form of 'drama-documentary' which was eventually produced for Radio Three by Hallam Tennyson. (It was a strange production, almost surreal in its unsettling effect on the actors, with Timothy West – a big, solid, confident figure like Gautier – superbly transforming his voice into the slight, unstable, tortured Nerval.) This is the last piece in this section, although the story itself – and my wanderings in France – were far from over. The discovery of radio, as a vehicle for biographical story-telling, moving effortlessly inside and outside its characters' minds, shifting with magical ease between different times and locations, was a revelation and an inspiration to me.

# MONSIEUR NADAR

OPPOSITE THE GOLD AND DORIC of the modern Hôtel Scribe, about three minutes' walk under the plane trees from the Place de l'Opéra, stands a crazed and yellowing façade of taciturn stucco, surmounted by a triplet of broken urns. This is 35 boulevard des Capucines, Paris 75008. It carries no plaque, no prefectural plate, no memorial. Yet there was a time when Victor Hugo, exiled in the Channel Islands, could have a letter delivered to this address with nothing more than the proprietor's name on the envelope.

A hundred years ago, the building was red: a bright, republican red. Its top two floors consisted of studio rooms into which the morning sun poured unhindered, by a daring system of plate-glass windows set in a trellis of wrought-iron that curved gracefully across the entire façade. Its corniches were capped by alabaster busts of three generously proportioned Muses, and its roof cluttered by a series of glass sheds, not unlike greenhouses, interspersed somewhat eccentrically by pots of ferns and small Christmas trees in tubs. At pavement level, a constant coming and going of hired cabs and smart landaus, a dashing of commissionaires with giant parasols (also red), of strollers and gapers – *les flâneurs de Paris* – indicated some unusually attractive centre of business, art or scandal.

As night fell, and the street-lamps swaying from their iron gibbets filled the thoroughfare with a garish, orange gaslight, and the cab-lamps jerked down the uncertain asphalting of the boulevard, a great arc of clear white light, the output from fifty Bunsen Static Batteries linked in series, flooded down from the windows of number 35. This unearthly glow was occasionally punctuated by the livid flash from a pan of magnesium, which gave rise –

not altogether unreasonably – to rumours of spirit-raising and necromancy.

Across the whole frontage, at the level of the third-storey balcony, in bold cursive lettering 10 feet high and 50 feet long, in a system of gas-tubes designed exclusively by Antoine Lumière, ran the proprietorial name: NADAR. That too was in red.

In the 1860s Felix Nadar was certainly the most celebrated photographer in France. In retrospect, his reputation still stands with David Octavius Hill and Julia Margaret Cameron, as one of the three indisputably great portrait photographers of the nineteenth century. His famous atelier at number 35 boulevard des Capucines had long been linked with the pioneering days of French photography, since the time when it had been rented as an undecorated shell of a building, in a then unfashionable quarter, by the early landscape daguerreotypers, the *frères* Bisson, and the painter turned seascape photographer Gustave Le Gray, in the 1850s. The building was to conclude its controversial associations on a high note, when after the fall of the Second Empire, and the crushing tragedy of the Commune, Nadar moved to smaller premises, and hired the studio out to the 'Société Anonyme des Artistes Peintres' for a public exposition which became known to posterity as the First Impressionist Exhibition of 1874.

The aesthetic revolution brought about by the early photographers, and especially Nadar, was no less far-reaching than that achieved by the Impressionists. But the impact of photography on European society was too rapid, and too widespread, to be grasped at the time. The Impressionists asserted new standards of private, idiosyncratic vision, which penetrated only slowly, and among the elite of the art world. But photographers established, in little more than a decade, entirely new and universal ideas about visual reality, and about what everyone could commonly accept and recognize as 'lifelikeness'. Photography was, from the start, irretrievably popular in its appeal and suspiciously democratic in its tendencies. Not surprisingly it took Paris by storm: in 1850 there were less than a dozen professional studios in the city; by the 1860s something over 200, with more than 33,000 people directly or indirectly employed. Of these, Nadar was the doyen.

Especially in these early days, photography gave rise to a host of questions and suspicions. Was the photographer an artist, or a scientist? Would he destroy painting? Would his portraits somehow dehumanize nature, and banish the soul? And how was it that photography, with all its mechanistic and chemical crudeness, had suddenly created a golden age of the human image? As Nadar himself put it with typical trenchancy: 'Photography is a fantastic discovery: a science which engages the most advanced intellects, and an art which provokes the most profound minds: and yet its use lies within the capacity of the shallowest idiot.'

The story of Nadar's early career is a reflection and to some extent an explanation of many of these issues. It is also a kind of comic-epic, continuously larger and more colourful than life, like his own person. For the Nadar who eventually occupied the boulevard des Capucines was 6 feet 4 inches tall, with blazing red hair once described by the poet de Banville as 'comet's fire', and having for his motto the untranslatable Parisian shrug in the face of an intractable universe: *mais, quand même!*

In fact Felix Nadar created himself. As he was born in 1820, he was merely Felix Tournachon, the eldest son of a provincial printer and publisher from Lyons. After a long but unsuccessful attempt to establish a business in Paris, selling translations of radical texts by Diderot, d'Holbach and Lamennais, his father Victor Tournachon went bankrupt and returned to die at the Lyons asylum in 1837. Felix, forced at seventeen to assume responsibility for his mother and his younger brother Adrien, worked in the local Lyons journals and studied medicine at night. One story persisted in the memory about his father: he was once said to have swum the Rhône for a dare, carrying an open book in one hand, and a hunting horn – which he blew occasionally – in the other. A Byronic gesture perhaps; but also something more *à la mode*, a brilliant act of self-publicity.

Within a year Felix Tournachon had taken his mother and his brother back to Paris, his heart set on the grand conquest his father had attempted, but failed. He had no *métier*, but many schemes. Between 1838 and 1844, the years of the bourgeois monarch with the furled umbrella, Tournachon plunged into the life of the Left Bank. His story became that of Henri Murger's *Scènes de la Vie de Bohème* (1849), the sloping attics of the sixth arrondissement, the cheap cafés round Notre Dame de Lorette, and the laundry girls and golden-hearted *grisette* of the quartier Breda.

A bewildering assortment of bad jobs and good contacts followed: stenographer, bookshop assistant, coalseller, pipeseller, cub reporter, private secretary, editorial hack. While writing theatre reviews for an ephemeral journal, he met Jean Duval – later Baudelaire's mulatto mistress – stealing the show in a bit part at the Porte-Saint-Antoine, and they became friends. His newspaper work brought him into touch with Gautier, Nerval, de Banville, Murger himself (who frequently shared his attic and his purse), Baudelaire, Dumas *père*, Champfleury, and even Balzac, hiding out from creditors in a chamber hung with gentian wallpaper in the rue de Richelieu.

A somewhat weary police dossier was opened on him. 'Yet another of those dangerous people sowing highly subversive doctrines in the Quartier Latin – he makes speeches about the Lamennaian socialist theory.' He was also notorious for his wild, unbourgeois-like generosity.

Tournachon cut a remarkable figure in the narrow, cobbled streets – huge, gangling, red-headed, with long twitching fingers and staring impudent eyes. But it was some time before he settled upon his public image, a concept of singular importance to him. The journalist Charles Bataille first met him climbing down, with ostentatious stealth, from a fifth-floor attic in the rue Neuve des Martyres *by the outside* 'like a huge scrawny cat', presumably to avoid the concierge. Having reached the relative safety of terra firma, he arranged an eye-catching 'bull's blood' jacket round his shoulders, pulled on an elegant pair of gloves and, carefully neglecting to button cuff or cravat, loped off with a boyish grin to impress his new editor. This mixture of craft and sartorial naïveté always remained: at the height of his fame he attended a Fancy Dress Ball with Gustave Doré, dressed as a baby with orange beads and a cotton bib.

By 1842, Tournachon had landed his first regular job, as Letters Editor on *Le Commerce* (he wrote them himself), and he began publishing short stories of Bohemian life, and finally a novel, *La Robe de Déjanire* (1846). These showed his lifelong understanding of poverty, and a characteristic combination of fulsome sentiment and black humour. He had also found his name: from

Tournachon to Tournadard, an obscure, epistemological gallic joke, referring either to his satirical *sting*, or else to the tongue of *flame* (also *dard*) above his brow; and thence to the more economical and generally more marketable, Nadar. This signature now began to appear below little matchstick drawings, and at the age of twenty-seven, Nadar published a first caricature on the inside page of *Charivari*, the celebrated illustrated journal edited by Charles Philipon. Pictures, not words, suddenly began to flow from his pen.

The revolutionary events of 1848 precipitated Nadar into perhaps the most quixotic adventure of his entire career. It was nothing less than the liberation of Poland from the Prussians, by a volunteer column of 500 ultra-red republican Parisians, inspired by the rhetoric of the ageing Lamartine and the exiled Mickiewicz. Nadar proudly showed his falsified Polish passport round the cafés: 'Age 27 years, height 1.98 metres, hair rust red, eyes protuberant, complexion bilious.' The expedition ended in a prison near Magdeburg, but Nadar, irrepressible, was soon back in Paris looking for work with a Polish astrakhan cap perched proudly on his wild locks. Gérard de Nerval introduced him to a friendly editor: 'This is Tournachon; he's got lots of spirit, but he's very crazy.' The poet and the ex-Pole worked night shifts together, discussing ballooning – a shared enthusiasm – and politics, and sleeping on top of the warm printing presses. All the time, Nadar's long fingers were drawing.

In the following spring, the editor Charles Philipon began to use Nadar's caricatures regularly for his new illustrated magazine, *Le Journal Pour Rire*. Nadar's professional friendship with the forty-three-year-old editor was to be the most influential of his life. A collection of eighty manuscript letters, which lies in the archives of the Bibliothèque Nationale, still unpublished, vividly traces the growth of a fraught but chaotically fruitful partnership. Philipon appears always thoughtful, severe, appreciative, fatherly; while Nadar is rumbustious, multifarious, and ceaselessly late with copy. Like Emile de Girardin of *La Presse*, Philipon belonged to the first great generation of mass-circulation editors in Paris, and Nadar rapidly became his star. By 1851 Nadar was being asked to produce as many as 100 separate caricatures a month.

It was thus that sheer pressure of demand created the first

atelier Nadar, a vital cooperative formation which was to extend subsequently to his photographic work. Up to a dozen fellow craftsmen were soon employed on Nadar's inimitable sketches and ideas, and transferring them to the wooden blocks sent for printing all over Paris. The atelier became a kind of syndicate, and his ubiquitous spidery N changed from an artist's signature to 'marque de fabrication'. In a press now forbidden, by Imperial decree, all direct political commentary, Nadar spawned an entire world of grotesque little *homunculi*, a myriad *croquetons*, in which all the famous writers, actors and painters of the day danced and gibbered in manic processions across the tabloids of Paris. 'So then, we are lost', sighed the *frères* Goncourt, 'Nadar has now learnt to draw.'

But for Nadar himself, drawing remained the means only, not the long-sought object. The *image*, the outward physical projection of the inner, private, spiritual man, still obsessed him. How to capture it? And especially, how to capture it in that most elusive of creatures, his fellow writer? 'How to draw out, for example,' he asked himself, 'in the wonderfully sympathetic face of Dumas *père*, the hints of exotic blood, how to press the simian analogy in a profile which seems a living proof of Darwin, and yet to emphasize above all the predominant note in his character, his extreme and inexhaustible generosity . . . without ever forgetting, as a final detail, the increased reduction of the conch of his already microscopic ear.' Of Gautier, he wondered, 'how not to travesty that oriental beauty, that Olympian serenity'; and of Baudelaire, how one might trace the fantastic combination of 'strangeness and perfect sincerity' in that 'native from the land of the Griffin and the Chimera'. Always it was this good-humoured, but relentless search for the *ressemblance morale* of his subject.

Nadar's files in the atelier now contained over 800 studies, including even interview notes and daguerreotypes. From this massive repository of images, Nadar created – with Philipon's aid and advice – his first distinctive masterpiece, in 1854. This was his celebrated 'Pantheon Nadar', a vast single-sheet lithograph cartoon, showing a spiral cortege of over 240 contemporary writers and journalists, each minutely transformed into a jostling gargoyle of the creative spirit. With a printing investment of 200,000 francs, Nadar sold out; the sensation of the season.

Nadar was now thirty-four. He bought a house at 113 rue Saint-Lazare, married, and gave dinner parties for his Bohemian friends, many like him now distinguished. Meanwhile the decisive discovery of his ideal medium occurred almost unnoticed. A painter friend left a second-hand photographic apparatus in the corner of the atelier. *Mais, quand même* . . . With predestined ease, Nadar learnt to prepare the wet-collodion glass plates; and his friends, long accustomed to his vagaries, learned to sit unselfconsciously under the hard, searching exposures – between 30 and 120 seconds – in blazing sunlight. From the garden he moved to the attic, which was soon fitted with glass tiles. Nadar's strange combination of artistic and commercial gifts, and his flair for the new craft of publicity, found its instant culmination. At last the image could be trapped. In the spring of 1855, with the 'Pantheon' still fresh from the lithographic stone, Nadar set up as a photographer.

By 1856, with dazzling speed, he had temporarily transformed himself into 'Nadar et Cie' to capitalize the business, and he won the *grande medaille d'or* for photography at the Brussels Exhibition that summer. A legal battle with his younger brother, Adrien, finally won him, in 1857, exclusive right to the 'marque de fabrication' of Nadar. Significantly, it was the first time in France that an artistic pseudonym had been disputed as a commercial property. Felix Tournachon's transformation was now complete: he was *'Nadar Photographe'*.

Within the next fifteen years, the atelier Nadar produced one of the greatest sets of contemporary portraits ever made. From 500,000 or so remaining glass and emulsion negatives, perhaps some 300 prints compose the *chef d'oeuvre* of the collection. For the most part these are of writers. They cover the whole panorama of mid-nineteenth-century French literature: Baudelaire, Gautier, Nerval, de Banville, Lamartine, Hugo, Dumas *père et fils*, George Sand, Du Camp, Daudet, Verne, Scribe, Murger, Champfleury, the *frères* Goncourt, Sainte-Beuve, Michelet, Charles Philipon and Emile de Girardin, and literally scores and scores of others. But there are many musicians as well – Berlioz, Rossini, Offenbach; and painters – Delacroix, Corbet, Corot, Monet. There is also a set of Sarah Bernhardt, and a charming nude study of Henri Murger's mistress, the original Musette of the Bohemian stories. It is, in effect, a second 'Pantheon Nadar', except of infinitely greater human penetration. The best photographic portraits should be, wrote Nadar, 'ample like a Van Dyck, and elaborate like a Holbein'.

Nadar's portraits, in fact, owed much to painting, especially Ingres (who in turn used Nadar's photographs for his own studio work). The monumental simplicity of their presentation, the subtle use of their advancing and retreating shadow, and the bold play with the texture of a jacket, blouse or cape, to offset the flesh of face or hands, all are constant marks of Nadar's work. His best period, up to 1874, coincided with the use of the wet-plate collodion process: this rarely required poses of less than twenty seconds, and emphasized the sense of an intense, prolonged, revelatory gaze deep into the subject's psyche. After 1872–73, gelatine emulsion brought exposure times down to less than a second, and the subject could be 'snapped' without his cooperative effort in the process of capturing and holding the fugitive image.

Nadar defended the autonomy of his art, with force and pride.

> The theory of photography can be learnt in an hour, and the first practical steps in a day ... But what can be learnt far less readily is the moral nature of your subject; it is the rapid reflex which puts you in touch with your model, makes you grasp and judge his habitual style and ideas, and allows you to produce – not some superficial or lucky shot, some indifferent and tasteful reproduction within the range of the meanest laboratory assistant – but the most familiar and the most favourable likeness: *la resemblance intime.*

It was an assertion that expressed the effort and experience behind an entire career.

In 1860 Nadar moved to the address which he consecrated for French photography, on the boulevard des Capucines. He charged 50 francs for a half-plate portrait, and joyfully spread the old 'bull's blood' insignia across his whole decor, even down to the wrapping paper. He always continued to scorn Emperor and Court, leaving royal clientele to the Mediterranean beach-photographer Disderi, in the suitable vulgarity of the boulevard des Italiens. At the grand piano under the open studio windows, Jacques Offenbach was encouraged to play variations on the revolutionary Marseillaise, while the Imperial Guard – martial but tone-deaf – trotted in glittering ranks towards the Place de l'Opéra.

In 1862 Charles Philipon died, and thereafter Nadar's energies were increasingly expended in madcap projects. He pioneered flash and aerial photography, and founded a Society for the Promulgation of Heavier Than Air Machines. It was now Daumier's turn to caricature him, suspended in a balloon with his camera over the Arc de Triomphe, 'at the height of his art'. He squandered his resources almost to bankruptcy in his own immense scarlet publicity balloon, *Le Géant*, which the *Scientific American* stonily reported as capable of carrying eighty persons, a printing press, beds and lavabos, and of course a photographic laboratory. But in a night crash-landing near Hanover, *Le Géant* nearly killed both him and his faithful, long-suffering wife, and Victor Hugo was moved to propose a relief fund. The Secretary of the Heavier Than Air Society, the young Jules Verne, canonized Nadar as the hero of *De la Terre à la Lune* – the astronaut Michel Ardan, a final anagrammatic transformation of the fiery nomenclature. 'He was a dare-devil, a Phaeton driving the Sun's chariot at break-neck speed, an Icarus with replaceable wings.'

To the end of his life, Nadar always remained fascinated by the *rapport* between writers and the photographic image. In calm old age, in 1900, he recalled how Balzac refused to be photographed because he held a Lucretian theory of *spectres* (like the Sioux Indians), believing that each exposure dissolved some vital layer of life through the malign alchemy of the Dark Room. Nerval and Gautier had proposed a more gothic hypothesis, that each photograph somehow released a fiendish doppelgänger, who might pursue them across the ether until death. Nerval in fact was only ever photographed once, by Nadar in January 1855; it was about a fortnight before the poet committed suicide in the rue de la Vieille-Lanterne.

But it was Baudelaire who had led the most sustained attack on early photography, in his scathing, *salon* review of 1859. Pressing home a diatribe against the vapid popular taste for 'realism' in art, he thundered prophetically: 'A revengeful God has answered the supplications of the multitude. His Messiah was Monsieur Daguerre. And the multitude said: ". . . Art means Photography"'. From this moment forth, our vile society, like some Narcissus, rushed to contemplate its own trivial image in the metal plate. A madness, an extraordinary zealotry seized these new worshippers of sunlight. And strange abominations were brought forth.' It must have seemed ironic in retrospect. For Nadar's photographic series of Baudelaire between 1854 and 1862 is one of the most expressive documents available about the self-destructive force of the poet's own life. As it is also one of the triumphs of Nadar's art.

Before he died, Baudelaire in turn enshrined Nadar, the photographic witness of the doomed Empire, in one of his own superb images from the late prose poems.

> *In a vast plain of glowing embers, he saw Nadar who was collecting salamanders.*

Salamanders: those darting legendary ephemerae, who feed upon a flash of light, and flourish in the fiery heart of destruction.

# GAUTIER IN LONDON

As he walked down the Strand one surprisingly sunny morning in March, examining the patriotic engravings of Queen Victoria and Prince Albert smiling domestically from the royal tilbury,
Théophile Gautier came upon a barrow boy selling waterproof
mackintoshes. It was a matter of generally received knowledge
that the *imperméable*, like those other viscous phenomena, the
English glass of stout, the English fog, and the English phlegm,
contained something of the philosophical essence of Britain. So
Théophile Gautier, poet, litterateur, and – more practically – regular columnist for Paris's leading daily newspaper *La Presse*, drew
aside to observe.

It was March 1842. Gautier's first and most brilliant ballet *Giselle*
had just opened to packed houses in Her Majesty's Theatre. The
manager, Mr Benjamin Lumley, had remarked that the piece was
'admitted to be vastly pretty', a judgement which Gautier, who
spoke little or no English, received as a generous compliment.

In the peculiar absence of rain, the barrow boy was obviously
anxious to demonstrate that his mackintoshes were genuinely
waterproof. To Gautier's perplexity, he proceeded to nail the
circumference of one of the sacred garments to a horizontal
wooden frame, suspended alongside the stall. Into the shallow
canvas depression thus formed, he emptied a large enamel jug of
water. Into the water he tipped a bowl-full of engaging goldfish.
He then produced a handful of small fishing lines and, flourishing
them, inquired whether any of his customers would care to go
fishing.

Gautier walked on towards Trafalgar Square, where Lord

Nelson's column was gradually arising from a primal chaos of scaffolding and publicity hoardings. He passed the Duke of Northumberland's house, where a sculpted lion guarded the portal with its tail raised vertically in the air. 'It is the lion of Percy', Gautier noted with unaccountable irritation, 'and never has heraldic lion so grossly abused its right to affect fabulous shapes and forms.' The English were not only an unreliable and eccentric nation, they were positively *bizarre*.

It was Gautier's first visit to London. He was thirty-one, the esteemed author of an erotic novel *Mademoiselle de Maupin*, and an arbiter of French literary fashion. In the next twenty years he was to make some five more trips to the British capital, reporting for his newspaper, or simply for his friends, on a variety of national peculiarities, including the Ascot Races, methods of surviving 'incendiary' turtle soup, the paintings of Hogarth, the depressions of Sunday afternoon, the camels of Regent's Park Zoo, Covent Garden, and the Great Apotheosis at the Crystal Palace. Gautier came both as a private citizen of Paris, and as a public representative of civilization, roles that were not easily to be distinguished. Though he could not therefore, on principle, *admire* – he found himself by rapid turns amused, charmed, distressed, perplexed, outraged. But he never lost that original sense of strangeness, of the obstinate shadows clinging to that metropolis of the northern isles, like the ubiquitous soot which, he recorded with gallic frankness, made one blow black into one's handkerchief.

It had struck him, in the larger perspective, even as his steamboat the *Harlequin* first swung west into the yellow waters of the Thames Estuary at sunset, and a forest of dark chimneys gathered along the low banks, sculpted like colossal towers and obelisks, 'giving to the horizon an Egyptian air, a vague profile of Thebes or Babylon, of an antediluvian city, a capital of enormities and rebellious pride, something altogether extraordinary'. It was an impression that anticipated another European's, Joseph Conrad's in the opening pages of *Heart of Darkness*, by some fifty years.

Gautier saw the evidence of Empire in the jostling host of merchant craft, running between the lightships with their great lamps and scarlet paintwork: ships from India, reeking of oriental perfumes and with Lascar crews crowding the rigging, ships from the Baltic and the North Sea with crusts of ice still frozen to their bulwarks, ships from China and America freighted down with tea and sugar cane. But among all that vast fleet, 'you always recognise the English ships: their sails are black like those of Theseus's galleon departing for the Isle of Crete, a sombre livery of funeral mourning, rigged by the sad climate of London'. Gautier caught at the dominant motif, hanging there, mute, unexplained. 'London! –' he exclaimed almost with enthusiasm, ' – *la ville natale du spleen*'.

Yet returning from that first brief encounter, he was nonchalant, even rather knowing. He recorded the following dialogue at a family dinner table in the rue la Boétie. 'Did you see the Tunnel? – No, I didn't see the Tunnel. – And Westminster? – No, indeed. – And St Paul's? – Oh, no. – Then what on earth did you do in London? – I wandered about town observing Englishmen and, more particularly, observing English women. One cannot find their description in any guidebook, and they seemed to me quite as interesting as stones arranged one upon the other after a certain fashion.' Gautier added with some pain: 'since this occasion the good *bourgeois* have regarded me as somewhat mad, suspecting me vaguely of harbouring cannibalistic tendencies, and send their children up to bed when I come to call. I am seriously afraid that this will prejudice my marriage prospects.'

The Tunnel in question was Monsieur Brunel's tiled passageway between Wapping and Rotherhithe, and could not strictly be classed as a British marvel. Gautier later reported in *La Presse* that a friend, presumably English, was working on plans for a Tunnel beneath the entire *Manche*, connecting Folkestone with Calais, and containing railway carriages fired along by compressed air. He remarked that he had, as a conscientious journalist, already reserved his seat for the first crossing, scheduled to take place four years hence, in 1847.

But Gautier was in no sense, as he frequently pretended, and as Henry James later brashly assumed ('the broad-eyed gaze of a rustic at a fair'), an innocent abroad. As drama critic for *La Presse*, whose *feuilletons* ran on the front page beneath the political and business leaders of his exacting editor, the publishing magnate Émile de Girardin, he was normally tied to his regular evening descents upon the Paris boulevards. But in the formula of his lifelong friend and collaborator on *La Presse*, Gérard de Nerval, he was 'a traveller by instinct, a critic by circumstance'.

Almost every spring or summer for thirty years, Gautier made good his escape from Paris, usually in a retrospective flurry of apologies, forwarding addresses, and promises of exotic copy. These flights of the swallow, as they became in one of his most famous poems, '*Ce que disent les Hirondelles*', were made to Germany, Italy, Spain, North Africa, Egypt, Turkey, even eventually to Russia, and he subsequently published brilliantly coloured imagist accounts of all of them.

Even his apartment, in an italianate *hotel particulier* at 14 rue Navarin, off the place Pigalle on Montmartre's lower side, expressed his search for spiritual displacement. Indeed, it was almost a caricature of French Romantic aspirations, furnished as it was with Turkish carpets, Siamese cats, and Italian theatrical ladies, and perfumed with Spanish cooking, Cuban cigars and Algerian hashish. There was, finally, to be an English element, but that was to prove part of the more intimate *moeurs*.

Moreover, Gautier was acutely conscious of the curiously modern desperation, almost the death-wish, implicit in this passionate longing for other shores, other climes, the *other* itself. Many of his springtime *feuilletons* each year played upon this theme with deliberate irony, heralding the age of mass tourism in a distinctly minor key:

'Nowadays the dream of the masses is – *Speed*. By iron or steam they seek to conquer that "ancient weight upon all things suspended". It would seem that their sole concern is to devour Space. Do they do 12 or 15 leagues an hour simply to flee from *ennui*? If so, the enemy awaits them at the farther platform. Yet how strange is this wild urge for rapid locomotion, seizing people of all nations at the same instant. "The dead go swiftly", says the ballad. Are we dead then? Or could this be some presentiment of the approaching doom of our planet, possessing us to multiply the means of communication so we may travel over its entire surface in the little time left to us?' It feels odd to read this paragraph on the faint, blue microfilms for *La Presse* of 1843.

Yet Gautier's journeys to London, while part of this lifelong centrifugal urge, seem to have been of a different order. His notes have remained scattered through a score of essays, letters, articles, poems and reviews. London was less a place to visit, than a state of mind to ponder upon. It was a dark mirror, a smoky crystal ball. You could turn it in your hand. Gautier remained profoundly uninterested in its institutions, its monuments, even its literary associations. Rather, it was its atmosphere, its tone, its iridescent qualities, its curious undercurrent of black comedy, which continually drew him back.

On his second visit he summoned an English barber to his rooms at the Hotel Sablonniere, in Leicester Square. His ballet *La Péri*, with his untouchable amour Carlotta Grisi dancing the title role, was playing at the Theatre Royal, Drury Lane. He was due at the Lord Mayor's procession and banquet. He needed a shave. The barber knocked, entered, bowed: a thin man with the English whiteness of jowl, dressed entirely in black. In complete silence, with the flowing rapidity of a phantom, he shook out a crisp, white apron, adjusted a chair, and stropped a long razor. Gautier grew increasingly uneasy at each stroke, a victim of those unspeakable suspicions that separate native from foreigner, living from dead.

'Seeing him so chill, so pale, so mournful, I asked myself if he were not some ill-provisioned resurrectionist who wished to acquire a new subject. At the same time, I instinctively cast my eyes upon that part of the floorboards where my chair rested, anxious to ascertain whether or no there was a hidden trap door through which I should plunge into the cellar bearing a large slit in my throat.' On the point of calling off the whole operation, Gautier was saved by the inherited logic of Pascal and Voltaire. 'I made the calming reflexion that, since I was lodged upon the second floor of the hotel, there could hardly be a cellarage beneath my parquet, and that a trap door in opening would make me fall to the first floor, depositing me exactly on top of the pianoforte of an extremely pretty young opera-singer.' The *jolie cantatrice* was Ernesta, who subsequently bore Gautier twin daughters. So the English barber was possibly a better Figaro than Gautier concluded at the time.

At Drury Lane, Gautier made extensive notations on the flesh tones of the English girls in the audience. No native painter had ever done justice to their exquisiteness, Gautier felt, except possibly Sir Thomas Lawrence, who could be held ultimately responsible for the creation of the English Rose type, the bloom of a thousand keepsakes, whose torn and treasured leaves were pinned across the dressing-rooms of Europe. A connoisseur of textures, Gautier distinguished sharply between the opulent blonde and the tea-rose blonde, and gazed appreciatively at the complexion of cheek, neck and *gorge*, which made 'rice-paper, or the pulpy petal of the magnolia, or the inner pellicle of the egg, or the vellum on which the gothic miniaturists traced their delicate illuminations' look like coarse cloth by comparison. Yet the genial English passion for decorative gardens, when carried in all its stunning completeness of fruit trees, herbaceous borders and cockle shells, to the top of the English lady's *hat*, left him merely stoical.

In the middle of the ballet, Carlotta was required to perform a daring leap in the *pas de songe*, representing the descent of the *péri* from the heavenly sphere. It called for the greatest agility and nerve on her part, and perfect timing from her partner Petipa, whose task was to receive her bodily presence on the earth beneath. Occasionally, in Paris, this *saute de gazelle* had been muffed, and the French audiences, recalled Gautier, had hissed without mercy. At the third performance in London, Carlotta once more misjudged the dangerous jump. As she prepared for another attempt, a ripple ran through the English audience, and murmurs from the stalls were heard begging her not to risk such a frightful plunge a second time. Then a sympathetic voice, from the gods, loudly suggested that it would be better to give Petipa 'a stiff drink' first, as he could scarcely 'stand up on his pins'. Amidst a profound stillness, Carlotta leapt into space, Petipa fielded sinuously, and the house sprang to its feet and gave them three cheers.

But then the English were different in sporting matters. Boats and horses alone really brought out their enthusiasm. There were even moments suggesting lyrical depths, as on the day's outing at Royal Ascot. Clutching his *Oxley's Authentic Racing Card* – which with *Robinson Crusoe* and the Mansion House menu, was one of the few British texts Gautier ever claimed to have read in the original – he stared round him with calm satisfaction at the scene. There were lawns of 'vegetable velvet', ladies with shot-silk dresses and fringed parasols, champagne and Scotch Ale corks flying into the cerulean blue, gypsies dancing round the carriage wheels telling endlessly optimistic fortunes. In the distance, over the undulations of emerald turf, the 'cherry-red horses ran'. At the far turn, the brightly coloured silks of the jockeys' caps were 'like poppies, cornflowers and anemones carried away on the wind'. At the close of each race, the winner stood steaming peacefully in the Royal Enclosure, and a cluster of white pigeons were released into the sky like a shout of purest joy.

It was only later that Gautier learnt that the pigeons simply carried the listings of the betting odds and results to a hundred murky gambling parlours across the nation, which sufficed to transform the occasion into a rather more utilitarian event, 'a roulette or a Stock Exchange'.

After the mixed triumphs of *La Péri*, six years elapsed before Gautier next slipped across the Channel. Though his friend's Tunnel was still inexplicably incomplete, the years of middle age had brought increased travelling comforts. The *Chemin de Fer du Nord* already ran as far as Rouen, and together with the regular steam packet services, and the celebrated express from Dover, this combined to bring the two capitals within a single day of each other. By the spring of 1849, after nine months of almost continuous political upheavals in Paris, Gautier was already restive for London's paradoxes and gloomy, introspective charm. His *feuilleton* of 21 May complained of not being able to take advantage of a newly created package tour, which for 175 francs transported you, housed you, took you on guided tours round the Court, the museums, Richmond, Hampton Court Palace, Greenwich, and even brought you back 'with all intelligence and care'.

A month later, his column began mysteriously. 'In this unhappy week of cholera and insurrection which has just gone by, the theatres of Paris have played nothing. The announcement of some major performance would have brought us back in the twinkling of an eye, despite pestilence and politics: for it is on such evil days that Art has need of all its supporters. But the thunder in the street makes the Muses fall silent, and we would have had nothing to do at our post. So we have profited from this sad *congé* by accomplishing a voyage to China, no less than the intrepid Mac-Carthy or Monsieur de Langrenée. This voyage cost us two hours and two shillings.'

This unexpectedly exotic expedition turned out to have been a visit by the ferry from Hungerford Bridge to a Chinese junk moored at St Katharine's Dock. It brought Gautier a new sense of the equivocations of Progress and Empire, almost, very distantly, a sense of menace. Below decks on the junk, he listened distractedly to a Chinese orchestra, with four young men in dark blue silken smocks and pigtails, playing a melancholy composition on drums, gongs, violins and tambourines. Around them the cabin was cluttered with ornate, open-work ivory boxes, porcelain pots and huge grotesque mandrake roots, twisted into fantastical shapes. Gautier meditated on a pile of Chinese coffins in a dark corner, each hewn out of a single log, and painted a glistening vermilion, 'stacked there, no doubt, for the benefit of the crew in case of cholera or nostalgia'. He was thoughtful. 'When a concert is finished, one replaces the instrument in its case: when a life is finished, one slips the man into his coffin: and the rest is silence ... But why do violins have cases that resemble the bier? Is it because they have souls and voices, and groan like us?'

Returning on deck, under the leaden sky of London, Gautier gazed curiously at a large lacquer cabinet fitted under the poop of the junk which was carved like some gigantic dream-bird. The cabinet formed an open shrine for Buddhist worship, and in it three golden figurines representing the Chinese trinity. In front of them, coloured spills, jossticks and aromatic tapers sent their sweet oriental perfumes drifting heavily over the dark waters of the Thames.

Perhaps, thought Gautier, the traditional piety of the Chinese crew had not been dissolved 'by contact with the sceptical barbarians...' He bent down and peered closely at the little, squat buddhas, miniature replicas of the mighty idols he had earlier seen on display at an antiquarian collection in Hyde Park. He studied their impenetrable good humour ... 'but as for the gods themselves, those circumflex eyebrows, those equivocal smiles, and those gross little bellies, all express an attitude towards the worshipper that is ironic, and even irreverent. The devotee does not lack faith; but it seems that the idol itself lacks conviction. Perhaps all religions will come to an end through the agnosticism of their gods.'

It was a foretaste of a sensation he was to have on one of his last visits, in 1851, as he wandered through the imperial splendours of the Great Exhibition at the Crystal Palace. Dazzled by the endless displays of jewelled armaments, exotic plants, stuffed elephants, priceless fabrics, and amorous potions of liquid pearl, he yet remained inexplicably unexalted, doubtful. What he finally remembered was a barred compartment containing several imprisoned Thuggees, the religious stranglers of Durga, the 'monsterous wife of Shiva, god of destruction'. These men were sullenly engaged in weaving an immense carpet, 'of evidently European design . . . with a greyish background spotted with black and red ornaments resembling burns and badly cleaned bloodstains. Its appearance was infinitely sinister and funereal. (Indeed it was as ugly as a home-made English carpet.) What torture it must have been for those poor Thugs, instinctive lovers of beautiful patterns and harmonious colours, to sit weaving this abominable tapestry of expiation!' This was the picture that stayed in his mind, from all that palace of wonders. This, and the massive pistons and flywheels of the engineering displays.

Yet in the midst of these later trips, with their thickening associations and suggestions, fell a bright shaft. For London unexpectedly and generously provided Gautier with the last great romance of his life, in the elegant shape of a very pretty Italian widow whom he encountered in Bond Street. Marie Mattei had adopted a smart, fast, modern English style, wore charming white waistcoats, rolled her own cigarettes in 'papelitos', sucked peppermints and sipped tea, as Gautier fondly recorded in his sonnets. He rapidly made her his mistress, and back in Montmartre she transformed his 'small red bed with its spiral bedposts' into a paradise of sexual blue. And there, with a touch of the renowned English coolness in the heat of battle

> . . . quand le plaisir a brisé nos forces,
> Nonchalant entr'acte à la volupté,
> Nous fumons tous deux en prenant le thé.

But passion, like all things – except perhaps the art that recorded it – was transitory, no permanent gift. As Gautier grew old, and Paris closed round them like a familiar shawl, there came back the memory of the English Sunday, that Feast of Limbo, when shops and pubs and theatres closed, streets were deserted, and everyone seemed to flee the city by boat or coach or charabanc, until it was like a place of the dead, 'one of those cities peopled by inhabitants who have turned to stone, as Eastern Tales relate'. It haunted him, that vision of melancholy exuding from the very walls, and he wrote wryly: 'At such times one longed to have a little portable chemist's outfit, consisting of opium, prussic acid, and acetate of morphine. The thought of suicide is born in the most resolute heart; it is not prudent to fiddle with your pistols or to lean over the balustrades of the bridges . . . There is but one recourse, to make oneself abominably drunk, to fill one's stomach with a blazing sunset of rum-punch . . . but you have to be English for that.'

On those days the only serious British activity seemed to be attending funerals. But the London cemetery, so icy, stark, flowerless and abandoned, with its low graves retaining 'like mummies, sarcophagi with a vague appearance of the human corpse' filled him with nothing but lugubrious imaginings, and gave him only an intense desire to remain alive. He turned the dark shape in his hand. But then, finally, was one not a Parisian? He pulled upon a fresh cigar, and stroked the receptive fur of an attendant cat. He thought of the baroque magnificence of the cemetery of Père Lachaise, the swept alleys, the carved chapels, the bright wreaths of blossom. 'How can the English, a nation so absolutely wedded to "home and comfort", how *can* the English resign themselves to being so dreadfully ill at ease in the next world?'

# POOR PIERROT

IF YOU ENCOUNTERED PIERROT in Paris today, he would seem innocent enough, quite innocent. Besides, it would probably be in a children's toyshop. In the Passage Jouffroy, for example, one of those high melancholy ironwork arcades off the boulevard Montmartre, much frequented by Gérard de Nerval in the long autumn days before his suicide, there is a spacious old-fashioned boutique stuffed with cardboard theatres, packs of Petits Metamorphoses, Second Empire dolls' house furniture, musical boxes that play Chopin – and Pierrots, dozens of them.

There are Pierrot dolls, Pierrot marionettes, Pierrot paperweights, Pierrot glove-puppets, Pierrot mannikins, Pierrot pipecleaners, and Pierrot *pantins* with flat cardboard limbs linked up with string and brass eyelets, and strangely blank on their reverse sides as if their souls had somehow been misplaced. All of them conform religiously to the same uniform: loose white smock and cap, and austerely blanched face that stares back at you with weird intensity. At a distance, perched there in the arcade window, they look like a flock of fantail pigeons in mourning; close to, they are somewhere between clowns and purgatorial spirits.

The childlike symbolism of all this reminds one of those endearingly familiar nursery-rhymes that once announced the terrors and tragedies of popular history, the 'tishoos of plague, the cherrystones of murder. Pierrot's origins are mysterious; yet everyone can lament his plight, the gentle distracted *ami* of the seventeenthcentury air, '*Au clair de la lune*', the creature of laughter and sadness that we vaguely associate with Paris and unrequited love and the bittersweet light of the moon.

But who, in fact, was Pierrot, and why was he so unhappy? That simple question is one of the profound riddles of folk mythology, and the account that follows is merely one episode in what is perhaps an eternally recurring cycle in the human tragi-comedy. It concerns Jean-Gaspard Deburau, one of the legendary giants of the French Romantic theatre, and a figure almost as mysterious as the White Clown whom he rescued from three centuries of despised obscurity in the travelling fairgrounds and anonymous harlequinades of western Europe.

To begin at the beginning is impossible: but one may start with a birth. Deburau was born in Neukolin in 1796 and can correctly be called a Bohemian. The youngest member of a troupe of touring acrobats, he spent a rootless childhood crossing and recrossing a continent convulsed by Napoleonic dreams. Deburau's father seems to have been an army deserter, a shrewd businessman and a bully; his mother seems to have died young, exhausted by privations; neither had definite nationality. Deburau grew up into a tall, loose-limbed boy, with a long melancholy face, taciturn and withdrawn, a clumsy acrobat and consequently the comic butt of his nimbler brothers and sisters.

There was something dreamy and elusively ambitious about him. A persistent legend tells of a visit to the Sultan's palace in Constantinople, where the family troupe were commanded to perform in an apparently deserted hall, partitioned off at one end by a diaphanous curtain. For their finale, young Deburau was required to scamper to the top of a human pyramid: as he faltered on to his brother's shoulders, he was magically rewarded by a glimpse beyond the softly undulating veil. He was looking down on a secret audience, the entire Sultan's harem, a giddy vision of silks and jewels and curving flesh, forbidden to all mortal eyes on pain of death. He gazed, overbalanced, and fell.

The Deburau family seemed to have settled in Paris towards 1814, but it is not until 1822 that the father's name first appears on a cast list of the new pantomime theatre, the Funambules. Young Deburau was employed as a buffoon, and revealed a hidden talent for elegant and sometimes savage mimicry. His emotional life remains hidden: the city archives show that at twenty-three he married a flower girl called Adelaide, for whom he bought dresses on credit at the local *couturière*, so we may perhaps assume that she was beautiful, and that he loved her. But three months later Adelaide died, in a tiny upper lodgings at the Hôtel Bouffiers. A surviving inventory shows a bed with a straw mattress, a round dining table with two flaps, and a chest of drawers with a marble top.

After seven more years of penurious existence, Deburau *père* died, the family troupe began to disperse, and one has the sense of a tyranny dissolving. For Deburau, then aged thirty, it was a moment of late blossoming. At last he was able to sign his own contract with the Funambules management, and he concluded a solid three-year agreement with a weekly salary of 35 francs, which was about four times what the musicians earned. He was engaged to play one named role only: that of Pierrot, the White Faced Clown. The contract was dated 10 December 1826.

Until this critical moment in theatrical history, the stock part of Pierrot had been minor and ill-defined. Pierrot was loosely evolved from a number of auxiliary clown figures in the Italian Commedia dell'Arte troupes of the sixteenth and seventeenth centuries. He was a figure of fun, rather than of distinction. Experts are inclined to disagree, but Pierrot's ancestors have been variously identified with Pedrolino, the honest valet of Flaminio Scala's plays; the wise peasant Bertoldo whose struggles with the Prince of Bologna were first written down by Giulio Croce in the 1570s; the all-purpose buffoon of the fairground show, Il Pagliaccio (*Le Paillasse*, Old Strawbags); the Giglio or Gilles of the Neapolitan commedia; and the French Fool Gros-Guillaume (Fat Willy) who played in front of Cardinal Richelieu with a face plastered with baker's flour and two belts to restrain the catholicity of his belly, one above and one below.

Indeed, the 'poor Pierrot' whom Deburau inherited was so rich in ancestry that he was in effect perfectly illegitimate, a restless wanderer who sought his name in every city, a mongrel of the booths, a changeling outcast from the dignified family hierarchies of the traditional Commedia. He was quite simply the White Faced Clown, the *enfariné*, the Fool whose face is blanched – not with paint or wax – but with the homely naïveté of flour and water. In this single recurrent detail lies the probable foundation of his dramatic character and his earliest symbolism. The Clown with the face of flour seems to represent both servile bumpkin stupidity, and its opposite, an eternal peasant wisdom; he also stands for something of the natural fertility of the earth, as persistent and universal as wheat, from which comes both his greed and his amorousness (consider the appetites of Chaucer's Miller). These traits give Pierrot's most primitive psychology. It is essentially innocent.

By the eighteenth century the White-Faced Clown had established himself in supporting roles in many of the harlequinades in France, though the Italian Commedia itself had been banished from Paris in 1697 to protect the drama of Molière. The White Clown was a buffoon, valet, trickster and the eternally unsuccessful rival of Arlequin for the love of Columbine; and it is as 'Gilles' that he appears in the famous portrait by Watteau of 1721, executed in eight days as a billboard for the Théâtre de la Foire in Paris.

In a curious way, this painting is a premonition of Deburau. The White Clown stands forth in the parade, his limp arms dangling down his white *casaque*, his feet turned outwards, a proverb of naïveté. Yet he has become suddenly mysterious. Perhaps this is simply because it is one of Watteau's very last works, with a consumptive glow of loss and transfiguration about it. But perhaps also, it is because Pierrot is suddenly *without* his mask of flour. From the ageless anonymity of the White Clown, a completely individual face now looks out, enigmatically, with a faint smile of greeting or mockery, the rims of the eyes and the nostrils slightly swollen and red, as if he had been weeping for some reason yet to be revealed. All this is of course a hundred years before Deburau himself stood forward to be judged.

It began (or began again) with a summer newspaper article by Charles Nodier in the *Pandora* of 1828, heralding with a certain donnish humour the great new Gilles or Pierrot at the Funambules Theatre, a '*Satan naïf et bouffon*', who needed nothing but a large bank account and a smart carriage to give him a Parisian vogue. Nodier rented a box for a year, and wrote a pantomime especially for Deburau, called appropriately enough *Le Songe d'or*, a dream of riches.

Nodier's support was influential, for as the eccentric librarian of the Arsenal, and the intimate of Hugo and Sainte-Beuve, his flights of fancy were closely observed by Parisian intellectuals. Deburau and the pantomime soon gained a kind of cult following. The sharp young critic on the *Journal des Débats*, Jules Janin, headed it with a racy two-volume *Histoire du Théâtre à Quatre Sous*

(1832), proclaiming the classical theatre dead and wildly pane-gyrizing the Funambules. It was complete with commissioned por-traits of Deburau, and a fictionalized account of his early career, including a discussion supposed to have been held with Napoleon before Waterloo on the problems of French drama; and a lawsuit against the theatre management involving an impious toadstool said to have sprouted in the great clown's dressing-room.

The long-haired poets Gautier and Nerval, then both in their twenties, attended the Funambules so regularly that whenever Pierrot carried out one of his ritual abductions of jam-tarts or pies, a salutation of pastries would fly up to greet them where they sat at their posts in the front-of-house box. Many other writers and *feuilletonistes* later came to watch the pantomime, and those who have left records include Baudelaire, Champfleury, Alphonse Karr and George Sand.

But Gautier's summary is perhaps the best: 'The pantomime is the real *comédie humaine*; and even though it does not employ two thousand characters like Balzac's, it is none the less complete for that. It embraces everything in four or five type-parts. Cassandra represents the family; Columbine the ideal woman or the dream pursued, the flower of youth and beauty; Arlequin with his monkey's snout and snake-like body, his patchwork and his shower of spangles, represents Love, Wit, Impulse, Audacity, and all that glitters in vice or virtue; while Pierrot, poor haggard, pallid Pierrot in his glimmering draperies, always hungry and always beaten, is the antique slave and the modern proletarian, the pariah, the helpless and disinherited being, who witnesses the orgies and follies of his masters with mournful and yet cunning eyes.'

At the Funambules, Deburau began to give a peculiar and start-ling authority to the Pierrot, that *être passif et déshérité*. Partly this came from the conditions under which he played. The theatre, an erstwhile circus of performing dogs, Les Chiens Savants, was situated on the ancient boulevard du Temple, at the heart of the popular revolutionary quarter of Paris, between the market of Les Halles and the faubourg Saint Antoine. The *canaille* which crowded along the iron balustrade of the *paradis* – the gods, with its famous 4-*sous* seats – were the roughest, rowdiest, most unpre-dictable audience in Paris. Nerval recalled that to use a lorgnette in their presence was to incite a riot.

But it was just this audience that Deburau dominated. He did it, said George Sand, simply by expressing their own feelings. Moreover he did it in total silence. For in Deburau's masterly hands, Pierrot had become an entirely silent mime.

Originally, this silence had a political cause. Throughout its existence between 1816 and 1862, the Funambules never received a government licence to perform speaking plays, as these were regarded, in the circumstances, as subversive of morality, law and order. Instead it confined itself to a spectacular show of tightrope walking, tumbling, quick-change, flying traps, dancing, slapstick and popular music, based on the pantomime plots of the traditional harlequinade. In place of dialogue, it developed rather more visual and violent methods of exchanging ideas and emotions. There were three specialities: *cascades*, highly complex, balletic fights with clubs, punches and the celebrated leaping *pied au cul* – or kick up the arse – which the tall, muscular Deburau excelled in. Then the *sauts*, startling and often perilous leaps up and down counterweighted trapdoors. And finally *trucs*, bizarre instantaneous changes of scenery or stage-prop, so that a sheltering wardrobe might become a ravenous whale, or a cooling ice-cream – for Pierrot – a spluttering Roman candle.

Moving calmly, almost sardonically, through this stylized, rather brutal form of 'English' pantomime, the long pale figure of Deburau gradually became the dominating genius of the theatre. The White Clown came into his own kingdom. The extraordinary, hypnotic power of the blanched face, with mournful eyes and derisive lips thrown into vivid relief, gave Deburau a dramatic instrument infinitely more subtle than Arlequin's mask and spangles, or Columbine's skirts and prettiness. Moreover, the taciturn Bohemian revealed an astonishing inventiveness of gesture and grimace, an entire *argot* of winks, sneers, nods, gapes, twinkles and guffaws. The *paradis* hung upon his face.

George Sand wrote that along the seething balustrade an almost studious concentration would appear, in row upon row of cupped chins and gaping mouths: 'you really feel he is speaking, you could write down all his *bons mots*, all his caustic repartee, all his eloquent apologies. When the machinists make a noise backstage, the public, frightened of losing a single *word* of their Pierrot, howl "Silence in the wings", and he thanks them . . .'

Increasingly, Deburau instilled Pierrot with his own personality: mocking, subtly malicious, charming and yet bitter, perhaps even menacing. He removed the buffoon ruff of the Commedia clown, since it obscured his face in the lurid ramp-lights, and replaced Gilles's floppy hat with the severe black skullcap which further offset the white of his flour, and which henceforth became an obligatory part of the Parisian Pierrot's costume. More and more he played over the heads of the other characters, directly to his audience, assuming their complicity in his schemes, nonchalant, powerfully reserved. In some pantomimes it was now he, and not the wigged Arlequin, who clasped Columbine's waist in the traditional finale of flaring orange Bengal Flames.

By 1835, Deburau was undisputed master of the Funambules stage. His salary stood at 200 francs a month, and he had remarried. His second wife was the pretty, twenty-year-old daughter of a prosperous artisan; Deburau was thirty-nine, and his illegitimate son, Charles, from a previous liaison, was seven. He was an established professional man. At the theatre he played dominoes in his dressing-room, or criticized the other actors' improvisations from the wings. When Placide, the old comedian who had played Cassandra, came to retire, he was presented with a pair of silver candlesticks at the final curtain, and burst into tears. The cast gathered round and the audience shook with emotional applause: then suddenly Pierrot advanced with a huge bathsponge and mopped disapprovingly at an imaginary puddle round Cassandra's feet, thus instantly drawing laughter and then applause back to himself.

Gautier recalled sadly: 'With Deburau the role of Pierrot grew and expanded until he finished by occupying the whole piece and distorting his own nature till its origins were almost lost. Beneath the flour and smock of the illustrious Bohemian, Pierrot took on masterful airs and inappropriate aplomb. He still delivered his kicks but he received none in return. Arlequin scarcely dared dust his shoulders with the bat, and Cassandra thought twice before landing a clout. He kissed Columbine and wrapped his arm round her waist like a seducer from the Comic Opera. He directed the action just as it suited him, and arrived at a height of insolence and daring that seemed to threaten even his own good genius . . .'

For one teenage spectator, Henri Rivière, there were openly

sadistic moments in Deburau's weird by-play with the *paradis*. Much later he formed his impressions into a brilliant first novella, entitled lightly *Pierrot*. 'The audience would not have been entirely surprised if the bottle which he gave Cassandra marked "laudanum", had really contained poison; or if, when he pretended to shave him on stage, instead of merely making Cassandra shudder with a touch of the cold razor, he had actually opened his throat from ear to ear . . .'

It happened, finally, in 1836, in the spring. Pierrot killed a man. Or rather, Deburau did.

The transcripts of the trial have survived, and for the first and last time Pierrot stands forth and speaks to his public. It is a moment of acute human insight, heralded in that curious way by Watteau's unmasking of the White Clown a century before. On the surface the case was straightforward enough. Evidence was brought before the Assize to show that Deburau and his new wife had been out walking one sunny April afternoon in the suburb of Bagnolet. They were followed by a young apprentice called Nicholas Vielin, who unaccountably began to hurl taunts and insults at them: *'Eh, Pierrot! Eh Paillasse, méchant paillasse, te voilà avec ta margot, ta putain!'* Vielin pursued them along the streets for some time, shouting obscenities at the tall clown. Deburau remained obstinately and ominously silent. Then at last, in a sudden access of rage, he turned, strode back up the road and struck a single blow with his cane. The apprentice collapsed instantly on the cobbles, with a deep wound over his left temple. He died later that evening. He was seventeen.

Deburau, with his narrow ironic face, and quick blue eyes, came pale and weeping to the witness box. He wore a black suit and waistcoat. He gave his evidence with soft, precise assurance, in a court packed with theatregoers and fashionable ladies.

> *President of the court:* How were you holding your walking-stick?
> *Accused:* By the middle.
> *President:* With which end of it did you strike?
> *Accused:* The small end.
> *President:* What was your intention of making use of your cane?
> *Accused:* I repeat, I had no intention of striking at all.

That crucial evidence regarding the holding of the stick was not pursued. Other damaging evidence was turned adroitly aside.

> *President*: Once you realized the victim had died from the blow sustained, did you not instantly exclaim, 'If he's dead, too bad for him. When I'm in a rage, I don't know myself?'
> *Accused*: No Monsieur. That would not have been possible, since I did not know the young man was dead until the following day.

That non-sequitur was not picked up either.

But perhaps the most telling piece of character evidence came quite by chance, towards the end of the case, in the statement of a defence witness, a Monsieur Sartelet, obviously a man of some education. 'I then advised Monsieur Deburau to take my address, since I might be of use to him in the affair. I added that it was happy for him I had witnessed the scene, since I could provide a true account of the facts. He replied, "Ah Monsieur! It is happy for me – but unhappy too. For had you not been there, I would have continued to support those insults in silence. But seeing you there, I could no longer bear the humiliation of being insulted before onlookers any more; and so the unhappy event took place." (Gasps in court.)'

That surely was the evidence of the White Clown himself, the evidence of centuries.

The judge summed up the case favourably to Deburau. Young Vielin had been the aggressor, the provocation had been persistent and extreme; the death resulting from the blow was accidental. The jury returned a verdict of not guilty. Pierrot received an unconditional discharge and returned to the Funambules.

Yet Pierrot's trial was full of macabre resonances that escaped neither the *canaille*, nor the literary world. Not least was the revelation that Vielin had been a regular follower of Deburau's from the *paradis*, and discussed his performances passionately over the supper-table with his apprentice-master. As Alphonse Karr wrote in Nerval's theatrical magazine, *Le Monde Dramatique*:

'Before the fame brought by Janin's book, Deburau would never have considered himself insulted. He would have pulled a grimace at his mockers and made them laugh ... but instead of that,

Deburau, who has never been seen white-faced except for his flour, went white-faced with anger; and with a stroke of his cane he killed a peasant boy that he had probably nearly killed on ten previous occasions with laughter . . . Deburau has become tragic, while murder has become a farce.'

Deburau himself could hardly avoid making the transfer between the real and the stage world. The theatrical historian Paul Hugounet later published what he claimed was a letter of Deburau at this time: 'I can't touch a stick any more without burning my fingers . . . whatever I do that death will always come between me and my public. Whenever I twirl a slapstick on stage against the make-believe assailants the spectators will think of Pierrot *assassin* and that will turn their laughter into ice.'

Something irrevocable had indeed occurred. Poor Pierrot had killed his fellow man, his brother, his child, his mocker. The White Clown had encountered Death. Deburau had brought a tragic presence to the role. The evolution of Pierrot's dramatic character had made one more turn in the folk memory, and gathered one more layer of historic symbolism. The naïve flour-face, the mischievous moon-face, now also contained the deathly marble-face: white with anger, white with shock, black with knowledge. Through pride perhaps, very human pride, Pierrot had lost his innocence.

The full consequences of this are a matter of theatrical, literary and perhaps psychological history. The 1840s saw the sudden development of an entire pantomime of death, more conscious and more literary, heavy with political and moral prophecy. The *Marchand d'habits* (1842) in which Pierrot kills an old-clothes merchant in order to enter a society ball, gradually became Deburau's signature piece, brilliantly analysed by Gautier and a century later superbly mimed by Jean-Louis Barrault in Marcel Carné's celebration of the Funambules, *Les Enfants du Paradis* (1944). The *Marchand d'habits* was followed by *Pierrot, Valet de la Mort* (1846), *Pierrot Posthume* (1850), and many similar black pantomimes. Nerval wrote thoughtfully, and perhaps autobiographically, of Pierrot playing music in the halls of hell. Baudelaire produced his strange reflections on the *comique féroce* in a classic essay *The Soul of Laughter* (1855); and George Sand's stage-struck son, Maurice, turned back to Pierrot's pre-lapsarian days in the first authoritative history of the Commedia dell'Arte (1860).

But few of these high affairs concerned Deburau then, or need concern us now. For this is simply one story of the White Faced Clown as it happened in Paris. To imagine that Deburau's trial seriously affected his popularity would be to misunderstand his relations with the *paradis*. On the contrary: six months after his acquittal, Deburau signed a new ten-year contract with the management for an unprecedented fee of 250 francs a month with a 6 per cent pension scheme. He continued to dominate the stage for another nine years at the Funambules, though increasingly racked by asthma, that most psychosomatic of diseases. Accounts tell of him leaning in the wings against the woodland scenery flaps, beating his left side with his fist and gasping for air.

In February 1845, his fiftieth year, Deburau struck the back of his head badly while plunging down one of the spring-traps to the *troisième dessous*, traditionally associated with Hell in the theatrical world. He replied to George Sand's anxious inquiry on this occasion with his old flourish: 'I do not know in what terms to express my appreciation. My pen is like my voice on stage, but my heart is like my face.' The asthma gained relentlessly on him, and on 17 June 1846, Deburau died at three in the morning.

The young Jules Champfleury had witnessed his last night at the Funambules. They were playing the *Noces de Pierrot*. At the final curtain it was Deburau's turn to let fall a single tear which traced its dark line down the white *enfariné*. He left the theatre at midnight by the little side door into the rue Fossés-du-Temple, the white carnation of Pierrot's wedding feast pinned bravely to his dark lapel.

# INSIDE THE TOWER

*A radio-drama based on the life of the poet Gérard de Nerval. All Nerval's speeches are drawn from his own essays, letters and journals.*

*(fade in radiophonic music)*

HOLMES     In 1855 Paris suffered a bitterly cold winter. During most of January the city lay under thick snow. At night temperatures dropped below minus ten degrees centigrade. The gas-lamps glowed in the streets with a dull, blue flame. The horse-drawn omnibuses jammed in the icy ruts of the boulevard, and the café windows were opaque with frost. Down by the Seine, the washerwomen's sheets hung rigidly over the side of the laundry barges, and the river turned to ice under the Pont Neuf and the Pont Saint Michel. The wind blew cruelly through the cobbled back-streets. The beggars said the sun had died.

*(fade in over music the sound of wind; then muffled street noises, carriage wheels, coughing, footsteps crunching on snow, muffled swearing in French . . .)*

EYE WITNESS     I suppose it was about six-thirty in the morning, Friday 26th January. I was on my way to work across the Place du Châtelet, when I spotted a man in black uniform and a couple of policemen hurrying down a side-street. The beginning of the rue de la Tuerie was nothing but empty, boarded-up houses, but after a few steps there was the blackened shop of a key-cutter on the left, with a sign, shaped like a huge key, standing out from the wall overhead against the frosty, snow-laden sky. Further on, on the other side, was the entrance to a narrow iron flight of steps, one of those street staircases which begins with four steep steps down onto a sort of iron landing running across the width of the alley. At the bottom level the steps lead into a sordid alley which disappeared at the far end into a labyrinth of filthy back-streets. It was into this foul alleyway, known officially as the rue de la Vieille-Lanterne, I saw a man in black with two policemen going purpose-fully. I followed them.

The cobbles were covered in thick ice, and the iron banisters were loose in several places. At the bottom of the staircase I witnessed a grim scene. A man's body was stretched out in the alley, his head resting on the last step, and his feet sticking into the gutter of a sewage pipe that came out of the alley-wall beneath the iron landing. They had just cut him down from the bars of a low window, in the cellar-wall above the bottom steps, from which he had hanged himself . . . The man in black turned out to be the commissioner of police.

*(water, echoing footsteps and voices, the slap of wet clothes on marble . . .)*

MORTUARY ASSISTANT

Slab number 14. Twenty-sixth January 1855. Reception time: nine-thirty a.m. Sex: masculine. Age: forty-seven. Place of birth: Paris,

Seine. Civil status: bachelor. Clothes and pos-
sessions: one black jacket; two calico shirts;
two flannel waistcoats; one pair pale-grey
trousers; one pair patent-leather shoes; one
pair socks – red cotton *(fade)* . . .

*(fade in radiophonic music)*

POLICE
COMMISSIONER

Labrunie, Gérard. Also known as Gérard de
Nerval, man of letters. Temporary address at
the Hotel de Normandie, 13 rue des Bons-
Enfants. A case of suicide by strangulation.
This morning at approximately seven-thirty
a.m. the deceased was found hanging from
the bars of a locksmith's shop in the rue de
la Vieille-Lanterne. He had hanged himself
with a length of sash-cord; the body was
attached to the bars by means of the said
cord. There were no signs of violence on the
corpse.

MAXIME DU
CAMP

Very early on Friday morning I received a
message from Théophile Gautier informing
me that Gérard de Nerval had been found
hung . . . They'd sent for Gautier and Arsène
Houssaye to confirm the identification. Gautier was apparently moved to tears; he had a
long-standing affection for Gérard. It was
easy for me to see the body in the mortuary.
Poor Gérard was laid out flat on his back, his
eyes shut, and his tongue just slightly pro-
truding between parted lips. His fingers were
clenched inwards on his palms, but his face
was calm. His head was fractionally twisted
on to his left shoulder-blade, and the tips of
his feet were turned abnormally outwards.
There was no trace of violence, no bruising,
no contusions. Only, around the neck, there
ran a thin line – more brown, as I remember,

than red – which bore witness to the pressure of the cord, that piece of kitchen-cord which Gérard had shown me but six days previously – and which in his madness, he took for a seventeenth-century ladies' dress-cord, no less than the actual dress-cord of Madame de Maintenon!

*(tolling bell effect: radiophonics)*

HOLMES     Gérard's funeral took place on the 30th January, and a mass was said for him in a side chapel of Notre Dame. In order to obtain permission for him to be buried in consecrated ground at Père Lachaise cemetery, a special application was made to the Archbishop of Paris. Suicide, when committed while 'of unsound mind', does not cut the victim off from the consolations of Mother Church.

*(monks' choir singing the 'Dies Irae' in Gregorian chant. In the background the sound of digging, and wind blowing. Over this the scrape of a quill pen on paper and the voice of . . .)*

DR EMILE BLANCHE     My Lord Bishop: M. Labrunie, Gérard de Nerval, was suffering from extreme fits of mental alienation, which seized him on repeated occasions during these last few years, and for which he received treatment from both my father and myself, Dr Emile Blanche, in this institution . . . Though M. de Nerval was not ill enough to be confined in a mental asylum against his will, yet in my considered opinion his state of mind had not been healthy or normal for a long time previously.

He believed he had the same powers of

imagination, and the same aptitude for work, as he had in the old days, and he expected to support himself as before on the income from his writing. Certainly he worked harder than ever, but one may feel that he was disappointed in his hopes, perhaps. His natural independence and pride of character prevented him from accepting anything in the way of aid, from even his best-tried friends. As a result of these mental – or moral – pressures, his reason was driven further and further astray; and above all this was because he now saw his madness face to face. I therefore have no hesitation in declaring, my Lord Bishop, that it was certainly in an extreme fit of madness that M. Gérard de Nerval put an end to his days.

*(gradually fade out sound of the plainchant, the digging, and finally the wind, during the next voice-over. Towards the end, radiophonics reappear)*

MAXIME DU
CAMP

He was mad, though it was an intermittent kind of madness, which in its moments of calm left him with a personality both gentle and original, and a mode of life that was full of oddities. But when his state became critical, he was a danger both to himself and those around him, and he would be carried off to Passy, to the mental hospital in the old town house of the Duc de Penthièvre, run by Dr Emile Blanche. These fits would either depress him to the point of coma, or else excite him to the pitch of fury; but they rarely endured for more than six months at a time. He would emerge from them slowly, like someone only half-awake and still under the impression of a vivid dream. I often used to go and visit him in the asylum when he was recovering. He said to me on one occasion: It's so kind of you to come, Du Camp: you know our poor Dr Blanche is mad. He thinks he is running a mental hospital, and we all have to pretend to be mental patients in order to calm him down. I wonder if you could stand in for me a while, because I have to go over to Chantilly tomorrow morning to marry Mme de Feuchères. You will recall that Mme de Feuchères was the mistress of the last prince of the house of Condé, who hanged himself from a window with a silk handkerchief.

*(music starts faintly)*

HOLMES

The poet who called himself Gérard de Nerval spent many years recording his dreams and hallucinations. The analysis of memory became the central preoccupation of his life. 'Angelique', 'Sylvie', 'Pandora', 'Aurélia' – these are the names of the works by which he sought to justify his existence; and perhaps to explain his death. They are works which he regarded as both literary and to some degree scientific; as human evidence. But was he, in fact, mad?

*(the radiophonic music increases in volume, until rising through it comes the voice of . . .)*

NERVAL

Our dreams are a second life. I have never been able to penetrate those Gates of Ivory, or of Horn, that separate us from the invisible world, without shuddering. The first moments of sleep are the very image of death; a dark haze of drowsiness invades our thoughts, and we can never determine the

precise instant when the *self*, in its other
form, takes over the work of existence. A
vague subterranean region slowly brightens
out beneath us, and from the shadows of
the night emerge those pale figures, gravely
unmoving, that populate the worlds of limbo.
Then the picture takes shape, and a new light
begins to glow upon and animate the strange
apparitions – and the world of the Spirits
opens before us. I am going to try to set down
the impressions produced by a long malady,
which took place entirely within the mysteries of my spirit – and I do not know why
I employ the term 'malady', for never, as far
as my inward self was concerned, did I feel
myself to be in a healthier state. Sometimes
I believed that my physical strength and mental powers were doubled; it seemed as if I
knew everything, understood everything; my
imagination brought me infinite delights. In
recovering what men have chosen to call my
*reason*, should I regret having lost such
things?

HOLMES

Théophile Gautier and the other poets who
were his friends did not find it difficult to
accept Nerval's madness as a form of visionary power superior to mere reason.

GAUTIER

I had known Gérard since my college days.
He was a small, dreamy figure with a neat
brown beard cut in the German manner and
large grey eyes. There was something boyish
about this round, full face, and his mischievous conversation. He had a peculiar walk: his
elbows flapped at his sides, and in his short
Austrian cloak he looked a little like an
ostrich trying to take off from the boulevard,
as if he would like to flap away over the heads

of the crowd, over the carriage roofs, over the chestnut trees, over the balconies and sloping rooftops, and disappear into the Parisian sky.

I well remember him standing one day in front of the great marble fireplace in Victor Hugo's drawing-room, and holding forth on his favourite subject, which involved whirling together the Heavens and Hells of several different world religions with such studious impartiality that someone suddenly exclaimed: 'But Gérard! It's perfectly plain that you don't believe in any religion at all, really!'

*(Gautier chuckles to himself, remembering)*

Well Gérard simply transfixed the chap with those glittering grey eyes of his, all those weird scintillations, and announced with immense deliberation: 'No religion at all? *I* have no religion? – I tell you I have seventeen religions – seventeen at least.' Well you can imagine *that* brought the conversation to a pretty close!

*(Gautier goes on chuckling, and suddenly mutters . . .)*

HOLMES

In his twenties, Gérard developed a mysterious passion for a blonde singer in the Opéra-Comique, Jenny Colon. He bought a huge fourposter bed, carved with zodiac-signs, in which to consummate the affair; but Gautier, who knew about such things, said that Gérard was disappointed in his hopes. He travelled abroad, to Naples, to Brussels and Vienna, trying to forget her. By the spring of 1841 he returned to Paris for the carnival season, and took lodgings near Gautier again, in the cheerful *quartier* of small streets, cafés, flea-markets and fish shops, north of the boulevard Montmartre. It was the haunt of young painters, journalists and actresses, and during Mardi Gras the revels lasted all night long. The streets filled with decorated carriages, crowds of revellers in grotesque masks and provocative fancy-dress, the sound of music and dancing and fireworks. Gérard drank in the café Pelletier with his friends, and then wandered off alone through the streets. He was in a strange state, he seemed to fluctuate between exaltation and despair.

*(the carnival music which has continued softly in the background, now increases in volume)*

NERVAL

The hour was striking just as I passed the doorway of No. 37 rue Notre-Dame-de-Lorette, and on the doorstep I saw a woman, still quite young, but whose appearance filled me with surprise and horror. Her face was deadly pale, and her eyes were sunken into her skull. I said to myself: 'This is the figure of Death.' I went home to bed with the clear idea that the world was soon to end . . .

The next evening I returned to my usual café, where I held forth for hours on music and painting, with my various friends. I spun together all the elements of a theoretical system on the affinities of the human races, on the power of numbers, on the harmony of colours. Then midnight struck. For me it signified the fatal hour: though I wondered if the chronometer of the heavens did not perhaps correspond with our earthly clocks. I said to my friend Paul Chenevard, the painter, that I was leaving and setting out for my homeland, in the East. He came with me as far as the crossroads at Cadet. Here, finding myself at the confluence of several streets, I stopped uncertainly, and sat down on a bollard on the corner of the rue Coquenard. Paul used all his force to make me move on, but in vain. I felt nailed to the spot. Finally, at about one in the morning, he abandoned me, and finding myself alone I called out for help to two friends, Théophile Gautier and Alphonse Karr, whom I glimpsed in the crowd passing like shadows. It was a night of carnival, and a mass of carriages packed with people wearing masks were going up and down the street. I examined the carriage numbers with intense curiosity, and became engrossed in a mystical kind of numerical calculation. At last, above the roofs of the rue Hauteville, I saw a red star rising, encircled with a blue, hazy halo. I thought I recognized it as the distant star of Saturn, and getting to my feet with a great effort, I set off in that direction.

*(at this point the carnival music fades rapidly away, and Nerval's voice begins to speak in a kind of vacuum . . . radiophonics gradually appearing)*

Then I began to hear some strange and mysterious kind of singing, almost like a hymn, which filled me with wild joy. At the same time I began to take off my terrestrial garments, and fling them in a circle around me. When I got to the middle of the street, I found that I was suddenly surrounded by a night-patrol of soldiers. I realized that I had been endowed with superhuman physical force, and it seemed as if I only had to stretch out my hands in order to lay all the poor soldiers flat on the pavement, as one might smooth the fur of a fleece. But I did not want to deploy this magnetic force, and I allowed myself to be taken without resistance to the police-post in the Place Cadet.

They put me on a camp-bed, while my clothes were hung in front of the stove to dry. Then I had a vision. The sky opened before my eyes in a blaze of light, and the divinities of antiquity appeared in front of me. But the morning put an end to this dream. A change of guard replaced the soldiers who had brought me in, and they put me in the lock-up cells with a strange individual, arrested the same night as myself, who did not seem to know even his own name.

Then my friends came to collect me, and later they put me in a carriage and we found ourselves at the rue Picpus. They had brought me to a hospital . . .

*(radiophonic music)*

For three days I fell into a profound sleep, rarely interrupted by dreams. A woman dressed in black appeared at the foot of my bed and it seemed to me that her eyes were sunken in her skull. Only, at the bottom of their empty sockets, it seemed as if I could see tears welling slowly up, glistening like diamonds. To me, it seemed that this woman was the ghost of my mother, who had died long ago in Silesia.

HOLMES

Nerval was collected from the police-cells at the Place Cadet by Gautier and Alphonse Karr, who took him home to the rue Navarin. They were not entirely surprised. Gérard had once been arrested before, at the age of twenty-three, for street disturbance; and one summer in Belgium with Gautier he had behaved strangely, staring at the girls in the cafés, and walking around, in Gautier's benign phrase, 'in a state of alarming erection', being turned out 'because of his priapism'. But Nerval was now violent, a chair and a mirror were smashed, and the next evening Gautier took him in a carriage to the rue Picpus, where he remained for three weeks. He was discharged in March 1841, but shortly after had a relapse, and was taken to the celebrated asylum, then in Montmartre, run by Dr Esprit Blanche, the father of Émile. Gérard remained a patient there for eight months. He was visited constantly by his friends, Gautier, Alphonse Karr, Arsène Houssaye.

NERVAL

They will tell you that I have recovered what is conveniently called my 'reason', but don't believe a word of it. I am, and I have always been, the same, and the only thing that surprises me is that people found me *changed* for a few days last spring.

What really happened was that I had a fascinating dream, and that I now regret its passing. I even sometimes ask myself if the dream was not more strictly *truthful* then, than the natural explanation of those events today. But as there are doctors here, and officials, who guard against any extension of the field of poetry on to the public highway, I have not been definitely discharged and allowed out to roam among reasonable people until I have admitted, officially and formally, that I have indeed *been ill*: something which cost a lot both of my sense of self-respect and my sense of veracity. Confess! Confess! they shouted at me, just as they did in the old days with witches and heretics. And finally, to put an end to it all, I agreed to it, and let myself be categorized under the heading of an *ailment* which is variously defined and entitled by the doctors and by the Dictionary of Medicine, as 'Theomania' or indeed 'Demono-mania'. With the aid of these two terms, medical science appears to have the right to abolish or reduce to silence all the prophets and seers predicted by the Apocalypse, among whom I flatter myself to be! But I am resigned to my fate, and if I do not achieve my predestiny, I shall accuse Dr Blanche of having subtly suppressed the Holy Ghost.

I am fine now, my dear Janin, but for seven months, thanks to your pretended obituary of me in the 'Debats' on 1st March, I have passed for a *lunatic*. My complaint is just. Though I am always grateful for your help, I am no less affected by having to pass for a *sublime lunatic*, thanks to you, to Théophile Gautier, to Lucas, and so on. I shall never be able to go into society anywhere . . . I shall never be able to marry, I shall never get myself a serious hearing . . . nearly all my literary friends have followed your example, and agreed to make of me some sort of prophet, a visionary, whose reason was lost in Germany in the course of initiations to secret societies, and study of oriental symbolism. 'What a shame!' they all say, 'France has lost a genius who could have done her honour . . . Only his friends really knew him!' With the result, my dear Janin, that I am the living tomb of Gérard de Nerval whom you once loved, helped and encouraged.

*(change to music with Arab flavour)*

Perhaps I can escape the cold indifference of Paris by following the Eastern Star that leads me to my destiny.

GAUTIER

How much I wished, my dear Gérard, that I could have come and joined you at Cairo, as I had originally promised. Not that you will find this difficult to believe: I should far rather wander with you along the banks of the Nile, or hold long discussions in the gardens of Schoubrah, or climb the mountain of Mokattan to admire the beautiful view, than to polish my boot-soles on the various grades of asphalt and bitumen that stretch between the rue Navarin and the rue du Mont-Blanc. But who is the man who can do what he likes, except you perhaps? Like another Don César de Bazan, you see before you a host of yellow women, and black women, and blue women, and probably green women; you see the wild ibis, and the rats of the Pharaohs' tombs. You are fortunate indeed! While I have not even been able to leave Paris: there is always some invisible thread to pull me back to the ground just at the moment when I am about to take flight; without mentioning the wretched newspaper column . . .

NERVAL

Oh my old friend! how well the two of us seem to illustrate that nursery fable of those two men, one who went out to pursue his fortune in life, and the other who waited for it in his bed at home. Though it is not my fortune that I pursue: it is the ideal itself, colour, poetry, love perhaps; and all this comes to you, who remain where you are, and escapes from me, who pursues it . . . To me, it seems that I have already lost, kingdom by kingdom, province by province, the most beautiful half of the universe, and soon I shall not know where to find a refuge for my dreams. But it is Egypt that I most regret, having hunted it out of my imagination, only to find a sad lodging for it in my memories!

You still believe in the magic ibis, in the purple lotus flower, in the yellow Nile; you believe in the emerald palm tree, the nopal-bush, and even perhaps the camel . . . alas! the poor ibis is nothing but a wild bird, the lotus is a vulgar onion plant; the Nile is a dull red river with slate-grey reflections, the palm tree is like a moth-eaten hat feather, the nopal-bush is merely a cactus, the camel only exists as a dromedary, the *alma* dancing girls are actually men, and as for the women, well, you are fortunate never to have set eyes on them! No, I shall think no more of Cairo, the city of the Thousand and One Nights . . .

To sum it up, the East cannot compare with that waking dream which I went through two years ago in Paris; or rather, the Orient of that dream is more distant still, or higher perhaps. I have had enough of running after poetry: I now believe that you can find it on your own doorstep, and perhaps in your own bed. As yet I am still the man who runs after it, but I am going to try and stop myself, and wait.

*(the noise of Gérard's ship splashing through the waters of the Mediterranean continues for some moments, until it becomes faintly menacing. However, it fades gradually and gives way once more to the busy, Parisian music of Offenbach and this merges into radiophonics . . . )*

HOLMES   Nerval returned to Paris in January 1844, his thinning hair bleached from the desert sun, and his grey eyes seeming even paler and larger in his tanned face. His legend had grown in his absence, and he was now something of a celebrity. Besides being wined and dined by Gautier, he had his mystical sonnets 'Christ in the Garden of Olives' published in the *Artiste* by Balzac, and he began to be cultivated by the younger generation of poets such as Charles Baudelaire. Yet he still seemed restless, and he was the foremost among the group of painters and poets who went to the Hotel Pimodan on the Île Saint-Louis to smoke hashish, as his friend Alphonse Karr remembered.

*(the sound of the music begins to echo unnaturally, and distort, and fill with strange sounds of breathing and laughter . . . )*

ALPHONSE KARR   There were only a few of us, half a dozen at most I remember, among them Gérard, Théophile Gautier, and an extremely amusing fellow, Boissard, a painter . . . the luncheon was animated, and we took the drugs towards the end, infused in hot water like tea. During the meal I noticed that the doorbell rang constantly, which aroused my suspicions, and these were confirmed when we adjourned from the dining-room to the salon, an immense chamber with carved panelling, wall-mirrors, and nude goddesses painted on the ceiling. A dozen spectators were already assembled there, among them Esquirol, the famous specialist in mental diseases, and I realized we were to be put on exhibition . . . The influence of the hashish soon began to manifest itself: one young man leapt on to a table and began a long lecture which was complete nonsense. Boissard burst into tears and began to moan, 'Don't bother me, don't bother me, I am so happy!' Gautier put his head under some cushions and tried helplessly to stifle a mad outburst of laughter; and Gérard, with his same dreamy smile, began to sing ballads and songs, improvising the words . . . I heard Dr Esquirol whispering in a low voice: 'It's obvious that frequent use of this substance would endanger a man's reason . . .'

I am told that the painter Boissard subsequently fulfilled Esquirol's melancholy prediction. He became addicted to both hashish and opium, and died young, his health broken and his mind clouded. As for Gérard, I was frightened at the time that he might abandon himself to opium. He already liked wine, literary wines he used to say, meaning the wines celebrated by poets, the wines of Syracuse, the Rhine valley, Falerna, and so on. Certainly he smoked a lot, though I never saw him completely drugged.

GAUTIER

Gérard's peculiarities became increasingly exaggerated, and sometimes it was difficult to explain them away, for they moved from the purely intellectual into the physical realm. To Gérard's indignation, this made some kind of enlightened medical treatment a growing necessity. He could not conceive why doctors should be worried if, for example, he chose to walk in the gardens of the Palais-Royal leading a live lobster along on the end of a blue silk ribbon. 'Why should a lobster be any more ridiculous than a dog?' he used to ask, 'or for that matter, a cat, or

a gazelle, or a lion, or any other animal that
one chooses to take for a stroll? I have a
liking for lobsters. They are peaceful, serious
creatures. They know the secrets of the sea.
They don't bark, and they don't gnaw upon
one's *monadic* privacy like dogs do. And
Goethe had an aversion to dogs, and he
wasn't mad.' There were a thousand other
reasons, each more ingenuous than the last.
*(Gautier sighs)*

NERVAL

Dreams and madness. The red star. The longing for the Orient. Now Europe arises. The
dream is realized. Seas. Memories. Confusion
. . . It is *men* who have made me suffer. A new
land where my head can find rest. My love
abandoned in a tomb. I fled from her, I lost
her, I made her great . . . Brussels. Escaped
from the lead coffin. The new era. The
return of the gods.

*(sudden percussion arising out of ecstatic music)*

My dear Du Camp – something terrible's
happened, not just a delay, but a serious accident, I was nearly killed, I shall probably feel
the effects for the rest of my life . . . Isn't it
a kind of predestination? I was getting on
well with the article, nearly half the sheets
done, I would have completed it by tomorrow
at latest. Then yesterday I went to dine with
a friend at Montmartre, someone Théophile
knows. While descending one of the terraces,
I tripped and fell down a staircase, my chest
struck an angle of the ironwork and my right
knee buckled up under my whole weight.
The worst is the chest, this morning I have
a huge blue contusion . . . my knee hurt so
much I couldn't sleep at all last night. Can

we put off the article until next month? . . . I am so feverish . . . warn Théophile and Houssaye . . . Your devoted Gérard de Nerval.

*(return of visionary music)*

NERVAL   I was wandering in the countryside at Montmartre, preoccupied with an essay I was writing on various religious ideas . . . It was sunset, and going down the steps of a rustic staircase, I slipped and my chest struck heavily on the angle of ironwork. I had enough strength to get to my feet and stagger to the middle of the garden, believing I had received a death-blow. Before I died I wanted one last look at the setting sun . . . However, my collapse was only a fainting-fit, and I managed to get back to my lodgings and go to bed. I became feverish. When I recalled the exact point at which I had fallen, I remembered that I had been admiring a view over the cemetery. It was the very same that contained the tomb of Aurélia.

This fact did not actually occur to me until that moment; otherwise I might have attributed my fall to the feelings excited by such a view. But even this realization gave me the sense of a more absolute, exact predestination. I regretted, even more, that death had not reunited me with her. Then, as I thought this over, I told myself that I was not worthy. I recalled bitterly the life I had led since her death, reproaching myself – not with having forgotten her, for I had never really done so – but with having desecrated her memory with easy love affairs. The idea came to trouble my feverish sleep . . . I had confused dreams, mixed with scenes of bloodshed.

HOLMES

The tomb of Aurelia. The love abandoned in the tomb. Who was Aurelia? After his death, all his friends agreed that it was none other than the pretty, blonde Opéra-Comique singer, Jenny Colon, who had apparently rejected his love and his huge Renaissance fourposter bed, years previously. Jenny had last seen Gérard a few months before his arrest, in Brussels. She had died, tragically young, in 1842, shortly before Gérard set out for the East. She had been buried in the cemetery at Montmartre. Jenny and Aurelia had become identified in Gérard's mind.

A few weeks later in January 1852 Gérard suffered another, more disastrous setback. He had written a play with Joseph Méry.

MERY

Our play was chosen to reopen the Porte-Sainte-Martin Theatre, under new management. All our friends said a triumph was assured, but after only a score of performances, the management wrote me a letter to say that receipts were bad, and the play would have to come off. I arranged for Gérard, who had been out buying presents for the cast, to call at my apartment at eleven o'clock on the morning of 23rd January 1852.

It was impossible to keep Marc Fournier's letter secret. My dear old friend, I said to Gérard with a laugh, do you remember how Victor Hugo's play *Les Burgraves* only ran for fifteen nights? It was a lot better than our *Imagier* . . . Gérard stared at me: 'What on earth do you mean?' 'I mean one has to be ready for anything,' I said, 'even this letter.' And I passed it over to him. As Gérard read, he lifted both hands to his temples, as if to retain his reason. A burst of nervous laughter twisted his lips, but his eyes were dark and filled with tears. I tried everything I could think of to cheer him up, all the fatuous reasons to excuse our failure, but it was all wasted on him. Gérard was an acutely sensitive person, he couldn't take it lightly, he couldn't bounce back . . .

Finally he said, with another of those bursts of frightful laughter, 'In fact you are quite right; yes, *Les Burgraves* was much better than ours – There's only one play that ever works in Paris, the same play we have all been watching for thirty years, the same play we'll always watch. The cast consists of a mother and her son. Act One, the son is lost. Act Five, he's found again. The mother cries, *My son!* The son cries, *My mother!* The curtain falls, the audience weeps, the author is inundated with royalties' . . . Gérard burst out laughing, weeping, shook my hand, and left.

I followed him out on to the stairs, and asked him to come and see me again very soon. 'I prefer not to meet you again,' he said. 'Whyever not?' I asked. 'You tried to console me,' he said, and disappeared.

When next I saw my poor friend he was in the Maison Dubois, a municipal sanatorium in the faubourg Saint-Denis. He was admitted on that same day, 23rd January 1852, for a period of three weeks. The official diagnosis was feverish hysteria and swelling of the face, believed to be erysipelas.

NERVAL

A terrible idea began to dawn upon me. 'Man is double,' I told myself. 'I sense two men within my own breast,' one Father of the Church has written. The intercourse of two souls, at conception, places this double seed within one body, and offers for inspection two matching parts reproduced within all the organs of its physical structure.

In every man there is both a spectator, and an actor; the one who speaks and the one who answers. The oriental thinkers have seen in this two enemies, naturally opposed: the good and the evil genius.

'Am I the good, or am I the evil half?' I asked myself. In any case, the *other one* must be hostile to me. Who knows if there is not a certain set of circumstances, or a certain time of life, when these two spirits must separate? As both are attached to the same body by physical affinity, perhaps one of them is promised fame and happiness, while the other is destined to annihilation or eternal suffering?

At this point a fatal thought flashed through my dark confusion. Aurélia was no longer mine! I thought I had heard talk of a ceremony that was to take place elsewhere, and preparations for a mystic marriage, which was meant to be mine, but where the *other* was planning to take advantage and profit from the error of my friends, and of Aurelia herself.

*(behind all of Nerval's speeches that follow, the radiophonic themes continue to play very quietly, in alternation, fading away when other voices speak. The effect is to give Nerval's account its own continuity, isolated from the outside events described by others)*

From that moment that I knew for certain that I had been submitted to the trials of sacred initiation, an invincible force entered into my spirit. I considered myself to be a hero acting beneath the gaze of the gods.

Everything in nature took on an entirely new aspect, and secret voices spoke from the plants, the trees, the animals, and the humblest insects, to warn and encourage me. The talk of my companions contained mysterious implications whose sense I understood, and small inanimate objects fitted themselves to the workings of my mind: from chance combinations of pebbles; the shape of cracks, corners and openings; the outline of leaves, from a particular colour, or smell, or sound, I could see harmonies produced that I had never realized existed. I asked myself how I could have lived so long outside nature, and without identifying myself with her? Everything lives, everything moves, everything corresponds. Magnetic impulses emanate from me, and from others, and effortlessly traverse the infinite chain of created being; there is a transparent network that spreads across the whole world, and its extending threads communicate outwards, further and further, from the planets to the stars. Though I am captive at this moment upon earth, I converse with the choirs of stars, and the stars partake of my sorrows and joys!

I went down a dark staircase and found myself in the streets . . . People were talking of a wedding, and the bridegroom who was due to appear and announce the beginning of the festivities. An insane transport of anger swept over me. I suspected that the person they were waiting for was my *double*, who was about to marry Aurélia, and I made a violent scene that alarmed the whole assembly. I begged anyone who knew me to come to my aid. One old man said to me: 'But you must not behave like this, you are frightening everyone.' I shouted back: 'I know he has already struck me with his weapons, but I am not afraid, I am waiting for him, and I know the secret sign that will vanquish him.'

At this moment one of the metal workers from the workshop I had visited appeared. He was holding a long bar, the end of which was tipped with a red-hot metal ball. I wanted to throw myself at him, but the ball he was waving in front of him threatened my head. The people around me seemed to mock at my impotence. So I backed away as far as the throne, my soul full of speechless pride, and I raised my arm to make the sign which I thought had magic power. The scream of a woman, clear and penetrating and full of agonizing pain, woke me with a start! The syllables of some unknown word I was about to utter failed upon my lips.

I flung myself to the floor and began to pray fervently, in a flood of tears. But whose was that voice that had just rung out so painfully through the night? It did not belong to my dream; it was the voice of some living woman, and yet for me it was the very voice and accent of Aurélia. I opened my window. Outside all was peaceful, and the cry did not come again . . .

What had I done? I had troubled the harmony of the magic universe from which my soul drew the certitude of its own immortality. I was damned perhaps for having wished to pierce a redoubtable mystery and for offending against the divine law. I could expect nothing now except scorn and anger! The exasperated shadows fled away, with harsh cries, tracing fatal circles in the air, like birds at the approach of a storm.

I alone understand the ruin and disorder of the world. I know the cause, I alone know it. There are no remedies. But as for the cause, though I am forbidden to reveal it to anyone, I will tell you on condition that you say nothing to anyone, outside. The cause is this. *(long pause)* God is dead.

GAUTIER

Even when there was no shadow of doubt left that the sickness had touched his brain, Gérard conserved all his intellectual capacities intact. There was no darkening, no aberration, no failure of precision, to betray the wild disorder of his mental faculties ... When his fits of madness passed, he recovered full possession of himself, and used to recount what he had seen in his hallucinations with marvellous eloquence and poetry, things a hundred times superior to the fantasies produced by hashish or opium. It is a terrible pity that some stenographer did not record these amazing accounts.

NERVAL

The visions which came to me continually in my sleep had reduced me to such a state of despair that I could hardly speak; the company of my friends was only a vague distraction; my whole spirit seemed wrapped up with these delusions, and I could not respond to any other ideas. I was unable to read or write ten lines together ... One of my friends, called George Bell, undertook to overcome my utter discouragement. He took me off to various places in the country outside Paris, and kept gently talking even when I was silent, or only answered with a few incoherent phrases. His bearded face was strangely expressive, almost monkish ... One day we were eating together under a trellis of flowers, in one of the little villages on the outskirts of the city, when a woman came to sing beside our table. There was something I could not explain in her tired but sympathetic voice that reminded me of Aurélia. I gazed up at her: even her facial features were not unlike those I had loved. The café people sent her away, and I did not dare retain her, but I said to myself: who knows if Aurelia's spirit is not in that woman! And I was happy for the bit of money I had slipped her.

*(radiophonics)*

GEORGE BELL

He seemed to trust me, since I too had suffered as he was suffering now. During his worst hours, he never feared to reveal what was going on inside his mind to me. I undertook to try and cure him, and as the fine weather had come round again (it was the summer of '53), we started making a series of long expeditions on foot, sometimes lasting several days, in the countryside around Paris. While we walked along, usually in the woods around Meudon, Sèvres, Saint-Cloud, Versailles, and Saint-Germain, I tried to help him recover the feeling of confidence and enthusiasm which gives one the strength to write. When Gérard recounted to me memories of his childhood, or of his love affair, I was extremely careful to prevent him slipping back into his dream state, and continually emphasized the value and power of the reality-principle in literature. Bit by bit, he seemed to emerge from his torpor, and it was then that he wrote for the *Revue des Deux Mondes*, who always liked printing his pieces, the arcadian romance 'Sylvie', one of the most sensitive things he ever produced. But this was only a brief respite allowed by his sickness. The least accident could set it off again . . .

In despair, I went along in tears to Notre-Dame-de-Lorette, where I knelt at the altar of the Virgin, and asked pardon for my faults. Something inside me said: the Virgin is dead, and your prayers are useless . . . When I came to the Place de la Concorde, my idea was to destroy myself. Several times I made my way down to the Seine, but something always prevented me from carrying out my purpose. The stars were glittering in the firmament. Suddenly it seemed as if they had all gone out, all at the same time, like the candles I had seen in the church. I thought that the time had been accomplished, and that the end of the world was approaching as announced in the Apocalypse of St John. I thought I could see a black sun in the empty sky, and a blood-red sphere above the Tuileries gardens.

I said to myself: 'Eternal night is beginning, and it will be terrible. What will happen when men realize that there is no more sun?'

I came back by the rue Saint-Honoré, and pitied the belated workmen I encountered on the way. When I arrived at the Louvre, I walked as far as the *place*, and found a weird spectacle waiting for me. Through the scudding clouds I could see several different moons racing overhead. I imagined that the earth had gone out of its orbit, and was drifting helplessly through space like a dismasted ship, and that the stars grew large or diminished as we drew away from one and approached another. For two or three hours I stood contemplating this chaos, and finished by going off towards Les Halles. The country work people were carrying in their boxes of farm produce, and I said to myself: 'How astonished they will be when they see that the night is continuing, endlessly.' Yet the dogs began to bark in the distant streets, and the cocks crowed.

GEORGE BELL

The new crisis reached its climax at the end of August 1853, a few days after the publication of 'Sylvie'. Gérard became unable to sleep at all, and spent several nights on the hills above Montmartre, where he had walked as a boy, waiting obsessively for the sunrise. He then went down to the market at Les Halles, got into an argument with one of the porters, and knocked him down. Next he attacked a postman, pointing to his silver badge and saying he was an aristocrat and should not go into a low café, and threatening to kill him. He stood in the middle of the streets and threw money in the air. Then he went to visit his father, and finding him not at home, he left a bunch of marguerites. He crossed over the river to the Jardin des Plantes, and made a scene in front of the animal cages, and threw his hat to the hippopotamus. Returning to the Palais-Royal, he ran shouting through the arcades and joined in a circle of little girls dancing in the gardens. Then, pursued by a growing crowd, he rushed to the rue Saint-Honoré, and caused an uproar in a *tabac* trying to buy a cigar with a special seal. When he came out, he was surrounded by an angry mob; but just at this moment, I and two friends arrived, and dragged him into a café. Gérard was finally extricated, put into a cab, and taken off to the hospital of La Charité, where he was put in a straitjacket.

NERVAL

It seemed that the goddess appeared to me, saying: 'I am the same as Mary, the same as your mother, the same as all those others you have always loved in every guise. At each of your trials I have thrown off one of the masks which covers my true features, and soon you will see me as I really am . . .' During the night my delirium increased, but especially the following morning when I discovered that I was tied up. I managed to get out of the straitjacket and towards morning I began to walk through the other wards. Persuaded that I had become like a god, and had the power of healing, I laid hands on some of the patients, and coming to a statue of the Virgin, I took off her crown of artificial flowers and put them on my head to increase the powers which I believed I had been given. I walked with huge strides, talking with animation about the ignorance of men who believed they could cure people through Science alone. Noticing a flask of ether on a table, I swallowed it at one gulp.

One of the hospital housemen, with a face that I said was like an angel, came up and tried to stop me. We struggled, but I was filled with immense nervous energy, and I overcame him and was about to fling him to the floor when I stopped myself. I told him he did not understand my mission. Then other doctors arrived, and I continued my speech on the impotence of their medical art. Next I went down some stairs to the outside, even though I had no shoes, and coming to a garden I went in and wandered over the lawn and began to pick flowers.

One of my friends had come back to collect me. I left the garden with him, and while he was talking to me, they suddenly threw another straitjacket over my head, and forced me into a cab and drove me to an asylum outside Paris.

Seeing myself among the mental patients, I understood that up to then all this had been my delusions. Nevertheless, the promises that I attributed to the goddess Isis seemed to be realized in a series of trials that I was destined to undergo at the asylum. So I accepted them with resignation.

HOLMES

The asylum was the celebrated institution of Dr Émile Blanche, a large private clinic with a walled garden, at No. 2 rue du Seine, Passy. Gérard was to remain a patient there for the best part of twelve months, and was only finally discharged a few weeks before his death.

Blanche's asylum was famous throughout Europe. The worst kind of physical maltreatment had been abolished, accommodation was comfortable, and Blanche, who visited all his patients personally, was one of the pioneers in the use of art therapy. The garden walls were covered with grotesque murals, and the public rooms filled with strange paintings and sculptures, all done by patients.

The basis of Dr Blanche's system was the application of three ascending grades of treatment, known familiarly to the inmates as 'Hell', 'Purgatory' and 'Paradise'. In 'Hell', the most severely disturbed cases were subject to a regime of solitary confinement, straitjacket, severely reduced diets, and regular visitations to the dreaded baths in the cellar, where they were forcibly immersed in freezing-cold water. Once a patient's disposition improved, he passed into 'Purgatory', where he was encouraged to rest for long periods, eat well, and take limited recreation periods in the garden and public rooms. Finally, in 'Paradise', patients were given general freedom of the house and gardens; ate together at a common table with Dr Blanche and his senior assistants; and they were encouraged to invite friends to visit, and to take short accompanied day-trips back to Paris.

Gérard was to pass through all three of these stages of Dr Blanche's salvation, with several relapses, before attaining the status of a special patient, almost a friend of Blanche's, renting his own room. But his trials began in 'Hell'.

*(screams, laughter, water, echoes, horror . . .)*

NERVAL

Is my soul an indestructible molecule, a single bubble puffed with a bit of air, but always finding again its place in nature? Or is it simply this emptiness, this image of oblivion, disappearing in immensity? Will it always be a mortal particle, destined in all its transformations to suffer the vengeance of the powerful?

I saw myself having to call my whole life to account, and even my previous existences. In proving that I was good, I would prove that I had always been good. And if I had been evil, I told myself, then surely my present life would be a sufficient expiation? This thought reassured me, but did not stop me fearing that I would be classed for ever among the damned.

I felt myself plunged into cold water, and even colder water streaming over my skull. I concentrated my thoughts on the eternal Isis, the mother goddess and the sacred bride. All my longings, all my prayers were combined in this magic name. I felt myself come alive again in her, and sometimes she appeared to me in the form of the classical Venus, and sometimes also with the features of the Holy Virgin of the Christians. At night her dear apparition came again, more clearly, and yet I said to myself: 'What can she do for her poor children, being herself vanquished and perhaps persecuted?'

*(music bridge)*

One night, I was shouting and singing in a sort of ecstasy. One of the asylum attendants came to my cell and took me downstairs to a ground-floor room, and locked me in. I continued in my dream, and even though I was standing up, I thought I was shut inside a kind of oriental pavilion. I ran my hands along the sides, and saw that the room was octagonal. A low couch was fitted round the walls, and these seemed to be made of thick glass through which I could see treasures, rich shawls and tapestries shining. Through the iron trellis of the door appeared a moonlit landscape, and I thought I could make out the shapes of rocks and tree-trunks. I had already seen this place in some previous existence, and I seemed to recognize the deep mountain grottoes of Ellora in Egypt.

Little by little the faint blue light of early morning penetrated the pavilion, and filled it with bizarre images. I now thought I was in the midst of a vast slaughter-house, where the history of the universe was written in characters of blood. The body of a gigantic woman was depicted in front of me: only her various parts were cut in pieces as if by sabre strokes. The bodies of other women of different races, becoming larger and clearer at every moment, covered the other walls with a bleeding mass of jumbled limbs and heads, empresses and queens and humble peasant girls. This was the history of all crime, and it was enough to turn one's eyes to any point on the walls or ceiling, to behold some ghastly tragedy re-enacted there.

'This is the result of the power offered to men,' I said to myself. 'Bit by bit they have destroyed and slashed to a thousand pieces the eternal type of Beauty, until the human race has lost most that is energy and perfection.' And indeed, I could see along a particular line of shadow cast by a crack in the door, the descending inheritance of all future races.

At dawn I was at last dragged from my dark meditations. The kind and compassionate face of my excellent doctor brought me back to the land of the living.

*(music bridge and the sound of a pen scratching on paper)*

Passy, 2nd December 1853. My dear Papa . . . I'm working hard, though things are going round and round in the same circle rather; but my black ideas have left me . . . The peace I enjoy in this house fills me with delight and determination. It would be Paradise indeed if I could only have a bit more freedom. I hope Dr Blanche will decide as much himself: for my presence in Paris is becoming indispensable for dealing with my literary affairs, and winter is the time for preparing books for publishers. I am undertaking to write about my illness, and set down in detail all the impressions it has brought me. This will be a study not without value for medical discussion and science. I have never felt more capable of analysis and description. I hope you will judge so yourself . . . I embrace you. Your devoted son, Gérard Labrunie de Nerval.

GAUTIER

The study of his madness on which Gérard embarked is one of the most extraordinary creations ever to come from a writer's pen. It has been said of 'Aurélia, or The Dream and the Life' that it is the autobiography of Madness itself. But it would be more accurate to say that it was the memoirs of Madness *ghosted* by Reason. The philosopher is always present, calm and controlled, even in the midst of the wild hallucinations of the visionary.

NERVAL

Dr Blanche has given me a special room – it is at the topmost point of the sanatorium and it is the only one with the privilege of a window. It looks over the courtyard, over the thick leaves of a walnut tree, and two Chinese mulberries. Beyond them I can vaguely glimpse a busy street through the green-painted trellis of bars. At sunset, the whole horizon seems to expand. It is like looking down on a country village, with windows circled with climbing plants or cluttered with bird-cages, or strings of drying underwear; every now and then you see some young woman's face look out, or an old granny, or the pink head of a child. People shout across to each other, there is singing, and sudden bursts of laughter. It is cheerful to hear, or sad, depending on the time of day, and the mood you are in.

Here, surrounded by the debris of my different adventures I am writing once again.

ALEXANDRE
DUMAS

As far as men of science are concerned, poor Gérard is mentally sick and needing medical treatment; but we ourselves believe he is simply a better writer, a better dreamer, a better wit, and generally more cheerful (or more sad) than ever before. Sometimes he believes he is the eastern king Solomon, waiting for the Queen of Sheba; sometimes that he is Sheikh Ghera-Gherai wishing to declare war on the Emperor Nicholas; and sometimes that he is mad . . . Well, judge for yourselves. A few days ago he dropped into the office of the Musketeer when I was out (a rare thing), and while waiting, took pen and paper, and left the following verses by way of an amusing visiting card.

NERVAL

I am the shadow-man, the widower, the mourner,
The Prince of Aquitaine in the Broken Tower;
My only Star is dead, and my Zodiac Guitar
Shines with the Black Sun of Melancholia.

In the night of my Tomb, O you who appeased me,
Give back my Posilippo, and the bright sea of Italy;
Give back the Flower that eased my poor heart's pain,
The trellis-bower where the Rose embraced the Vine.

Am I Amor or Phoebus? Am I Lusignan or Byron?
My brow still burns with the Queen's red kiss;
I have dreamed in the Grotto where the watery Siren is.

And twice, oh twice victor, have I swum the dark Acheron
   Tuning and re-tuning on my Orphic lyre
The Holy Lady's sighs of woe,
      The Fairy Woman's cries of fire.

The countryside where I was brought up was full of strange legends and bizarre superstitions. One of my uncles, who had by far the greatest influence on my early education, had taken up collecting Roman and Celtic antiquities as his hobby. In his vegetable garden, or in the surrounding fields, he would sometimes dig up coins and statues carrying the images of the ancient gods and emperors. His admiration for them, as an antiquarian, made me look on them with veneration, and I studied their history in his books. A certain statue of Mars in gilded bronze, a Pallas Athene armed, a Neptune and Amphitryon carved above the village fountain, and, above all, the fat, kindly bearded face of a Pan smiling from the entrance of a grotto, among the festoons of myrtle and ivy, were the household gods and guardians of this remote retreat. I have to admit that they then inspired me with much greater veneration than the poor Christian images in the church, and the two shapeless saints above the church door, that certain local experts claimed – anyway – were really the twin gods Eaus and Cernunnos of the ancient Gauls.

I found myself confused in the midst of all these differing symbols, and one day I asked my uncle what God really was. 'God', said my uncle, 'is the sun.'

I was always surrounded by young girls; one of them was my aunt; two servants of the house, Jeanette and Fanchette, also lavished their attentions on me. My childish smile recalled my mother's, and my blond softly-curling hair covered my precocious forehead in a disorderly mop. I became enamoured of Fanchette, and I conceived the singular idea of taking her for my bride according to the rites of our ancestors. I celebrated the marriage service myself, acting out the ceremony with the aid of an old dress of my grandmother's thrown over my shoulders. My brow was encircled with a silver-spangled ribbon, and I had heightened the natural colour of my cheeks with a light touch of rouge. I called to witness the God of our fathers, and the Blessed Virgin, of whom I had a medallion, and everyone willingly joined in this naïve game.

Then there was the river Nonette, glittering in the meadows bordering the last houses of the village. Ah, the Nonette! One of those lovely little streams where I fished for crayfish; and on the other side of the forest runs her sister stream the Thève, where I was nearly drowned for not wanting to appear a fool in front of the little peasant girl, Célénie.

Célénie often appeared to me in my dreams, like a water-nymph, naïve temptress, wild and lightheaded from the scent of the meadows, crowned with water-lilies and wild celery, and revealing behind her childish laughter and dimpled cheeks, the pearly teeth of the Germanic water-sprite . . .

Célénie loved the grottoes lost in the woods of Chantilly, the old ruined chateaux, the crumbling temples and columns festooned with ivy, and the woodcutters' campfires, where she would sing and tell of the old legends, like the story of Madame de Montfort imprisoned in her tower, who would sometimes fly away in the shape of a swan.

I was seven years old, and playing heedlessly at my uncle's doorstep, when three military officers appeared in front of the house; the blackened gold of their uniforms shone dully beneath their helmets. The first one hugged me to him with such energy that I cried out: 'Father . . . you are hurting me!'

From that day hence my destiny altered. All three had returned from the Siege of Strasbourg. The eldest, saved from the retreat from Moscow, took me with him to learn what he called my duties. I was still a frail child, and the cheerfulness of his younger brother charmed me through my work. A soldier who served them as a batman had the idea of giving up some of his nights to me. He used to wake me before dawn, and take me for walks over the hills surrounding Paris, breakfasting me on fresh bread and cream from the farms and dairies.

And I remember, most of all, what I can never quite remember, what always hovers just beyond the reach of memory, beyond the horizon of recollection, beyond the endless searchings of the heart. This is the last, the deepest return. . . .

WOMAN'S VOICE   Marie-Antoinette Labrunie, née Laurent, born Paris 1785, died Gross-Glogau, Silesia, 1810. A brave simple woman who chose to accompany her husband to the wars, and to leave her only child behind in France. . . .

NERVAL   She died at the age of twenty-five from the exhaustions of the war, killed by a fever caught while crossing a bridge heaped with dead bodies, when her carriage nearly overturned. My father, who was forced to rejoin the army at Moscow, later lost her letters and her jewels in the rapids of the Beresina.

I never saw my mother; the portraits of her were either lost or stolen. I only know that she resembled an engraving of those times, made after Prud'hon or Fragonard, that was called 'Modesty'. The fever from which she died has had me in its grip three times, at moments which form in my life three regular, periodic divisions. Always, at these moments, I have felt my spirit overcome with the images of mourning and desolation that surrounded my cradle.

The letters that my mother wrote from the shores of the Baltic, or the banks of the river Sprey and the Danube, were read to me how many, many times! The feeling for the marvellous in life, the taste for distant travelling, were for me no doubt the result of these first impressions, and also the long period I spent in that remote countryside deep in the woods.

*(music bridge and the sound of a pen scratching)*

My dear friend: all is accomplished. I have been discharged by Dr Blanche. I have no one to accuse now except myself and my own impatience, that has led me to be excluded from the Paradise. Henceforth I work and give birth in labour . . . Officially I admit that I have been sick. But I cannot agree that I have been mad, or even subject to hallucinations. If I offend Medicine, then I shall throw myself at her feet – when she reveals herself as a goddess. Your friend, Gérard de Nerval, Initiate and Vestal.

GEORGE BELL  As autumn deepened into winter, Gérard's circle of endless walking gradually grew narrower. No longer did he visit Saint-Germain, the hills above Montmartre, or the crooked streets of Saint-Denis. He lodged in little hotels round the Louvre and Palais-Royal, haunts of his youth, and wandered about the back streets round Les Halles and Châtelet, scribbling on proofs in the public reading rooms, drinking at the cheap cafés, window-gazing in the arcades. He was badly in debt and hardly earned enough from his writing to keep body and soul together. We, his friends, caught the merest glimpses of him.

ALPHONSE KARR

Gérard had so many good friends, Gautier, Dumas, Méry, George Bell, Arsène Houssaye . . . all anxious to help him, to give him a meal, or a roof over his head. But Gérard refused, he refused steadfastly. It was quite simple. He feared that he would never be able to write anything again. You see he was sensitive, he was born in a certain way, he had a certain atti-tude . . . he was I suppose, a gentleman.

MAXIME DU
CAMP

On the 20th January the snow had fallen thick over Paris, it looked faintly sinister. Théophile Gautier had just turned up at the office to talk about his book *Captain Fracasse*, which he was having trouble in starting. Sud-denly Gérard walked in; he was wearing a black jacket that was so thin it made me shiver just to look at him. I said: 'You're dressed a bit lightly for going out in this bitter weather, aren't you?' He answered: 'No, I'm not, I'm wearing two shirts – noth-ing could be warmer.'

Gautier, as his old college friend and fel-low writer, had the right to greater frankness than I, and said: 'It's snowing pneumonia and pissing down bronchitis. There are plenty of people here with more than one overcoat who would be only too pleased to lend you one until your dying day!' Gérard said: 'No – the cold does you good. Look at the Eskimos, they never get ill.'

Then breaking the conversation, he said: 'I've bought something very rare, the junk sellers are so stupid that they never know what they are selling. I'll show you – it's the belt that Madame de Maintenon wore when she acted in *Esther* at Saint-Cyr.' Carefully unwrapping a piece of crumpled paper, he took out a piece of kitchen sash-cord. It was thin, tightly plaited, strong and looked brand new. Gautier and I exchanged a wink: 'Yes, it's very interesting.'

All three of us left the office together. The weather was freezing. The carriage wheels grated and groaned as they drove through the packed snow. Gautier said: 'Gérard, come and lunch with me. I'll give you one of my famous risottos!' Gérard refused. I said: 'Look, it really is very cold, I've got a spare room for you at my apartment.' Gérard pulled out a twenty-franc coin that he had just been given. I can see it now: a Louis Dix-Huit piece dating from 1814, the end of the Napoleonic War. Gérard said: 'Thank you, but I don't need anything, I'm all right for the week.' Then he left us; I think he was frightened we would press him. The next time I saw him was at the mortuary.

NERVAL 24th January 1855 . . .

My dear, kind aunt: tell your son that he does not know that you are the best of mothers, and of aunts. When I shall have tri-umphed over everything, you will have your place in my Olympus, just as I have my place in your house. Do not expect me this evening, for the night will be black and white.

*(music bridge)*

That night I had a delicious dream, the first for a long, long time. I was in a tower that went so deeply into the earth, and so high into the sky, that it seemed as if my entire life would be consumed in climbing up and going down. Already all my strength was spent, and I was on the point of giving up, when a door in the side of the tower appeared. A spirit appeared before me and said: 'Come with me, my brother! . . .' He had the looks of one of the poor mental patients I had helped to nurse, but transfigured and full of understanding. I do not know why I thought he was called Saturnus.

We were now in a countryside filled with the fiery glow of stars. We stood still gazing up at this spectacle, and the spirit placed his hand on my forehead . . . All at once, one of the stars I had been watching in the sky began suddenly to grow and expand, and the divinity of all my dreams appeared before me, smiling. She was dressed in a sort of Indian costume, as I had once seen her many years before. She walked along between us, and wherever her feet touched, flowers and plants and sweet meadow grass rose from the earth behind her.

She said to me: 'The trial to which you were submitted has come to its end. These stairs without number where you have exhausted yourself, climbing up and going down, were the stages of the ancient illusions which confused your thought. And now you may recall that day when you turned to the Blessed Virgin, and sought relief from delirium. It was necessary that your prayer should be carried to her by a simple soul, free from all earthly ties. Such a soul you have found beside you, and that is why it is permitted for me to come and encourage you.'

The joy this dream spread through my

heart brought me a sweet awakening. Dawn was about to break. I wanted to leave a material sign of the apparition that had consoled me, and I wrote on the wall these words: 'You visited me this night.'

EYE WITNESS   There was the blackened shop of a key-cutter on the left, with a sign, shaped like a huge key, standing out against the frosty snow-laden sky.

COMMISSIONER   This morning at approximately seven-thirty
OF POLICE   a.m. the deceased was found hanging from the bars of a locksmith's shop in the Rue de la Vieille-Lanterne ... He had hanged himself with a length of sash-cord. There were no signs of violence on the corpse.

NERVAL

When Christ, raising his thin arms to the sky
As poets do, under the sacred trees,
Had lost himself in long dumb miseries,
Thinking ungrateful friends planned treachery:

He turned to those awaiting him below
(Kings, sages, prophets, in their dreams by day,
But now in sleep they dully lay),
And cried aloud: 'There is no God! Oh, no!'

Unstirred they slept. 'My brothers, have you heard?
My brow has touched the timeless vault of heaven
Bleeding and torn, I suffered many days.

'I cheated you. Abyss! abyss! abyss!
God shuns the victim to the altar given
There is no God ... no God!' They slept unstirred.

# III

# Five Gothic Shadows

# INTRODUCTION

THE BLEAK, URBAN MELANCHOLY of Nerval's story had haunted the end of my time in France. When I got back to England I went to ground for a year in a shepherd's cottage in a little hamlet called Stone-cum-Ebony, on the edge of Romney Marsh on the Kent–Sussex border. It was a small, beautiful land of orchards and sheep fields, where I grew vegetables, chopped fire-wood, brewed my own beer, drove an ancient motorbike to the local co-op, and took a more earthy and extroverted approach to life and work. I was luckier in love, too: Joanna, who worked as a student nurse in the local hospital, came to teach me apple-picking in the long summer evenings, and wander with me along the frozen dikes in winter, talking to the grave solitary herons that watched us with unblinking eye.

I was still hunting my Romantic subjects, and still obsessed with their images of loneliness and despair, but now slowly I began to find a new tone, a lighter tune. I turned back to English writers, and sought among the sturdy eccentrics of the Regency and the Victorians for some different path towards another major figure. But it was a long time before I could really escape from Shelley. Meanwhile, I was encouraged by a noble succession of literary editors at *The Times*, without whom I would have been marooned and penniless: Michael Ratcliffe, Ion Trewin and Philip Howard. I shall never forget their patience with my deadlines, and their generosity with my copy-corrections, often phoned through from a wind-blasted red call-box that stood at the crossroads between Stone and Appledore. Philip once told me that he employed a special sub-editor exclusively to correct what he kindly called my 'eighteenth-century spelling'.

Through them I was free to produce a whole series of strange, rapid character sketches and historical essays, what Lytton Strachey once called 'portraits in miniature'. I now think these are fundamental to the art of biography, the ability to give a snapshot impression of a whole life caught from one fleeting but revealing angle. It is the very opposite (or complementary) discipline to the huge, factually accumulated chronicle; and really great biography (that rare thing) invariably contains both.

Often these pieces were inspired by that sound – but much mocked – journalistic standby, the centenary article. I learned to honour this convention, because it is the opportunity for some lost or undervalued fragment of human history to be recovered. It is the chance for some partly-forgotten figure to step back – if only for a moment – into the modern limelight. It is the chance of a second lifetime, as it were. I came to believe that this is a vital part of the biographer's special contract with the past: *all is not lost, your time will come again, justice may yet be done.*

These sketches gave me a new freedom to experiment with biographical style and story-telling. I tried out different narrative voices, entered into each Life at odd angles, read facts dangerously through fiction or poetry, risked melodrama, facetiousness and sentimentality. The great thing was simply to summon up for one moment a living breathing shape, to make the dead walk again, to make the reader *see* a figure and *hear* a voice. (Hence perhaps my fascination at this time for ghost-stories, which are of course not realities but metaphors for reality.) Above all I aimed for a new lightness of touch, and speed of effect, trying to give each piece the shape of a short story. My editors counselled that ideally such a piece should be capable of holding any reader's attention in a crowded train, to the point *where they missed their station.* Indeed, to the point where they are sidetracked.

Not so easy, of course. I once observed someone reading one of my pieces on a train, between Tonbridge and Ashford, on the way back to Romney Marsh one winter's evening. It was a salutary experience. Over several minutes an expression of lively interest steadily faded to one of judicial blankness, soon followed by deep and blameless sleep. Later I cheered myself with the thought that perhaps I had succeeded in *sidetracking their dreams.*

The five pieces I have gathered here are united by such an ambition. The eccentricity of their subjects, Romantic themes gone astray, gothic grotesques, gargoyles, ghost tales, were in fact my renewed attempt to find my way back to the solid central ground of Romanticism: passion, idealism, shared endeavour. (The glimpse of Mill's life with Harriet Taylor promised this.) They were also, I now suppose, a kind of personal exorcism that had to take place, there on Romney Marsh (where the first piece begins). The last, which goes back much further, to a single gothic incident in Tudor history, began innocently enough as an admiring book review. I include it (the only review) because it became a kind of talisman: the example of a superbly dedicated scholar who demonstrated how wonderfully the true track of the past – in this case another kind of sidetrack – could still be recovered.

# THE SINGULAR AFFAIR OF
# THE REVEREND MR BARHAM

THE CASE OF the Reverend Richard Harris Barham, a minor canon of St Paul's and the pseudonymous author of the once universally popular *Ingoldsby Legends*, is in every respect a most singular affair.

The curious reader may possibly recall a tale told by M. R. James entitled 'The Stalls of Barchester' in which an apparently pious and exemplary cleric is revealed in his private diaries to have been the victim of a series of appalling visitations which lead to his eventual destruction. Though Barham was to hold, in real life, a Divinity Lectureship and the honorary position of Senior Cardinal's Stall, there can be naturally no evidence that the late Provost of Eton intended anything like a personal reference in his fiction. Nevertheless, certain uncomfortable resemblances between the romance and the reality are not altogether easy to shake off. In the course of my researches in the archives of Canterbury, across the wild sheep fens and treacherous byways of Romney Marsh, and under the lone lamp of my attic study, I was continually and not always agreeably reminded of them.

The external facts of Barham's life are, except for a number of odd *lacunae*, a charming picture of the buoyant, clubbable Anglican life of Regency and early-Victorian England. Barham was born in the cathedral city of Canterbury in December 1788, only son of Alderman Barham, a local worthy who lived a few yards away from the Precinct Gates at 61 Burgate Street. The Alderman was a great drinker of port, and on his decease he weighed 27 stone and his front door had to be especially widened for the exit of his coffin. Of Barham's mother, little was at first known except for contradictory rumours of high spirits and low health.

Barham was sent to St Paul's School, Westminster, where he successfully combined the roles of inveterate hoaxer and head boy, and then to Brasenose, Oxford, where he joined a crack dining and debating club, the Phoenix, and ran somewhat wildly into debt and dissipation, but survived to collect a degree in 1811. Among his friends were Richard Bentley, the future publisher, and Theodore Hook, the bohemian novelist. Back at Canterbury, he came into the estate of Tappington Everard, was articled to an attorney, and pursued a frolicsome life among the theatrical set, forming another club – the Wigs – where on at least one occasion port and eloquence degenerated into swords and prejudice.

Then abruptly, at the age of twenty-five, Barham reformed. He took clerical orders, and moved to a series of somnolent rural curacies at Ashford, Westwell, and finally at Warehorne on the very edge of the hills overlooking Romney Marsh – that 'recondite region', as he later wrote, productive only of sheep, eels, smuggling, witchcraft and pestiferous mildews. He married a local girl, kept a gun, a dog and a vegetable patch, and resolutely bred children. For four years, between 1817 and 1821, he lived in this remote seclusion, keeping a diary, composing certain literary papers, and riding between the stout Georgian brick church of Warehorne on the knoll, and the low, flint, Early English chapel of Snargate in the misty depths of the Marsh below, where, through the genial plurality of the Anglican Establishment, he also occupied the incumbency as parson. Warehorne, it might have seemed, was the last outpost of the civilized world. Snargate, with the baleful invitation of its name, the first outpost of an altogether different region.

In Barham's thirty-fourth year came another abrupt transformation. Through the unexpected intervention of a friend in London, he captured a minor canonry at St Paul's, moved to Lincoln's Inn Fields, rose to an appointment in the Chapel Royal, and made a rapid path in gentlemanly journalism, contributing to *John Bull* and *Blackwood's*. In 1831 he was a founder member of the Garrick Club, and soon his squat, humorous figure, with its curious drooping left eyelid and pale, almost white eyelashes, was a regular feature of the literary dining tables, along with Hook, Sydney

Smith, young Boz, Cruickshank and Harrison Ainsworth. In 1837, Bentley asked him to contribute a comic series to the newly founded *Miscellany*, and the first issues saw *Oliver Twist* running at the front, and what were to become the opening numbers of *The Ingoldsby Legends* – verse and prose stories from 'Tom Ingoldsby's' family chest – bringing up the rear.

Barham's existence, now comfortably established at Amen Corner, seemed to be settled in an unalterable rotundity of good works, good humour and good living. But mortality shadowed him in the terrible, ineluctable death of five of his beloved children, until in 1840, on the loss of his favourite son Ned, he went into a decline, became ill in 1844, and died prematurely the following June from a throat infection, which gave him, he wrote, 'the not very pleasant sensation of slowly hanging'.

*The Ingoldsby Legends*, however, achieved a spectacular life of their own. In the next half-century, Bentley produced no less than eighty-eight separate editions: the Popular Edition of 1881 sold more than 60,000 copies on the first day of publication, and by 1900 more than half a million 'Ingoldsby's' were in circulation. They became a favourite with illustrators – Cruickshank, Tenniel, Leech, and perhaps finest of all, in 1907, Arthur Rackham who released a cobwebby thermal of witches and goblins from their pages. One poem, 'The Jackdaw of Rheims', became a classroom classic, while the whole volume received that *imprimatur* of good literature, an entry in the Papal *Index Librorum Prohibitorum.*

With Pickwick, Ingoldsby became a byword for Victorian amiability, the apogee of hearthside fun and Christmas good cheer. Comparisons bounced roisterously between Chaucer and W. S. Gilbert, and the virtuosity of the sprinting, cartwheeling verse – with its smart slang, outrageous rhymes and riproaring metres designed specifically for parlour recitation – was universally acclaimed. Moreover, the 'Legends' were strictly, or rather jovially, moral in intention, as Thomas Ingoldsby himself wrote (one almost forgot the Rev. B.) in the envoy to 'The Witches' Frolic':

> Don't flirt with young ladies;
>     don't practise soft speeches;
> Avoid waltzes, quadrilles,
>     pumps, silk hose, and knee-breeches; –
> Frequent not grey Ruins –

> shun riots and revelry,
> Hocus Pocus, and Conjuring,
>   and all sorts of devilry; –
> Don't meddle with broomsticks, –
>   they're Beelzebub's switches;
> Of cellars, keep clear – they're
>   the devil's own ditches;
> And beware of balls,
>   banqueting, brandy and – witches!
> Above all! don't run after
>   black eyes! – if you do, –
> Depend on't you'll find what I
>   say will come true
> Old Nick, some fine morning,
>   will 'hey after you'!

Only one early critic drew back from the convivial glow into the surrounding shadow: how was it, asked Richard Hengist Horne in 1844, that Barham seemed obsessed by certain bestial themes which he 'systematically *ripped up* for amusement'? Why was it that the canon seemed sometimes deliberately 'to gambol and slide in crimson horror'? No one wanted to know.

Public reputations are frail, and fame is only one of the more transient forms of visitation. The house at Burgate Street no longer stands, and no complete edition of *The Ingoldsby Legends* is currently in print, though old ones may be found brooding in coffined rows in the darker corners of seaside secondhand bookshops. The Ingoldsby Club, which once junketed at the Freemason's Arms off Great Queen Street, is long since defunct, though the lone pilgrim may still sip a port at the Jackdaw at Denton and meditate upon the Cruickshanks. I have walked in the graveyard at Warehorne, where the west wind moans across the Marsh from Rye, and climbed the shadowy timbers of Snargate belfry, where the smugglers once stacked Dutch tobacco in the eaves, and in the failing afternoon light heard the rattle of ash leaves on the slates, and the scuff of what I took to be sheep against the chancel door.

But I first definitely began to suspect something of the truth on examination in the British Museum of the now very rare three-volume definitive edition, annotated by Barham's daughter Fanny

(Mrs Francis Bond), of 1894. It became clear from this that many of the 'Legends', especially the 'Lays' which were lifted by Barham from the *Legenda Aurea* as convenient mode of attacking the monkish wing of the Tractarians – 'Pale' Pusey and the New-manites – are not essential to the collection, and indeed disguise its true nature.

The core of *The Ingoldsby Legends* is in fact a Kentish regional literature (with an occasional import from other counties), in which the countryside lying roughly in the triangle of Canterbury, Rye and Dover forms a sort of hermetic map or chart of Barham's spiritual geography. It is a haunted landscape, across which many grim apparitions move. Moreover, the 'Legends', far from being an anthology of *Myth and Marvels* (Bentley's, not Barham's, reassuring subtitle) are of the darkest kind of black comedy, packed with obsessionally repeated acts of violence and supernatural revenge, and redolent with a kind of succulent bawdy, in which the pleasures of feasting constantly substitute for those of love-making. The central stories, both prose and verse, contain a brand of tortured autobiography, and furtively connect with some of the more curious entries in his Diaries, and some of the forgotten details of the Rev. Barham's life.

Barham's Diaries, extant between 1803 and 1844, are filled primarily with genealogical and antiquarian notes, records of after-dinner conversations and ghost-stories. The fascination with genealogy was the symptom of a profound doubt about his own identity. In later life, with ironic bravado, he traced his tree to William FitzUrse, one of the knights who murdered Becket at Canterbury Cathedral; but the real roots of uncertainty lay close in childhood, not safely in history. Inspection of Alderman Barham's Will, and the obituary columns of *The Gentleman's Magazine*, reveal that his father sired not one but two children, by different women, and neither was immediately legitimate. The first, a girl, Sarah Bolden, died after a long illness in 1798 aged twenty-one. The second, Barham himself, was the child not of a Kentish Harris, but of the Alderman's humble housekeeper, Elizabeth Fox.

Moreover Barham's father died when the boy was only six, and he was removed from his mother's care (unsuitable rather than unhealthy, one suspects), and fostered out to maiden aunts called Dix. The effect of this early separation from his true mother, and the apparent banishment and eventual loss of his elder half-sister Sarah, may be imagined. A Kentish authority (S. M. Ellis, 1917) says – without realizing the significance – that he found 'Sara' together with Barham's initials scratched on a window at the house in Burgate Street, a mute appeal. Or perhaps an early incantation?

Barham grew up with a sense of banished or suppressed being, a double identity, emphasized by a crisis over his inheritance (£8,000 of the estate was misappropriated), and clearly expressed in the wild fluctuations between the persona of the Oxford buck and the rustic cleric. All these themes duly appeared in two early and long-forgotten novels, *Baldwin* (a Minerva Press blue-back thriller of 1819), and *My Cousin Nicholas* (1836, but largely drafted at Warehorne), during that strange but crucial period of self-exile by Romney Marsh. Disinheritance, hoaxes, double identities, patricide and fratricide, a loved one haunting her half-brother, even the first hint of demonic possession – all are set forth in shadowy, uncertain form. The haunted Fortescue, from the latter book, vividly recalls one part of Barham's youth:

> The tales of [his mother], herself a mine of legendary lore, had not, even in his childhood, tended to diminish his propensity to the sombre and the marvellous; Fetches and Banshees, the warnings of good angels and the shrieking of bad ones, 'black spirits and white, blue spirits and grey', omens, prognostications, and presentiments of death or desolation, with all the mysterious machinery of an invisible world, formed no slight portion of her creed. The very act that drove her and her foster-child from the paternal hearth, had been as plainly predicted to her as death-watches, dreams and candle-snuffs could shadow it forth.

By maturity, Barham's mind had developed a deeply macabre twist, which is resonant in the sick humour of his casually recorded jokes. He loved collecting epitaphs and an early gem reads, 'On a Man with a Remarkably Large Mouth':

> Reader! tread lightly o'er this sod
> For if he gapes you're gone by G–d

Asked once if he liked children (six altogether had died), 'Yes, Ma'am,' he replied, 'boiled with greens.'. He adored cats, and preferred to write after midnight with one perched, like some familiar gargoyle, on his shoulder. His daughter Fanny was encouraged to treat these as people: one, disguised as a baby, leapt out of its cradle and savaged an innocently cooing Bentley; while his son Dalton recalled that in Jacobean times it would have brought them 'in disagreeable communication with his Majesty's Witch Finder General'. When planning to move house, Barham announced: 'Your mother . . . is to be moved tomorrow, taking care to preserve as much of the earth about her roots as possible, across the Churchyard into Amen Corner, under a hot wall with a southern aspect.' Of an absent friend, Barham mused that he was probably still alive somewhere since 'none of the vergers have yet seen his ghost in the gloaming wandering about the north aisle'. It was wit, but it had quicklime on it.

Barham was also strangely fascinated by forensic matters. He was befriended by Richard Birnie, chief magistrate of Bow Street, and the two celebrated 'runners' Ruthven and Townshend. He attended the trial of the Cato Street conspirators in 1820, that of Cephas Quested, the Marsh smuggler the following year, and was conducted by Ruthven round the still fresh scene of the notorious Donatty stabbing off Gray's Inn Road in 1822. His Diaries are packed with other descriptions of weird cases of suicides, mesmerism, hauntings, houndings and visitations – many eventually transmuted into the raw material of the 'Legends'.

Barham's first serious attempt to grapple with the phantasmagoria that occupied the dark underside of his mind, was a fantastic precursor of Edgar Allan Poe's tale, 'The Trance'. Conceived at Warehorne, later published in *Blackwood's* and finally in *The Legends*, it was inspired by a story of Kentish witchcraft and 'ventriloquism' from Scott's *Dictionary of Witchcraft* (1654), compounded with Barham's own experience (so he said) of the bedside confessions of an adolescent girl. 'The Trance' tells of a wild and degenerate Oxford student 'Frederick S–' who lives a double life and discovers the satanic power of 'summoning' the spirits of sleeping people. While away studying in the Low Countries, Frederick practises on his innocent seventeen-year-old lover, transports her, and forces her to perform acts of horror and 'damning pollutions'.

Ultimately, all are destroyed, except the Reverend narrator, who is left appalled by his own unspeakable discoveries. The tale is brilliantly and intricately unfolded, through several frames of ironically bewildered narration, and points eventually towards R. L. Stevenson's *Dr Jekyll and Mr Hyde*. In a painful gesture of autobiography, Barham eventually entitled the story, 'A Singular Passage in the Life of the Late Henry Harris, Doctor in Divinity'. In what sense Barham himself believed he had witnessed these powers, one hesitates to speculate.

He finally succeeded in harnessing the doppelgänger theme in the Kentish 'Legend' of 'The Leech of Folkestone'. (Barham first used the word 'double-goer' in a letter of 1828, two years before the OED first registers the appearance of 'double-ganger' in English.) This story provides the key to the symbolic geography of *Ingoldsby*. It tells of a country gentleman, Master Marston, who is being poisoned and bewitched (wax doll and steel hatpins) by a Folkestone doctor – the Leech. Marston is met by a second, and far more mysterious 'leech', who appears with a travelling fair on the edge of Romney Marsh and offers to save him, if he will accompany him into the wilderness at the rising of the moon. The black magic combat for Marston's life is a combat between mainland and marshland forces. Mainland represents civilization, rationality, domestic government (though it is evil); while the Marsh represents a dark, unconscious region of disorder, hallucination and drunken violent comedy (which can be used for good). The Marsh wins, and Master Marston is saved. It is the old opposition between Warehorne and Snargate, but drawn large, to express a whole spiritual state.

Barham's sly, grimly humorous introduction of the Marsh is one of his justly famous regional passages and is still quoted in local literature:

> Reader, were you ever bewitched? – I do not mean by a 'white wench's black eye', or by love-potions imbibed from a ruby lip; – but were you ever really and bona fide bewitched in the true Matthew Hopkins's sense of the word? . . . The world, according to the best geographers, is divided into Europe, Asia, Africa, America, and Romney Marsh. In this last named, and fifth quarter of the globe, a Witch may still be occasionally discovered in favourable, i.e. stormy, seasons, weathering Dungeness Point, in an eggshell, or careering on her broomstick over Dymchurch wall.

The whole story, with its fine Brueghel-like description of the gingerbread fair at Aldington, is a masterly combination of black humour, folklore and parapsychology.

After the 'Leech' (1827, his sixth 'Legend'), Barham was able to break free from the artificial, rather Pickwickian formula of the 'Ingoldsby' household at Tappington, and ran deliriously through the folk mythology of Canterbury, Dover, Reculver, Barham Down, St Romwold's, Sandwich and other Kentish locations. The old symbolic oppositions and identities frequently occur (see 'Smuggler's Leap', or 'The Brothers of Birchington', or 'The Witches' Frolic'), but other themes and obsessions were now entangled.

One, 'Nell Cook!', returns to the losses and humiliations of Canterbury, with particular poetic force and psychological insight. It is a tale of the 'Dark Entry', a haunted gateway in the Cathedral Precincts. Nell is the servant and lover of a libidinous canon, a situation with obvious autobiographical undertones. Her charms are described with typical appreciation in terms of the delicacies of her *haute cuisine*. 'Her manchets fine were quite divine, her cakes were nicely browned' &c. All goes sweetly until Nell is jilted, when in vengeance she kills her master and his new lady, with a poisoned warden pie: 'The Canon's head lies on the bed – his "Niece" lies on the floor! They are as dead as any nail that is in any door.' Nell's punishment is to be entombed under the flagstones of the gateway, with a piece of the fatal 'kissing-crust' (*viz* the 'soft part of the pie or loaf where it has touched another in baking', a fiendish resolution of the culinary and erotic metaphor). Nell's murderous ghost, with 'eyes askew', ever after guards the Dark Entry at dusk, to the terror of the schoolboy narrator, for she breathes death. By the end of the poem, the 'Dark Entry' seems to command a mass of childhood symbolism, the gateway to memory, the gateway to sexual experience, the gateway to the Inferno.

But perhaps the wildest and most horrifying of all Barham's visitations are those of dismemberment. They feature notably in 'The Hand of Glory', 'St Gengulphus' and 'Bloudie Jack'. As a boy, Barham's arm had been crippled in a coach crash on the way to London, and a surgeon had threatened him with amputation, though in the event an instrument of catgut and silver rings was substituted. But the memory, itself perhaps a metaphor of disintegration and disinheritance, stayed with him. In 'Bloudie Jack'

(1840) – an English Bluebeard who murders eight wives, the ninth called Fanny – it reaches a grotesque climax when the villain is himself dismantled by a vengeful mob:

> They have pulled off your arms
> and your legs, Bloudie Jackie!
> As the naughty boys serve the blue flies;
> And they've torn from their sockets,
> And put in their pockets
> Your fingers and thumbs for a prize.
> And your eyes
> A Doctor has bottled – from Guy's.

Judiciously annotating these stories in her edition of 1894, Fanny Barham observed that many images were taken from her father's Bow Street interests, particularly the ghastly Greenacre murder involving a professional 'resurrectionist'. They lead ultimately to those two most beloved figures of late-Victorian horror mythology, Count Dracula and Jack the Ripper. No doubt it was a blessed release that Barham never lived to encounter these last grim incarnations of his private world, stalking the north aisle of St Paul's or rising from the mists around Old Romney. At least I hope he did not, though there is the question of the very late story, softly entitled 'Jerry Jervis's Wig'.

Barham, and it would appear his *Ingoldsby Legends*, for the present lie at peace. Most of his papers slumber in transatlantic libraries, his volumes doze on dusty shelves. But when I walk under the bare woods of Aldington Fright, and hear the rooks calling in the gathering gloom, it is difficult to dismiss from my mind the small, hurrying figure of that singular canon, and the poor cursed Jackdaw that the world half-remembers him by:

> He cursed him in sleeping, that every night
> He should dream of the devil, and wake in a fright;
> He cursed him in eating, he cursed him in drinking,
> He cursed him in coughing, in sneezing, in winking;
> He cursed him in sitting, in standing, in lying,
> He cursed him in walking, in riding, in flying,
> He cursed him in living, he cursed him in dying! –
> Never was heard such a terrible curse!!
> But what gave rise to no little surprise,
> Nobody seem'd one penny the worse!

# THE REVEREND MATURIN
# AND MR MELMOTH

WHEN OSCAR WILDE was released from Reading Gaol in 1897, you will recall that he fled to France under a rather remarkable pseudonym – Monsieur Sebastian Melmoth. His travel bags were initialled S. M., and his letters and melodious telegrams were signed 'Melmoth'. From the Hotel d'Alsace, Paris, he wrote to a friend explaining:

> You asked me about 'Melmoth' . . . to prevent the post-man having fits I sometimes have my letters inscribed with the name of a curious novel by my great-uncle, Maturin: a novel that was part of the romantic revival of the early century, and though imperfect, a pioneer: it is still read in France and Germany; Bentley republished it (in England) some years ago. I laugh at it, but it thrilled Europe.

Exactly why poor Oscar should have hit upon this lugubrious title remains to be seen. For the moment it is sufficient to remember that he chose it in prison, and that he carried it with him into exile and – quite soon – into death.

Wilde's grand-uncle (on his mother's side) was the Reverend Charles Robert Maturin, an eccentric Irish curate of St Peter's, Dublin. In 1820, at the age of forty, the Reverend Maturin startled his parishioners by publishing the extraordinary piece of Gothic fiction known as *Melmoth the Wanderer: A Tale*. Despite its modest subtitle, it ran to four substantial volumes, and was constructed in a most intricate, not to say devious manner, from a whole series of interlocking stories, each one nesting inside the other on the principle of a set of Chinese boxes or Russian dolls.

It was rumoured to be replete with all the terrors of the genre – comfortably outdoing the haunted castles of Horace Walpole, the fiendish monasteries of Monk Lewis, and the vapouring heroines of Mrs Radcliffe. Naturally, it was much mocked by the English reviewers of the day, who regarded Gothic Horror as irretrievably down-market. Croker growled in the *Quarterly*: 'Mr Maturin has contrived, by a "*curiosa infelicitas*" to unite in this work all the worst peculiarities of the worst modern novels. Compared with it, Lady Morgan (author of *The Wild Irish Girl*) is almost intelligible – *The Monk*, decent – *The Vampire*, amiable – and *Frankenstein*, natural.'

No doubt because of this, the novel leapt into a second edition, was adapted for the stage, and was shortly translated into French (twice by 1822), and later German and Spanish. Its European popularity has never waned since, and a Russian translation in a heavy black cover like a Bible appeared only four years ago.

Much more surprising, however, it became a *cause célèbre* among the leading Romantic and Symbolist writers in France. Balzac glorified it in *L'Elixir de longue vie*, and even wrote a satirical sequence, *Melmoth Réconcilié* (1835). Admiring references and epigraphs can be found in the works of Hugo, Baudelaire, Gautier, Eugène Sue, Villiers de l'Isle Adam, and Lautréamont, whose *Chants de Maldoror* pinches several morbid scenes.

Baudelaire, writing *On My Contemporaries* (1865), observed majestically: 'Beethoven began to stir up those worlds of melancholy and unappeasable despair which massed like thunderclouds on the inner horizon of man. Maturin in the novel, Byron in poetry, Poe in the analytical romance ... all admirably expressed the blasphemous element in human passion. They cast splendid, dazzling shafts of light on the hidden Lucifer figure who is enthroned deep in every human heart. I wish to suggest by this that modern art is essentially demoniac in tendency.'

This places the Reverend Maturin in unexpectedly influential company. Nor was Baudelaire referring to conventional, cardboard 'demons'. Certainly, the hero of *Melmoth* is on closer inspection no ordinary fiend. In fact, apart from a certain contract made with the powers of darkness, he seems to have been a rather studious and distinguished Anglo-Irish gentleman of the seventeenth century. 'There was nothing remarkable in his figure,' said one in the novel who had met him on his travels in Madrid (and lived to tell the tale). His demeanour was quiet, his dress sober, he did not carry a sword. Only there was something about his expression – 'the eyes particularly' – which could not fail to appal.

> Accustomed to look on and converse with all things revolting to nature and to man – for ever exploring the madhouse, the jail, or the Inquisition, the den of famine, the dungeon of crime, or the death-bed of despair – his eyes had acquired a light and language of their own – a light that none could gaze on, and a language that few dare understand.

Who *was* Mr Melmoth, that he frequented such grim institutions and dark secret places of the heart? He was a man, whatever else he might be, on a lifelong – a more than lifelong – pilgrimage. What he sought was a single victim. Someone whose life was so terrible, so tormented, so trapped, that as an act of rational choice – an act of madness, or delirium, was not valid – they would agree to change places with him. In this bargain they would purchase their freedom in exchange for 'an unutterable condition' which Melmoth proposed.

It is typical of Maturin that in the course of this long novel we never learn precisely what this 'unutterable condition' is. But it becomes clear that Melmoth has sold his soul in exchange for certain kinds of physical and intellectual gifts, and an extension of his natural life for a term of 150 years. The one way he can escape from final payment on this transaction is to transfer the deal to another human being before his time is up. It is a kind of diabolic mortgage. Hence Melmoth's ghastly search among the suffering and oppressed.

The legend of the Satanic pact is, of course, one of the most venerable in European folklore and literature. The figures of Cain, Dr Faustus, Ahasuerus the Wandering Jew, all express it; and Marlowe, Goethe, Byron, Coleridge and Thomas Mann have based masterpieces on it. It also had wide popular currency in English thriller writing of the nineteenth century – William Godwin's *St Leon* (1799), Robert Louis Stevenson's *The Bottle Imp*, and M. R. James's *Casting the Runes* are notable variations.

But Maturin's originality lay in transferring attention from the mythology of the horrendous pact, to the human psychology of those *in extremis* tempted to give way to it. What kind of despair could endanger them? The Tempter, Melmoth, is human. Apart from its outer frame-story, the novel is very little concerned with supernatural stage business. It is fundamentally a study in oppression – particularly the oppression of institutions and customs – explored in various convenient Gothic forms.

There are six main tales, though only a flow-chart could show how they follow, drop through, open out, and close back round each other, like some mad emperor's mechanical puzzle. The first concerns Stanton, an Englishman lured into a lunatic asylum; the second Monçada, a young Spaniard trapped in a monastery and then an Inquisition prison; the third, Immalee, an 'Indian' maiden marooned on a palm-tree island; the fourth Isaidora, a Spanish debutante doomed to an arranged marriage; the fifth, the Walbergs, a loving German Protestant family torn apart by sudden poverty and unemployment; and the sixth, Elinor and John Sandal, two Shropshire lovers ruined by a greedy mother. Each one also contains several sub-tales and anecdotes. But every one of them concerns some sort of imprisonment of the body or the spirit. Even when someone plays chess in Maturin, they break off leaving the Queen *en prise*.

The pains that most of these intended victims undergo are mental rather than physical, though they can reach forms of torment where the borderline is blurred in hallucination or dream. Here, in a celebrated passage, the young monk Monçada suffers a nightmare on the eve of his interrogation by the Spanish Inquisition:

> The next moment I was chained to my chair again –
> the fires were lit, the bells rang out, the litanies were
> sung – my feet were scorched to a cinder – my muscles
> cracked, my blood and marrow hissed, my flesh con-
> sumed like shrinking leather – the bones of my legs
> hung two black withering and moveless sticks in the
> ascending blaze – it ascended, caught my hair – I was
> crowned with fire – my head was a ball of molten metal
> – my eyes flashed and melted in their sockets – I opened
> my mouth, it drank fire – I closed it, the fire was within
> – and still the bells rung on, and the crowd shouted,

and the king and queen, and all the nobility as I burned
and burned! ... *Misericordia por amor di Dios!* My own
screams awoke me – I was in prison, and beside me
stood the Tempter.

Strikingly horrible as this passage is (and pointing, in its rhythms
especially, towards Edgar Allan Poe), it remains within the hyper-
bolic conventions of eighteenth-century Gothicism, only a breath
away from outright laughter. Indeed it is in this suppressed laughter, on the reader's part, that much of its grotesque power probably
lies. Not for nothing Maturin was dubbed 'the Fuseli of novelists'.

Who was the obscure Irish curate who created Melmoth and
his labyrinth of victims? How did he become such an epicure of
terror and oppression? Charles Robert Maturin was no clerical
jailbird or insurrectionary priest, and he lived quietly through the
upheavals of the French Revolution and the first bloody outbreaks
of Irish nationalism in Dublin, under Wolfe Tone and Emmet.
Yet these things left their inner mark, and later in life he claimed
that a Huguenot ancestor had spent twenty-six years in the Bastille.

Born in 1780, the youngest son of a prosperous Irish civil servant, Maturin graduated at Trinity College, Dublin, and took Holy
Orders in the Protestant Church. His first curacy was at the remote
country town of Loughrea, in Galway, and here he came in touch
with the profound superstition and misery of the local people. By
the age of twenty-four, however, he had been appointed as one
of the curates of St Peter's, living in the fashionable quarter of
St Stephen's Green in Dublin, with a stipend of some £80 per
annum. He was a youthful, elegant figure – his portrait shows
something of a clerical dandy, with open shirt and graceful fingers
– and he quickly married his childhood sweetheart, Henrietta
Kingsbury, who had musical talents and useful connections with
the Irish Episcopacy.

But Maturin was disappointed in his hopes of early preferment.
His seniors found him too colourful and unstable: a love of dancing, amateur theatricals and mischievous mimicry, alternated with
strange fits of melancholy and distraction. He also revealed an
inconvenient literary bent – publishing in rapid succession a series
of garish romances: *The Fatal Revenge* in 1807, *The Wild Irish Boy*
in 1808, and *The Milesian Chief* in 1812. This was not the curriculum vitae of a future bishop.

Maturin's Preface to the latter work is revealing of his situation as he saw it at the age of thirty-two: 'If I possess any talent, it is that of darkening the gloomy, and deepening the sad; of painting life in the extremes, and representing the struggles of passion when the soul trembles on the verge of the unlawful and the unhallowed. In the following pages I have tried to apply these to the scenes of actual life: and I have chosen my own country for the scene, because I believe it is the only country on earth where, from the strange existing opposition of religion, politics and manners, the extremes of refinement and barbarism are united and the most wild and incredible situations of romantic story are hourly passing before modern eyes. In my first work I attempted to explore the ground forbidden to man; the sources of visionary terror; "the formless and the void": in my present I have tried the equally obscure recesses of the human heart. If I fail in both, I shall – write again.'

Maturin's sense of being trapped in Ireland, his clerical career frustrated and literary recognition remote, was now compounded by financial crises. His father was sacked from his senior position in the Dublin Post Office on an unfounded charge of malfeasance; and a distant relative, possibly a rascally cousin, inveigled Maturin into going security on a business that promptly went bankrupt. Plunged into debt, and with a household now including nine dependants and his difficult old father, Maturin desperately took on private pupils, and wrote away more furiously than ever. The autobiographical basis of one of Melmoth's tales – the Walberg family – was already taking shape.

Then in 1816, Maturin's fortunes dramatically changed. He had decided to try his luck with a stage melodrama, and the resulting script – *Bertram, or the Castle of St Aldobrand* – reached the notice of Walter Scott, who passed it on with an amused recommendation to Byron, then chairman of the Drury Lane Theatre Committee. A single stage-direction catches the flavour of the piece: 'The Rocks – The Sea – A Storm – The Convent illuminated in the background –The Bell tolls at intervals – A group of Monks on the Rocks with Torches – A Vessel in Distress.'

To Maturin's amazement, the play was immediately accepted and a brilliantly successful production was mounted in May 1816, with Kean in the star role. Byron sent him fifty guineas; John

Murray bought the book copyright for £350; and box office receipts earned him more than £500. Maturin visited London (the only time in his life he ever left Ireland), was applauded at Drury Lane, and did a breathless round of the literary drawing-rooms. For a brief, brief moment he was famous, and what is more, *free*.

Back in Dublin he lived in a dreamlike whirl. He was the hero of his own household. He bought Turkey carpets, ottomans, marble tables, silk wallpapers, elaborate lustres, and had his parlour expensively panelled with painted *boiserie* depicting the scenes from his novels. He became a habitué of Lady Morgan's Dublin salon, and indulged his passion for dancing 'with young persons', even joining a racy Gavotte Society that met three mornings a week. (There are some nasty dancing metaphors in *Melmoth*.)

'His character, habits and opinions seemed to undergo a total alteration,' a friend later wrote. 'He returned to Ireland, gave up his tuitions, indulged in the intoxications of society, and became a man of fashion, living upon the fame of his genius.' He was thirty-six.

At this time he was said to sit composing amid his own house parties, with a red patch pasted on his forehead to indicate that he was in the throes of creation. Subsequently that patch must have come to seem like the mark of Cain.

Maturin's time of triumph was bitterly short – less than a year. His subsequent melodramas – *Manuel* (1817) and *Fredolfo* (1819) – flopped hopelessly at Drury Lane and Covent Garden. Coleridge wrote a destructive review of his work, which he unkindly republished in the *Biographia Literaria*. A scheme of Byron's, to make over the royalties from his poems, fell through because of Murray's objections ('It could be in no respect different to you – whether I paid to a whore or a hospital – or assisted a man of talent in distress,' complained Milord) – and the three intended beneficiaries, Maturin, Godwin, and ironically Coleridge, received nothing.

Maturin's old debts absorbed all his remaining royalties. He was soon writing to Murray: 'There is not a shilling I have made by *Bertram* that has not been expended to pay the debts of a scoundrel for whom I had the misfortune to go security, so here I am with scarce a pound in my pocket, simpering at congratulations on having made a fortune.' One catches the bitter lilt of his voice.

By 1817, the complaints had become more pathetic. 'Let me beg you to write to me. I cannot describe to you the effect of an English letter on my spirits; it is like the wind to an Aeolian harp. I cannot produce a note without it. Give me advice, abuse, news, anything or nothing (if it were possible that you could write nothing), but write –.'

For Maturin the iron door of circumstance had clanged shut once more, and this time for ever. 'There is no room for Irishmen in England,' he groaned.

It was in this dark mood that he began to scrawl down the first wild tales that turned into the maze of Melmoth's wanderings across Europe in search of salvation. Much of his adolescent reading, from the *Arabian Nights* and Glanville's *History of Witchcraft*, to Percy and Ossian and *La Religieuse* of Diderot, swam back into his mind; so too did personal memories of the Dublin street riots, the English suppressions, and the deathbed visions of his country parishioners (many footnotes in *Melmoth* attest to these). But the master-idea, said Maturin, came to him during the course of a late Sunday evening's sermon at St Peter's in 1817.

He was speaking gloomily of the infinite mercy of God, and looking down at his little flock amid the flickering candlelight, he suddenly exclaimed: 'At this moment is there one of us present, however we may have departed from the Lord, disobeyed his will, and disregarded his word – is there one of us who would, at this moment, accept all that man could bestow, or earth afford, to resign the hope of his salvation? No, there is not one – not such a fool on earth, were the enemy of mankind to traverse it with the offer!'

A silence fell in the church, the wind howled, and as the French say an angel – or something worse – walked overhead. Maturin testifies that, in that silence, he reflected on his own lot, and somewhere a pair of baleful eyes first opened their lurid lights, and Melmoth was born – or reborn – and began walking on the wild cliff tops of County Wicklow. The passage can still be read in his published *Sermons* (1819).

While he wrote *Melmoth*, Maturin seems to have become a ghost of his former self. He had gone bald. The expensive furnishings of his house in York Street were progressively sold off, and even the stone flagged corridors left uncarpeted.

He no longer composed in the cheerful parlour, but took long solitary afternoon walks and returned after dark to shut himself up in his study to write. As he worked, he seemed to withdraw into some kind of bleak inner world, his quill pen moving with sinister speed as if under dictation. A Dublin friend recalled of this time:

> I have remained with him repeatedly, looking over some of his loose manuscripts, till three in the morning, while he was composing his wild romance of *Melmoth*. Brandy-and-water supplied to him the excitement that opium yields to others, but it had no intoxicating effect on him; its action was, if possible, more strange, and indeed terrible to witness. His mind travelling in the dark regions of romance, seemed altogether to have deserted his body, and left behind a mere physical organism; his long pale face acquired the appearance of a cast taken from the face of a dead body; and his large prominent eyes took a glassy look; so that when, at the witching hour, he suddenly without speaking raised himself and extended a thin and bony hand, to grasp the silver branch with which he lighted me downstairs, I have often started and gazed on him as a spectral illusion of his own creation.

No doubt this description has gained a certain blarney in the retelling. Yet it corresponds oddly with the sensation of blind, headlong speed in Maturin's narrative, which makes it so readable, and prompted the *New Monthly Review* critic of 1821 to observe: 'Maturin will ransack the forgotten records of crime, or the dusty museums of natural history, to discover a new horror. He is a passionate connoisseur in agony. His taste for strong emotion evidently hurries him on *almost without the concurrence of the will*.' A hundred years later, André Breton recognized in it the *écriture automatique* of Surrealism.

Maturin's publisher – now Constable of Edinburgh – reacted more frostily. Why did the chaotic instalments of manuscript have no pagination? Where were the logical links between the tales? What was the title to be? How could a reader ever reach the end without chapter summaries? And anyway, why was it so late?

In retrospect, it is clear that the asymmetrical, labyrinthine structure of the tales is one of the main sources of their weird power. The further the reader enters in, the more he is overcome by a nightmare sense of suffocation and apprehension. Yet all the time the narrative moves at relentless pace. It is like a prisoner rushing to escape through a Piranesi-style series of bifurcating, subterranean vaults, which only appear to lead him deeper and deeper underground. At each twist or intersection, sooner or later, we glimpse the figure of Melmoth, lurching from the shadows, grimly proposing his bargain. The final effort may even strike the modern reader with an uncanny sense of premonition – here already is something like the dark, closed universe of Kafka's *Castle* or Solzhenitsyn's *Gulag Archipelago*.

In the most avowedly Romantic of the tales, the story of the innocent Indian maiden Immalee on her beautiful desert island, Melmoth himself is her demon lover. He tries deviously to corrupt her mind with distorted accounts of mainland civilization, which he shows her – in a scene surely predestined for the stage – through a powerful telescope. Immalee is the figure who comes closest to redeeming Melmoth by falling in love with him. She is a potential Ariadne. He is the first human being she has ever seen ('the daughter of a palm tree'), and she unravels his sophistries with innocent guile. Through her we realize the limitations of Melmoth's satanically purchased powers, and the paradoxical truth that it is he who is more deeply imprisoned than all his intended victims. Many of their dialogues, full of Rousseauesque naïvetés, have a quaint poetic charm.

'The tempter was departing gloomily, when he saw tears start from the bright eyes of Immalee, and caught a wild and dark omen from their innocent grief. "And you weep, Immalee?" – "Yes", said the beautiful being, "I always weep when I see the sun set in clouds; and will you, the sun of my heart, set in darkness too? and will you not rise again? will you not?" and with the graceful confidence of pure innocence, she pressed her red delicious lips to his hand as she spoke. "Will you not?"'

In the end Melmoth simply cannot bring himself to seduce her, and he bitterly abandons her to the lonely island of peacocks and blossom, as a shadow passes over the moon. But the idyll is brief, and the labyrinth here doubles back with particular cruelty. Under the name of Isadora, Immalee turns up again in Madrid, rescued, educated and refined. She is swiftly carried off, seduced and married against her parents' will, and ends her days in yet another dungeon, with a dead child in her arms. There is no escape for anyone.

Yet Melmoth is never successful in his temptations. Not one of his victims finally gives way, and by the end of the novel it is Melmoth himself, returned after 150 years to the remote ancestral house on the coast of Wicklow, who is at last called to account. A touch of the Irish charm does not quite desert him, though. 'His hairs were as white as snow, his mouth had fallen in, the muscles of his face were relaxed and withered – he was the very image of hoary decrepit debility. He started himself at the impression which his appearance visibly made on the intruders. "You see what I feel," he exclaimed, "the hour then is come. I am summoned, and I must obey the summons – my master has other work for me! When a meteor blazes in your atmosphere – when a comet pursues its burning path towards the sun – look up, and perhaps you may think of the spirit condemned to guide the blazing and erratic orb."'

Maturin leaves open one unsettling possibility. Melmoth might continue to rove the world, 'seeking for whom he might devour', in centuries to come – 'should the fearful terms of his existence be renewed'.

Maturin eventually received £500 from Constable for his overdue manuscript, but the terms of his own contract were never renewed. A mere four years after the publication of his masterpiece, he died in gloom and genteel poverty, aged forty-four. Fame never reached him properly again. When Walter Scott, the most faithful of his literary supporters, journeyed to Dublin in order to collect materials for a biography, he found that most of Maturin's private papers had been destroyed by his family.

Maturin had written that he was 'one who has hitherto known little of life but labour, distress and difficulty, and who has borrowed the gloomy colouring of his own pages from the shade of obscurity and misfortune under which his existence has been wasted'. In *Melmoth* he added: 'Let those who smile at me, ask themselves whether they have been indebted most to imagination or reality for all they have enjoyed – if indeed they have enjoyed anything.'

Despite its Gothicism, much of the deepest inspiration of *Melmoth the Wanderer* is profoundly and timelessly Irish. It draws on images of age-old subjection and persecution, but lights them with a fantastic charm and exuberance. It touches upon the spiritual nature of captivity – social, religious, political – in a way that has often been more accessible to the European than the English mind. Perhaps this will always be so. But surely this was one of the reasons why Wilde, with a kind of posthumous gallantry, adopted his grand-uncle's strange creation when he went into sad exile in France.

How oddly delighted the Reverend Maturin would have been, if he had lived even to a legitimate ripe old age, to learn that Charles Baudelaire – that other spoilt priest – had proposed to translate *Melmoth* unabridged into French; and how moved he might have been to read the following passage from his 'Poème du Haschisch' (1858):

> Let us remember Melmoth, that admirable emblem.
> His horrific suffering lies in the disproportion between
> his marvellous faculties, acquired instantly by a satanic
> pact, and the everyday world in which, as a creature of
> God, he is condemned to live. And none of those whom
> he wishes to seduce consent to purchase, on those same
> conditions, his terrible privilege. In effect, any man who
> does not accept the conditions of life, sells his own soul.

Yet one stranger speculation remains. If Melmoth's contract was renewed – *where is he now?*

# M. R. JAMES AND OTHERS

AT THIS SEASON, the darkness slides out of the fens and begins to gather in Cambridge towards five o'clock. It is the late afternoon, *entre chien et loup*. From the tall windows of the panelled library of King's College, one looks north in the half-light over the neat, shaved lawns towards Wilkins' Building, and the four mace-like spires of King's Chapel, where the choristers will soon be vesting for Evensong. Outside, in the sharp wind, muffled figures hurry round the flagged terraces and disappear over the hump of the bridge into the rustling gloom of the Backs. As for the thin shapes that occasionally glide at angles across the forbidden centres of the grass, they are vaguely identified, by ancient notices, as Senior Members of the College, which their fluttering draperies would seem to confirm.

To the south, the library windows gaze down upon the shadowy brickwork of Webb's Court, and the Provost's gateway, above which the initials M. R. J. may be seen carved in relief above the casements, with sinuous trefoils and elaborate tentacles of stonework binding the letters of his name to the cold fabric in a tight, labyrinthine, and presumably benevolent embrace.

All this is as it was, and, almost, as it should be. The career of Montague Rhodes James was inextricably bound up with the life of King's College. Here he came as a scholar from Eton in 1882; here he took a Double First in Classics, and was appointed in faultless progression Dean, Provost and Vice-Chancellor of the university; and it was from here that he retired back to King's sister college Eton in 1918, to a second benign and much-loved Provostship, now the ageing friend of schoolboys, choristers and cats.

Montague James was a tall, solidly built man, with large

impassive features, rather severely cut, round black spectacles, and great physical strength, which seemed to find little outlet except in bicycling and demon patience. He never married. His life was essentially scholastic and collegiate in the old academic pattern, that rare blend of monastic loneliness and mischievous, faintly boyish, good fellowship. He presided at the end of the golden age of assured continuity between Eton and King's. In the field of medieval manuscripts he gained an international reputation as a palaeographer and antiquarian. His great work, a definitive edition of the Apocryphal New Testament, was published in 1924. He received the Order of Merit in 1930. He died, listening to Christmas carols, in 1936. He left a humorous, oddly impersonal autobiography called *Eton and King's* – subtitled 'Recollections, mostly trivial'. It was in its way a model life, smooth, well-trimmed, distinguished and without interruptions: indeed, much like the lawns of the college. Only, what were those shapes that glided across it, occasionally, in the dusk?

For there is the little matter of the ghost-stories.

Dons, of course, had strange quirks of humour in those days. They liked weird jokes lurking in footnotes; conundrums in Latin vulgate; etymological anecdotes about diseases; imaginary friendships with domestic animals; or domestic friendships with imaginary ones. (No doubt it has all changed now.) Montague James's ghost-stories fitted into all these categories of cloister recreation. Yet this does not entirely account for them.

There is, for example, the sudden and unexpected occasion of their advent, at an October meeting of the Chitchat Society, in 1893, a rather prosaic institution dedicated to 'the promotion of rational conversation' and habituated to nothing wilder than dissertations on church portals or Breton ballads. The minute still exists: the 601st meeting, eleven members present, and 'Mr James read Two Ghost Stories'. There were serious scholars in attendance: Walter Headlam, and Dr Waldstein of the Fitzwilliam Museum (where James was to follow as director); yet no explanation of this aberration is forthcoming.

We know only that the first story was 'Canon Alberic's Scrapbook', one of the most horribly violent and deliberately autobiographical of them all: in it, a travelling antiquarian, clearly identified with James, is set upon one lonely night in his *auberge* bedroom by a fiend whose picture he has just discovered in a priceless folio of medieval manuscripts.

> His attention was caught by an object lying on the red cloth just by his left elbow. Two or three ideas of what it might be flitted through his brain with their own incalculable quickness. 'A pen-wiper? No, no such thing in the house. A rat? No, too black. A large spider? I trust to goodness not – no, Good God! A hand like the hand in that picture!' In another infinitesimal flash he had taken it in. Pale, dusky skin, covering nothing but bones and tendons of appalling strength; coarse black hairs, longer than ever grew on a human hand; nails rising from the ends of the fingers and curving sharply down and forward ... The shape, whose left hand rested on the table, was rising to a standing posture behind his seat, its right hand crooked above his scalp ... he screamed with the voice of an animal in hideous pain.

Montague James was appointed Dean at King's in the year of this story.

Then there is the question of the regularity of the ghost-stories, which if not obsessive was certainly ritual. James was thirty-one, and he produced approximately one story every year for the next quarter of a century. The dates of the collections speak for themselves: *Ghost Stories of an Antiquary*, 1904; *More Ghost Stories*, 1911; *A Thin Ghost and Others*, 1919; and *A Warning to the Curious*, 1925. *The Collected Ghost Stories* appeared in 1931, and were reissued this autumn. Nor did James resort to any other form of fiction, except one, *The Five Jars*. But this was to be a deliberate piece of 'white magic', dedicated to a particular little girl with a very special place in James's existence.

Next there are James's oddly insistent denials, for he rarely insisted on anything, which belong to the end of his life. 'First, whether the stories are based on my own experience? To this the answer is No: except in one case, specified in the text, where a dream furnished a suggestion. Or again, whether they are versions of other people's experiences? No. Or suggested by books? This is more difficult to answer concisely . . .'

Against these has to be set the fact that we now know that virtually all of them have direct links with places that James visited, or with work he was engaged upon. The old Cambridge University Library, the Fitzwilliam and Ashmolean museums, the favourite seaside resorts of Felixstowe and Aldeburgh, country houses in Devon and Lincolnshire, his prep school at East Sheen, the cathedral manuscript library at Canterbury, vacational visits to Scandinavia, Austria and France, his lifelong study of witch trials – all may be found under the thinnest of disguises in the stories. A professor from Poitiers University has recently written to praise James on the accuracy of his architectural description of the little church of St Bertrand de Comminges, in the Pyrenees, which the fiend frequented in 'Canon Alberic': particularly the detail of the stuffed crocodile in the nave.

In general the ghost-stories reflect the everyday minutiae of James's own Edwardian scholar's world: the late-night studies, the panelled libraries, the rural taverns, the cathedral precincts, the out-of-season seaside hotels, the blustery golf-links, the closed cabs, the winking servants, the lawyers' deed boxes, the mouldering chapels, the lonely lanes and the stretching beaches of long, introspective expeditions with a thin walking stick in the late afternoon. Indeed, James always insisted that it was just these precise, slightly old-fashioned but absolutely faithful scenarios that were the major factor in the power of his stories to 'summon'.

A moment's consideration, however, serves to delay the looming conclusion that the occurrences in the stories were actually autobiographical. '*Deux fois je l'ai vu; mille fois je l'ai senti*' is the way the sacristan puts it in 'Canon Alberic'. A man who saw all James's demons would do presumably anything rather than write Christmas tales about them, although the diaries of Arthur Benson, the Master at Magdalene, suggests that he might resort to other forms of written record; and there is the case of Algernon Blackwood. But such literal transcriptions would be merely frightful, pathological fragments, not the beautifully balanced and thoroughly gentlemanly accounts of James's fiction.

Instead, one is led to ask, what after all is the nature of the ghost-story, beyond that of pure entertainment? If it is not literally true, what kind of truth might it embody? Or what kind of response does it summon? Or what kind of catharsis does it provide?

Is there not, perhaps, an element of something like *automatic writing* within the purely mechanical arrangement of the suspense? While the outward narrative is deliberate, and in James's case finely worked to a really masterly pitch of understatement and implied unpleasantness, the inner encounter is perhaps symbolic and not so deliberate. Indeed it may even be quite uncontrolled.

To this extent, the ghost-story may have some of the properties of the dream. As James practised it, it might be one of the few genuinely successful forms of English surrealism. It has a power to summon and embody – the words have a particular force of meaning in James's horribly muscular, crouching, taloned apparitions – certain unformulated threats and contradictions both inside the narrator's own mind, and, even more, outside it, in the conditions of his life and social circumstance. The ghosts are, perhaps, the true historical witnesses, far more honest and solid than the poor, fleeing men of flesh whom they hound and harrow.

Here, too, it may be recalled that the basic action of almost all James's ghost-stories is that of the investigation or research, which disturbs malign forces far more powerful than the investigator ever bargained for.

The sheltered, outmoded and somewhat peculiar tenor of James's life at King's, already contained, openly and on its surface, many of those qualities of the grotesque which were to be expressed at far greater intensity in the stories. This grotesquerie was of a special, English kind: farcically funny, the macabre and the cruel – strongly reminiscent, in fact, of those dribbling gargoyles which everywhere ornament the stolid church architecture of the East Anglian fens. The autobiography *Eton and King's* is packed with such tales of the eccentricities of fellow dons – of the ageing adolescent, Oscar Browning; or of the crippled J. E. Nixon, who lacked one hand and one eye, and was said to have been composed of *two dons* compacted in a railway accident near Euston Station. Typically, James recorded with a sort of professional interest the baiting of another old retainer by King's undergraduates:

> They sat at their window looking out into the court and
> saw Mozley coming out of his staircase, intent on a brisk
> walk. They then gave a low but penetrating whistle.
> Mozley started, looked round and stopped dead, and
> if the whistle was repeated ran back into his staircase
> like a rabbit. In a minute or two he would peep out
> again, looking cautiously about. Again they whistled, of
> course, keeping themselves concealed: again he ran
> back.

This entertainment might, apparently, go on for an entire afternoon. How close it already lies to the theme of the story 'O
Whistle and I'll Come to You, My Lad' is evident. But James's only
comment is: 'Are dons so odd nowadays as they were then? It can
hardly be. Most of them are married and lead normal family lives.'

By comparison, Nathaniel Wedd, a classical tutor at King's, has
recalled in an unpublished memoir one of James's own peculiarly
donnish superstitions which is equally suspended between the
sense of prank and of real fear. 'I lived in the rooms beneath him
in Fellow's Building. At about 2am I used to knock the ashes of
my pipe out, tapping on the mantelpiece. Monty told me how
often and often when in bed he heard the tap, tap, tap, he used
to lie shivering with horror. He couldn't believe it wasn't a ghost
in his outer room, though he knew all the time exactly how the
sounds were produced. At heart he believed in ghosts and in their
malevolence.'

James revelled in the company of undergraduates, especially in
the evenings, when as Provost he had the Lodge lock replaced by
a simple handle. Card games, mimicry, jigsaw puzzles, whisky and
soda, and such hybrid university sports as tossing up coins
freighted with licked postage stamps (the object being to frank
the ceiling), went on far into the early hours. The cast of humour
among the inner circle was exemplified by one of James's reviews
written for private performance at the ADC, a burlesque on the
Marlowe Society's *Faust*. The Jamesian Faust is an undergraduate
tempted by his Mephisphelean tutor to specialize in Occult
Studies for Part II of the Tripos. Significantly enough, it is the
lady domestic, his bedmaker, who pleads with him:

> O Sir, don't take that 'orrid Necromancy;
> Whatever would your poor dear huncle say?

I 'ad a gent took Necromancy once
And he was *come for* in his second year.
O! such a turn it give me! and the mess
And smell of sulphur in the furniture!
It took me weeks on weeks to clean the rooms.

But all in vain; for the undergraduate's final appearance is in the palm of his tutor's hand, as 'a small piece of meat'.

How far these leanings accompanied James into the serious scholastic side of his life and work as a palaeographer is difficult to assess. The Apocrypha is itself a somewhat twilight field, neither orthodox Biblical Studies, nor entirely medieval folklore, and it contains many strange presences, such as Solomon and the Demons. Several of James's short studies suggest occult attractions, such as the monograph on the medieval bibliophile and necromancer John Dee (1921); the essay on the legend of St Stephen and the crowing capon (1902); the paper in the *English Historical Review* on twelve medieval Latin ghost-story fragments; and the curious passage on the 'elixir of the palaeographer' in an educational pamphlet on *The Wanderings of Manuscripts* (1919). James was also fascinated by the medieval bestiaries, and produced several scholarly editions for the Roxburghe Club of these rather ambiguous manuscripts, which are part treatises on morality, part zoological catalogues and part demonological romances. Some of his descriptive entries, both in their subject matter and in their understated style, have an uncomfortable sense of *déjà vu*. Here, for example, is folio 156 Ms Ii 4.26 in the University Library Cambridge, published in 1928:

> *Cocodrillus.* Under three shallow arches: a plain pillar
> at each end. The beast has a ridged and serrated back
> and tail and legs, and tremendous talons, a tuft under
> its throat and a horned head. It faces right, and seizes
> a nude man in its great teeth, by the middle: he is
> writhing and crying out.

When James was received back at Eton, the official honorific speech of welcome contained a list of his scholarly achievements and interests, which terminated with a pointed reference to 'Lemuros istos'; at which phrase it is recorded that 'a grim smile for a second curved the lips of the new Provost'.

At the deeper emotional level, there can be even less certainty. It is possibly suggestive that the date of the first ghost-story, 1893, coincides with the arrival at King's of Jim McBryde, a talented undergraduate, who later studied at the Slade. The close friendship which sprang up between James and McBryde was perhaps, outside his immediate family of whom we know so little, the most important in James's life. McBryde's sunny, sympathetic nature, his gifts as an illustrator and raconteur, seem to have done much to draw James out of himself and free his imaginative powers. It was McBryde's naïve but extraordinarily evocative pen drawings which illustrated the first of James's ghost collections in 1904, with a directness – not untouched by amusement – that has not been rivalled since. McBryde travelled on many of James's cycling expeditions, and their trip to Scandinavia, together with another undergraduate, Will Stone, yielded 'The Story of a Troll-Hunt', a charming comic-strip essay about their attempt (successful) to capture a specimen of this legendary monster with the help of some alcohol and a parrot cage. Other, less direct consequences of this voyage seem to have been James's ghost-stories, 'Number 13' and the gruesome 'Count Magnus', in which the victim's face is sucked off his skull.

One has the sense that Jim McBryde was in many ways James's great emotional catalyst, and the friendship continued to blossom when he later married and settled in London. Then, suddenly and tragically, McBryde died at the age of thirty. Thereafter, James acted as the friend and adviser to his widow, Gwendolen, and as the guardian to his brilliantly pretty, golden-haired daughter, Jane. They, in turn, seem to have provided James with some of the steadiness and affection of a family.

James's wildly imaginative and amusing letters to Jane, especially when she was between the ages of six and twelve, are some of the most delightful and intimate things he ever wrote. They consist, very largely, in long dialogues between the Provost and the Provost's cat on the subject of young Jane's welfare. It was for Jane that 'The Five Jars', a unique and gentle piece of fairy-tale exorcism, was written in 1922.

But the subject of cats, who always played an ambivalent role in James's imagination, leads back remorselessly and inevitably to the various beasts and monstrosities of that darker world. James's ghost-stories as a whole may be said to form a kind of malign bestiary of the scholar's heart, for their fiends invariably show themselves in some furious sub-animal form which clutches rapaciously at the exposed weaknesses of a man who is alone. This bestial manifestation can be observed most literally in 'The Stalls of Barchester Cathedral', where the guilty prelate is first beginning to feel the presence of his familiar as he dozes in the choir at Evensong.

> During the Magnificat . . . my hand was resting on the back of the carved figure of a cat which is the nearest to me of the three figures on the end of my stall. I was not aware of this, for I was not looking in that direction, until I was startled by what seemed a softness, a feeling as of rather rough and coarse fur, and a sudden move-ment as if the creature were twisting round its head to bite me . . . I must have uttered a suppressed excla-mation, for I noticed that Mr Treasurer turned his head quickly in my direction.

In the 'Diary of Mr Poynter', the catlike creature is not identified with such certainty. But the progressive materialization of a physi-cal presence, with that particular feline *viciousness* so characteristic of James's notion of the terrible, and with the corresponding wince of revulsion from physical contact, is given one of its most subtle presentations.

> As he dashed into the baize door that cut the passage in two, and – forgetting that it opened towards him – beat against it with all the force in him, he felt a soft ineffectual tearing at his back which, all the same, seemed to be growing in power, as if the hand, or whatever worse than a hand was there, were becoming more material as the pursuer's rage was more concen-trated.

From the feline, one moves through the catalogue of James's bestial aggressors towards the unavoidable notion of the feminine. Here I think one may be close upon the central horror. There are several specifically female apparitions in the ghost-stories. Noticeable among them are the flapping, goose-like shape of Anne Clark in 'Martin's Close' as she rises from the pond on the moor to take revenge upon her lover; and the ghastly, antiquated lump of Mrs Sadleir in 'The Uncommon Prayer Book', who like 'a great roll of shabby white flannel', falls from a dark cupboard on the neck of the luckless antiquarian, 'more like a ferret going for a rabbit than anything else', as a Cockney witness observes, at a mercifully safe distance, through a glass partition.

But it is the unspecifically feminine, the stiffening ectoplasm of *feminality* which seems to carry in the end the maximum emotional charge in James's fiction. The long, darting, dress-like sheet and 'intensely horrible face of crumpled linen' belonging to the occupant of the empty bed in the moonlit hotel room of 'O Whistle and I'll Come to You, My Lad', which was so grimly caught by McBryde in his last illustration, is one of the nastiest and most unforgettable of these vengeful apparitions. 'It leapt towards him upon the instant, and the next moment he was halfway through the window backwards, uttering cry upon cry at the utmost pitch of his voice, and the linen face was thrust close into his own.'

Yet there remains one which is still more climactic. The ultimate intention of physical seizure and possession becomes explicit in the soft, dank, fleshly thing of 'The Treasure of Abbott Thomas'. The scholar investigator has located his prize at the bottom of a gloomy well, and momentarily separated from his bluff man-servant, he gropes for it in a deep cavity in the brickwork. 'Just give me a glass of cognac, Brown, I'll go on in a moment . . . Well, I felt to the right, and my fingers touched something curved, that felt – yes – more or less like leather; dampish it was, and evidently part of a heavy, full thing. There was nothing, I must say, to alarm one. I grew bolder, and putting both hands in as well as I could I pulled it to me, and it came. It was heavy, but moved more easily than I had expected. As I pulled it towards the entrance, my left elbow knocked over and extinguished the candle . . . I went on pulling out the great bag, in complete darkness. It hung for an instant on the edge of the hole, then slipped forward on to my chest, and *put its arms round my neck.*'

The italics belong to the Provost James, not to me. At this point, I think, the purely literary commentator calls a halt. The psychologist may wish to deploy certain comforting dictums of Freud. The sociologist will want to study the evolution of Cambridge away from an elite celibate, Victorian stronghold of great genius and great prejudice. The historian of education will perhaps trace the advent of women's degrees (which James voted against in the Senate House during the riot of 1897), and the graceful arrival of women dons and undergraduates, who have, incidentally, been officially resident at King's College since 1972. The ghost-story writer will merely nod, and reach once more for his quill.

For myself, I shall call to mind only the view from the College Library, as the dark finally settles into the courts and very faintly the sound of Evensong drifts on the chill air in the sweet, harmonious voices of the King's choristers and here and there a scholar twitches his curtains, sports his oak, and draws up his chair to the pool of light beneath his solitary, gazing lamp.

# JOHN STUART MILL

---

'IT IS WHOLLY the life of a logic-chopping machine,' pronounced Thomas Carlyle through his prophetic beard a few
months after Mill's death in 1873. 'Little more human in it than
if it had been done by a thing of mechanized iron. Autobiography
of a steam engine . . .' So it seemed to the Hero, besieged by an
age of railways and foundries and stovepipe hats; and there did
indeed appear something metallic, something patented and incor-
porated and water-cooled in the public life of John Stuart Mill.

From his birth in 1806, Mill had been exclusively assigned to
the Utilitarian inheritance, a product of the most celebrated cram
of the nineteenth century – Greek at three, calculus at eight,
political economy at twelve. Milton, it was said by admiring Benthamites, lisped in numbers; young Mill in syllogisms. From the
ages of seventeen to fifty-two, Mill was an administrative piston of
the East India Company, taking his boiled egg at ten sharp each
morning, eventually rising to the post of Chief Examiner, and on
resignation in 1858 being presented with a silver inkstand.

Most of his active life was passed at the end of that 100-yard-
long gaslit corridor in Leadenhall Street, behind a thick green
baize door, in a high bare office smelling of coconut matting and
ink and coal dust, inditing the sealed instructions of Imperial
administration. He wrote erect at a mahogany lectern, and gazed
through windows overlooking a brickwall yard, where a City clock
could be heard but not seen. He dressed habitually in a black
frockcoat of old-fashioned angular cut, with a black silk necktie
pulled tight round a white cotton wing-collar. He was a tall, bony,
slightly stooping figure who shook hands stiffly from the shoulder
and was prematurely bald at the age of thirty. There was that
indefinable ministerial quality of a dissenting clergyman.

His face was small, dry and circumstantial, deeply lined from early age, nose chiselled out and lips hydraulically compressed and narrow, the mouth drawn down at the corners by the imponderable weights of Utility. Then there was one curious thing: the eyes were preternaturally bright and rapid, permanently dancing like sparks in that hard coaltip of a face, and the right eye – the right eye never stood still at all: there was a permanent, perceptible twitch flickering the lid and eyebrow like a heliograph; and above it, strangest of all, a large inexplicable bump, a sort of dome, as if something alien had taken up occupation.

As a writer, Mill had always been intended to inherit the leaden mantle of the Benthamites, those great organizational rationalists of the turn of the nineteenth century, the Long Legged Scissor Men of Efficiency and Public Systems. Mill's father – James Mill, the great disciple of Jeremy Bentham – had personally educated Mill at his own writing desk, first in Newington Green and later in Westminster; and he was for many years Mill's immediate superior at India House. Mill senior was of Scots crofter stock, brilliant, severe and despotic; he had written a History of India in nine volumes and once projected a book to 'make the human mind as plain as the road from Charing Cross to St Paul's'.

Mill's own two *magna opera* were recognizably in this tradition: *A System of Logic, Ratiocinative and Inductive* published at thirty-seven; and *Principles of Political Economy* produced four years later in 1848, the year of the liberal revolutions in Europe and of the *Communist Manifesto*. Both became standard university textbooks of the period: the former as a discussion of methodology for natural scientists (it ran to thirty-two editions before the end of the century), the latter as a reference work for economists. Even today there are enthusiasts who by partial selection still claim Mill as an authority on Sociological Method (Ronald Fletcher, 1971), on a so-called school of philosophical 'Inductivism' (Alan Ryan, 1970), and on the neo-Malthusian propaganda for a 'steady state' society (*The Ecologist*, 1972).

Yet in reality, Mill's two massive works are lost brontosauri of the early-Victorian intellect, and to rehabilitate them is a museum act of fond anachronism. In conception their whole universe is pre-Darwinian; they are largely innocent of the forces of class and economic production analysed by Marx; and they are irretrievably stranded beyond that black crack in consciousness that Freud's work opened in the foundations of rationalism. Mill's godson, Bertrand Russell, accurately summarized their position in 1953: 'I do not think Mill ever imaginatively conceived of man as one among animals or escaped from the eighteenth-century belief that man is fundamentally rational . . . In the intellectual realm, James Mill continued to reign supreme over his son's sub-conscious.'

In the gardens to the east of Temple Station, between the Law Courts and the Thames Embankment, where the tramps doze fitfully in the summer rain, John Stuart Mill now sits encased in bronze, his metal hand welded to his metal book, fulfilling the judgement of his old friend and opponent Carlyle. And yet there were nightingales in his story.

Today we are perhaps more familiar with the kind of schoolboy prodigy that Mill senior laboured to manufacture in his son. It produces chess champions, adolescent mathematics dons, sectarian fanatics, burnt-out business directors, breakdowns and suicides. Mill suffered all these harsh incarnations to a degree, and yet he is unique because he transcended each and left behind a written record so acute and morally sensitive, that, properly collated, it forms one of the greatest pieces of personal and philosophical literature produced during the nineteenth century. It is a record that will certainly stand by Dickens's *Hard Times*, George Eliot's *Felix Holt* or Turgenev's *Fathers and Children*. In this achievement, and indeed as the condition of his very survival, Mill underwent an agonizing love affair and managed a sustained act of intellectual collaboration with a remarkable woman, the fruits of which were a moral and political manifesto of lasting value.

Mill's first breakdown came in a dreary November of 1826, at the age of twenty, for he was precocious in everything. He had just exhausted himself in editing Bentham's *Rationale of Judicial Evidence*, when he was seized by an overwhelming vertigo of despair. The passage in his *Autobiography* is well known: the sudden realization of the hollowness of the Benthamite 'greatest happiness' principle; the suicidal depression; the tirade against the 'dissolving' acids of intellectual analysis which seemed to wither all feeling from the bone; the desperate recourse to Wordsworth's poetry, walks by the Thames, the 'cultivation' of new friends and sensations.

Closer examination reveals the strong but apparently subconscious undercurrents of hatred for the father, a revulsive horror of the hard, dominating, systematized, patriarchal attitude of the Victorian male so perfectly expressed in the Benthamite doctrine, the doctrine of the Iron Men who built railways, capitalized financial empires and ruled inferior races.

> A small ray of light broke in upon my gloom. I was reading, accidentally, Marmontel's *Memoirs*, and came to the passage which relates his father's death, the distressed position of the family, and the sudden inspiration by which he, then a mere boy, felt and made them feel that he would be everything to them – would supply the place of all that they had lost. A vivid conception of the scene came over me and I was moved to tears.

What is less well known is the fact that Mill's text is incomplete. It is based on a manuscript made in old age, but omitting much that Mill originally wrote. Very recently Mill's original draft, made at the age of forty-seven, has come to light (Mill-Hollander MS 1853–5) and in a number of crucial and vivid sequences this has rendered the standard World Classics edition obsolete. Here are some of the passages that Mill so painfully set down, which not only enormously enhance the evident degree of his self-awareness, but slowly provide the reader with a key to the driving radicalism that came to characterize all his best writings.

> I was far longer than children generally are before I could put on my clothes. I know not how many years passed before I could tie a knot. My articulation was long imperfect; one letter, r, I could not pronounce until I was nearly sixteen. I never could nor can I now, do anything requiring the smallest manual dexterity . . . I was, my father continually told me, like a person who had not the organs of sense: my eyes and ears seemed of no use to me . . . both as a boy and as a youth I was incessantly smarting under his severe admonitions on the subject. He could not endure stupidity . . . He resembled almost all Englishmen in being ashamed at the signs of feeling, and by the absence of demonstration, starving the feeling themselves . . . I do

not mean that things were worse in this respect than in most English families, in which genuine affection is altogether exceptional; what is usually found being more or less an attachment of mere habit, like that to inanimate objects, and a few conventional proprieties of phrase and demonstration . . . That rarity in England, a really warm hearted mother, would in the first place have made my father a totally different being, and in the second would have made the children grow up loving and being loved. But my mother with the very best intentions, only knew how to pass her life in drudging for them . . . I thus grew up in the absence of love and in the presence of fear: and many and indelible are the effects of this bringing-up, in the stunting of my moral growth . . . I grew up with an instinct of closeness . . . my conscience never speaking except by my father's voice.

This was not merely an extraordinary confession, but also a formidable indictment. Mill moved, once and for all, far beyond his Victorian setting. All the seeds of later and passionately held beliefs were germinated here. The hatred of paternal or state authority which crushed instead of protecting freedom; the acute sensitiveness to social pressures; the intense loathing of those qualities in bourgeois English life which ground down high aspirations and feelings to trivial domestic conventions; and finally, the dawning realization of the oppression of women in society – the insidious moral oppression of the typical marriage of unequals, and the loveless, destructive influences unleashed by the tacit assumption of female inferiority. Mill knew he had been damaged by all these, and against them he raised one standard: a radical conception of the free growth of the individual in society.

But in his own case it was love, not philosophy, that now brought him into the light. He met her first in 1830 – he just twenty-three, she two years younger. Harriet Taylor was a pale, willowy, huge-eyed woman with her hair in dark, luxuriant ringlets; but no conventional drawing-room beauty. Her Unitarian upbringing had given her exceptional independence of mind: forceful, sharp-spoken, with strong egalitarian leanings, and the quick, direct temperament of the feminist. When they met at a dinner party in north London, the recognition was instantaneous. Carlyle, for all his mockery, caught and remembered something of the flash.

> She had dark, black, hard eyes, and an inquisitive nature, and was ponderin' on many questions that worried her, and could get no answers ... [she heard] there was a young philosopher of remarkable qualities ... and so Mill with great difficulty was brought to see her, and that man, who up to that time had never looked a female creature, not even a cow, in the face, found himself opposite those great dark eyes, that were flashing unutterable things, while he was discoursing unutterables concernin' all sorts o' high topics.

There was only one difficulty. Harriet Taylor was married and sat at her husband's table with two children sleeping peacefully in the room above.

It was an age and a society where divorce was a ruinous abomination and only husbands had the right to friendships beyond the domestic hearth. Over the next four years an intense struggle of loyalties and emotions took place – secret letters, confessions, denials, confrontations. Mill was honourable but indefatigable in his suit. He rowed with his father, quarrelled with acquaintances, treated the husband, John Taylor, with icy courtesy, and communed – oblivious to the world – with Harriet.

Mill's powers of imagination flourished, his independence grew, his political outlook was revolutionized. He walked in the country and wrote notes about the unfathomable darkness of the sea. Harriet confirmed his nascent feminist views, and eagerly discussed socialist and cooperative ventures, the St Simonian experiments in France, the philosophical poetry of Shelley. Mill went to Paris after the summer insurrection of 1830, and the following year cast his eyes round London. 'I should not care though a revolution were to exterminate every person in Great Britain and Ireland who has £500 a year.' This angry, faintly Jacobin fuse lit by Harriet was never entirely extinguished in Mill's mind, and sixteen years later, on the eve of 1848, he noted in private that the English ruling classes still averted political change with soup kitchens.

I often think that a violent revolution is very much needed, in order to give that general shake-up to the torpid mind of the nation which the French Revolution gave to Continental Europe. England has never had a general break-up of old associations and hence the extreme difficulty of getting any ideas into its stupid head.

In 1834, Mill and Harriet slipped away to Paris – city of love and rebellion – in an attempt to solve the deadlock, while John Taylor sombrely awaited the outcome in London. In the event a strange – but for that period not altogether exceptional – compromise was reached. It was an unofficial *ménage à trois*, with Harriet remaining as Taylor's wife in public, and as Mill's intimate in private. Mill visited at Kent Terrace, while Taylor went to the club at St James's. But one condition was rigid: Harriet had no sexual relations with either man. The arrangement lasted until Taylor's death fifteen years later in 1849, a frosty sunlight.

But even in that cold springtime, Mill blossomed. At twenty-nine he shared the editorship of the new *London Review*, and championed the cause of the Philosophical Radicals, a group that under his influence moved from strict Utilitarianism to wider, more humane attitudes. Mill directed attention to practical politics and contemporary literature, giving space to the young Coleridgean and conservative writers in an attempt to dissolve sectarian animosities and speed the cause of radical reform. He himself gave large reviews to Tennyson's early poetry, Alfred de Vigny, and Carlyle's *French Revolution* which – having burnt the first manuscript by mistake – he established as 'a great epic poem'.

Two paired essays in the *London Review*, on 'Bentham' (1838) and on 'Coleridge' (1840), first set forth Mill's matured attack on those rigid masculine forces which his father represented philosophically, and attempted to soften and combine them with the meditative, imaginative and feminine principles of conservation and growth which he now recognized in Coleridge. 'By Bentham, beyond all others, men have been led to ask themselves, Is it true? and by Coleridge, What is the meaning of it? . . . Whoever could master the premises and combine the methods of both, would possess the entire English philosophy of his age.' This was Mill's first masterpiece, a dazzling historical portrait and analysis of the conflicts inherited from eighteenth-century ideology. It contained some of the operatic, virtuoso dialectic of Peacock's novels of debate and crotchety eccentricities. But it was deepened, shaded and haunted by its autobiographical presences.

Mill's intimacy with Harriet became all-absorbing. She took a private retreat at Walton-on-Thames, where he attended discreetly at weekends. Frequently they holidayed together abroad. Intellectually and spiritually it was a brilliant match. Harriet edited his manuscripts, challenged his arguments, indicated more forceful positions. Her aggressive and imaginative conversation and letters stimulated Mill to his most significant work, giving him the confidence to write with a boldness and breadth and humanity that the Benthamites had never conceived. The direct results were the great essay 'On Liberty' (1859), and the fine complementary tract on freedom and oppression in the family, 'The Subjection of Women' (1869). He attacked with lasting effect the stereotyped social versions of 'masculine' and 'feminine' character, and the oppression of frozen married relationships.

> I believe men are afraid, not lest women should be unwilling to marry, for I do not think that anyone in reality has that apprehension; but lest they should insist that marriage should be on equal conditions: lest all women of spirit and capacity should prefer almost anything else, not in their own eyes degrading, rather than marry, when marrying is giving themselves a master.

Yet if Harriet gave Mill the key to his spiritual freedom, it was bought at a terrible price. Over the years the green baize door at India House became the portal to an anchorite's cell; society was rigidly excluded. The ghost of his father still chained Mill to the family home, fulfilling the task of Marmontel's boyish hero as head of the household – a household where Harriet was never mentioned. His life was split, his breakdowns recurred, and his right eye began its perpetual, jangling dance. Paradoxically, John Taylor's death provided no solution. Mill married Harriet in 1851, but the wounds were too deep, they could not face a life in society and Mill abruptly and bitterly broke off all relations even with his own family.

They retreated to a rambling house in Blackheath, with a white cat called Placidia, and a grand piano. Mill's stepson vividly recalled him playing with extraordinary passion, 'music entirely of his own composition, on the spur of the moment', and when Harriet asked what it was about, it would be storms and battlefields and triumphal processions.

The happiness they did achieve was brief. Both Mill and Harriet contracted consumption – another Benthamite inheritance – and only seven years after their long-sought marriage, Harriet died at Avignon on the way south to recuperate in 1858. Mill had been making the earliest draft of his *Autobiography* for their vindication, and the manuscript passages set forth her profound influence on his life and writing. A decade of puzzled textual scholars have found them strangely exaggerated for the 'high priest of rationalism', unaware in their own dryness that what Mill was writing was a love letter to his dying wife: 'the best thing that I, in particular, could do for the world would be to serve as a sort of prose interpreter of her poetry'.

In the year after Harriet's death, 'On Liberty' was published, at first in a bound edition, and later in cheap copies for 1s 4d designed for working men and women and from which Mill refused to take a royalty. It had been completed in collaboration with Harriet, and everywhere it is resonant with the personal experience of their own struggles, Mill's most profoundly radicalizing experience. It is a classic text, whose arguments have been compared to a line of Spartan infantry, any one of which may be demolished without breaking the stubborn fighting posture of the whole chain. No political policy or system can be based on Mill's 'Liberty', but for precisely that reason wherever individuals or minorities are under legal or social pressure, Mill's cold-eyed Spartans continue to be invoked. Mill wrote:

> The 'Liberty' is likely to survive longer than anything else that I have written ... because the conjunction of her mind with mine has rendered it a kind of philosophic text-book of a single truth, which the changes progressively taking place in modern society tend to bring out into ever stronger relief: the importance, to man and society, of a large variety in types of character, and of giving full freedom to human nature to expand itself in innumerable and conflicting directions.

Mill's own life smouldered on for thirteen years after Harriet's death. For one Parliamentary session he was MP for Westminster, and another year he toured the Cévennes in solitude. He had purchased a little whitewashed cottage at Avignon, from the back upper bedroom of which he could see Harriet's grave in *la cimetière* St Veran, and it was here he came home to die in May 1873. The cottage was densely surrounded by willows and poplars which gave the evening air a chill dampness that precipitated his final and fatal attack of bronchitis. Mill had been advised to have the trees cut down, but the man of bronze could not bear to disturb the nightingales that sang among their branches long into the lonely night.

# LORD LISLE AND
# THE TUDOR NIXON TAPES

How close can we really get to the ordinary men and women of the distant past? Can we know what they gossiped about each day and worried about each night? Can we catch the sound of their voices across the centuries? This is a question that has increasingly concerned modern historians like Laurence Stone, Barbara Tuchman and Richard Cobb, and it has led to the search for a new kind of documentary source that can take us more intimately into the *recherche du temps perdu*. The six volumes of *The Lisle Letters*, dating from the mid-sixteenth century, published recently by the University of Chicago Press, offer one of the greatest sources of 'eavesdropping' history ever discovered: to be compared with the seventeenth-century diaries of Samuel Pepys. But they are something more: a revelation of the world of power politics that could be more properly compared to the Nixon tapes.

We owe the existence of the Lisle letters to a charge of conspiracy and high treason that burst upon the head of a distinguished and unsuspecting Tudor diplomat one spring evening in London some 441 years ago: which turns out to be little more than the day before yesterday. Listen for a moment to the tale. In April 1540, King Henry VIII of England, dangerously poised between the beds of his fourth and fifth wives, and between anti-Papist diplomatic alliances with France and the Habsburg Empire, recalled home to court one Arthur Plantagenet, Viscount Lisle, who had been serving for the past seven years as his lord deputy (or civilian governor) in Calais. The port of Calais, twenty-two miles across the channel from Dover Castle, was the last English outpost on the continent: a garrison town, a hotbed of customs evasion and political intrigue. As the historian A. L. Rowse has written, six-teenth-century Calais was exposed 'to all the winds of doctrine that blew, whether from France or the Netherlands, from Rome or the obscure recesses of Germany'.

Lord Lisle was really too nice a man for this sort of thing, and anyway close to retirement age. He was the illegitimate son of Edward IV, and thereby King Henry's elderly uncle on the wrong side of the blanket. His career had been marked largely by avuncular festive duties: he had been a member of Henry's Privy Chamber, an attendant at the Field of the Cloth of Gold, and the Chief Panter at the wedding celebrations of poor Queen Anne Boleyn. He had served seven years in windy, woebegone Calais with great goodwill, and now he came home with hopeful heart, modestly expecting an earldom, a small slice of monastic lands, and an honourable semi-retirement to his estates in Hampshire and the West Country, with his wife, Honor Lisle, and his extensive family from their two previous marriages. He was an expatriate Englishman coming quietly home to his native land; English history had mercifully brushed him on the shoulder and passed him gently by.

Lisle briefly took his seat in the House of Lords, and then boated down the Thames to attend the King and his first minister, Thomas Cromwell, for the Whit Sunday jollifications. It was the same fateful route taken just four years previously by another trusted servant of the King, Sir Thomas More. What happened next is recorded in a secret dispatch by Marillac, the French ambassador in London, dated May 21, 1540.

> Two days ago, at ten o'clock at night, my Lord Lisle, Deputy of Calais, uncle of this King, was led prisoner to the Tower, where before had been committed three of his servants, and similarly today a chaplain of his who is come out of Flanders in a ship. The cause thereof hath not yet been so certified unto me that I can write it for truth; but it is bruited that he is accused of having had secret intelligence with the Cardinal Pole who is his near relative, and of other practices to deliver up to him the town of Calais. Howsoever it may be, the said Lord Lisle is in a very strait prison, and from the which none escape save by miracle.

Cardinal Reginald Pole, the detested nephew of the King, was based in Rome and credited with any subversive pro-Catholic scheme that Henry's spies could unearth. The charge thus involved heresy, treason and family disloyalty, a lethal cocktail.

Back in Calais, with the terrifying speed and ruthless efficiency that characterized the Tudor state machine, Lisle's whole family, including Honor, was placed under house arrest. His goods were impounded 'that afternoon, in the twilight', and a general seizure of his private papers and correspondence began. Nothing in the end was missed except a few love letters, written by one of his stepdaughters to a secret French fiancé, which were 'cast into the jakes' (the toilet) by a servant girl at the very moment that the royal commissioners burst into the Lisle apartments. Ironically, this was the one act that could have seriously compromised Lisle, though it was utterly beyond his control.

All the rest – some 3,000 letters, written almost daily during the seven crucial years of Henry VIII's reign between March 1533 and April 1540 (both the letters from Calais and the replies from England), and covering every possible aspect of Tudor life, from the purchase of a red silk nightcap to the popular view of Anne Boleyn's adulteries – were assembled in a massive dossier for the sifting of the King's experts in treachery and disaffection, those twin obsessions of the Tudor monarchy. They were eventually filed in eighteen manuscript volumes in the Public Record Office, where they survived fire, flood and Hitler's blitz, to find their destiny in the hands of a remarkable British scholar of grassroots history, Muriel St Clare Byrne.

Miss Byrne, now eighty-six, began work on her edition of the Lisle letters half a century ago. The project was commissioned by T. S. Eliot, who was an editor at the British publishing firm of Faber and Faber. By the time it finally appeared last year (with the University of Chicago Press as co-publisher), the project had grown to six volumes of letters and supporting documents. Altogether it amounts to nearly 4,000 pages, or close to two million words: a created world roughly equivalent to that of all Dickens's major novels.

Here is Miss Byrne's initial reaction to the inventory of Lisle's seized household goods, which to other historians might have been a mere lifeless list of chattels (twenty-one printed pages of it):

> They make almost unbearable reading, these lists, stab-
> bing the imagination with their meticulous, automatic
> enumerating of such things as 'two old pieces of tap-
> estry,' 'two old carpets,' and 'three old worn dripping
> pans.' There is something at once pitiful and terrifying
> about their mechanical throwing open of cupboard
> doors upon the skeletons of ostentation and careful-
> ness, the gay apparel and the gorgeous jewels, the poor
> little shifts and the worn-out splendours . . . and the
> memories, the standing cup with H for Henry and A
> for dead and forgotten Anne Boleyn on its cover, the
> standing cup with Henry's Tudor rose and Katherine
> of Aragon's pomegranate badge.

The Lisle documents were known to Victorian scholars, but it took Miss Byrne to grasp their full historical significance. Without her labours, the Lisle family would have remained a tragic piece of flotsam in the Henrician revolution, immersed in the tidal movements of Tudor history: the break with the Roman Church, the dissolution of the monasteries, the creation of the Tudor bureaucracy, the rise and fall of great churchmen and ministers like Wolsey, More and Cromwell, and the enduringly lubricious legend of Henry's six wives. Miss Byrne was the first to see not only that the Lisles were acute witnesses to much of this but that by virtue of their position in Calais (perched, as it were, just outside the court's window, anxious for every crumb of news) the letters written to them had equal, or even greater, value. They form a matchless anthology of Tudor prose, sparkling with life in a period described by C. S. Lewis as 'the Drab and Transitional'. They show the living language that Shakespeare was heir to. For the letters written to Lisle and his wife come from all parts of English society: from privy councillors and archbishops; from country squires and yeoman farmers (on the estates back home); from bailiffs and chaplains, jailbirds and midwives. For seven pre-cious years, a complete world comes back to life and speech.

Because of Lisle's position, of course, that world is filled with many of the great names of Tudor history. Besides the King himself, constantly on the horizon like some brilliant summer storm, we glimpse at least four of his wives: Katherine of Aragon, Anne Boleyn, Jane Seymour and Anne of Cleves.

The period 1533 to 1540 corresponds exactly with the rise and fall of Thomas Cromwell, the cold and clever architect of the new state. Many other (frequently doomed) luminaries move before our eyes: Archbishop Cranmer of the Prayer Book; Sir Richard Riche, the sinister solicitor-general; the poets Thomas Wyatt and Thomas Howard, Earl of Surrey; and Princess Mary (later Bloody, who died with the loss of Calais [1558] engraved on her heart).

Yet for all their glamour, it is not these figures who dominate the correspondence. It is the little people: the captain who has lost his ship; the chaplain who has preached a dangerous sermon; the serving wench who is unjustly thrown into jail; the old retainer who gives recipes or medical advice. One figure, especially, steps from anonymity straight into Tudor history: Master John Husee, the Lisles' agent, estate manager and matchless confidant.

The collection includes no less than 515 of John Husee's letters, making him the choric voice of the whole drama. The son of a London merchant, in his mid-thirties, bachelor and self-styled gentleman, he is a born organizer of other people's affairs, and absolutely dedicated to Lisle and Honor – 'Your lordship's own man bounden', 'Your ladyship's own man'. He is meticulous, gossipy, observant, wise in the ways of 'this wily world', and capable of turning his hand to any task, diplomatic or domestic.

Husee's exploits in the Lisle service frequently teeter on the edge of comic epic, or comic opera: a Tudor Figaro. He will extract the contents of a man's will before the will is read, or even before the man is dead (and then describe the death most movingly); he will curse the Abbot of Westminster, a noted bon viveur, in suitable style – 'I would he had a tun of wine, and the cask, in his belly!'; he will wheedle away Honor's favourite pet dog, little Porky, because he knows it has caught another lady's fancy, and later replace it with a rare South American monkey.

Husee directs us into the heart of the Lisle letters, which is a theme straight out of Shakespeare's history plays: the exercise of power, influence and personal affection in a dangerous world where no one is safe.

The outward sign of this is an astonishing, ceaseless carrying of gifts and remembrances to and from friends, clients, businessmen, political allies, family relations, religious advisers, ancient retainers and the great panjandrums of the Tudor state. There is scarcely a letter that does not mention some form of material benefit or bounty. Money itself was almost never sent. As Christopher Hill has observed, probably the nearest thing to ready cash was wine (just as tobacco still forms the ready currency of a modern closed hierarchy like the prison or penitentiary). Other favourite gifts included game, pies, spices and conserves, pet animals (the rarer the better), horses and armour, dress materials and jewels, and the famous cramp rings, blessed by the King, against rheumatism and chronic ills. These gifts were more than Tudor eccentricities. They express the continuous functioning of the Tudor hierarchy of power. Their emphasis on the rare and strange and special is a recognition of the critical individuality of power. Being genuinely personal, they carry genuine goodwill, although it is frail and requires constant renewal.

The ultimate gifts in the King's power, of course, were land and position. Lisle's salary as deputy of Calais was negligible – perhaps £200 a year. What kept him going, through mounting debts and an inability even to pay his own household, was the promise of royal reward: land, gifts, new 'rooms' or posts he could assign, and thus receive gifts for himself. Such a system explains a dominant characteristic of Tudor political life: that as personal wealth and prestige increased, personal security and expectation, being dependent on the King's favour, grew more tenuous – terrifyingly so. Hence the vital importance of a man like John Husee, the go-between, the intelligencer (a word coined about 1580), the gift-presenter, the manipulator, the man who knows more than his master.

Here is Husee's account of presenting Lisle's New Year gift and greeting at court in January 1538, just over two years before his fall. He interprets every nuance of gesture or phrase, for each one carries perilous weight. (The Lord Privy Seal is Cromwell; Sir Brian Tuke is the steely-eyed Royal Treasurer.)

> I delivered on New Year's Day your gift to the King's
> Majesty in his own hands; and as soon as I was within

the Chamber of Presence, going to present the same as accustomed, my Lord Privy Seal smiled and said to the King's Grace, 'here cometh my Lord Lisle's man!'; and the King spake merrily unto him again, but what his Highness said I cannot tell. So that, after I had done my duty, his Grace received it of me smiling, and thanking your lordship did ask heartily how you and my lady did. His Grace spake few words that day to those that came. As far as I could perceive he spake to no man so much as he did unto me, which was no more words but this: 'I thank my lord. How doth my lord and my lady? Are they merry?' It was gently done of my Lord Privy Seal to have your lordship in remembrance, setting the matter so well forward. The King stood leaning against the cupboard, receiving all things; and Mr Tuke at the end of the same cupboard, penning all things that were presented . . . There was but a small Court.

It is but a small scene, yet an immensely telling one. History lives. We hear the King's bluff laughter, and then the whispered joke (about Husee? about Lisle?). We see Husee practically counting the King's words, and we listen, like him, for the faintest trace of sarcasm in the word 'merry' (*too* merry in Calais?). We see how Cromwell has monopolized access to the King, and how he alone can 'set matters forward'. We see the accountant's quill pen, as much a symbol of the Tudor state as the headsman's axe, 'penning all things'. We even catch a hint of the King's lassitude and obesity, as he leans against the cupboard, casual but lethal: a slumbering tiger ready to spring.

Husee's shrewdness of observation and political tact became Lisle's most valuable weapon in the struggle for survival. He knows, for example, the danger of Lisle's writing over-long letters to the King; and the absolute necessity of watching the shadows behind Cromwell. Most of all, he understands his own master's greatest weakness: Lisle's tendency to be temperamental, to be thrown into panic or depression by any hint of official disfavour or criticism. He is too nice, too anxious not to give offence. This made Lisle especially vulnerable to Cromwell, who had perfected the art of pressuring his subordinates by unspoken threats, nuances of displeasure, meaningful silences, or sudden tiny cold splinters of criticism – his notorious 'sharp' letters – that slid beneath the skin like glass. 'If your lordship had received such another letter,' wrote Husee bracingly to Lisle on one occasion, 'I am well assured that you would not 'a slept well in seven nights following!'

In one celebrated instance Husee actually confronted Cromwell with one of these sharp letters to Lisle, and boldly informed the Lord Privy Seal 'that if his lordship did not the sooner write some other loving letter unto you [Lisle] that I stood in doubt that your Lordship might take such conceit [imaginary fear] thereon that might perchance put you in hazard of some disease or peril of your life'. One can almost see Cromwell's narrow lips – in the famous Holbein portrait – draw back in a disarming, deadly smile: 'he answered and said that he thought your Lordship was wiser than to take it after any such manner; for whatsoever he wrote, he was and is and would remain still your Lordship's sincere and very friend.'

Part of the fascination of this interview is that it takes place between the second most powerful man in the kingdom and an ordinary citizen, a nobody who, apart from the master he serves so faithfully, is a cipher, a walk-on part in the conventional drama of history. Yet Husee and Cromwell talked, argued, even joked after a fashion (though he had spent 'half the day in seeking of him'); and that is history too. Thanks to Miss Byrne we can still hear it as it really happened. If we were Frenchmen we would surely find a philosophical distinction to make about this: between *l'histoire apprise*, or history as it is normally learned and heard, and *l'histoire surprise*, or overheard history. The Lisle letters are overheard history, *par excellence*.

But we must end with our tale. Husee warned Lisle three years before his fall that anything to do with heresy, renegade preachers or religious heterodoxy at Calais must be treated like gunpowder. Regarding church matters, he cautions Lisle, 'be no less earnest and precise than you would be in causes of high treason.' Lisle, the genial, ageing, anxious administrator – who was not much concerned with religion anyway, except that his wife inconveniently favoured the 'old' Papist rituals – would have been only too happy to oblige. But in the Tudor state, events easily outstripped men and all their contrivances.

1540 was one of the deadliest years for Tudor career-makers, rivalled only by 1536, when Anne Boleyn's fall dragged so many with her to the block. Not only was Lisle suddenly incarcerated in the Tower, but his opposite number in Dublin, Leonard, Lord Grey, deputy of Ireland, was recalled, arrested and – black augury – summarily executed. The most shattering blow, however, was the fate of My Lord Privy Seal himself. After a long battle in Council throughout the spring of 1540, Cromwell apparently consolidated his position. He was created Earl of Essex in April, at the very moment of Lisle's recall. But Cromwell's safety, no less than Lisle's, was illusory. In June he was arrested on charges of heresy and expropriation, and on July 28 he was beheaded with little ceremony on the lawns within the Tower, probably within earshot of Lisle. His last letter to the King, abandoning all his wonted coolness and icy circumspection, begged for 'mercy, mercy, mercy'. He was found guilty of, among many other things, pro-Lutheran leanings and favouring the 'Sacramentaries' (who challenged the conservative doctrine of transubstantiation in the Mass): there had been many such in Calais.

This sequence of events has naturally led historians to suppose that Lisle was himself dragged down in the general attack on Cromwell, ostensibly for administrative incompetence and for not enforcing religious orthodoxy among the fractious garrison and townfolk of Calais, just as Husee had feared. But the facts are far stranger and more ironic. The appalling truth seems to be that Cromwell ('your very friend') framed Lisle. In a desperate last attempt to defend his position against his religious right-wing enemies in Council, Cromwell used the machinations of Lisle's chaplain in Rome to discredit Lisle's entire administration in Calais. He thereby hoped to cover up his own involvement in protecting the Sacramentaries (or left wing) in Calais. Cromwell alone knew that old Lisle was perfectly innocent; perhaps he even meant to save him when the danger was past. But then the mantrap closed on his own head. The details are complex and fascinating, but what emerges in the end is a terrible and convincing picture of Cromwell ruthlessly and vainly sacrificing Lisle to the royal fury. The letters between Lisle's stepdaughter and her French lover added a final twist: that they were hastily disposed of at the time of arrest could mean only one thing to the Tudor mind – treason.

So one more Tudor family fell, public life destroying private, power annihilating human trust.

The administration changed in Calais, then, but the axe did not fall in London. Ambassador Marillac, reporting Cromwell's demise, noted perplexedly: 'As to the other prisoners, people know not what to say except that there is good hope as regards the Deputy of Calais, of whom the King has said he could not think the Deputy erred through malice but rather through ignorance.' It still sounded perilously like an epitaph. For eighteen months the position hung in the balance. We would give anything to know of Husee's frantic efforts on behalf of his beloved master: but there are no further letters. Miss Byrne observes that Mistress Anne Basset, Honor Lisle's daughter, remained a favoured lady at Henry's court against all odds, and it is impossible not to imagine Husee's skilful, ever-faithful hand guiding Anne's conduct and making her bide her time.

Then, in February 1541, according to the account of a Welsh chronicler, Elis Gruffudd (yet another of Miss Byrne's documentary discoveries), the following poignant incident took place:

> The next Friday the King's Grace moved down the river in his barge from York Place to Greenwich, and at the time Lord Lisle his uncle, who was a bastard of King Edward IV, raised his hands high, and shouted hoarsely from the Tower where he was imprisoned for mercy and release from the prison. The King took it graciously and sent his secretary to the Tower to the Lord to show him the King had given him his pardon and that he would have his freedom and release from prison two or three days later and that he would get back his possessions and offices.

It is an extraordinary scene. Old Lisle up on the 'leads' of the Tower (where privileged prisoners could exercise); the King's barge floating down the wintry Thames beneath its forbidding walls; the voices echoing across the chilly waters between them. It almost re-enacts, as in a pageant play, Lisle's whole career in Calais – exiled across the estranging sea from his King. Perhaps John Husee had planned the whole scene: 'Be sure, my lord, to be up on the roof betimes . . .' Who knows?

But that something like this did indeed happen, we can be certain, for Ralph Holinshed, the British chronicler, corroborates the royal pardon, and adds the detail that it was sealed with a gift – the last of so many that fill the Lisle story. It was a ring, and 'a rich diamond, for a token from him, and to tell him to be of good cheer'. Miss Byrne quotes the genealogist Francis Sandford about what happened next. The night following Lisle's receipt of Henry's gift, his heart was so 'overcharged' with joy that 'he yielded up the Ghost; which makes it observable that this King's Mercy was as fatal as his Judgements'. Lord Lisle's body, Sandford goes on to say, 'was honourably buried in the Tower of London'.

But not his letters. And not their voices.

# IV

## A Philosophical Love Story

# INTRODUCTION

I was now back in London, in a flat below Highgate Hill. The figure of Coleridge (glimpsed again in the Melmoth piece) was walking slowly down that hill, at what Keats called 'his alderman after-dinner pace', towards me. I often wandered over Hampstead Heath, up the small lane 'by Lord Mansfield's house' where Coleridge met Keats one spring afternoon in 1819, and talked of poetry, dreams, monsters and nightingales. I longed to join in that conversation, and hear Coleridge's voice myself. Instead I stood silently under the chestnut trees outside No. 3 The Grove, and looked up at the third-floor study where he had spent the last decade of his life, watching for any encouraging movement at the window. Very frequently, it seemed to start raining. Later I found that Coleridge's room in fact looked out over the garden, at the back, where he wrote many of his last poems, and this was a lesson in the presumption of the biographer who assumes he can step like a tourist into the past.

This question of how the biographer achieves authenticity now began to trouble me. How much is constructed from broken evidence, a scattered bundle of letters, the chance survival of a diary? How much is lost, forgotten, changed beyond recognition? What secret thoughts are never recorded, what movements of the heart are never put into words? And more than this, by the very act of biographical empathy, how much does the biographer create the *fiction* of a past life, the projection of his – or her – own personality into a story which is dramatically convincing, even historically correct, but simply *not the human truth as it happened*? It was these reflections that led me to write *Footsteps*, an experiment in which the biographer cross-questions his own art and the impulses that drive him on a quest for understanding that may be, ultimately, ephemeral.

But if that book convinced me of one thing, it was that biography is a human exchange, what I have called 'a handshake across time'. It is an act of human solidarity, and in its own way an act of recognition and of love. Perhaps its Romantic subjectivity is precisely its strength. It confirms our need to find the self in the other, not always to be alone.

This simple, almost naïve, idea radically altered the path of my own research. I now became interested in the way earlier biographers had undertaken their work, and the feelings and emotions that had propelled them. I also saw that my attraction to lonely, extreme, isolated figures – often on the edge of madness or suicide – produced a very partial account of Romanticism. What of Romantic friendship, what of Romantic couples, what of Romantic love? In *Footsteps* I had touched on the early story of the feminist Mary Wollstonecraft, and I now found that her husband, the philosopher William Godwin, had written her biography as a memorial to their own brief but passionate marriage.

Here my two themes were wonderfully combined: biography and love. I convinced Penguin Classics to republish Godwin's *Memoir*, alongside a forgotten Scandinavian travel book by Wollstonecraft. The essay that follows is an expanded version of my Introduction. It is, I suppose, what the eighteenth century would call a study in *sentiment*. I now see it was also partly inspired by the earlier piece about John Stuart Mill and Harriet Taylor and the nightingales. It held out the possibility that the Romantic spirit was not necessarily doomed to obsession and solitude, an important idea for me personally. It was, after all, my first attempt to write a love story.

# THE FEMINIST AND THE PHILOSOPHER:
## A LOVE STORY

---

## I

### 'Fire and Ice'

WHAT FOLLOWS is a love story, set in England at the end of the eighteenth century.

But it is much else besides. It is the story of an 'experiment in living', an attempt to liberate the conditions of daily life from the restrictions of convention, in a way that may still concern us today. It is the story of a struggle for self-expression, a search for new literary forms in the art of 'life-writing', which has helped us define our modern ideas of biography and autobiography. And it is, finally, the story of a treasure-hunt.

These elements combine to produce a rich human testament, capable of varied interpretation, but whose appeal will last as long as men and women strive to live happily – or shall I say, to live less unhappily – together, and seek to tell the truth – the inward, difficult truth – about themselves and their experiences of the heart.

Writing as an experimental biographer myself, fascinated equally by lives as they are lived, and lives as they are told (which is not of course the same thing), I have chosen to present this love story from a number of different angles. The reader must be patient if it does not unfold with the satisfying simplicity of a Romantic fairy-tale.

The true chronology of the heart is complex. The past tense shapes the present tense. Our memories alter our future hopes. The very act of *telling* our lives seems to redefine the way we once lived them. Death, especially, is a Grand Reinterpreter of History, and profound loss can paradoxically give back what once seemed unattainable, in a different form.

Bearing all this in mind, I have worked back and forth through the story somewhat in the manner of a literary detective, pursuing the evidence along several lines of inquiry. I have combined historical research with literary criticism. But above all I have concentrated on the two remarkable books in which my protagonists speak most openly for themselves: *A Short Residence in Sweden, Norway and Denmark* and *Memoirs of the Author of the Rights of Woman*. These are two largely forgotten classics of English eighteenth-century non-fiction, and if I have done nothing else, I will at least have found them the new European readers they so wonderfully merit.

The first is a travel book, which tells of a solitary journey, undertaken in mysterious circumstances, through Scandinavia. The second is a life-history of the extraordinary woman who made that journey (and many others), as seen by the man who subsequently became her lover, and then her husband. They were written within a few months of each other, in the closing years of the 1790s, that great decade of revolution in human affairs throughout Europe, when the possibilities of happiness and justice seemed for a moment infinitely extendable, and then in another moment, infinitely remote.

Both works are short, factual, readable and, in different ways, intensely passionate. Both are oddly untypical of their authors, or at least of the stereotypes by which they are known to history: the Feminist and the Philosopher. Yet, as literature, these are arguably the best books that either wrote.

Mary Wollstonecraft and William Godwin first met at a publisher's dinner-party in London on 13 November 1791. It was given in honour of Tom Paine, the best-selling author of *The Rights of Man*, to celebrate his imminent departure for Paris. He was going to take up his seat as the delegate for the Pas de Calais in the French Revolutionary Convention. Their host was Joseph Johnson, the leading radical publisher of the day (his list would include Paine, Priestley, Coleridge, Wordsworth and Blake). The atmosphere was heady with the talk of rights, revolution and reform, and the Golden Age of Liberty which had dawned across the Channel.

Wollstonecraft and Godwin were the junior members of the party. She was thirty-two and he was thirty-five, and neither had yet published the works that were to make them famous, *The Rights of Woman* (1792) and *Political Justice* (1793). Both were known as reviewers and essayists for Johnson's magazine, the *Analytical Review* (a sort of *New Statesman* of its time), and had reputations for advanced political views within the small circle of North London radicalism. But neither was a national figure like Paine, and by normal standards of behaviour they should have taken a back seat in the evening's proceedings, listening politely as the master expounded the cause of Liberty.

However, normal behaviour – by eighteenth-century standards – was never to be their forte. Indeed, they promptly dominated the dinner-table with a series of noisy and increasingly angry arguments, which seem to have ended by practically reducing Paine and Johnson to silence. Whatever else it suggests (and to my mind it suggests a great deal), this incident shows that nothing so ordinary as love at first sight could ever be expected of these two remarkable authors.

Godwin presents this memorable evening with almost disconcerting candour seven years later in the *Memoirs*. He makes no sentimental attempt to disguise the clash of characters that occurred. He lists the subjects discussed, the grounds of disagreement, and his own growing irritation.

> The interview was not fortunate. Mary and myself parted, mutually displeased with each other. I had not read her *Rights of Woman*. I had barely looked into her *Answer to Burke*, and been displeased, as literary men are apt to be, with a few offenses against grammar and other minute points of composition. I had therefore little curiosity to see Mrs Wollstonecraft, and a very great curiosity to see Thomas Paine. Paine, in his general habits, is no great talker, and, though he threw in occasionally some shrewd and striking remarks, the conversation lay principally between me and Mary. I, of consequence, heard her, very frequently when I wished to hear Paine.
>
> We touched on a considerable variety of topics, and particularly on the characters and habits of certain

eminent men. Mary, as has already been observed, had acquired in a very blameable degree the practice of seeing every thing on the gloomy side, and bestowing censure with a plentiful hand, where circumstances were in any respect doubtful. I, on the contrary, had a strong propensity to favourable construction, and particularly, where I found unequivocal marks of genius, strongly to incline to the supposition of generous and manly virtues. We ventilated in this way the characters of Voltaire and others, who have obtained from some individuals an ardent admiration, while the greater number have treated them with extreme moral severity. Mary was at last provoked to tell me, that praise, lavished in the way that I lavished it, could do no credit either to the commended or the commender. We discussed some questions on the subject of religion, in which her opinions approached much nearer to the received one, than mine. As the conversation proceeded, I became dissatisfied with the tone of my own share in it. We touched upon all topics, without treating forcibly and connectedly upon any. Meanwhile, I did her the justice, in giving an account of the conversation to a party in which I supped, though I was not sparing of my blame, to yield to her the praise of a person of active and independent thinking. On her side, she did me no part of what perhaps I considered as justice.

We met two or three times in the course of the following year, but made a very small degree of progress towards a cordial acquaintance. (Chapter 6)

The whole scene serves to suggest the lack of conventionality, and the passion for sincere feeling, which was to be the hallmark of their lives. They were both clever, difficult, highly original people, and this is partly what gives their writings such lasting fascination and intellectual bite. It also demonstrates why their friends thought them such an unlikely combination: feminist fire in hissing contact with benign but philosophical ice.

They were not to meet again for another four years, until the spring of 1796. A great deal had happened to them, and to the world, in the intervening period. They had matured, but they had also seen their political hopes darken.

After the publication of her great work on women's rights and education, Mary Wollstonecraft had herself gone to Paris for over two years, and witnessed the trial and execution of the French king and the coming of the Terror. She had seen many of her close friends among the Girondists, including Manon Roland, guillotined, and Tom Paine imprisoned under sentence of death and reduced to alcoholism. She had had a love affair with an American adventurer, Gilbert Imlay, conceived and borne his illegitimate child, and returned to London only to find their relationship slowly and agonizingly collapse, amidst her recriminations and his betrayal of her with another woman. She had subsequently travelled in Scandinavia, twice tried to commit suicide, and somehow managed to write the account of her experiences that is central to our story. She had become famous and, as is the way of the world, she had suffered deeply for it. Everything she believed in, and above all her vision of woman's independence and equality, had been tested to breaking point.

William Godwin's career had run a smoother but no less demanding course. *Political Justice*, his millennial work attacking oppressive government and advocating an anarchist society based on absolute reason and sincerity, had brought him to what Hazlitt later called 'the very zenith of a sultry and unwholesome popularity'. His novel *Caleb Williams* (1794), dramatizing the same issues in the form of a political thriller, had broadened his reputation. But his brave intervention before the Treason Trials of the same year, in favour of his friends, the defendants Thomas Holcroft and Horne Tooke, had made him a marked man for the gathering forces of political reaction. He lived an isolated, scholarly bachelor's life in Somers Town, North London, varied only by dining out and theatre-going. While he flirted ineffectually with the blue-stocking ladies of his narrow circle (Mary Hays, Mrs Inchbald, Amelia Alderson), his fame only brought him increasing loneliness and anxiety, and a strange lack of emotional commitment. He took pupils, kept a meticulous diary, and sometimes wore racy yellow waistcoats. But he felt himself to be an unlovable man: childless, stiff in company, and uneasily dependent on his old mother, who still lived far away in Norwich. It was only when Mary Wollstonecraft returned to England and published *A Short Residence* in January 1796 that a new light seems slowly to have risen over his cool, rational, philosophical horizon.

Godwin vividly describes his reaction to the work in Chapter 8 of the *Memoirs*, making perhaps the best of all introductions to it.

> The narrative of (her) voyage is before the world, and perhaps a book of travels that so irresistibly seizes on the heart, never, in any other instance, found its way from the press. The occasional harshness and ruggedness of character that diversify her *Vindication of the Rights of Woman*, here totally disappear. If ever there was a book calculated to make a man in love with its author, this appears to me to be the book. She speaks of her sorrows, in a way that fills us with melancholy, and dissolves us in tenderness, at the same time that she displays a genius which commands all our admiration.

It was, characteristically, Mary Wollstonecraft who now took the decisive step to renew their acquaintance, by calling uninvited and unchaperoned (another breach of eighteenth-century proprieties) at Godwin's house in Chalton Street, near the present site of St Pancras railway station and the new British Library, on 14 April 1796.

Godwin found himself gazing on a mature woman of thirty-six, her face fuller and softer than he had remembered, but with the same large brown eyes and striking mass of auburn hair worn short, unpowdered, and falling carelessly over her left brow. Wollstonecraft found a stocky, energetic, balding man whose eyes sparkled behind round gold spectacles, and whose manner had grown patient, humorous and surprisingly tender. They now instantly accepted each other as fellow authors and intellectual colleagues.

Neither thought initially in terms of love, let alone marriage. Godwin had written scathingly of matrimony in *Political Justice*, adding a long appendix against what he called 'the most odious of monopolies'. He analysed the evils of 'cohabitation', seeing it as a Romantic delusion, in which true friendship and sincerity were inevitably compromised in an unequal relationship based on transient physical passion. He proposed the abolition of 'the system of marriage as it is at present practised in European countries'. Instead he discussed at length a free and open relationship based on intellectual parity and mutual respect. 'So long as I seek, by despotic and artificial means, to maintain my possession of a woman, I am guilty of the most odious selfishness ... No ties ought to be imposed on either party, preventing them quitting the attachment, whenever their judgement directs them to quit it ... The mutual kindness of persons of an opposite sex will, in such a state, fall under the same system as any other species of friendship ... I shall assiduously cultivate the intercourse of that woman whose moral and intellectual accomplishments strike me in the most powerful manner' (*Political Justice*, Book 8, Chapter 8, Appendix). It is evident that, at long last, Mary Wollstonecraft was this woman.

Wollstonecraft herself had bitterly attacked the injustices of marriage in *The Rights of Woman*. She particularly exposed the fashionable Rousseauist view of women as children of nature, Romantic playthings equally exploited by indulgent or tyrannical husbands. She argued that if women were not educated as men's equals, and treated as genuine partners, they would always be oppressed within the social system. She had bitterly experienced the inequality of this relationship in her affair with Imlay. She too clung to the ideal of an attachment 'founded on esteem', and mutual independence like friendship. 'Friendship is a serious affection, the most sublime of all affections, because it is founded on principle, and cemented in time. The very reverse may be said of love' (*The Rights of Woman*, Chapter 4). A lively and familiar correspondence sprang up between them during the early summer. Godwin was sensitive to her sufferings and violent swings of mood, while Mary Wollstonecraft instinctively understood his fear of emotions that might get out of hand and compromise him. They complemented each other, and they reassured each other, until they found, quite simply, that they were well matched.

Godwin embraced the language of love, by making it both funny and sincere, playful and adult, with surprising ease. He wrote in July: 'I love your imagination, your delicate epicurism, the malicious leer of your eye, in short every thing that constitutes the bewitching toute ensemble of the celebrated Mary ... Shall I write a love letter? May Lucifer fly away with me, if I do: No, when I make love, it shall be with the eloquent tones of my voice, with dying accents, with speaking glances (through the glass of my spectacles), with all the witching of that irresistible, universal passion. Curse on the mechanical icy medium of pen and paper. When I make love, it shall be in a storm, as Jupiter made love to Semele, & turned her at once to a cinder. Do these menaces terrify you? ... Or shall I write to citizeness Wollstonecraft a congratulatory epistle upon the victories of Buonaparti?'

In Chapter 9 of the *Memoirs* Godwin tenderly describes the growth of their intimacy, though scorning any idea of a conventional courtship. 'It grew with equal advances in the mind of each ... One sex did not take the priority which long-established custom has awarded it, nor the other overstep that delicacy which is so severely imposed.' Instead, in a passage of remarkable sensuousness, he tells how they secretly became lovers.

> It was friendship melting into love. Previously to our mutual declaration, each felt half-assured, yet each felt a certain trembling anxiety to have assurance complete ... Mary rested her head upon the shoulder of her lover, hoping to find a heart with which she might safely treasure her world of affection – fearing to commit a mistake, yet, in spite of her melancholy experience, fraught with that generous confidence, which, in a great soul, is never extinguished. I had never loved till now, or, at least, had never nourished a passion to the same growth, or met with an object so consummately worthy. We did not marry.

It is a most striking paragraph for the chilly philosopher of absolute reason to have written. In fact it indicates a revolution far deeper than politics, and in the end, far more influential.

Godwin's diary shows that they were lovers by August 1796. But both held strong views on practical independence, and Mary Wollstonecraft took a separate flat for herself and her child (little Fanny Imlay, now two years old) at 16 Judd Place West, near Chalton Street, so that both could continue their literary work. They met in the evenings, and Fanny would anxiously ask after 'Man', as she called Godwin, who quickly became fond of her. In the winter Mary Wollstonecraft became pregnant, and after much discussion, the two antimatrimonialists were finally married at Old St Pancras Church on 29 March 1797. They moved into 29 The Polygon, Chalton Street, but continued to work and often dine out independently, determined to avoid what they saw as the evils of 'cohabitation', while exploring the novel delights of domesticity.

While we lived as near neighbours only, and before our last removal, Mary's mind had attained considerable tranquillity, and was visited but seldom with those emotions of anguish, which had been but too familiar to her. But the improvement in this respect, which accrued upon our removal and establishment, was extremely obvious. She was a worshipper of domestic life. She loved to observe the growth of affection between me and her daughter, then three years of age, as well as my anxiety respecting the child not yet born. Pregnancy itself, unequal as the decree of nature seems to be in this respect, is the source of a thousand endearments. No one knew better than Mary how to extract sentiments of exquisite delight from trifles, which a suspicious and formal wisdom would scarcely deign to remark. A little ride in the country with myself and the child, has sometimes produced a sort of opening of the heart, a general expression of confidence and affectionate soul, a sort of infantile, yet dignified endearment, which those who have felt may understand, but which I should in vain attempt to portray.

In addition to our domestic pleasures, I was fortunate enough to introduce her to some of my acquaintances of both sexes, to whom she attached herself with all the ardour of approbation and friendship.

Ours was not an ideal happiness, a paradise of selfish and transitory pleasures. It is perhaps scarcely necessary to mention, that, influenced by the ideas I had long entertained upon the subject of cohabitation, I engaged an apartment, about twenty doors from our house in the Polygon, Somers Town, which I designed for the purpose of my study and literary occupations. We were both of us of opinion, that it was impossible for two persons to be uniformly in each other's society. Influenced by that opinion, it was my practice to repair to the apartment I have mentioned as soon as I rose, and frequently not to make my appearance in the Polygon, till the hour of dinner. We agreed in condemning the notion, prevalent in many situations in life, that a man and his wife cannot visit in mixed society, but in company with each other, and we rather sought occasions of deviating from, than of complying with, this rule. By these means, though, for the most part, we spent the latter half of each day in one another's society, yet we were in no danger of satiety. We seemed to combine, in a considerable degree, the novelty and lively sensation of a visit, with the more delicious and heart-felt pleasures of domestic life.

Whatever may be thought, in other respects, of the plan we laid down to ourselves, we probably derived a real advantage from it, as to the constancy and uninterruptedness of our literary pursuits. (Chapter 9)

The open marriage caused gossip among their radical circle, much of it malicious, and several friends hypocritically refused to recognize the couple socially, as Godwin painfully recalls in the *Memoirs*. *The Times* noted jocosely in its Court and Social column that 'Mr Godwin, author of a pamphlet against matrimony' had clandestinely wedded 'the famous Mrs Wollstonecraft, who wrote in support of the Rights of Woman'. But the letters that continued to flit between the two addresses show how happy and supportive of each other they were.

Mary wrote that she did not like 'to lose my Philosopher even in my Lover'. They read each other's essays, and criticized each other's style and arguments. They exchanged books and newspapers, and avidly discussed the Parliamentary debates. They speculated on ideal forms of government, on a system of national education for children (here Wollstonecraft altered Godwin's views decisively), and on the proofs for the existence of God. At the same time they argued cheerfully about door-keys, dealing with tradesmen, buying each other theatre-tickets, and whether Godwin was spoiling little Fanny by giving her butter on top of her pudding.

Mary occasionally lapsed into her old gloom and despondency. Once Godwin stayed away too long on an expedition to the Midlands (he stopped to see a carnival with a half-naked Lady Godiva on a horse), and once he was too responsive to the flirtatious attentions of a pretty young blue-stocking, Miss Pinkerton. But these jealousies – quickly patched up – only reflected the sensual vitality of their own relationship. In one note, Mary wrote: 'I have seldom seen so much live fire running about my features as this morning when recollections – very dear – called forth the blush of pleasure, as I adjusted my hair.' In another, shortly before her baby was due, she exclaimed in her forthright manner: 'I begin to love this little creature, and to anticipate his birth as a fresh twist to a knot, which I do not wish to untie. Men are spoilt by frankness, I believe, yet I must tell you that I love you better than I supposed I did, when I promised to love you for ever ... You are a tender, affectionate creature, and I feel it thrilling through my frame giving and promising pleasure.'

The denouement was tragically brief. Their love-child, the future Mary Shelley, was born five months later on 30 August. Mary Wollstonecraft contracted septicaemia after the delivery, and eleven days later, after much suffering, she died, on 10 September 1797. William Godwin, the unemotional philosopher, quietly wrote, 'It is impossible to represent in words the total revolution this event made in my existence. It was as if in a single moment "sun and moon were in the flat sea sunk".' Struggling to control his grief, he moved his study into Mary Wollstonecraft's own room at the Polygon, and immersed himself in her papers, and began to re-read all her books.

In October he began to write like a man possessed, and ten weeks later the entire *Memoirs* was drafted. He consulted with their old friend Joseph Johnson, and the work was finally published – together with a small four-volume edition of *The Posthumous Works* – in January 1798. It was the same year that marked the appearance of the *Lyrical Ballads*.

## II

## 'A Dead Wife Naked'

IT IS FAIR TO SAY that most readers were appalled by the *Memoirs of the Author of a Vindication of the Rights of Woman*. There was no precedent for biography of this kind. Godwin's candour and

plain-speaking about his own wife filled them with horrid fascination. The *Historical Magazine* called the *Memoirs* 'the most hurtful
book' of 1798. The poet Robert Southey accused Godwin of 'a
want of all feeling in stripping his dead wife naked'. The *European
Magazine* described the work as 'the history of a philosophical
wanton', and was sure that it would be read 'with detestation by
everyone attached to the interests of religion and morality, and
with indignation by any one who might feel any regard for the
unhappy woman, whose frailties should have been buried in
oblivion'.

For a start, the book belied its title. It was not a pious family
memorial, or a work of feminist hagiography. It was a complete
biography in miniature, intimate in detail and often critical of
Wollstonecraft's behaviour, though always understanding and
passionately committed to her genius.

It recounted each phase of her life with complete openness,
making no allowance for conventional proprieties. No one had
ever written about a woman like this before, except perhaps as
the fictitious, incorrigible heroines of Daniel Defoe. Godwin completely rejected the old idea of biography as a tale of 'success', or
a moral exemplum. He was interested, in an entirely new way, in
the manner in which the character was formed by inheritance
and circumstance, and in the essential element of struggle against
adversity by which real achievements are slowly hammered out of
the unyielding conditions of daily life. He saw Mary's character
as dynamic and steadily maturing. He presented her whole career
as an inextricable mixture of tragedy and triumph, active, per-
severing, and heroic, a new kind of independent woman within
an old kind of prejudiced society.

He described her restless and unhappy childhood, dominated
by a brutal and feckless father whose hopeless business affairs
determined her to seek financial independence in later life. He
saw the importance of her 'fervent' early friendship with Fanny
Blood, which led her to improve her own education, and eventually took her on her first remarkable voyage to Portugal. He
showed her growing confidence as a teacher, governess and educational writer, which also took her to Ireland. He emphasized
the courage of her decision to seek work as a woman freelance
writer in London, and the great help she received from her

publisher and friend Joseph Johnson. He showed her passionate feminist response to the French Revolution, and the way it produced *The Rights of Woman*. Then, unflinching, he described an ill-judged affair with the painter Henry Fuseli, her expedition to revolutionary Paris, her falling in love with Gilbert Imlay, and the birth of their illegitimate child, Fanny. He analysed brilliantly how the daring of her solitary voyage to Scandinavia was so closely involved with her intense personal depression and two attempts at suicide in 1795. Finally, with tender simplicity he described their own liaison and marriage, and at great length, and in almost gynaecological detail, her tragic death after bearing her second daughter, Mary.

It was Godwin's frankness over Mary Wollstonecraft's love affairs and suicide attempts that seemed to cause the most immediate offence. Yet it would be impossible to understand anything of her remarkable temperament, that mixture of extraverted courage and introverted melancholy which made her such an original writer, without the fullest knowledge of these. The *Monthly Review,* previously her supporter, now wrote with hypocritical disapproval in May 1798: 'blushes would suffuse the cheeks of most husbands if they were forced to relate those anecdotes of their wives which Mr Godwin voluntarily proclaims to the world. The extreme eccentricity of Mr Godwin's sentiments will account for this conduct. Virtue and vice are weighed by him in a balance of his own. He neither looks to marriage with respect, nor to suicide with horror.'

It was hypocritical, because Godwin in fact took great care to explain what he and Wollstonecraft sought in a true marriage of real trust, and analyses at length the motives for suicide, and why they are almost invariably mistaken. But his objectivity as a biographer, and his willingness to examine the violence of Wollstonecraft's emotions and her frequent depressions (which had good cause), merely shocked. This itself is an interesting point of literary history. The biographer had not yet gained his independent status, he was seen simply as an unfeeling husband who betrayed family secrets.

Godwin's frankness and sincerity were of course nothing less than revolutionary at the time. They arise directly from the anarchist principles of sincerity and plain-speaking which he enshrined in *Political Justice*. In literary terms his biography was as courageous an act as his earlier intervention, with a brilliant pamphlet, on behalf of his friend Thomas Holcroft, before the Treason Trials. Both sprang from the same set of convictions, that a writer's duty was to carry honest feeling from private into public life. But even his friends thought he was naïve, and many thought he was completely inhuman. The lawyer William Roscoe, friend of Fuseli and one of Wollstonecraft's greatest admirers and warmest correspondents, wrote the following bitter quatrain in his copy of the *Memoirs*:

> Hard was thy fate in all the scenes of life
> As daughter, sister, mother, friend and wife,
> But harder still, thy fate in death we own,
> Thus mourn'd by Godwin with a heart of stone.

Godwin's enemies naturally had a field day. They saw that the revelations of the *Memoirs* could be used to attack, and finally (as they thought) put to flight the whole monstrous regiment of feminists, free-thinkers and radical reformers. The *Anti-Jacobin* delivered a general onslaught on the immorality of everything Mary Wollstonecraft was supposed to represent, from independent sexual behaviour and the formal education of young women, to disrespect for parental authority and non-payment of creditors. It implied that the case was even worse than Godwin made out – 'the biographer does not mention many of her amours' – and indexed the book under 'Prostitution: see Mary Wollstonecraft'. It concluded on a note of high sententiousness: 'Intended by (Mr Godwin) for a beacon, it serves for a buoy, if it does not show what it is wise to pursue, it manifests what it is wise to avoid.'

The *Anti-Jacobin* and other magazines kept up these attacks for months, and indeed years, descending to increasing scurrility and causing Godwin endless private anguish. One example, from a poem published in 1801, 'The Vision of Liberty', will suffice:

> William hath penn'd a waggon-load of stuff
> And Mary's life at last he needs must write,
> Thinking her whoredoms were not known enough,
> Till fairly printed off in black and white.
> With wondrous glee and pride, this simple wight
> Her brothel feats of wantonness sets down,

Being her spouse, he tells, with huge delight,
How oft she cuckolded the silly clown,
And lent, O lovely piece!, herself to half the town.

But perhaps the most damaging, and certainly the saddest, reaction came from those women writers who were essentially sympathetic to Wollstonecraft's cause, but who were dismayed to see it personalized in the actual details of her life. The facts of Wollstonecraft's sufferings, and the truths of her difficult personality, frightened them. They felt Godwin had written too much about her emotional life and too little about her intellectual achievement. They thought that the very form of the biography betrayed the ideology of feminism. It made Mary Wollstonecraft seem too romantic and too dangerous a figure.

Mary Hays, quoted anonymously in the *Analytical,* regretted the intimate details of Wollstonecraft's life and criticized what she saw as Godwin's failure to explain the reasons behind her feminist principles. When, five years later, she compiled her five-volume *Dictionary of Female Biography* (1803), though she gave extensive entries on Manon Roland, Catharine Macaulay and Mary Astell, she completely omitted Wollstonecraft. The same astonishing omission occurs in Matilda Bentham's *Dictionary of Celebrated Women* (1804).

Wollstonecraft's young admirer, Amelia Alderson, now married to John Opie, who had painted the celebrated last portrait of Wollstonecraft which always hung in Godwin's study, radically revised her views. Using Wollstonecraft's story, she produced a fictional account of a disastrous saga of unmarried love in *Adeline Mowbray* (1805). (It was this novel that the young Harriet Westbrook sent meaningfully to Shelley before their elopement to Scotland in 1811.) Maria Edgeworth wrote a comic attack on the Wollstonecraft type in the person of Harriet Freke, who appears in *Belinda* (1801). She observed that 'women of the Wollstonecraft order . . . do infinite mischief and for my part, I do not wish to have any thing to do with them', adding that she was neither 'a safe example, nor a successful champion of Woman and her Rights'.

This hostility to Godwin's revealing portrait still frequently occurs in modern biographers, who draw freely on all its details, but remain uneasy about its placing of feminism within the particular context of Wollstonecraft's personality. The cause, they believe, must always be greater than the woman who champions it. Even Claire Tomalin, Wollstonecraft's best modern defender, tends to take this line. 'In their own way, even the *Memoirs* had diminished and distorted Mary's real importance: by minimizing her claim to be taken seriously for her ideas, and presenting her instead as the female Werther, a romantic and tragic heroine, (Godwin) may have been giving the truth as he wanted to see it, but he was very far from serving the cause she had believed in. He made no attempt to discuss her intellectual development, and he was unwilling to consider the validity of her feminist ideas in any detail.'

In fact the first six of Godwin's chapters concentrate almost exclusively on Wollstonecraft's intellectual development, through the particular influence of the radical Unitarian Dr Richard Price, through her experience of teaching at Newington Green, through her journeys to Lisbon and Dublin, through her reading of Burke and Rousseau and translating for the *Analytical*, and through the 'vehement concussion' produced by the general ideas of the French Revolution. It is true that he does not analyse her feminism in any detail, but he makes it clear at every point that he regarded the *Rights of Woman* as her major work and the one that she was 'destined' to write. He regards it as her 'most celebrated production' and her outstanding contribution to 'the public welfare and improvement'. He saw it as the focus of her career, and the passion of her life.

> Never did any author enter into a cause, with a more ardent desire to be found ... an effectual champion. She considered herself as standing forth in defence of one half of the human species, labouring under a yoke which, through all the records of time, had degraded them from the station of rational beings ... She regarded her sex, in the language of Calista, as 'in every state of life the slaves of man': the rich as alternately under the despotism of a father, a brother, and a husband, and the middling and poorer classes shut out from the acquisition of bread with independence.

Though he justly criticizes the literary style and intellectual structure of the *Rights of Woman*, observing that it was written at white
heat in 'no more than six weeks', he is more forthright on its
historic importance than any other male writer before John Stuart
Mill:

> But when we consider the importance of its doctrines,
> and the eminence of genius it displays, it seems not very
> improbable that it will be read as long as the English
> language endures. The publication of this book forms
> an epocha in the subject to which it belongs, and Mary
> Wollstonecraft will perhaps here-after be found to have
> performed more substantial service for the cause of her
> sex, than all the other writers, male or female, that ever
> felt themselves animated by the contemplation of their
> oppressed and injured state. (Chapter 6, second edition
> wording)

It is difficult to see how Godwin could have nailed her colours
(and his) more firmly to the mast.

Nevertheless, the symphony of outrage that the *Memoirs* caused
in almost every quarter gave him a profound shock. In no other
subsequent work – either philosophical or fictional – did he write
again with such daring against the conventions of the age. The
veiled and softened portraits that he draws of his wife in the novels
*St Leon* (1799) and *Fleetwood* (1805) are milky and sentimental
by comparison, though in the Preface to the former he freely
acknowledges her influence on his thinking.

After anxious discussions with Joseph Johnson, Godwin decided
to issue an amended second edition of the *Memoirs*, which swiftly
appeared at the end of 1798. He made many small, discreet
changes of phrase, and deleted some personal references (such
as that to the powerful Wedgwood family) which had caused
offence. He also sensibly changed phrases that were taken (to his
pain and surprise) as sexually ambiguous, such as the 'particular
gratification' Wollstonecraft found in her friendship with the revolutionary Irishman A. H. Rowan during the dark days in Paris.
But the second edition is very far from being a biographical retreat
or betrayal, as has frequently been suggested. In fact Godwin
added many new, crisply analytical paragraphs which increase our
understanding of Wollstonecraft's impetuous character, and show

the sensitivity with which Godwin pursued his task and responsibility as a biographer. Indeed some of these additions, such as his reflection on the bitter irony of Wollstonecraft's suicide attempt at Putney Bridge, suggest that new levels of feeling and eloquence had been released in him:

> It is sufficient to say that the wretchedness of the night which succeeded this fatal discovery of Imlay's unfaithfulness, impressed her with the feeling, that she would sooner suffer a thousand deaths, than pass another of equal misery.
>
> The agony of her mind determined her, and that determination gave her a sort of desperate serenity. She resolved to plunge herself in the Thames, and, not satisfied with any spot nearer to London, she took a boat and rowed to Putney. Her first thought had led her to Battersea-bridge, but she found it too public and accordingly proceeded further up the river. It was night when she arrived at Putney, and by that time it had begun to rain with great violence. The rain suggested to her the idea of walking up and down the bridge, till her clothes were thoroughly drenched and heavy with the wet, which she did for half an hour without meeting a human being. She then leaped from the top of the bridge, but still seemed to find a difficulty in sinking, which she endeavoured to counteract by pressing her clothes closely round her. After some time she became insensible, but she always spoke of the pain she underwent as such, that, though she could afterwards have determined upon almost any other species of voluntary death, it would have been impossible for her to resolve upon encountering the same sensations again. I am doubtful, whether this is to be ascribed to the mere nature of suffocation, or was not rather owing to the preternatural action of a desperate spirit.
>
> How strange is the condition of our nature! The whole scene of human life may at least be pronounced a delusion! Speculation for ever deceives us, and is the appropriate office of castle-builders, but the active concerns of life cheat us still more! Mary was in the first instance mistaken in the object of her attachment, imputing to him qualities which, in the trial, proved to

be imaginary. By insensible degrees she proceeded to stake her life upon the consequences of her error, for the disappointment of this choice, for a consideration so foreign to the true end of her powers and cultivation, she was willing to consign those powers and that cultivation, pregnant as they were with pleasure to herself and gratification to others, formed to adorn society, and give a relish the most delicate and unrivalled to domestic life, as well as, through the medium of the press, to delight, instruct, and reform mankind – she was willing, I say, to consign all these to premature destruction! How often is the sagacity of our moral judgment reserved for the hour of meditation, and how little does it sometimes bestead us in the time of our greatest need!

After having been for a considerable time insensible, she was recovered by the exertions of those by whom the body was found. She had sought, with cool and deliberate firmness, to put a period to her existence, and yet she lived to have every prospect of a long possession of enjoyment and happiness. It is perhaps not an unfrequent case with suicides, that we find reason to suppose, if they had survived their gloomy purpose, that they would, at a subsequent period, have been considerably happy. It arises indeed, in some measure, out of the very nature of a spirit of self-destruction, which implies a degree of anguish, that the constitution of the human mind will not suffer to remain long undiminished. This is a serious reflection. Probably no man would destroy himself from an impatience of present pain, if he felt a moral certainty that there were years of enjoyment still in reserve for him.

It testifies greatly to his courage as a biographer that, despite all protests, he removed nothing of real significance from Wollstonecraft's story, and made no attempt to modify his account of her social or political beliefs.

Of the three short passages (they total less than four pages) which he subsequently rewrote, the first concerns her friendship with Henry Fuseli (in Chapter 6), the second describes his own view of marriage (Chapter 9), and the third consists of a final summary of Wollstonecraft's 'intellectual character' (in Chapter

10). The basic effect of these revisions was to replace Godwin's usual bold, clear-cut handling of issues with a more tentative, obfuscating style of explanation. But they are understandable, given the antagonisms he had aroused, and, except in one place, they are hardly crucial to his interpretation.

In the Fuseli passage, the first edition had allowed the casual or hostile reader to suppose that Wollstonecraft had a sexual relationship with the painter; she 'conceived a personal and ardent affection for him', and she 'made light' of the circumstance that he was already married. This was not only untrue, but it weakened Godwin's marvellously perceptive account, in Chapter 7, of how she later became infatuated with Gilbert Imlay. In the second edition Godwin clarifies the sexual situation, and adds a long explanation of Wollstonecraft's scornful attitude to the social proprieties. But the revision is rambling and retreats to generalities, and one is left with the intriguing impression that Godwin himself was slightly at a loss to explain the exact nature of their friendship.

In the matrimonial passage, Godwin was largely concerned to palliate his own, evidently naïve early views on the desirability of avoiding wedlock. He also wished to distinguish them from Wollstonecraft's much more searching critique of contemporary marriage as an institution of social oppression. Nevertheless, he also deleted several fine sentences about the early, premarital stage of their love affair, and it is evident that he had given way to the well-meaning but cautious advice of his friends. For once he seems to have found a private truth that it was prudent to disguise from the public gaze. Yet the fact of their unorthodox love affair – 'we did not immediately marry' – still stands, daring and provocative. And their 'experiment in living' is still celebrated as the crown of life together.

The third passage that Godwin rewrote occurs at the very end of the *Memoirs*. In fact both versions are strangely unsatisfactory, and they for once clearly reflect Godwin's emotional state at the time he wrote. To 'summarize' Mary Wollstonecraft's mind in the way he attempted was a curious reflex of the philosopher, and I shall return to it in a moment.

No changes or explanations, however, could make the biography more popular or more acceptable to contemporary opinion.

It remained a work of astonishing outspokenness, revolutionary in its implications. As such, it was inevitably condemned to obscurity. Though translations appeared in Germany (1799) and France (1802), no new English edition was published for over a hundred years. Even in America, beyond two small editions in 1700 and 1804, there was silence. Not until William Clark Durant's scholarly reprint and supplement, a labour of love, appeared in New York in 1927, was there the slightest recognition of what Godwin had achieved.

## III

### 'Fervent Friendships'

THE MODERN READER is immediately struck by two outstanding qualities of the *Memoirs*: their coolness of tone and their authority of judgement. Though composed at a time of passionate grief, the portrait is lucid and thoughtful at every point. Here is a detached biographer, who has meditated deeply on his subject, and who is quietly intent on showing how such a remarkable character and mind was formed. His view of Wollstonecraft's psychology is complex, without lacking a moral discrimination which is sometimes Johnsonian in its weight. In common with a modern biographer, Godwin sees Mary Wollstonecraft's strengths as inextricably involved with her weaknesses of character, the one growing out of the other, as he makes explicit in a sentence from Chapter 9 of the second edition: 'She had errors, but her errors, which were not those of a sordid mind, were connected and interwoven with qualities most characteristic of her disposition and genius.' The slight shock of surprise with which we register the use of that dispassionate phrase 'sordid mind', and then its utter rejection, is typical of the effect of Godwin's bold and unflinching style. It keeps us continuously alert and engaged.

Godwin's very modern interest in the psychology of Wollstonecraft's personality is evident throughout. He was fascinated by the way character was shaped by early environment. 'The writer of this narrative, when he has met with persons, that in any degree created to themselves an interest and attachment in his mind, has always felt a curiosity to be acquainted with the scenes through which they had passed, and the incidents that had contributed to form their understandings and character. Impelled by this sentiment, he repeatedly led the conversation of Mary to topics of this sort, and, once or twice, made notes in her presence.' In this way (in Chapter 1) he shrewdly deduced the troubled relationship between her parents – the bullying, violent, erratic father and the over-submissive, son-worshipping, Irish wife – and found in it the source of Mary's later outlook on life, divided between driving idealism and disabling depression.

> Mary experienced in the first period of her existence, but few of those indulgences and marks of affection, which are principally calculated to soothe the subjection and sorrows of our early years. She was not the favourite either of her father or mother. Her father was a man of a quick, impetuous disposition, subject to alternate fits of kindness and cruelty. In his family he was a despot, and his wife appears to have been the first, and most submissive of his subjects. The mother's partiality was fixed upon the eldest son, and her system of government relative to Mary, was characterized by considerable rigour. She, at length, became convinced of her mistake, and adopted a different plan with her younger daughter. When, in her novel the *Wrongs of Woman*, Mary speaks of 'the petty cares which obscured the morning of her heroine's life, continual restraint in the most trivial matters, unconditional submission to orders, which, as a mere child, she soon discovered to be unreasonable, because inconsistent and contradictory, and the being often obliged to sit, in the presence of her parents, for three or four hours together, without daring to utter a word,' she is, I believe, to be considered as copying the outline of the first period of her own existence.
>
> But it was in vain that the blighting winds of unkindness or indifference, seemed destined to counteract the superiority of Mary's mind. It surmounted every obstacle, and by degrees, from a person little con-

sidered in the family, she became in some sort its director and umpire. The despotism of her education cost
her many a heart-ache. She was not formed to be the
contented and unresisting subject of a despot, but I
have heard her remark more than once, that, when she
felt she had done wrong, the reproof or chastisement
of her mother, instead of being a terror to her, she
found to be the only thing capable of reconciling her
to herself. The blows of her father, on the contrary,
which were the mere ebullitions of a passionate temper,
instead of humbling her roused her indignation. Upon
such occasions she felt her superiority, and was apt to
betray marks of contempt. The quickness of her father's
temper, led him sometimes to threaten similar violence
towards his wife. When that was the case, Mary would
often throw herself between the despot and his victim,
with the purpose to receive upon her own person the
blows that might be directed against her mother. She
has even laid whole nights upon the landing-place near
their chamber-door, when, mistakenly, or with reason,
she apprehended that her father might break out into
paroxysms of violence.

From this early experience of sexual warfare, she emerged a natural fighter: 'Mary was what Dr Johnson would have called, "a very
good hater"' (Chapter 1). Godwin sees the formative significance
of her intensely emotional friendship with Fanny Blood, and the
way the balance of the relationship slowly altered, with Wollstonecraft emerging as the dominant partner:

But a connection more memorable originated about
this time, between Mary and a person of her own sex,
for whom she contracted a friendship so fervent as for
years to have constituted the ruling passion of her mind.
The name of this person was Frances Blood, she was
two years older than Mary. Her residence was at that
time at Newington Butts, a village near the southern
extremity of the metropolis. The acquaintance of Fanny
contributed to ripen the immature talents of Mary.

The situation in which Mary was introduced to her,
bore a resemblance to the first interview of Werther
with Charlotte. She was conducted to the door of a

small house, but furnished with peculiar neatness and propriety. The first object that caught her sight, was a young woman of a slender and elegant form, and eighteen years of age, busily employed in feeding and managing some children, born of the same parents, but considerably inferior to her in age. The impression Mary received from this spectacle was indelible, and, before the interview was concluded, she had taken, in her heart, the vows of an eternal friendship.

Fanny was a young woman of extraordinary accomplishments. She sung and played with taste. She drew with exquisite fidelity and neatness, and, by the employment of this talent, for some time maintained her father, mother and family, but ultimately ruined her health by her extraordinary exertions. She read and wrote with considerable application, and the same ideas of minute and delicate propriety followed her in these, as in her other occupations.

Mary, a wild but animated and aspiring girl of sixteen, contemplated Fanny, in thc first instance, with sentiments of inferiority and reverence. Though they were much together, yet the distance of their habitations being considerable, they supplied the want of more frequent interviews by an assiduous correspondence. Mary found Fanny's letters better spelt and better indited than her own, and felt herself abashed. She had hitherto paid but a superficial attention to literature. She had read, to gratify the ardour of an inextinguishable thirst of knowledge, but she had not thought of writing as an art. Her ambition to excel was now awakened, and she applied herself with passion and earnestness. Fanny undertook to be her instructor, and, so far as related to accuracy and method, her lessons were given with considerable skill.

Godwin traced with delicate tact the development of this passionate female friendship. He described how Mary began as Fanny's younger pupil, and then became her intimate companion and confidante. Together, they set up a school for young children in Newington Green, a first decisive step of independence. Later, when Fanny became weakened by consumption, Mary selflessly encouraged her to marry, and travel with her young husband to seek health in the warmer climate of Portugal. When Fanny's health was further threatened by her pregnancy, Mary unhesitatingly abandoned her school and her professional prospects in London, and journeyed alone to Lisbon to nurse her friend in November 1785.

Fanny Blood's death in childbirth was a formative (as well as a prophetic) tragedy. It resolved Mary's spirit, rather than weakening it. She returned to England in 1786 more than ever intent on pursuing an independent professional life, working first as a tutor and governess in Ireland, and then as a freelance journalist in London. She told Joseph Johnson that she would be 'the first of a new genus'. She published the earliest of her ideological works, *Thoughts on the Education of Daughters* (1788), and from then on determined to fight in whatever way she could for women's rights. She also became increasingly aware of her own powers and inward strength.

> The first feeling with which Mary had contemplated her friend, was a sentiment of inferiority and reverence, but that, from the operation of a ten years' acquaintance was considerably changed. Fanny had originally been far before her in literary attainments; this disparity no longer existed. In whatever degree Mary might endeavour to free herself from the delusions of self-esteem, this period of observation upon her own mind and that of her friend, could not pass, without her perceiving that there were some essential characteristics of genius, which she possessed, and in which her friend was deficient. The principal of these was a firmness of mind, an unconquerable greatness of soul, by which, after a short internal struggle, she was accustomed to rise above difficulties and suffering. Whatever Mary undertook, she perhaps in all instances accomplished, and, to her lofty spirit, scarcely any thing she desired, appeared hard to perform. Fanny, on the contrary, was a woman of a timid and irresolute nature, accustomed to yield to difficulties, and probably priding herself in this morbid softness of her temper.

This tenacity of purpose and 'firmness of mind' emerges as one of Wollstonecraft's greatest virtues as a woman. Godwin identifies it in many telling instances: dealing successfully with a difficult employer Mrs Dawson, in Bath, when she was still only nineteen; persuading the captain of a British ship to change his mind, off Lisbon; disciplining the hitherto ungovernable Kingsborough children in Dublin; exclaiming against the savagery of the guillotinings in Paris so as to endanger her own life; and completing the journey through Scandinavia at a period when she was almost disabled by suicidal thoughts.

At the same time he gives us a penetrating and tender account of her emotional vulnerability, most especially in the affairs with Fuseli and Imlay. The masterpiece of his analysis occurs in a long passage in Chapter 7, going right back again to her childhood, and then retracing her emotional development in terms of her relations with her father, with Fanny Blood, with Fuseli, and finally with Imlay himself. This is indeed a 'romantic' interpretation – he calls her, in a phrase that became notorious, 'a female Werther' – yet to my mind it carries extraordinary conviction. It ends with a celebration of her full sexual awakening, in beautiful pre-Freudian imagery:

> Mary was now arrived at the situation, which, for two or three preceding years, her reason had pointed out to her as affording the most substantial prospect of happiness. She had been tossed and agitated by the waves of misfortune. Her childhood, as she often said, had known few of the endearments, which constitute the principal happiness of childhood. The temper of her father had early given to her mind a severe cast of thought, and substituted the inflexibility of resistance for the confidence of affection. The cheerfulness of her entrance upon womanhood, had been darkened, by an attendance upon the death-bed of her mother, and the still more afflicting calamity of her eldest sister. Her exertions to create a joint independence for her sisters and herself, had been attended, neither with the success, nor the pleasure, she had hoped for them. Her first youthful passion, her friendship with Fanny, had encountered many disappointments, and, in fine, a melancholy and premature catastrophe. Soon after these accumulated mortifications, she was engaged in a contest with a near relation, whom she regarded as unprin-

cipled, respecting the wreck of her father's fortune. In this affair she suffered the double pain, which arises from moral indignation, and disappointed benevolence. Her exertions to assist almost every member of her family, were great and unremitted. Finally, when she indulged a romantic affection for Mr Fuseli, and fondly imagined that she should find in it the solace of her cares, she perceived too late, that, by continually impressing on her mind fruitless images of unreserved affection and domestic felicity, it only served to give new pungency to the sensibility that was destroying her.

Some persons may be inclined to observe, that the evils here enumerated, are not among the heaviest in the catalogue of human calamities. But evils take their rank more from the temper of the mind that suffers them, than from their abstract nature. Upon a man of a hard and insensible disposition, the shafts of misfortune often fall pointless and impotent. There are persons, by no means hard and insensible, who, from an elastic and sanguine turn of mind, are continually prompted to look on the fair side of things, and, having suffered one fall, immediately rise again, to pursue their course, with the same eagerness, the same hope, and the same gaiety, as before. On the other hand, we not unfrequently meet with persons, endowed with the most exquisite and delicate sensibility, whose minds seem almost of too fine a texture to encounter the vicissitudes of human affairs, to whom pleasure is transport, and disappointment is agony indescribable. This character is finely portrayed by the author of *The Sorrows of Werther*. Mary was in this respect a female Werther.

She brought then, in the present instance, a wounded and sick heart, to take refuge in the bosom of a chosen friend. Let it not however be imagined, that she brought a heart, querulous, and ruined in its taste for pleasure. No; her whole character seemed to change with a change of fortune. Her sorrows, the depression of her spirits, were forgotten, and she assumed all the simplicity and the vivacity of a youthful mind. She was like a serpent on a rock, that casts its slough, and appears again with brilliancy, the sleekness, and the elastic activity of its happiest age. She was playful, full of confidence, kindness and sympathy. Her eyes assumed new lustre, and her cheeks new colour and smoothness. Her voice became cheerful, her temper overflowing with universal kindness, and that smile of bewitching tenderness from day to day illuminated her countenance, which all who knew her will so well recollect, and which won, both heart and soul, the affection of almost every one that beheld it.

Many things could be said of this passage, not least Godwin's generosity as the biographer-husband in writing it. But it is perhaps enough to note that its snake imagery was taken up almost word for word, in Shelley's triumphant chorus from *Hellas*, which carries forward Mary Wollstonecraft's hopes for happiness in a better world, like a flame passed from hand to hand:

> The world's great age begins anew,
>   The golden years return,
> The earth does like a snake renew
>   Her winter's weeds outworn . . .

Godwin's powers of moral analysis as a biographer are matched – particularly in the second half of the *Memoirs* – by a considerable narrative gift. This is in a sense unexpected, until we recall that the philosopher was also a novelist. He recounts with great effect the rapid and fatal development of the love affair with Imlay in Paris (Chapter 7), the suicide attempt from Putney Bridge (Chapter 8), and above all the agonizingly detailed account of Wollstonecraft's death which occupies almost an entire chapter (Chapter 10).

This last scene is itself a revolution in the biographer's art, depleted of all the traditional religious and literary comforts, but harrowing in its medical details and Godwin's supreme use of understatement to express unspoken emotion. It was perhaps this chapter which most shocked his intimate friends, and the modern reader may still find it strangely disturbing. He was much criticized for making no formal reference to Wollstonecraft's religious feelings at this time (though they are fully discussed in Chapter 3) – 'her religion was almost entirely of her own creating'. Yet Godwin's overwhelming grief – which we know from his later letters – seems to gain tremendous force from his effort to contain it. The precise, laconic sentences observe terminal illness as a domestic event, surrounded by mundane bustle and the grotesque details of medical treatment. But they also carry a world of metaphysical pain:

In the evening she had a second shivering fit, the symptoms of which were in the highest degree alarming. Every muscle of the body trembled, the teeth chattered, and the bed shook under her. This continued probably for five minutes. She told me, after it was over, that it had been a struggle between life and death, and that she had been more than once, in the course of it, at the point of expiring. I now apprehend these to have been the symptoms of a decided mortification, occasioned by the part of the placenta that remained in the womb. At the time however I was far from considering it in that light. When I went for Dr Poignand, between two and three o'clock on the morning of Thursday, despair was in my heart. The fact of the adhesion of the placenta was stated to me, and, ignorant as I was of obstetrical science, I felt as if the death of Mary was in a manner decided. But hope had revisited my bosom, and her cheerings were so delightful, that I hugged her obstinately to my heart. I was only mortified at what appeared to me a new delay in the recovery I so earnestly longed for. I immediately sent for Dr Fordyce, who had been with her in the morning, as well as on the three preceding days. Dr Poignand had also called this morning, but declined paying any further visits, as we had thought proper to call in Dr Fordyce.

The progress of the disease was not uninterrupted. On Tuesday I found it necessary again to call in Dr Fordyce in the afternoon, who brought with him Dr Clarke of New Burlington-street, under the idea that some operation might be necessary. I have already said, that I pertinaciously persisted in viewing the fair side of things, and therefore the interval between Sunday and Tuesday evening, did not pass without some mixture of cheerfulness. On Monday, Dr Fordyce forbad the child's having the breast and we therefore procured puppies to draw off the milk. This occasioned some pleasantry of Mary with me and the other attendants.

Nothing could exceed the equanimity, the patience and affectionateness of the poor sufferer. I intreated her to recover, and I dwelt with trembling fondness on every favourable circumstance, and, as far as it was possible in so dreadful a situation, she, by her smiles and kind speeches, rewarded my affection.

Wednesday was to me the day of greatest torture in the melancholy series. It was now decided that the only chance of supporting her through what she had to suffer, was by supplying her freely with wine. This task was devolved upon me. I began about four o'clock in the afternoon. But for me, totally ignorant of the nature of diseases and of the human frame, thus to play with a life that now seemed all that was dear to me in the universe, was too dreadful a task. I knew neither what was too much, nor what was too little. Having begun, I felt compelled, under every disadvantage, to go on. This lasted for three hours. Towards the end of that time, I happened foolishly to ask the servant who came out of the room, 'What she thought of her mistress?' She replied, 'that, in her judgement, she was going as fast as possible.'

Such a passage lets us into entirely new areas of personal intimacy and grief, in a way that is without precedent in eighteenth-century life-writing. There is nothing quite like this, even in Boswell. It acknowledges human vulnerability, and draws strength and solidarity from it, in a recognizably modern way.

Yet for all this, Godwin does have certain important limitations as a biographer which must be briefly acknowledged. First, he lacked several sources. He had full access to Wollstonecraft's professional papers, and had private information from many of her closest friends: Joseph Johnson, Hugh Skeys, Mary Hays, Mrs Christie, and several others. But Wollstonecraft's family refused to cooperate with him, and her sister Everina Wollstonecraft withheld all correspondence. Equally, Henry Fuseli angrily refused to let Godwin even glance over Wollstonecraft's letters of 1791. Most significant of all, perhaps, Gilbert Imlay's side of the correspondence with Wollstonecraft in Paris, London and Scandinavia was never recovered. This is a lacuna which has probably affected all subsequent accounts of their affair. In general it meant that

Godwin was always interpreting these emotional events through Mary Wollstonecraft's own account of them (in her own letters, and in her private talks with Godwin when they first fell in love). If there is any 'romanticizing' its cause lies here – in the kind of literary projection that we shall see in *A Short Residence* – rather than in Godwin's deliberate attempt to present an acceptable heroine to the age.

In the second place, Godwin's literary style as a biographer lacks a strong visual sense. (This was something first noted by Hazlitt, the painter turned critic, in his fine essay on Godwin in *The Spirit of the Age*.) This means that we are given very little awareness of Mary Wollstonecraft's physical presence, which must have been so striking: how she looked, the famous auburn hair, how she dressed, how she moved and talked in company. But more than that, and so crucial for a traveller like her, we have no impression of all those formative places that she visited – Lisbon, Dublin, Paris, Gothenburg, Christiania, Hamburg. In Godwin's mind, she always moves and lives in something of an abstract void. We cannot even easily imagine her little apartment in Store Street, with that cat, or her parlour in the Polygon with little Fanny. As I shall show, her own manner in *A Short Residence* is so much the opposite of this abstraction, that the stylistic contrast between the two works – the biographic and the autobiographic vision – itself says more than anything else about the contrasting temperaments of their authors.

Finally, for all his astonishing detachment and sense of objective judgement, Godwin was far more influenced by Mary Wollstonecraft's intellect than he then realized. One has the sense that he could see round her character far better than he could see round her mind. In an unphilosophical moment he admitted that her personality had 'a kind of witchcraft'. When he wrote the *Memoirs* he was still trying to digest the full implication of her ideas, and even his professional philosophic work was never to be the same again. This becomes most evident in his unavailing attempts to write a summary of 'the leading intellectual traits of her character' at the end of his book. He tried it twice, in the first and the second edition, and both are deeply unsatisfactory. In fact they tell us much less than he had already managed to show in the body of his narrative. His biographic explorations are far more convincing than his philosophic ones.

What he tries to do is enforce an arbitrary distinction between their two 'kinds' of intellect. In the first edition, he puts it like this: 'We had cultivated our powers (if I may venture to use this sort of language) in different directions; I chiefly an attempt at logical and metaphysical distinction, she a taste for the picturesque' (Chapter 10).

This strikes one as so ludicrously inadequate – and so far below what he had already brilliantly shown of her developing 'powers' – that one loses confidence in a way that happens nowhere else in the book. Godwin himself seems to have been vaguely aware of something going wrong when he makes the apologetic parenthesis about using 'this sort of language'. One is hardly surprised to find a little later the absurd statement that 'in the strict sense of the term, she reasoned little'. We seem to have collapsed into an inferior mode of discourse.

In the second edition, he explores the distinction again, but now attempting to see their intellectual companionship on a grand scale. It becomes an archetype of the universal reconciliation between the two sexes. Each supplies what the other most lacks, in a prophetic partnership between the powers of Reason (male) and Imagination (female).

> Mary and myself perhaps each carried farther than to its common extent the characteristic of the sexes to which we belonged. I have been stimulated, as long as I can remember, by the love of intellectual distinction; but, as long as I can remember, I have been discouraged, when casting the sum of my intellectual value, by finding that I did not possess, in the degree of some other persons, an intuitive sense of the pleasures of the imagination. Perhaps I feel them as vividly as most men; but it is often rather by an attentive consideration, than an instantaneous survey. They have been liable to fail of their effect in the first experiment, and my scepticism has often led me anxiously to call in the approved decisions of taste, as a guide to my judgement, or a countenance to my enthusiasm. One of the leading passions of my mind has been an anxious desire not to be deceived. This has led me to view the topics of my reflection on all sides, and to examine and re-examine without end the questions that interest me. Endless

disquisition however is not always the parent of certainty.

What I wanted in this respect, Mary possessed in a degree superior to any other person I ever knew. Her feelings had a character of peculiar strength and decision, and the discovery of them, whether in matters of taste or of moral virtue, she found herself unable to control. She had viewed the objects of nature with a lively sense and an ardent admiration, and had developed their beauties. Her education had been fortunately free from the prejudices of system and bigotry, and her sensitive and generous spirit was left to the spontaneous exercise of its own decisions. The warmth of her heart defended her from artificial rules of judgement, and it is therefore surprising what a degree of soundness pervaded her sentiments. In the strict sense of the term, she had reasoned comparatively little, and she was therefore little subject to diffidence and scepticism. Yet a mind more candid in perceiving and retracting error, when it was pointed out to her, perhaps never existed. This arose naturally out of the directness of her sentiments, and her fearless and unstudied veracity.

A companion like this, excites and animates the mind. From such a one we imbibe, what perhaps I principally wanted, the habit of minutely attending to first impressions, and justly appreciating them. Her taste awakened mine, her sensibility determined me to a careful development of my feelings. She delighted to open her heart to the beauties of nature, and her propensity in this respect led me to a more intimate contemplation of them. My scepticism in judging, yielded to the coincidence of another's judgement, and especially when the judgement of that other was such, that the more I made experiment of it, the more was I convinced of its rectitude.

The improvement I had reason to promise myself, was however yet in its commencement, when a fatal event, hostile to the moral interests of mankind, ravished from me the light of my steps, and left to me nothing but the consciousness of what I had possessed, and must now possess no more! (Chapter 10)

This is a shrewd, and in places intensely moving, analysis of the relationship. It clearly contains much truth, and must have required considerable humility for Godwin to write, at a time when he was considered one of the leading philosophers of the age. Yet it is based, inescapably, on a prejudiced assumption about the nature of the sexes (and one which Wollstonecraft would never for a moment have accepted). It is that the Man reasons, while the Woman merely feels. Godwin has here so far declined into the conventions of eighteenth-century thinking (and even modern cliché), that one cannot take him entirely seriously.

Yet it is his only major lapse as a biographer, and on reflection it is an instructive and even a touching one. Reading through both versions, I think one can see what has happened. In the first place he was really trying to describe the way in which Wollstone-craft had 'improved' the inadequacies of his own intellectual make-up, as he was now beginning to see them. It was her feeling, her imagination, her intuition, that he most valued. It was not that she merely felt, but that he merely reasoned – until he met her. 'What I wanted in this respect, Mary possessed in a degree superior to any other person I ever knew ... my oscillation and scepticism were fixed by her boldness.' For once, and only once, he was speaking with overwhelming subjectivity.

In the second place, Godwin was indeed reverting to another, and more conventional mode of literary discourse. For one crucial and revealing moment he was turning his back on the revolution-ary vision and style he had forged as a biographer. He was reverting to the grand, dusty philosophic commonplaces of the previous age: the age which they had both so courageously stormed and subverted. He was attempting to generalize like a philosopher of the Enlightenment, on an experience they had lived out together with the passionate particularity of the Roman-tic poets and lovers.

## IV

## 'Love in a Cold Climate'

GODWIN'S BIOGRAPHY leaves us finally with a sense of the mystery of Mary Wollstonecraft's character. I do not think this is a weakness. On the contrary, by acknowledging a whole new world of Romantic impetuosity and idealism which could not be defined in conventional terms, it draws us on to explore and investigate further for ourselves. This is a new achievement in life-writing. It is not *lapidary* in the old sense; it does not lay a formal tombstone on her life. But rather, it opens a window back into the extraordinary way she lived and wrote. It compels us to try and get closer to her, and to look further into the experiences which finally brought her and Godwin together. We must go back over the story again from her own viewpoint. I am convinced that no single piece of literary evidence shows this so well as her remarkable account of the journey she made to Scandinavia, and the impact it made on her contemporaries. It is this work, even more than *The Rights of Woman*, which reveals her originality, and her adventurous qualities of mind and spirit. As Godwin himself said, it was the book calculated to make any reader fall in love with its author.

From the first, *A Short Residence* must have seemed a highly unusual book. Not only was its narrator an unaccompanied woman, travelling first with her child and a maid, and later entirely on her own. But stranger than this, she was travelling not to Europe, but to Scandinavia – a largely unknown region, almost indeed a boreal wilderness. The poet Robert Southey wrote excitedly to his publisher friend Joseph Cottle: 'Have you met with Mary Wollstonecraft's (travel book)? She has made me in love with a cold climate, and frost and snow, with modern moonlight.'

Even the most mundane details of Scandinavian life – the feather-filled duvets, the wood-burning stoves, the salty fish and meats of the smorgasbord, the huge pine forests, the steep meadows with their bell-hung cattle, the wild cataracts and the glassy fjords – struck the reader as something 'rich and strange'. The novelty of this in cultural terms cannot be overestimated. Hitherto the English literary traveller (for the great part male, well-heeled and accompanied by guides, valets or tutors) had adhered to a well-defined circuit through Europe and the Levant that over three centuries had become known as the Grand Tour. 'The grand object of travel', pronounced Dr Johnson, 'is to visit the shores of the Mediterranean' – though he himself got no further than Paris.

Sterne, Smollett, Gray, Walpole had all limited their itineraries to France and Italy, or those parts of Germany and Switzerland reached by the river Rhine. The essential attraction was towards the cities and civilizations of the south. To go north and east – beyond say the international port of Hamburg and the old walled and turreted medieval city of Lübeck, was to journey beyond the pale of Western culture. The shores of the distant Baltic, and the half-legendary lands of the midnight sun beyond, were terra incognita for all but a few hardy sailors, merchants, diplomats and the new race of commercial travellers. The latter were a significant class of whom Wollstonecraft had a great deal to say.

Her own itinerary was therefore remarkable in itself, and should be glanced at on the map. From Gothenburg in Sweden she travelled north across the Norwegian border as far as Halden. She crossed the Skaggerak to the wild, rocky shores beyond Larvik. She remained for several weeks at Tonsberg, and sailed west as far as Risor. Next she returned via Oslo (then Christiania) and travelled south again, crossing the Kattegat into Denmark, where she stayed in Copenhagen. Finally she crossed the straits to Schleswig, and so to Hamburg, where she took a regular ship home to Dover. The whole journey lasted three and a half months, from late June to early October 1795, at a time when the rest of Europe was at war with France, and all travel was generally hazardous.

The little that was then known about Scandinavian society, its arts, languages, social customs, laws and forms of government, is skilfully sketched in by Wollstonecraft during the course of her narrative, and brought alive by her sharp eye for detail and – even more – by her willingness to ask pertinent questions. She is characteristically pleased when her first host in Sweden, a naval district pilot and customs officer, remarks bluntly at supper 'that I was a woman of observation, for I asked him men's questions'.

We learn from her of the political domination of Denmark over its neighbour Norway, and to a lesser extent Sweden; and the commanding influence of the great Danish statesman Count A. P. Bernstorff, who had put the whole of Scandinavia on a footing of 'armed neutrality' towards the conflicting powers in Europe. The dramatic assassination of the Swedish King Gustav III in 1792, and the amorous intrigues of Princess Matilda at the Danish court with the royal physician Struensee, both subjects of popular interest in England, also draw Wollstonecraft's attention.

But equally we feel we are entering a beautiful, unexplored world of Nature, which serves above all as a backdrop – sometimes poetically intense – for Wollstonecraft's own reflections and memories. Almost the only previous topographical work on the subject was William Coxe's *Voyages and Travels* (1784), which provided little more than a series of geographical and economic notes. The main link between Britain and Scandinavia remained the trade in raw materials and naval stores – timber, rope and certain minerals. Beyond the confines of the royal courts at Christiania and Copenhagen, it was considered to be a primitive world, on which the ideas of the Enlightenment, and the possibilities of political liberty touched off by the French Revolution were only just beginning to impinge. The northernmost state, Norway, with which Mary Wollstonecraft fell in love, was free only by the fact of its remoteness from Copenhagen. It had no proper constitution until 1814, no university until that founded at Christiania in 1811, and did not gain full political independence until more than a century later in 1905. It was on the other hand the first state in northern Europe to grant women the vote, in 1907.

The immediate question that arises, therefore, is the motive for Wollstonecraft's travels. What was she doing in Scandinavia at all, and why did she follow the curious, looping itinerary to the tiny ports of western Norway? The mystery is deepened by the sense of weariness and reluctance which strikes the opening chord of the book – not at all the light-hearted eagerness of the conventional, picturesque traveller. The tone grows steadily more thoughtful and melancholy as the journey progresses.

Part of the answer is provided by Godwin's *Memoirs*. The idea for the voyage was Gilbert Imlay's. After Wollstonecraft's return from France in the spring of 1795, and her first attempt at suicide in London, he was anxious to distract her and give her the chance to reflect on their situation. The shipping business he had embarked on when they were together the previous year at Le Havre had run into difficulties, and he suggested that she go as his agent to sort out the problems with his business partner Elias Backman, who was based in Gothenburg. This arrangement explains the immediate form of *A Short Residence*, which is written as a series of twenty-five letters to an unnamed correspondent in London, who, it becomes clear, has been the narrator's lover. The whole book is, in effect, addressed to Gilbert Imlay and makes frequent half-veiled references to their previous life together in France. This provides the essential confessional thread of the work.

It had long been thought that this curious business venture was largely a cynical manoeuvre of Imlay's to put Mary Wollstonecraft at a safe distance from himself. Yet this leaves out of the account several other factors. Having been brought up in various parts of England by her shiftless father, Wollstonecraft in adulthood was naturally restless. She was a born traveller and an instinctive seeker after new horizons and new societies. She could never rest very long in one place, she was always half-consciously looking for an ideal form of existence, a Golden Age.

In the previous ten years she had been not only in France (living in both Paris and Normandy), but also in Ireland and Portugal. This was exceptional, especially for a woman of that time. She had always longed to go to America, and had she lived, I suspect she would have persuaded Godwin to make a new life there. In all this she expresses that yearning spirit of Romanticism, half practical pioneering and half visionary Utopia, which becomes so explicit in the writers who followed her; Southey's and Coleridge's dream of Pantisocracy on the banks of the Susquehanna; Lord Byron's excursions into Greece; Shelley's lifelong search for some ideal commune in Switzerland or Italy. These are all the direct reflections of the same voyaging, unappeased spirit.

Wollstonecraft added Norway to the list of enchanted destinations which fascinated the Romantics. Writing to Imlay from Christiania, in a characteristic passage, she conjures up one of those enduring images of the ideal life that is always just out of reach. Here the bitterness of her past experience lies in the balance with her unquenched hopes. It is a vivid piece of self-portraiture, the kind of thing with which Godwin (rather than Imlay) fell in love; and it is difficult to believe that it was written by a woman for whom travel was not a deep reflex, a profound need of intellect and heart.

She describes how autumn has come to Christiania, and the gathering clouds urge her to depart southwards. Yet despite the 'calls of business and affection', she feels a strange urge to press onward into yet remoter regions. She continues:

> You will ask perhaps, why I wished to go further northward. Why? not only because the country, from all I can gather, is most romantic, abounding in forests and lakes, and the air pure, but I have heard much of the intelligence of the inhabitants, substantial farmers, who have none of that cunning to contaminate their simplicity, which displeased me so much in the conduct of the people on the sea coast ... The description I received of them carried me back to the fables of the golden age: independence and virtue; affluence without vice; cultivation of mind, without depravity of heart; with 'ever smiling liberty', the nymph of the mountain. – I want faith! My imagination hurries me forward to seek an asylum in such a retreat from all the disappointments I am threatened with; but reason drags me back, whispering that the world is still the world, and man the same compound of weakness and folly, who must occasionally excite love and disgust, admiration and contempt. (Letter 14)

This was not written by a woman who could be sent away on a fool's errand. It was written by one of nature's pilgrims, who would always seek, hoping against hope to find. If she quotes from the old Republican poet Milton, the spirit in which she admonishes and then encourages herself is not far from Bunyan.

## V

## 'The Treasure Ship'

YET THERE IS fascinating evidence, of a different kind, that her journey was more than a romantic literary adventure. It was also a genuine business enterprise, and Imlay had expressed remarkable confidence in her talents by putting it into her hands. Wollstonecraft was indeed a serious commercial traveller. Modern research has slowly revealed that she was responsible for the legal recovery of a very large sum of money: in fact nothing less than a treasure ship. As this extraordinary story is never revealed in her book, despite her long polemic passages on the commercial spirit and the destructive effect of the mercantile outlook (passages all aimed directly at Imlay), it is worth investigating it in some detail. It gives us a striking new perspective on Mary Wollstonecraft's exceptional abilities, and goes a long way to explaining both the itinerary she travelled and the daring nature of what she undertook.

Wollstonecraft's first modern editor, William Clark Durant, discovered in the Abinger Papers a remarkable legal document drawn up by Imlay, in which she is appointed his legal representative and given power of attorney throughout Scandinavia. It states:

> Know all men by these presents, that I, Gilbert Imlay, citizen of the United States of America, at present residing in London, do appoint Mary Imlay, my best friend and wife, to take the sole management of my affairs and business which I had placed in the hands of Mr Elias Backman, negotiant, Gottenburg, or those of Messers Myburg and Co, Copenhagen ... For which this letter shall be a sufficient power, enabling her to receive all the money that may be recovered from Peter Ellyson, whatever the issue of the trial now carrying on, instituted by Mr Elias Backman, as my agent, for the violation of trust which I had reposed in his integrity. (William Clark Durant, ed., *Memoirs of Mary Wollstonecraft*, 1927, p. 295)

The exact implications of this document have for long remained obscure. Backman – a shrewd commercial fixer who subsequently became the first American Consul in Sweden – was known as Imlay's agent in a semi-legal trading business, shipping much-needed raw materials from Gothenburg to Le Havre, and running the British blockade round the neutral Baltic ports into wartime France. This was a business undertaken by British and American sympathizers with France, and connived at by firms like Myburg, but which was strictly speaking a 'traitorous correspondence' with the enemy. Nevertheless excise records show that similar businesses – in gold coin, tobacco and spirits – were illegally maintained throughout the war from almost all the ports of southern England. Operations through Hamburg, Copenhagen, Gothenburg or Arendal were considerably more respectable, though not necessarily safer.

But the identity of 'Peter Ellyson', the reason for his 'trial', and the exact nature of his 'violation of trust' have not been known to modern biographers. They have therefore tended to discount Imlay's document, and to give little credence to its concluding statement: 'Thus, confiding in the talent, zeal, and earnestness of my dearly beloved friend and companion, I submit the management of these affairs entirely and implicitly to her discretion.'

Yet zeal and discretion were most certainly demanded of Mary Wollstonecraft. To what degree has been revealed, only recently, by a modern governor of Gothenburg, Mr Per Nystrom. In the late 1970s Nystrom began to interest himself in the early shipping records of his city. The result of his researches appeared in a little pamphlet published by the Royal Society of Arts and Sciences of Gothenburg in 1980 (*Mary Wollstonecraft's Scandinavian Journey*, RSAS Gothenburg, Humaniora No. 17, 1980). What he shows is that Mary Wollstonecraft was in pursuit of a stolen treasure ship, packed with silver and Bourbon plate. The ship had been spirited away by its Norwegian captain from Imlay's trading company, which owned the vessel and its cargo. It represented the greater part of Imlay's assets. In fact, Wollstonecraft was on a treasure-hunt in Scandinavia.

The extraordinary story, as unfolded by Nystrom, is briefly this. In June 1794, registration documents show that Gilbert Imlay purchased a cargo ship called *La Liberté* from a group of French merchants at the Normandy port of Le Havre. Imlay had already had some success with his blockade-running business, probably with cargoes shipped from Hamburg on Danish ships, and he now decided to set up on his own account as a clandestine importer of alum and naval construction materials from the Baltic. He was in an optimistic mood and full of schemes. He had recently rented a house for Mary Wollstonecraft in Le Havre, and the month before their daughter Fanny had been safely born. He felt expansive.

The ship was ideal for the task – fast and highly manoeuvrable – and only required false papers to disguise her mission. To this purpose, he renamed her *Maria and Margaretha* (perhaps there was a private joke here, using the Italian version of his wife's name, Mary, and her maid's, Marguerite). He then hired a twenty-five-year-old Norwegian sailor to be her captain. The sailor's name was Peder Ellefsen, the son of a well-known merchant family from Risor, the small port between Larvik and Arendal on the Skagerrak.

Imlay was now able to apply through Ellefsen to the Danish Consul in Le Havre (who dealt with all Scandinavian shipping), and re-register the ship as a neutral vessel. According to these new papers the *Maria and Margaretha* was a Norwegian cargo ship, based in Kristiansund, owned by Ellefsen himself, and carrying ballast back to Copenhagen. The flag of convenience was complete. Imlay now secretly loaded up his ship with its real cargo, intended as the convertible currency with which he would purchase the stores at Gothenburg, under Elias Backman's supervision. Nystrom is able to show what this cargo was, from subsequent documents connected with the 'trial' of Peder Ellefsen. It consisted of thirty-two bars of silver, and thirty-six pieces of plate, some of it rumoured to carry the royal Bourbon coat of arms. The total value was £35,000; an enormous sum, equivalent to perhaps a million pounds in modern currency.

How Imlay ever obtained such valuables remains a mystery. Perhaps it was through his connections in Paris, perhaps it was confiscated or even stolen aristocratic property, perhaps through some Franco-American syndicate involving his old friend Thomas Christie. At all events it was a capital investment far beyond his private means, and to lose it would have meant ruin. There can be no doubt that Mary Wollstonecraft, at the time she was acting as his agent in 1795, must have been fully briefed on all these details.

The ensuing events can be traced. The ship was dispatched under Ellefsen's command in August 1794 to run the British blockade through the North Sea. Norwegian shipping records show that she reached the shores of the Skagerrak safely on 20 August, and put in at one of the small ports near Arendal. But she never reached her destination port of Gothenburg, down the coast in Sweden. In reply to his urgent requests for information, Backman was first told that the treasure ship had sunk. But further inquiries during the autumn confirmed that Peder Ellefsen was in fact safely back in his home port of Risor. There were independent reports that the treasure had been taken off in a small boat by the captain, and that the first mate (who was English) had been given the ship as the price of his silence. Whatever the exact details, by the winter of 1794–95 when he had returned to London, Gilbert Imlay was aware that his venture had disastrously miscarried. The *Maria and Margaretha* had disappeared, the silver and plate had been misappropriated, and Peder Ellefsen had 'violated his trust'. It was, one may think, a case of poacher poached.

Legally speaking, of course, the situation was extremely delicate. It throws new light on all those mysterious business worries for which Wollstonecraft was continually reproaching Imlay, and which cast their shadow over *A Short Residence* in the tirades against the profit motive, and the obsession with trade, in Letters 23 and 24, from Hamburg. French law had no jurisdiction in the case; British law would have regarded both parties as criminal. Imlay's only recourse was to the Danish courts, and he instructed Backman to apply to Copenhagen, in an attempt to bring some kind of pressure to bear on the merchant community in Norway. To his great surprise, and perhaps through the influence of American traders with A. P. Bernstorff, the motions at least of legal redress were forthcoming.

Nystrom's evidence is less clear-cut from this point onwards, but it appears that a preliminary Board of Inquiry was appointed according to the Danish protocol in dealing with Norwegian matters. This consisted of three local judges or commissioners drawn from leading members of the Norwegian business community. The great significance of Nystrom's researches on this point is his identification of the Scandinavian towns in which they lived. Christoffer Nordberg and A. J. Ungar came from Stromstad, north of Gothenburg, on the Swedish–Norwegian border. Jacob Wulfsberg came from Tonsberg, on the southern Norwegian coast. If we add to these Peter Ellefsen's home port of Risor, we have at last the complete outline of Mary Wollstonecraft's Scandinavian itinerary in the summer of 1795.

It is now clear that, after an indecisive preliminary investigation by the Board of Inquiry in the spring of that year, Imlay had confided to 'his best friend and wife' the task of trying to reach some legal settlement through personal intervention. She was to discover the fate of the treasure ship, the attitude of all parties concerned, and to reach if possible some financial agreement, probably on an 'out of court' basis. It was by any standards an onerous undertaking, involving a foreign legal system, a series of delicate interviews, a six-hundred-mile round trip from Gothenburg and the prospect of an extremely difficult meeting with Peder Ellefsen himself on his home ground at Risor. Only someone as daring and determined as Mary Wollstonecraft would have attempted it.

## VI

## 'A Dark Speck of Life'

FOR THE LITERARY PURPOSES of *A Short Residence*, no explicit reference is made to this saga of the treasure ship. But Nystrom's discoveries allow us to plot the stages of Wollstonecraft's northern journey with new understanding. They also help us to appreciate better than before the extraordinary skill with which she transformed a prosaic business venture into a poetic revelation of her character and philosophy.

The range of Wollstonecraft's practical interests is both delightful and formidable. She has strong views on everything from gardening to prison reform and even sea-monsters. She may spend her time visiting a salt works, discussing farmers' land rights, going sea-bathing, studying divorce laws, chatting to domestic servants, or simply climbing a cliff at sunset to blow a hunting horn and listen to its echoes swelling and fading among the distant, shadowy promontories. All these things tell us as much about her as about Scandinavia, and her individual observations vividly reveal her cast of mind:

> The women and children were cutting off branches from the beech, birch, oak, &c, and leaving them to dry – This way of helping out their fodder, injures the trees. But the winters are so long, that the poor cannot afford to lay in a sufficient stock of hay. By such means they just keep life in the poor cows, for little milk can be expected when they are so miserably fed.
>
> It was Saturday, and the evening was uncommonly serene. In the villages I every where saw preparations for Sunday, and I passed by a little car loaded with rye, that presented, for the pencil and heart, the sweetest picture of a harvest home I had ever beheld! A little girl was mounted astraddle on a shaggy horse, brandishing a stick over its head; the father was walking at the side of the car with a child in his arms, who must have come to meet him with tottering steps, the little creature was stretching out its arms to cling around his neck; and a boy, just above petticoats, was labouring hard, with a fork, behind, to keep the sheaves from falling.
>
> My eyes followed them to the cottage, and an involuntary sigh whispered to my heart, that I envied the mother, much as I dislike cooking, who was preparing their pottage. I was returning to my babe, who may never experience a father's care or tenderness. The bosom that nurtured her, heaved with a pang at the thought which only an unhappy mother could feel.
> (Letter 16)

Wollstonecraft also uses certain intense, often solitary, moments of her travel, almost like Wordsworthian 'spots of time', to establish the confessional themes, the hopes and fears, that give the book its inward and Romantic quality. Often these are achieved by the way in which, with perfect naturalness, she places herself within a landscape, or minutely observes it.

In Letters 5 and 6 she describes how she sets out alone in a small open boat to cross the Christiania Sound for Larvik. She adopts the dauntless tone that vividly caught the imagination of her readers.

> The wind had changed on the night, and my boat was ready. A dish of coffee, and fresh linen, recruited my spirits; and I directly set out again for Norway; proposing to land much higher up the coast. Wrapping my great coat around me, I lay down on some sails at the bottom of the boat, its motion rocking me to rest, till a discourteous wave interrupted my slumbers, and obliged me to rise and feel a solitariness which was not so soothing as that of the past night . . . The sea was boisterous; but, as I had an experienced pilot, I did not apprehend any danger. Sometimes, I was told, boats are driven far out and lost. However, I seldom calculate chances so nicely – sufficient for the day is the obvious evil! We had to steer amongst islands and huge rocks, rarely losing sight of the shore, though it now and then appeared only a mist that bordered the water's edge. (Letters 5 and 6)

In this description of the solitary voyager, sailing through dangerous waters towards an unknown, misty shoreline, Mary Wollstonecraft's whole life seems for a moment to be symbolized. But more than that, something of the Romantic predicament itself is prophesied. How many other boats would be driven 'far out and lost'!

At the old merchant town of Tonsberg her business with Judge Wulfsberg detained her for three weeks. She settled into an inn overlooking the sea, walked daily over the rocks, rowed in the bay, and began to write her travel book (Letters 6 to 9). For the first time she sounds cheerful – 'I have recovered my activity, even whilst attaining a little embonpoint' – and her quick eye and inquiring spirit rove with marvellous freedom through these chapters. She notices everything: the sea captains who sing Republican songs but still venerate the Danish prince; the women who dress so charmingly but are ill-paid as domestic servants; the criminal who was branded on his third conviction, but who praised Judge Wulfsberg for providing him with financial relief afterwards (she sends him some money herself). But the most revealing of all is the way she shifts with startling ease from an abstract, sententious, philosophic reflection in the eighteenth-century manner, to a minute and poetically detailed observation of nature, which reminds us of nothing so much as the *Notebooks* of Coleridge or the *Journals* of Dorothy Wordsworth.

> I wished to avail myself of my vicinity to the sea, and bathe; but it was not possible near the town; there was no convenience. The young woman whom I mentioned to you, proposed rowing me across the water, amongst the rocks; but as she was pregnant, I insisted on taking one of the oars, and learning to row. It was not difficult; and I do not know a pleasanter exercise. I soon became expert, and my train of thinking kept time, as it were, with the oars, or I suffered the boat to be carried along by the current, indulging a pleasing forgetfulness, or fallacious hopes. – How fallacious! yet, without hope, what is to sustain life, but the fear of annihilation – the only thing of which I have ever felt a dread – I cannot bear to think of being no more – of losing myself – though existence is often but a painful consciousness of misery; nay, it appears to me impossible that I should cease to exist, or that this active, restless spirit, equally alive to joy and sorrow, should only be organized dust – ready to fly abroad the moment the spring snaps, or the spark goes out, which kept it together. Surely something resides in this heart that is not perishable – and life is more than a dream.
>
> Sometimes, to take up my oar, once more, when the sea was calm, I was amused by disturbing the unnumerable young jelly fish which floated just below the surface: I had never observed them before; for they have not a hard shell, like those which I have seen on the sea-shore. They look like thickened water, with a white edge; and four purple circles, of different forms, were in the middle, over an incredible number of fibres, or white lines. Touching them, the cloudy substance would turn or close, first on one side, then on the other, very gracefully; but when I took one of them up in the ladle with which I heaved the water out of the boat, it appeared only a colourless jelly.
>
> I did not see any of the seals, numbers of which followed our boat when we landed in Sweden; for

though I like to sport in the water, I should have had
no desire to join in their gambols.

It is in the close combination of these two kinds of observation that
her romantic genius is so well displayed. Her intense awareness of
inner life and identity, is projected on to even the most humble
forms of nature.

At Peder Ellefsen's home port of Risør, hidden away among
wild rocky headlands some 150 miles out from Christiania, she is
overcome by fears. They are vividly expressed in her description
of the claustrophobic, primitive and backward place, where a 'con-
traband trade makes the basis of their profit'. They seem, too, to
have revived memories of the old regime in France, and the terrors
of imprisonment, the deepest nightmare, perhaps, of her spirit.

> We were a considerable time entering amongst the
> islands, before we saw about two hundred houses
> crowded together, under a very high rock – still higher
> appearing above. Talk not of bastilles! To be born here,
> was to be bastilled by nature – shut out from all that
> opens the understanding, or enlarges the heart.
> Huddled one behind another, not more than a quarter
> of the dwellings even had a prospect of the sea . . . The
> ocean, and these tremendous bulwarks, enclosed me
> on every side. I felt the confinement, and wished for
> wings to reach still loftier cliffs . . . I felt my breath
> oppressed, though nothing could be clearer than the
> atmosphere. (Letter 11)

Of the business finally transacted here, she says little, except that
she was 'prevailed upon to dine with the English vice-consul'. One
is amazed to learn such a person existed in such a place. For the
rest she notes only her utter relief on departing after several days
– 'It seemed to me a sort of emancipation.'

Returning to Christiania (Letters 13 and 14) she was notably
well entertained by the family of Bernhard Anker, an anglophile
and one of the leading merchants in Norway. Anker was a Fellow
of the Royal Society, and besides owning the best private library
in Norway and a fine collection of scientific instruments, he was
also proprietor of a hundred of the 136 licensed saw mills in the
district. No doubt she was still trying to get support and advice

over the Ellefsen affair. But she also had time to tour the city (quarrelling with William Coxe's description in his *Voyages and Travels*), and to be taken out to the younger Anker's country estate, with its famous English-style gardens.

Here occurs one of those touching details which suddenly bring a sort of intimacy to our knowledge of the past. Four years later, in the summer of 1799, another young English traveller, Edward Daniel Clarke, also came to the Ankers' country estate. Wandering out of the house, he came upon an unexpected sight, which he must be allowed to tell in his own words. 'In the gardens we were shown an old Norwegian dwelling, preserved as a specimen of what the Norwegian houses were two centuries before, with all its furniture and other appurtenances, as it then stood. Upon the walls of this building we observed the names of many travellers who had visited the spot, and, among others, that of the late Mrs Godwin, thus inscribed, with a pencil, near the door – "Mary Wollstonecraft"' (*Travels in Various Countries*, 1824, Vol. 10, p. 389).

It is difficult to say which is the more memorable aspect of this sudden, homely detail; that she wrote her name like any other English traveller (though modestly, in pencil, 'near the door'). Or that she signed herself not 'Imlay', but her real name, her writing name, 'Wollstonecraft'. It must have been worth the glimpse of a dozen 'Byrons' scrawled over the monuments of Europe.

Almost her last sight in Norway was the dramatic cascades near Frederikstad, which she approached through a devastated pine forest leading down to a dark, narrow valley booming with the sound of roaring water. This place seems to have hypnotized her, with its white crashing waters bursting out against the black rocks and overhanging trees, an elemental force both thrilling and disturbing. The ideas of death – suicide perhaps – but also rebirth and immortality, filled her mind. It is a passage that I think may particularly have struck Coleridge when he read it the following year at Nether Stowey, and we shall return to it:

> Reaching the cascade, or rather cataract, the roaring
> of which had a long time announced its vicinity,
> my soul was hurried by the falls into a new train of
> reflections. The impetuous dashing of the rebounding

torrent from the dark cavities which mocked the exploring eye, produced an equal activity in my mind: my
thoughts darted from earth to heaven, and I asked
myself why I was chained to life and its misery? Still the
tumultuous emotions this sublime object excited were
very pleasurable; and, viewing it, my soul rose, with
renewed dignity, above its cares – grasping at immortality – it seemed as impossible to stop the current of my
thoughts, as of the always varying, still the same, torrent
before me – I stretched out my hand to eternity, bound-
ing over the dark speck of life to come. (Letter 15)

But her observations on the pine woods themselves, those living
symbols of wild nature throughout Scandinavia, have remarkable
particularity and philosophic power. Beginning with almost botanical precision, and curiously foreshadowing the Darwinian notion
of the 'struggle for existence', they move characteristically towards
a poetic vision of death as a kind of regeneration of the spirit,
of 'something getting free'. The organic society of the woods,
Wollstonecraft seems to suggest, reflects the evolutionary possibilities of the human spirit. This was to become a major theme, a commanding vision, for later Romantic poets; and one can glimpse,
perhaps, the shadowy outline of some future ode by Shelley.

The spiral tops of the pines are loaded with ripening
seed, and the sun gives a glow to their light green tinge,
which is changing into purple, one tree more or less
advanced, contrasting with another. The profusion with
which nature has decked them, with pendant honours,
prevents all surprise at seeing, in every crevice, some
sapling struggling for existence. Vast masses of stone
are thus encircled; and roots, torn up by the storms,
become a shelter for a young generation ... The grey
cobweb-like appearance of the aged pines is a much
finer image of decay; the fibres whitening as they lose
their moisture, imprisoned life seems to be stealing
away. I cannot tell why – but death, under every form,
appears to me like something getting free – to expand
in I know not what element; nay I feel that this conscious being must be as unfettered, have the wings of
thought, before it can be happy. (Letter 15)

At Copenhagen she seems to have obtained an audience with Count Bernstorff himself on the Ellefsen affair. But she describes the city at length – it had recently been gutted by fire – with detailed reflections on the Danish government (Letters 18 to 21). The story of Princess Mathilda and Struensee obviously touched her deeply – she suggests their error was in attempting to push through liberal reforms too quickly. She criticizes many aspects of Danish life, from the heavy drinking to the public execution of criminals. She looks 'in vain for the sprightly gait of the Norwegians' and their sense of liberty – and was repelled both by the 'promiscuous amours of the men of the middling class with their female servants' and the 'gross debaucheries' of the lower orders. 'Love here seems to corrupt the morals, without polishing the manners, by banishing confidence and truth, the charm as well as the cement of domestic life.' She particularly criticizes the 'cunning and wantonness' of the Danish women, and the illiberal and tyrannical behaviour of Danish husbands.

> I have every where been struck by one characteristic difference in the conduct of the two sexes; women, in general, are seduced by their superiors, and men jilted by their inferiors; rank and manners awe the one, and cunning and wantonness subjugate the other; ambition creeping into the woman's passion, and tyranny giving force to the man's; for most men treat their mistresses as kings do their favourites: ergo is not man then the tyrant of the creation? (Letter 19)

This letter is her most explicitly feminist chapter, and in a revealing aside she quickly meets the sarcastic objections that she feels sure Imlay, and perhaps other readers, will raise. 'Still harping on the same subject, you will exclaim – How can I avoid it, when most of the struggles of an eventful life have been occasioned by the oppressed state of my sex: we reason deeply, when we forcibly feel.' It is a remark that rings out with heartfelt conviction, and makes any idea that Mary Wollstonecraft had trimmed her views in later life not only absurd, but impertinent.

Yet the more tender side of her beliefs is also evident in the pleasure with which she describes the sexual freedom of the young people in Scandinavia (a subject which became notorious in

Victorian England), and the 'kind of interregnum between the reign of the father and the husband' which the young women enjoyed in courtship.

> Young people, who are attached to each other, with the consent of their friends, exchange rings, and are permitted to enjoy a degree of liberty together, which I have never noticed in any other country. The days of courtship are therefore prolonged, till it be perfectly convenient to marry: the intimacy often becomes very tender; and if the lover obtain the privilege of a husband, it can only be termed half by stealth, because the family is wilfully blind. It happens very rarely that these honorary engagements are dissolved or disregarded. (Letter 19)

This liberal praise of premarital sexual understanding is typical of Wollstonecraft's lack of hypocrisy in such matters, and her fearlessness in saying exactly what she means. It is a fearlessness matched by Godwin, when he made it clear in the *Memoirs* that it was just such a relationship that he and Mary shared in 1796.

Much at Copenhagen reminds her of her previous sojourn in France, of the fate of the émigrés, and the pretensions of rulers. At the Rosenberg Palace she reflects on the 'cabinets full of baubles and gems and swords' which once symbolized royal power in Denmark. 'It is a pity', she remarks mischievously, 'they do not lend them to the actors, instead of allowing them to perish ingloriously.' Yet with a very modern reflex, she also sees the historical interest of the building. 'Every object carried me back to past times, and impressed the manners of the age forcibly on my mind. In this point of view the preservation of old palaces, and their tarnished furniture, is useful; for they may be considered as historical documents.' She does not seem entirely immune, either, to the wayward charm of the 'large silver lions' mounted at the entrance to the banqueting rooms.

Several times she remarks that had she travelled in such primitive, or at least under-developed, societies before going to France, she would have taken a very different view of the French, and especially of the 'common people' and their behaviour during the Revolution. The concept of the 'Noble Savage' seems more than ever meaningless to her. What was achieved in France depended very greatly on the degree of sophistication which society in general had already reached. The 'virtues of a nation', she is more than ever convinced, 'bear an exact proportion to their scientific improvements'.

This reflection leads her to a view of travel which strikingly rejects the old eighteenth-century idea of the Grand Tour as an extension of classical education and the reverential study of the masterpieces of antiquity. Travel should be, she argues, a kind of sociological inquiry, which brings us a much more critical and comparative idea of how societies develop and progress. We should be interested in the primitive for the light it throws on the 'more polished'. We should be more forward-looking, and more conscious of social evolution. We should travel more intelligently and more self-critically. 'If travelling, as the completion of a liberal education, were to be adopted on rational grounds, the northern states ought to be visited before the more polished parts of Europe, to serve as the elements even of the knowledge of manners, only to be acquired by tracing the various shades in different countries' (Letter 19). This attitude foreshadows much of the more strictly anthropological travelling of the nineteenth century, with its emphasis on comparative studies of particular societies and climates.

## VII

### 'Demon Lover'

THE GENERAL TONE of philosophic detachment is hardly sustained through the final stages of the journey, which caused Wollstonecraft increasing frustration and exhaustion. The maid Marguerite, with her amusing Parisian chatter about German fashions, and 'the arch, agreeable vanity peculiar to the French' with which she retold her adventures at Gothenburg, had 'a *gaieté du coeur* worth all my philosophy', thought Wollstonecraft with a sigh. Her own ennui and depression returned with her approach to Hamburg. She could no longer avoid the realization that Gilbert Imlay had had no change of heart about meeting her, despite all her efforts in the Ellefsen affair. Her open appeals to Imlay dominate the last letters of the book, describing her arrival in the German city and her restless stay in the nearby suburb of Altona, determined to 'sail with the first fair wind for England'. She speaks of the 'cruellest of disappointments, last spring' – a barely veiled reference to her return to London from Paris, and the first suicide attempt – and describes herself as 'playing the child' and weeping at the recollection (Letter 22).

Her disenchantment is intense, though she still sees things (and smells them) vividly. Her vision of the river Elbe – with its ironic reference to 'treasure' – reminds us of the paintings of Caspar David Friedrich, with the symbolic overtones of 'Die Frau am Fenster', waiting perhaps for her lover:

> My lodgings at Altona are tolerably comfortable, though not in any proportion to the price I pay, but, owing to the present circumstances, all the necessaries of life are here extravagantly dear. Considering it as a temporary residence, the chief inconvenience of which, I am inclined to complain, is the rough streets that must be passed before Marguerite and the child can reach a level road.
>
> The views of the Elbe, in the vicinity of the town, are pleasant, particularly as the prospects here afford so little variety. I attempted to descend, and walk close to the water's edge, but there was no path, and the smell of glue, hanging to dry, an extensive manufactory of which is carried on close to the beach, I found extremely disagreeable. But to commerce every thing must give way, profit and profit are the only specu-lations – 'double – double, toil and trouble'. I have seldom entered a shady walk without being soon obliged to turn aside to make room for the rope-makers, and the only tree, I have seen, that appeared to be planted by the hand of taste, is in the churchyard, to shade the tomb of the poet Klopstock's wife.
>
> Most of the merchants have country houses to retire to, during the summer, and many of them are situated on the banks of the Elbe, where they have the pleasure of seeing the packet-boats arrive, the periods of most consequence to divide their week.

The moving picture, consisting of large vessels and small-craft, which are continually changing their position with the tide, renders this noble river, the vital stream of Hamburg, very interesting, and the windings have sometimes a very fine effect, two or three turns being visible, at once, intersecting the flat meadows: a sudden bend often increasing the magnitude of the river, and the silvery expanse, scarcely gliding, though bearing on its bosom so much treasure, looks for a moment, like a tranquil lake.

Nothing can be stronger than the contrast which this flat country and strand afford, compared with the mountains, and rocky coast, I have so lately dwelt so much among. In fancy I return to a favourite spot, where I seemed to have retired from man and wretchedness, but the din of trade drags me back to all the care I left behind, when lost in sublime emotions. Rocks aspiring towards the heavens, and, as it were, shutting out sorrow, surrounded me, whilst peace appeared to steal along the lake to calm my bosom, modulating the wind that agitated the neighbouring poplars. Now I hear only an account of the tricks of trade, or listen to the distressful tale of some victim of ambition. (Letter 24)

Her tirades against the commercial spirit here reach their climax. She sees Hamburg as 'an ill, close-built, swarming' city, and as a symbol of everything that has corrupted Imlay and come between them. She bitterly attacks the profit motive, and 'the mushroom fortunes' that have started up during the war. She excoriates a race of traders and dealers who are insolent, vulgar and 'seem of the species of the fungus' themselves. These are among her most savage passages. She describes these 'sordid accumulators of cent per cent' as the most degraded form of masculine ambition, brutishly opposed to everything that is finest and most progressive in the spirit of the age.

Mary Wollstonecraft is caught here in a terrible paradox, of course. For her own journey in search of the treasure ship had been undertaken partly for commercial reasons and to help Imlay in the recovery of a 'mushroom fortune' of war. Not only must she have felt betrayed by Imlay, but to some extent self-betrayed.

It is this, surely, that gives such despair to her final accusation, a passage which threatens to overturn the entire form of *A Short Residence*, transforming the voice of the literary traveller into that of the abandoned lover. Many previous passages in the book press towards this final act of self-exposure, giving what I have called the confessional tension to the entire work. But here it is most explicit, and most moving.

> Situation seems to be the mould in which men's characters are formed; so much so, inferring from what I have lately seen, that I mean not to be severe when I add, previously asking why priests are in general cunning, and statesmen false? that men entirely devoted to commerce never acquire, or lose, all taste and greatness of mind. An ostentatious display of wealth without elegance, and a greedy enjoyment of pleasure without sentiment, embrutes them till they term all virtues, of an heroic cast, romantic attempts at something above our nature, and anxiety about the welfare of others, a search after misery, in which we have no concern. But you will say that I am growing bitter, perhaps personal. Ah! shall I whisper to you – that you – yourself, are strangely altered, since you have entered deeply into commerce – more than you are aware of – never allowing yourself to reflect, and keeping your mind, or rather passions in a continual state of agitation – Nature has given you talents, which lie dormant, or are wasted in ignoble pursuits – you will rouse yourself, and shake off the vile dust that obscures you, or my understanding, as well as my heart, deceives me, egregiously – only tell me when? . . . Men are strange machines, and their whole system of morality is in general held together by one grand principle, which loses its force the moment they allow themselves to break with impunity over the bounds which secured their self-respect. A man ceases to love humanity, and then individuals, as he advances in the chase after wealth, as one clashes with his interest, the other with his pleasures: to business, as it is termed, every thing must give way, nay, is sacrificed, and all the endearing charities of citizen, husband, father, brother, become empty names. But – but what? Why, to snap the chain of thought, I must say farewell. Cassandra was

> not the only prophetess whose warning voice has been
> disregarded. How much easier is it to meet with love
> in the world, than affection! (Letter 23)

The distance between this, and the most passionate of the private letters, is less than 'the thickness of a piece of paper'.

The strangely desultory and gloomy note on which the book ends – passing in a single anxious paragraph from Hamburg to Dover – makes the reader more than ever curious to know what was the practical outcome of Mary Wollstonecraft's journey. What was the upshot of the Ellefsen affair? The way the book breaks off suggests that negotiations were broken off too. We know tantalizingly little. Nystrom was never able to establish if the crucial interview with Peder Ellefsen in Risor actually took place, or if the sympathetic Judge Wulfsberg of Tonsberg was able to arrange an out-of-court settlement. Yet there is one piece of evidence which might suggest that Wollstonecraft's efforts were by no means in vain. For the treasure ship itself was mysteriously recovered that autumn.

Swedish shipping records show that on 6 October 1795 a light cargo boat called the *Maria and Margaretha* was re-registered at Gothenburg as the property of Imlay's partner, Elias Backman. Its tonnage was slightly increased from that registered at Le Havre, which might perhaps mean that she had been refitted and re-rigged. It is not impossible that this could have been done at Ellefsen's expense, and thus represented some form of settlement and quid pro quo. The proximity of the re-registration date to that of Wollstonecraft's departure from Hamburg on the 17 September 1795 suggests that the two events were at least connected. The record is of course inconclusive, and the affair ends as mysteriously as it began. No authority knows what happened to the Bourbon plate. Yet the possibility that Mary Wollstonecraft had pulled off a most delicate piece of business negotiation, in a twilight world of wartime illegality, remains provokingly open. It seems quite within the scope of her extraordinary talents. One would certainly like to believe it.

The affair of the treasure ship is also important for the peculiar tension and atmosphere it lends her book. Though never once referred to explicitly in the text, it exerts its unseen pressure on the narrative of *A Short Residence*. It gives Wollstonecraft's travels their secret urgency, their sense of a mysterious, almost nightmare pursuit. It adds immeasurably to the feeling of inexplicable anxiety, of gloomy foreboding, which so marks Wollstonecraft's reflections on men and affairs and drives her continually to seek Romantic solace in the wilderness of the Scandinavian landscape, hoping to escape into a sublime vision of grand, impartial Nature: its magnificent forests, waterfalls and seashores, so remote from the petty concerns of men.

It also, if I am not mistaken, subtly alters our perception of Gilbert Imlay, her unnamed correspondent. Mary Wollstonecraft's unrequited love for him, increasingly desperate and bitter, already casts him in the role of Romantic villain, withholding his affections and cruel in his absence. (How just or unjust this picture was, in biographical terms, is a subject more fully explored in Godwin's *Memoirs*.) But the additional knowledge of his business interest in Wollstonecraft's expedition, adds – however unfairly – to our sense that he is exploiting her. In the context of the book, he becomes an almost demonic figure, driving her on to the limits of her physical, emotional and intellectual resources. I have already suggested that, in real life, I do not think this entirely reflected Imlay's attitude to his 'best friend and wife'. But in purely literary terms, the portrait she draws of him (always anonymously) is both haunting and convincing. It is a brilliant piece of emotional projection. Imlay is slowly transformed into her demon lover, and his shadow comes to brood over the Scandinavian countryside like something out of the Icelandic sagas or the enchanted folk music of Edvard Grieg. He tempts her over dizzy gulfs or the edge of precipitous waterfalls, he tortures her with the delusive promises of love and treasure and happiness. I do not wish to over-emphasize this aspect; it is nothing more than a mist that occasionally thickens round the largely factual and inquiring style of the narrative. But I think it is there, and that the later Romantic poets – especially Coleridge and Shelley – deeply and instinctively responded to it in their own work. And so did William Godwin.

## VIII

## 'Wild Geese'

*Letters Written during a Short Residence in Sweden, Norway, and Denmark* was published by Joseph Johnson in January 1796. It was the most popular book Wollstonecraft ever wrote, and she must have been delighted with its reception. After the miseries and desperation of the previous year, the suicide attempts and the end of her relationship with Imlay, it represented a personal triumph over her circumstances. The professional writer had regained her self-respect, and also found a new readership. The reviews were widespread and favourable. The book was swiftly translated into Dutch, German, Swedish and Portuguese. An American edition appeared in Wilmington, Delaware, through the good offices of her friend, the Irish revolutionary, Archibald Hamilton Rowan. A second edition was published by Johnson in 1802. The younger generation of writers were fascinated with it, and admiring references appear in the journals, poems or correspondence of Coleridge, Southey, Wordsworth and Hazlitt. Though only one further nineteenth-century edition was published (by Cassell's Library, 1886), its underground reputation remained secure. Shelley and Mary took a copy with them when they eloped to France in 1814, and I have recently discovered that Robert Louis Stevenson had a copy of the first edition when he went to Samoa in 1890, which still exists in a private collection, sporting his Vailima bookplate.

The book was generally admired in Godwin's circle, among those who knew the full circumstances surrounding its writing. Anna Seward and Mary Hays praised it, and the young Amelia Alderson, then an unknown and aspiring writer, wrote a fan letter which expressed the feelings of many of her younger contemporaries: 'I remember the time when my desire of seeing you was expressed by fear – but as soon as I read your letters from Norway, the cold awe which the philosopher has excited, was lost in the tender sympathy called forth by the woman. I saw nothing but the interesting creature of feeling and imagination.'

Some indeed felt that the feminist philosopher had sacrificed too much to 'feeling and imagination', and indulged rather shockingly in the modish melancholy and emotional self-revelations of the New Sensibility. (Though Godwin, as we have seen, turned this point to her literary advantage, by describing her in the *Memoirs* as a sort of 'female Werther'.) The acid and amusing French traveller-writer, Bernard de la Tocnaye, made several criticisms of her observations in his *Promenade en Suède*, and added that she had caused great offence to the ladies of Gothenburg by criticizing their bad teeth. But his greatest mockery was reserved for her highly emotional style in the description of landscape (failing to note that this is balanced by her accurate observations of natural phenomena). He summarizes in the following passage, which I have translated from his sprightly and sarcastic French:

> In her book [Mary Wollstonecraft] often makes use of that special new vocabulary which is deemed senti-mental, the grotesque linguistic garb adapted from Laurence Sterne, and the new-fangled 'moonlight and apparitions' style of writing. So we meet with nothing but cowbells a-tinkling on the hillsides – the waves mur-muring their melodies – the spirits of peace wandering o'er the hills – eternity in every moment – the sylphs dancing in the air – the dews gently falling – the cres-cent moon in the ethereal vault – and everything invit-ing her to turn aside her steps and wander afar, etc., etc., etc. In short, it's all modish nonsense. (*Une Promen-ade en Suède*, 1801, Vol. 1, pp. 25–9)

Well, there are no sylphs in Mary Wollstonecraft (though there are nymphs and one satyr). But it is true that her book was consciously literary in many aspects. This is partly what so excited her readers. She understood a great deal about the traditional genre of travel-writing, and had perceptively reviewed and criticized the short-comings of earlier works for Johnson's *Analytical*. These included the picturesque outpourings of Gilpin's *Tours*, Jean-Pierre Brissot's dry, topographical account of North America, and J. G. Forster's wild visions of the stars and icebergs of the southern seas (which fascinated Coleridge). Her private letters also show how fond she was of Sterne's *Sentimental Journey* and Rousseau's *Promenades*, and the image of her as a 'solitary walker' became a kind of private joke between her and Godwin. Throughout the text of *A Short Residence* she quotes freely from a small group of favourite eighteenth-century authors of an introspective kind – especially Thomas Gray, William Cowper and Edward Young of the *Night Thoughts*. She shows a marked tendency to identify with Shakespeare's Hamlet – that Danish Prince of melancholy. Many of her more empurpled landscape descriptions are direct extensions of Edmund Burke's doctrine of the sublime in nature, which so influenced the Romantic poets, reaching towards the fusion of the human spirit with some half-perceived and animating world-soul.

From the cliffs above Tonsberg she wrote:

> The fishermen were calmly casting their nets, whilst the seagulls hovered over the unruffled deep. Everything seemed to harmonize into tranquillity – even the mournful call of the bittern was in cadence with the tinkling bells on the necks of the cows, that, pacing slowly one after the other along an inviting path in the vale below, were repairing to the cottages to be milked. With what ineffable pleasure have I not gazed – and gazed again, losing my breath through my eyes – my very soul diffused itself in the scene – and, seeming to become all senses, glided in the scarcely-agitated waves, melted in the freshening breeze ... Imperceptibly recalling the reveries of childhood, I bowed before the awful throne of my Creator. (Letter 8)

One may have sympathy with de la Tocnaye's impatient 'etc., etc., etc.' reading such passages as these. Yet if we compare them with the kind of verse landscape description soon to be written by Wordsworth and, especially, Coleridge, one can appreciate the kind of impact they had. A masterly poem like 'This Lime Tree Bower My Prison', composed by Coleridge at Stowey in 1797, seems to show an almost direct influence in places:

> ... So my friend
> Struck with deep joy may stand, as I have stood,
> Silent with swimming sense, yea, gazing round
> On the wide landscape, gaze till all doth seem
> Less gross than bodily, and of such hues
> As veil the Almighty Spirit, when yet he makes
> Spirits perceive his presence.

The emotional drama of the book – the solitary, outcast woman dreaming of her faithless lover – also had its literary effect. There is some evidence to suggest that Wordsworth's narrative poem 'Ruth', written in Germany in 1799, drew on the story of Imlay and Wollstonecraft, as well as on his own abandonment of Annette Vallon. Ruth's lover is a 'youth from Georgia's shore', who eventually deserts her to return to his old, wild life 'with roving bands of Indians in the West'. Ruth ends her life as Wollstonecraft might have done, had it not been for Godwin. She lives in solitude, half maddened by her memories, 'an innocent life, yet far astray'.

But the strangest, and most intriguing, of these influences may have been on the composition of Coleridge's mysterious poem 'Kubla Khan' in the autumn of 1797. There is probably no other short poem in the English language which has been credited, not to say over-endowed, with so many possible literary sources – from Plato, Purchas and Milton onwards. To add one more may seem like an unfriendly act. Yet the great bibliographic scholar, John Livingston Lowes, has already remarked on several explicit verbal echoes between the two works in his study, *The Road to Xanadu* (1927). Wollstonecraft's description of the falls and cataracts at Frederikstad and those at Trollhattan shows close similarities to Coleridge's hypnotic description of the sacred river in Xanadu:

> And from this chasm, with ceaseless turmoil seething,
> As if this earth in fast thick pants were breathing,
> A mighty fountain momently was forced:
> Amid whose swift half-intermitted burst
> Huge fragments vaulted like rebounding hail . . .

Where Wollstonecraft wrote of 'the impetuous dashing of the rebounding torrent from the dark cavities', and later of 'the various cataracts, rushing from different falls, struggling with the huge masses of rock, and rebounding from the profound cavities . . . (so) that fancy might easily imagine a vast fountain, throwing up its waters from the very centre of the earth', it is hard not to believe that the great echo-chamber of Coleridge's mind did not half-hear those Scandinavian waters amidst so many others.

But there is also a broader, emotional resemblance between this central part of the poem and Mary Wollstonecraft's particular situation in Scandinavia which has not previously been noticed. The misery she feels in being separated from Imlay presses hard upon the narrative during the return journey from Risor to Gothenburg, and is never far from the surface of her thoughts. In Letter 13, for example, she suddenly breaks off a formal discussion of dishonesty and stealing among the Norwegians, to exclaim passionately, 'These are, perhaps, the vapourings of a heart ill at ease – the effusions of a sensibility wounded almost to madness. But enough of this – we will discuss the subject in another stage of existence – where truth and justice will reign. How cruel are the injuries which make us quarrel with human nature! – At present black melancholy hovers round my footsteps, and sorrow sheds a mildew over all the future prospects, which hope no longer gilds.'

This impression of 'a sensibility wounded almost to madness' by Imlay's cruelties is felt nowhere more strongly than in her meditations on the terrible but beautiful waterfalls at Frederikstad and Trollhattan. Gazing down into the rushing waters, she seems hypnotically drawn in, and her thoughts flit round the dark possibilities of suicide. 'The impetuous dashing of the rebounding torrent from the dark cavities which mocked the exploring eye, produced an equal activity in my mind: my thoughts darted from earth to heaven, and I asked myself why I was chained to life and its misery?' These reflections gain a grim authenticity from her subsequent attempt at watery suicide by throwing herself into the Thames from Putney Bridge in October 1795.

Coleridge was deeply touched by this picture of the solitary woman lamenting her lost lover in such a wild and distant place. It is an image which has something of the archetypal force of the old Border ballads which so fascinated him. (He records in his *Notebooks* that he intended to write to her about the need for 'religion'.) This must surely lead us to speculate whether the 'deep Romantic chasm' of 'Kubla Khan' was not imaginatively located, at least in part, in that far north country of Scandinavia, and whether Coleridge did not – at some level of poetic correspondence – have Mary Wollstonecraft in mind when he wrote those inspired and thrilling lines:

> A savage place! – as holy and enchanted
> As e'er beneath a waning moon was haunted
> By woman wailing for her demon lover!

There is of course no certainty in such matters, no certainty above all in a poem which was itself composed in a dream. But the ripples spread out intriguingly into the mainstream of nineteenth-century poetry.

How far, and how strangely, that seed was sometimes scattered may be seen in one last and wholly unexpected literary tribute. In 1816 the Professor of Moral Philosophy at Edinburgh University published a poem entitled 'The Wanderer in Norway'. Dr Thomas Brown was not a scholar to whom the principles of feminism would normally have appealed, yet he was so captivated by the figure of Mary Wollstonecraft on her travels, that the whole work is inspired by her example. In the Preface to his poem, he movingly describes *A Short Residence*:

> It is a volume which cannot be read without interest –
> in some degree a picture of the country through which
> she passed, and of the manners of its inhabitants – but
> still more as a picture of her who beheld what she
> describes, with feelings of which no traveller before her
> has left a record, and which few, if it is to be trusted,
> are again to have the sad fortune of recording. Mary
> was more than a sentimental traveller, she was truly an
> impassioned traveller – a traveller suffering deeply, and
> seeing Nature in those wildly contrasted views, with
> which Misery looks on it, in the moments of its greatest
> anguish, and in those strange gleams of hope, which
> sometimes fling a brightness more than natural on
> every object, – even when Misery herself is the gazer.
> (*The Wanderer in Norway and Other Poems*, 1816,
> pp. 21–2)

Here it is clear that Mary Wollstonecraft has already been almost completely transformed into a Romantic heroine, even of the Byronic type. This is fully amplified in the course of Dr Brown's verses, which picture her arriving off the coast of Norway in a midnight storm, standing 'dim on the prow . . . with bosom bare', her 'loose tresses' flying in the wind, and her 'vacant eye' conscious only of the gusts of passion raging within her wounded heart.

> As though with passion's fiercer swell opprest,
> She sought the tempest to her burning breast.

Brown had responded to her work, like so many others, in terms of its confessional value, but she saw her whole life as a moral exemplum, with a purely tragic significance. For him, the great experiment of Romanticism was essentially a noble failure, and Mary Wollstonecraft, with her 'sad fortune', was one of its most tragic victims whose time had not yet come.

But we can now see how very differently it must have spoken to William Godwin, in 1796. Mary's revelations must have sped as directly as any arrow to the Philosopher's heart. Originally addressed to one lover, Gilbert Imlay, the faithless, by an exquisite irony it found another, Godwin, the wise and faithful. How many passages must have seemed like letters written for him alone, holding out the promise of their great and simple experiment in living and sincerity:

> I cannot write composedly – I am every instant sinking into reveries – my heart flutters, I know not why. Fool! It is time thou were at rest.
>
> Friendship and domestic happiness are continually praised, yet how little is there of either in the world, because it requires more cultivation of mind to keep awake affection, even in our own hearts, than the common run of people suppose. Besides, few like to be seen as they really are, and a degree of simplicity, and of undisguised confidence, which, to uninterested observers, would almost border on weakness, is the charm, nay the essence of love or friendship: all the bewitching graces of childhood again appearing. As objects merely to exercise my taste, I therefore like to see people together who have an affection for each other, every turn of their features touches me, and remains pictured on my imagination in indelible characters. Why am I talking of friendship, after which I have had such a wild-goose chase – I thought only of telling that the crows, as well as wild-geese, are here birds of passage. (Letter 12)

*A Short Residence* may be said to have entered into the literary mythology of Romanticism within a single generation. Its combination of progressive social views – Wollstonecraft's 'favourite subject of contemplation, the future improvement of the world' –

with melancholy self-revelation and heart-searching, came to have an almost symbolic force within that extraordinary circle of poets, travellers, philosophers and autobiographers. Mary Wollstonecraft projected herself through the book as a model of the literary woman: audacious, intelligent, independent and free-thinking, and yet, equally, one who suffers endlessly and inevitably in a society which is not yet honest and just enough to accept her for what she is. The model, and the book, were to be largely forgotten in Victorian England, and to disappear for over a hundred years, except where fleetingly recalled by such rare woman traveller-writers as Isabella Bird and Mary Kingsley. But the seed was sown, and like Shelley's 'Ashes and sparks, my words among mankind', they waited to burn up bright again in a different, freer world.

IX

'The New Empire of Feeling'

IF THE HISTORY OF human affections can be said to have its epochs and turning-points, like those of science and politics and literature, then the liaison between Mary Wollstonecraft and William Godwin was surely one of the most significant. Their brief union marks the beginning of a new phase of human aspirations, as certainly as any historic treaty or geographical discovery of some *terra nova* over the horizon.

Their love story can itself be seen as a new kind of journey, and the long-sought treasure ship as containing a different sort of gold.

Virginia Woolf wrote in 1932: 'Mary's life had been an experiment from the start, an attempt to make human conventions conform more closely to human needs. And her marriage with William Godwin was only a beginning, all sorts of things were to follow after ... As we read her books and letters, and listen to her arguments and consider her experiments, above all that most fruitful experiment, her relation with Godwin, and realise the high-handed and hot-blooded manner in which she cut her way to the quick of life, one form of immortality is hers undoubtedly: she is alive and active, she argues and experiments, we hear her voice and trace her influence even now among the living . . .' (*The Common Reader: Second Series*, 1932, p. 163).

Even at the time, their marriage was understood as something symbolic. To the forces of reaction, as represented by the *Anti-Jacobin Magazine*, and now strongly in the ascendant, it was of course an unholy alliance – atheism, anarchism, feminism, French Revolutionary politics and free love, all brought together in one unseemly bed, and now swiftly and properly punished by Divine Providence. But to the small group of beleaguered radicals, to the larger body of liberal opinion, and to many of the younger writers of the day, it was a kind of culmination: a consecration of that New Sensibility in which the rational hopes of the Enlightenment were catalysed by that element of imagination and personal rebellion which we now know as Romanticism.

Godwin and Wollstonecraft were seen to bring together, through their books, their complementary views, their experiment in living, two most powerful strands in the tradition of progressive reform. They were seen as transitional figures, pointing towards a freer life and a more just society, and the new 'empire of feeling'. Coleridge, with his genius for identifying the abstract principle embodied in human affairs, put his finger on this in one of his brilliant, conversational asides recorded by the young William Hazlitt as they walked together in the West Country in 1797. 'He asked me', recalls Hazlitt, 'if I had ever seen Mary Wollstonecraft, and I said I had once for a few moments, and that she seemed to me to turn off Godwin's objections to something she advanced with quite a playful, easy air. He replied, that this was only one instance of the ascendancy which people of imagination exercised over those of mere intellect' ('My First Acquaintance with Poets' in *The Liberal*, No. 3, 1823). Coleridge would alter his views on Godwin's 'mere' intellect, but the point was well made. Here was a significant new marriage between Imagination and Reason.

Both Wollstonecraft's *A Short Residence* and Godwin's *Memoirs* are, in my view, crucial documents of this historic moment of transition and the Romantic renewal of hope and feeling, but their literary quality has never been properly recognized before. They are also records of the intense disruption it caused. They are full of pain, discontent and frustrated happiness. Though adopting different literary forms – the travel book and the biography – they are both essentially confessional. They are most intimately linked by the fact that they both give us portraits of Mary Wollstonecraft, but seen from the two distinct and opposite poles of life-writing: the autobiography and the biography, self-revelation and the objective character-study. These correspond wonderfully to the natural gifts of their authors. Yet both are alike in the urgency of their testament, swiftly composed at times of grief, when many of the barriers of reticence were down.

The result seems to me to be nothing less than a revolution in literary genres. Originally cast within certain well-accepted eighteenth-century conventions – the topographical travelogue and the pious family memoir – they explode these at a number of significant points through sheer intensity of feeling and sincerity of emotion. Wollstonecraft does this through a new wilderness and richness of emotional rhetoric, Godwin through a new frankness and understatement. Both – paradoxically – are characteristic of Romanticism.

For the student of literature – and we are all in some sense that – I would put my claim for these beloved and unjustly neglected works precisely. Mary Wollstonecraft's is the most imaginative English travel book since Sterne's *A Sentimental Journey* (1768). Godwin's is the most significant and revolutionary short biography since Johnson's *Life of Richard Savage* (1744). Both mark the shift, as well as anything can, from an eighteenth-century to a modern world of feeling. Both bring the inner life of a human being significantly closer to our own experience of it.

For the student of love, I would add in my modest role as biographer: *'bon voyage, et bonne chance'*.

# V

## Shelley's Ghost

# INTRODUCTION

IN THE INTERVAL, so to speak, Coleridge had arrived. His was the richest, most complicated biography I had ever attempted. The quiet, contemplative view of his study window overlooking the Heath was wholly illusory. One of the greatest intellectuals of the Romantic age, Coleridge led a life which also revealed itself as an emotional maelstrom: the passionate friendship with Wordsworth, the broken marriage with Sara, the unrequited love affair with Asra, the tragedy of his son Hartley, the struggles with opium addiction, the political manoeuvring with revolutionary politics, the literary plagiarism, the soul-searching and spiritual breakdowns, the dreams and the nightmares, the pain and the puns, and always the ceaseless and wonderful *talk*. '*Avec Monsieur Coleridge*,' said Madame de Staël, '*c'est tout à fait un monologue.*'

Sailing through that Ancient Mariner storm, holding course over that 'trackless ocean', was to occupy me for some fifteen exhausting and exhilarating years. But while travelling in the phosphorescent wake of his biography – in London, the English West Country, the Lake District, Scotland, Germany, Malta and Italy – the ghosts of past subjects would sometimes rise up and call for my attention back at home. The most powerful presence was undoubtedly that of Shelley, a curiously mischievous one too.

Shelley never met Coleridge, although he spent the winter of 1811 waiting in a cottage outside Keswick for the great man to arrive. This non-meeting was one of the first temptations I ever had to invent a biographical scene: several local Keswick newspapers wrote about Shelley's wild household – dancing naked round a bonfire, firing pistols in the night – and surely one file describing the historic encounter, 'Mr Coleridge Rebukes An Atheist', might have been overlooked? But Shelley did successfully ambush me on a number of occasions, two of which I include here.

He sprang out first from a battered old leather suitcase, lined in Regency polka-dot. The suitcase belonged to Lord Byron's friend Scrope Davies, and was unearthed from the cellars of a Pall Mall bank. The scholars were ravished by the manuscripts it contained – two completely unknown poems by Shelley, among much else – and I was called in to give a biographical opinion. But this was a case of pure sidetracking. What came to fascinate me was Scrope Davies's own story, a perfect example of the Romantic past lying in wait, hidden in the shadows of greater reputations, and yet crying out to be told. I wrote it up for an American magazine, who then wondered if there was a whole book to be done about Romantic gamblers, 'from Davies to Dostoyevsky, say?'. But this was too far, even for me.

Yet the possibility of lost manuscripts, or the urge to invent them, remained. What tempting gaps in the record could be filled, what ghosts could be summoned! I am sure one day biographers will attempt this, if only in homage to W. S. Landor's *Imaginary Conversations*. Shelley's last days in Italy came back to me. There was a third person who drowned in his yacht in the Gulf of Spezia, the 'English boatboy' Charles Vivian.

Suppose Vivian had kept a diary which survived the wreck, and which turned up in another trunk in a bank in Livorno? So I actually wrote this diary, in a little green morocco notebook, a pure biographer's fiction. Yet in the end it seemed to answer none of my questions, and I did not attempt to publish it. But finally, in the bi-centenary of Shelley's birth, I turned again to radio and transformed my nagging speculations into a drama. 'To The Tempest Given' contains no forgery, and is accurately based on the varied accounts of the last three weeks of Shelley's life at the Casa Magni in 1822. Every word that Shelley speaks has textual authority, only the voice of 'Holmes' sometimes has another hidden identity, that of the lost Charles Vivian.

# SCROPE'S LAST THROW

SCROPE BERDMORE DAVIES, whose remarkable trunk caused considerable excitement in London literary circles this winter, was a university don and a society gambler – a combination of *métiers* that would have interested Dostoyevsky, and which certainly fascinated Lord Byron. His strange dragonfly career (1783–1852), in some ways typical of the wits and dandies of the English Regency, seems to have hung on the fall of a card at Watier's Club, or the fall of a hoof at Newmarket; and it ended abruptly and tragically in his thirty-seventh year, with spectacular financial ruin leading not to suicide but to a long, dismal and penurious exile in the anonymous, small seaside hotels of northern France. Byron himself observed, helplessly, that 'such a man's destiny ought not to be in a dice-box'. But in a dice-box it always remained. The curious thing is that Scrope may have won on his last throw.

Up to now, astonishingly little has been known about Scrope considering he was one of Byron's closest friends ('one of the cleverest men I ever knew, in conversation') and thus belongs to a period of literary history that has been more minutely excavated by scholars – English, American, Italian and German – than any other, including Shakespeare's. No one has written his life; no one has collected his letters; no one possesses even a picture of him. The exhaustive *Dictionary of National Biography* honours him with no entry; and the author-authoritative *Byron's Letters and Journals*, edited by Leslie A. Marchand, grants him but one footnote, in which it is recorded that he was educated at Eton and had 'an irresistible stammer'. Uncertain monument.

Yet Scrope was undoubtedly one of Byron's most important

confidants up to 1816. He was part of the inner circle, with Hobhouse the future politician and Kinnaird the banker, when Byron
was at Cambridge; and is credited with, among other things, the
discovery that Byron slept *en papillote*, that is to say, in paper curlers
('Aha! Byron I have at last caught you acting the part of Sleeping
Beauty'). It was Scrope who provided Byron with £4,000 (about
£80,000 today) to finance his first journey to Greece and Turkey
in 1809, upon which Byron's early literary successes – *Childe Harold
I and II, The Giaour, The Bride of Abydos* – entirely depended. It was
to Scrope that Byron turned on the deaths of his mother and his
Cambridge friend Charles Skinner Matthews, in one terrible week
of August 1811; and it was to Scrope that he wrote from Calais:
'Sincerely, you are among one of the few things in England that
I leave with regret, and shall return to with pleasure.'

Scrope, with Hobhouse, was the only London friend invited to
visit the Byron–Shelley circle in the famous summer in Switzerland
of 1816; and it was to Scrope that Byron entrusted a fair copy of
*Childe Harold III* to carry back to London for publication by
Murray, together with secret presents of rock crystal for his
beloved half-sister, Augusta Leigh. It was a commission that Scrope
undertook, but did not entirely discharge, as we shall see. Finally,
it was in nostalgic recollection of Scrope's incurable wit and feck-
lessness that Byron perpetrated one of his most delightful bad
puns which incidentally established for posterity the correct pro-
nounciation of that bent, Dickensian name: 'Tell me of Scrope –
is he as full of "fierce embraces" as when I last saw him? – I wish
he would marry and beget some Scrooples; it is a pity the dynasty
should not be prolonged.'

Alas, the dynasty was never founded. Thirty-two years after his
enforced exile in 1820, Scrope Davies died forgotten, intestate
and scroopleless, in Paris in May 1852. He was remembered only
by one garrulous memoir writer of the period, a certain Capt.
Rees-Howell Gronow, who recalled in an uncharacteristically
gentle passage of his *Reminiscences*:

> Scrope Davies bore with perfect resignation the loss of
> the wealth he had once possessed; and though his
> annual income (provided by his faithful Cambridge col-
> lege) was very limited, he made no complaints of pov-
> erty. He daily sat himself down on a bench in his garden

of the Tuileries, where he received those whose
acquaintance he desired, and then returned to his
study, where he wrote notes upon the men of his day,
which have unfortunately disappeared.

Those precious notes have yet to be rediscovered – though
I learn that the librarians at King's College are now hopefully
ransacking the archives – but the forgotten trunk, never mentioned by Scrope himself, reappeared 124 years later in the private
deposit vault of Barclay's Bank. To understand how this extraordinary find occurred, it is necessary to recall the circumstances of
Scrope's ruin. First, consider the famous trunk itself.

It is actually rather small: a battered leather chest perhaps three
feet wide and one foot deep, with a central lock and a faint smell
of old riding boots. It is studded with brass rivets along the leading
edges and around the joint of the lid; the studs elegantly follow
the leather crescents where the corners are reinforced, and form
a diamond pattern on the front. The lid opens low down, so the
trunk seems to split apart like a drinks hamper or a pistol case –
both pleasant associations for Scrope. Inside it is sportively lined
in Regency polka-dot, and the lid is held by two silk stays. A
decorative label, like an *ex libris* slip, is stuck to the back panel.

Everything that Scrope valued, and much that he did not, was
hurled into the trunk during the space of one evening's hectic
packing in his Cambridge rooms in January 1820. The scene was
later described by a historian of King's College, W. H. Tucker:

> He had possessed himself, as admitted and known in
> College, by slow – or other – degrees of some £20,000
> at Newmarket; and as was most natural in betting men
> tried to double it, or more: in modern phrase, he rather
> plunged. On a certain evening he came into his rooms
> rather hurriedly, and with Mrs Hazel's help began to
> pack up his personal effects. 'What is it, Sir?' she
> enquired. 'Ruin! I've lost all I had, and as much more;
> and must leave tonight. Tomorrow will be too late.'

Scrope fled by the overnight coach to London, deposited the
trunk at his bankers, Morland, Ransom & Co. of No. 1 Pall Mall
East (where Byron also banked, and Kinnaird was senior partner),
and departed into obscurity: some accounts say Calais, some say

Ostend, some say Bruges. Thereafter, he never dared to return to England for fear of arrest, bankruptcy, public disgrace and inevitable imprisonment. In the end, he may have forgotten about the contents of the trunk, or, a more tantalizing possibility, he simply could never risk reclaiming it. After Byron's death at Missolonghi in 1824, and the scandalous success of Thomas Moore's *Life and Letters* (1830), the temptation to reclaim it would have been agonizing. But the trunk was out of reach – though not out of play.

Time passed, as it does in England. Morland, Ransom & Co. merged with several other private banks to form Barclay's. The building became Kinnaird House. But for 100 years, the old private deposit vault was undisturbed. In 1922 the trunk was restacked and relabelled, a little vaguely, S. Davies, but still it was not opened. Only in November 1976 did a literary-minded director of Barclay's, Christopher Norman-Butler, finally alight once more upon the chest and guess at its potentialities. The present John Murray of Albermarle Street, the direct descendant of Byron's original publisher, and Daniel Waley of the Department of Western Manuscripts of the British Library, were immediately called in; and two distant kinsmen of Scrope's were approached in confidence. These were Martin R. Davies, a solicitor from Bristol, and Bevis Hillier, an art collector and critic, who happens also to be a regular contributor to the London *Times*. At a dinner party of Byron scholars at the Athenaeum Club on December 14, heady rumours buzzed across the smoked trout and white Burgundy, and Mr Murray had a peculiar glint in his eye. But it was not until 20 December that the story finally broke in an old-fashioned, front-page literary scoop in the London *Times*, brilliantly executed by Hillier, and copied next morning by the *New York Times*. Leading articles appeared throughout the English-speaking press, the television filmed Mr Norman-Butler handing over the trunk (now empty) to Lord Eccles of the British Library, and Lord Eccles handing the trunk back (still empty) to Mr Norman-Butler for another go, and the BBC World Service network carried the discovery as its premier item. Scrope was news!

What did the trunk contain? Martin Davies well described its chaotic interior, so redolent of poor Scrope's last hectic hours in

England, as 'a sort of miniature Pompeii of the late Regency period'. The first impression was of scores and scores of unpaid bills and betting slips pinned on wire desk spikes; then an immaculate pair of white kid evening gloves; several embossed invitations from Lady Holland and the Duke of Wellington; letters and drawings from Scrope's younger brother, Decimus, who guarded Napoleon on his last journey to St Helena (another exile); and a packet of love letters from Lady Frances Webster, a noted society beauty of the day, an early flame of Byron's, and a later mistress of the Iron Duke's. In one letter, a perfectly preserved and lustrous lock of her hair.

Then there were the dandy's tailor's bills – a pair of red lounging slippers, a pair of white tennis shoes, twelve guineas' worth of shirts from C. H. Hemans, half-a-dozen Indian muslin handkerchiefs; traders' advertisements for expensive wine and cheap brandy ('Fine cognac at 9 shillings a gallon'); small account slips from Watier's Club for dining and gambling; collections of after-dinner jokes and aphorisms, both in English and Latin, all carefully prepared, like Oscar Wilde's, for 'spontaneous' repartee over the seltzer. More letters, in a jumble, from Thomas Moore, from Hobhouse, from Augusta Leigh. Then the legal documents, like a gathering tide, showing Scrope fighting at the Court of Common Pleas in 1818 for sums over £7,000; and the sinister shoal of tiny personal betting books, annotated with a minuteness that is already obsessional.

Finally, buried beneath this jackdaw heap, the sensational prizes: first, twenty unknown letters from Byron to Scrope written through the decade 1809–19, the seals torn open and the flakes of red wax still lying in the fresh folds. Second, a scarlet morocco-bound notebook containing Byron's lost copy of *Childe Harold III*, which Scrope had evidently kept for himself instead of delivering to Murray in 1816, and marked with Scrope's proud annotation: 'This Ms was given by Lord Byron to Scrope Davies at Geneva, September 2nd 1816.' (Fortunately, Shelley did deliver the fair copy Byron had given him that same summer.) Third – and perhaps most surprising of all – a pair of matching notebooks, bound in almost identical blue-and-orange marbled board, emanating from the Shelley circle. One contains a fair copy of Byron's 'Prisoner of Chillon', beautifully written out in round, childish hand by Claire Clairmont – Mary Shelley's stepsister, and Byron's mistress of that summer, aged eighteen, desperately in love, and so anxious to prove her worth. The other contains fair copies of four Shelley poems of the Swiss period: two unknown sonnets (one fragmented, the other entitled 'To Laughter'), the famous 'Hymn to Intellectual Beauty', and the philosophical poem 'Mont Blanc' with Shelley's annotation, 'Scene – Pont Pellisier in the Vale of Joux'.

This fantastic hoard has stunned scholars and antiquarians, and full assessment will obviously take most of this year. What are the manuscripts worth (a single copy of Byron's 'Beppo' was sold at Sotheby's for £55,000 – about $94,000 – in 1976)? Where should they be kept? What new light do they throw on the Byron–Shelley circle in 1816? What do they tell us about the Regency dandies? The answers to such immediate questions will only be pieced together slowly. It is not even clear yet to whom the trunk actually belongs, but for the time being it has been put on loan to the British Library.

Some perspectives, and also some puzzles, are emerging. The copyright of the twenty new Byron letters lies in the control and keeping of John Murray, but extensive extracts are being published by the London Byron Society *Journal* this spring, when some judgement of their value will be possible. It is already evident that Scrope's place in Byron's emotional development, his role of model dandy and confidential rake, will be assured by them. Those letters written from Italy also contain strikingly bitter revelations of Byron's attitude to English society and his own exile. Meditating in Venice on the rumours concerning his estranged wife and his half-sister that had originally driven him abroad, Byron remarks cuttingly, 'If they were *true* I was unfit for England, if *false* England is unfit for me.' He confides to Scrope in a mood of weary sarcasm:

> You recollect that with the exception of a few friends (yourself among the foremost of those who staid by me) I was detested and blackened by all . . . nothing can ever atone to me for the atrocious caprice – the unsupported – almost unasserted – the kind of hinted persecution – and shrugging Conspiracy – of which I was attempted to be made the victim – if the tables were to be turned – if they were to decree me all the

columns of the Morning Post – and all the tavern-signs
of Wellington – I would not accept them.

The full text of letters such as these, when they finally appear,
will obviously give a fascinating, if melancholy, picture of Byron's
home thoughts from abroad, and explain something of the mood
in which he transformed himself into Don Juan, the greatest of
all poetic dandies, the dandy adrift, the dandy who's gone to the
devil.

The 'Childe Harold' notebook, for all its value, perhaps tells
us more about Scrope's character than Byron's poetry. Jerome
McGann, of Johns Hopkins University, who is preparing an
exhaustive new edition of the poetry for Oxford University Press,
flew to London to examine the manuscript as it was being cata-
logued. He told me, as we stood among the debris of the trunk,
drinking tea and reading Scrope's wine lists, that his first impression was that the new readings of the poem would amount to little
more than variorum footnotes, with minor alterations of adjectives
and punctuation. The notebook does contain Byron's amusing
political footnotes, which were later suppressed. Scholars are however naturally cautious, and McGann's final assessment will appear
when his great opus, begun in 1970, finally surfaces.

Caution is justified. When the 'Mont Blanc' notebook was
initially put on public display in mid-January, it was naturally
assumed that all the poems were in Shelley's own hand. But
another eagle-eyed American scholar, Judith Chernaik, quickly
spotted that this was not so. Timothy Burnet of the Manuscript
Department swiftly brought out a pile of contemporary holo-
graphs by Shelley, Mary Shelley and Claire Clairmont, and a somewhat bizarre but very English kind of conference was instantly
convened over the glass display cases as the library was closing for
the night, amidst a small posse of anxious, peak-capped attendants, indulgently checking their watches and the priceless manuscripts in benign alternation. The revised opinion now stands that
the first three poems are in Mary's hand, and the fourth, 'Mont
Blanc', in Shelley's.

This notebook remains the most puzzling of all. How on earth
did Shelley's poems come to be in Scrope's trunk at all? Scrope
and Shelley were not friends; nor would Byron have dreamed of

sending Shelley's notebook back to Murray with Scrope. Did Scrope somehow purloin it, and keep it like the 'Child Harold' and 'Chillon' notebooks? Or was there some genuine muddle-up with Claire's copy, which looks so like it (both notebooks, incidentally, carry English watermarks for 1813)? It is intriguing.

One interesting possibility is that Mary copied out Shelley's Swiss poems at Byron's own request, as their summer together drew to a close, so that the notebook might form a kind of literary souvenir; and that Byron subsequently allowed it to fall into Scrope's clutches. This speculation serves to draw attention to the best of the two new sonnets, 'To Laughter'. Its subject – an attack on the cynical worldly humour, the sort that 'mocks at truth and Innocency', frequently indulged in by Byron's friends – may have been of special interest, or relevance, to Scrope. Indeed, it may conceivably have been about him.

Scrope and Hobhouse arrived at Byron's lakeside residence, the Villa Diodati, on August 26 1816, and their stay overlapped with Shelley's by three days. We know from Mary's *Journal* that Shelley spent at least two evenings in their company. The temperamental differences between Shelley and Scrope would have been very great – the earnest atheist meeting the roué – and it is not difficult to imagine Shelley's sonnet as an 'occasional' piece dashed off after such an encounter. It certainly has the sense of a violent personal attack. Here it is, transcribed from the manuscript:

### To Laughter

Thy friends were never mine thou heartless fiend:
 Silence and solitude & calm & storm,
Hope, before whose veiléd shrine all spirits bend
 In worship, & the rainbow vested form
 Of conscience, that within thy hollow heart
Can find no throne – the love of such great powers
 Which has requited mine in many hours
 Of loneliness, thou ne'er hast felt; depart!
Thou canst not bear the moon's great eye, thou fearest
A fair child clothed in smiles – aught that is high
 Or good or beautiful – Thy voice is dearest
 To those who mock at truth & Innocency.
I, now alone, weep without shame to see
How many broken hearts lie bare to thee.

The most soaring line in this rather tortuous poem, 'Thou canst not bear the moon's great eye', lends the whole piece the silvery atmosphere of a nocturnal soliloquy, and one recalls Shelley's meditative midnight walks down the little track through the vine fields that linked Byron's villa with his own cottage of Montalegré. Shelley's high-minded defence of 'aught that is high or good or beautiful' is typical of his immature Platonism, and would have tickled Scrope. It is also possible to see a reference to Claire in the 'fair child clothed with smiles': for Claire, though pregnant, was already in the role of Byron's cast-off mistress and may well have been the butt of some sly remarks at the Diodati ('How many broken hearts lie bare to thee').

Shelley's general complaint in the sonnet is that none of the 'great powers' which he himself worships – Silence, Solitude, Hope and Conscience – finds a place in Laughter's 'hollow heart'. It is an interesting coincidence that this sentiment finds an exact echo in Byron's own, slightly ambivalent, response to Scrope's indefatigable wit. When Scrope came to visit him at Newstead Abbey, after the death of their mutual friend Matthews in 1811, Byron wrote:

> Davies has been here, and has invited me to Cambridge for a week in October, so that, peradventure, we may encounter glass to glass. His gaiety (death cannot mar it) has done me service; but, after all, ours was a hollow laughter. You will write to me? I am solitary.

Did Byron perhaps confide something of the same feeling to Shelley in 1816 at the Diodati? And was the sonnet the result? It is certainly a possibility.

Yet this is all speculation. How and why Scrope got his hands on the little notebook, whether Byron was malicious or merely muddled in letting him see it, and how the angry sonnet 'To Laughter' came to disappear without trace in Shelley's (or Mary's) other papers must all remain mysteries. Some fuller explanation may be forthcoming when Dr Chernaik and Mr Burnet publish their complete transcription of the notebook in *The Times Literary Supplement* this spring.

For scholars, as indeed for bankers and antiquarians, the cardinal interest of the trunk must lie in the minute evaluation of the

Byron and Shelley prizes therein. But for a biographer, a rather different kind of enchantment flits and winks through the sad ruins of that paper Pompeii. All mysteries, all clues, all speculations seem to lead inexorably back to the elusive character and career of Scrope himself. Beside the 'Mont Blanc' notebook, now enshrined in its glass case, lies a tiny, ragged-edged betting book, much thumbed and covered in columns of jottings. Bend closer; the ink is a little faded, the writing a little ... tipsy. 'Won at shooting – 5 shillings. Lost at billiards – 10 shillings. Lost at fishing – 5 shillings. Won at Throwing Stones – 18 shillings. Lost at *chicken* driving – £1.' It is not much of a poem, perhaps, but it is still a vivid revelation of poor Scrope's obsessions and contradictions.

In his own way, Scrope was as much of a Romantic extremist, as much a representative of the 'spirit of the age' as his more illustrious companions. When we discover that Byron calculated that his friend was still worth £50,000 in 1816 (say, a round million pounds in contemporary currency) the suddenness and stunning size of his ruin within four years takes on something like magnificence, something that Gatsby might have felt 'truly grand'.

Moreover, his wit – by all accounts a fine, high-strung mixture of academic pedantry, gaming slang, religiosity and smoking-room farce – was obviously memorable (if only as Shelley remembered it) and renowned throughout London and Cambridge, while his sense of social deportment and rigid code of honour (which extended to duelling, if not to manuscripts) had a far finer tone than the mannered punctiliousness of the average St James's dandy. His exile, like Beau Brummell's, was a last gesture of good taste. It is touching, in the circumstances, that Byron chose to praise him in the following terms: 'Whatever Davies *says* I will *swear* to – and *that's* more than *he* would.'

Morally, Scrope was flawed, to an almost tragic degree, and it is this darker dimension that the minutiae of his trunk seem to establish for the first time. His gambling, like his drinking, has a kind of remorseless self-destructiveness that one can see piling up, bet by bet, bill by bill, debt by debt, in the account books. Yet he remained curiously lucid about his own fate, curiously self-mocking and detached, so that when the end came he could accept it with a good grace, almost a spirituality, that Gronow seems to hint at years later in the Tuileries gardens.

Two anecdotes – one from Byron, one from Gronow – sum up this quality, this scroopishness, shall we say, better than all others. The first dates from 1814, when Byron and he dined one night together at the Cocoa-Tree. Byron recounts:

> Sat from six till midnight – drank between us one bottle of champagne and six of claret, neither of which wines ever affect me. Offered to take Scrope home in my carriage; but he was typsy and pious, and I was obliged to leave him on his knees praying to I know not what purpose or pagod.

It is an expressive picture, Scrope Davies, drunk but still elegant, kneeling by a clubland dining table, silently saying his prayers as the servants carried away the bottles, snuffed the candles, and counted the small change.

The second anecdote has no date, but belongs perhaps to Scrope's last years in England, for it has a sense of imminent departure about it. In a single night of cards, Scrope had succeeded in entirely dispossessing a young aristocrat of everything he owned. As dawn filtered through the curtains,

> the poor youth sank down upon a sofa, in abject misery, when he reflected that he was a beggar; for he was on the point of marriage. Scrope Davies, touched by his despair, entered into conversation with him, and ended by giving him back the whole of his losses, upon a solemn promise that he never would play again. The only thing that Scrope retained of his winnings was one of the little carriages of that day, called a *dormeuse*, from its being fixed up with a bed; for he said, 'When I travel in it I shall sleep the better for having acted rightly.'

The story is exquisitely scroopish in its blend of kindness and cynicism, the don and the gambler ironically reconciled; and yet it is also shadowed by the same tragic quality, the sense of the inevitable, lonely, ruined exile awaiting him – in the long years of shiftless beds in small, squalid, foreign hotels, alone with his debts and his memories.

Now finally he has returned with his trunk: his last *dormeuse*, his 'dice-box', his dustbin, his monument. And he seems, in the end, to have won: his story is the talk of clubs and common rooms once more, and his name has come home from obscurity. A long-planned biography by Hillier and Davies will no doubt be with us soon; the letters will take their place in Professor Marchand's great edition in a fine flurry of appendices; and his position in the Romantic saga will be assured. Moreover, there is one other circumstance that would have pleased Scrope. The entire contents of his trunk will probably prove to be worth between one and two million dollars: so, in the end, he doubled his stakes and swept the board.

# TO THE TEMPEST GIVEN

*A radio-play based on Shelley's last days in Italy*

*wind, storm and sea*

SHELLEY

> The breath whose might I have invoked in Song
> Descends on me: my spirit's bark is driven
> Far from the shore, far from the trembling throng
> Whose sails were never to the Tempest given;
> The massy earth and spheréd skies are riven!
> I am born darkly, fearfully afar . . .

*fades to seaside, gulls, modern children on holiday*

HOLMES

. . . Yes, my 'spirit's bark'. Shelley always loved boats. At Eton, at Oxford, on Highgate ponds it was paper boats, at Pisa a skiff. That's what brought him to San Terenzo in April 1822, a sailing holiday really, far away from the crowds, the 'trembling throng'. He rented a beach house, Casa Magni, right at the sea's edge, miles from anywhere.

It still exists: seven white-washed arches below, four white-washed rooms above, and a long open balcony directly overlooking the surf: a primitive, magical place. Shelley loved the whole set-up. He had a 24-foot yacht especially built for him at the naval dockyards up the coast at Genoa. Typically it had too much sail and too much ballast: very fast and very unstable.

SHELLEY

Like Anacreon's swallow, I have left my Nile, and have taken up my summer quarters here, in a lonely house close to the sea side, surrounded by the soft and sublime scenery of the Gulph of Spezia. – I do not write. – I have lived too long near Lord Byron and the sun has extinguished the glowworm ... We have been out now several days in our boat, the Don Juan, although we have sought in vain for an opportunity of trying her against the feluccas or other large craft in the bay: she passes the small ones as a Comet might pass the dullest planets in heaven.

HOLMES

On the surface, Shelley was as happy as he'd ever been, suntanned, healthy, revelling in the outdoor life; bathing, sailing, picnicking. His clever young wife, Mary, was with him; and various friends and children packed into the four inhabitable rooms of the Casa Magni. From the various accounts they have left of these last weeks, we can discover a great deal about what was going on, especially from Mary. But it is not always easy to understand at first.

MARY

Our house, Casa Magni, was close to the village of Lerici; the sea came up to the door, a steep wooded hill sheltered it from behind. The proprietor of the estate on which it was situated was insane ... The scene was of unimaginable beauty. The blue extent of the waters, the almost landlocked bay, the near castle of Lerici shutting it in to the east, and distant Porto Venere to the west, formed a picture such as one sees in Salvator Rosa's landscapes only ... But sometimes the gales and squalls surrounded the bay with foam, and the sea roared unremittingly, so that we almost fancied ourselves on board a ship.

HOLMES   In reality, what was going on at Casa Magni, below the holiday surface, was very mysterious, very strange. To begin with, a small point, in May and June, one by one all their Italian servants – their cook, their nanny, their odd-job man – left them, saying the place was too remote, too peculiar. Then it became clear that Shelley's wife Mary, who had travelled as happily as a gypsy with him all over Italy for the last four years, was uneasy about this place.

MARY   The sense of misfortune hung over my spirits. No words can tell you how I hated our house and the country about it. Shelley reproached me for this – his health was good and the place quite after his own heart – What could I answer? – No words could describe my feelings – the beauty of the woods made me weep and shudder ... My only moments of peace were on board that unhappy boat, when lying down with my head on his knees, I shut my eyes and felt the wind and our swift motion alone.

HOLMES   Of course, the biographer has to intervene here and say that we are hearing Mary in retrospect. She may have been the cool, intellectual daughter of the philosopher William Godwin; but she was also a novelist and the author of *Frankenstein*. She was an imaginative woman, and surely her testimony was affected by the appalling series of things that subsequently occurred? Perhaps so: truth is a shimmering, uncertain element, that is refracted through time, like sunlight through shifting water. Yet there is one letter of hers, actually written at this moment, to a friend in Livorno, Leigh Hunt, who was planning to visit them after coming out especially all the way from England. In it Mary already expresses the same feelings of unease, of menacing beauty, and everything being somehow out of control. And more than that.

MARY

My dear friend, I know that Shelley has some idea of persuading you to come here. I am too ill to write the reasonings, only let me entreat you, let *no persuasions* induce you to come. Selfish feelings, you may be sure, do not dictate me – but it would be complete madness to come. I wish I could write more, I wish I could break my chains and leave this dungeon.

HOLMES

The idea of being held captive, of being trapped in some enchanted prison at Casa Magni, affected other members of the holiday party with Shelley. His old friend Edward Williams, who was there with his beautiful rather sporty young wife Jane, was a solid, extravert type not given to fanciful notions. Williams had been to Eton (like Shelley), served in the navy, and then as an officer in the East India Company army. Throughout his time with the Shelleys he kept a daily Journal, in a bluff matter-of-fact manner, which nevertheless seems almost unconsciously to reflect the disturbing atmosphere of the place, and sense of imminent disaster.

WILLIAMS

4th May. Went fishing with Shelley – no sport. Returned late, a heavy swell getting up. I think if there are no tides in the Mediterranean that there are strong currents on which the moon both at the full and change has a very powerful effect.

5th May. Kept awake during the whole night by a heavy swell, which made a noise upon the beach like the discharge of heavy artillery.

7th May. In the afternoon I made an effort with Jane in the rowing boat to put to sea ... but a wave struck her on the bow while launching and almost swamped her. I landed Jane half drowned on the rocks. In the evening a heavy thunderstorm passed over – one flash of lightning over Lerici was particularly vivid. The steeple of the place has already been struck, and the inhabitants say at a time when there was not a cloud to be seen.

HOLMES

But at the centre of this seascape of beauty and disturbance was always Shelley himself, acting in ways that came to seem increasingly strange, as if he was himself the eye of some invisible storm. Within a week of arriving at Casa Magni, an uncanny incident occurred.

*surf*

WILLIAMS

After tea while walking with Shelley on the terrace and observing the effect of moonlight on the waters, he complained of being unusually nervous, and stopping short he grasped me violently by the arm and stared steadily on the white surf that broke upon the beach under our feet. Observing him sensibly affected, I demanded of him if he were in pain – but he only answered, saying 'There it is again! – there!' He recovered after some time, and declared that he saw, as plainly as then he saw me, a naked child rise from the sea, clap its hands as if in joy and smiling at him. This was a trance that it required some reasoning and philosophy entirely to wake him from, so forcibly had the vision operated on his mind.

HOLMES

There can be no doubt that Williams, who did not live to correct or add to this Journal, was telling the truth as he experienced it at the time that evening on the terrace. But what did the vision mean, and who was the child? Williams himself put it down to a 'rather melancholy' conversation he had had with Shelley, probably about the very recent death of Allegra, Claire Clairmont's illegitimate child by Byron.

Claire had only been told of this death three days earlier at the Casa Magni; at the first shock of the news Shelley feared she would go mad, and he himself felt bitterly guilty at ever letting Byron take custody of the child. Williams put the vision itself down to Shelley's 'ever wandering and lively imagination'; to which one might add a dose of laudanum which Shelley sometimes took when under stress. But there were other children that Shelley might have been haunted by, in connection with his wife. As Byron said pointedly, Shelley's manner of life killed off children very effectively. His first child by Mary had died after a premature birth; his little daughter Clara had died from travel-sickness in Venice; his favourite son, little Willmouse, had died of fever in Rome. His surviving son Percy was frail, and Mary was again suffering from an uncomfortable pregnancy, which the primitive conditions at Casa Magni – washing in the sea, carrying water in pails, cooking on open fires, really as if they were camping – did nothing to ease.

SHELLEY

Mary is at present about three months advanced in pregnancy, and the irritability and languor which accompany this state is always distressing and sometimes alarming ... She still continues to suffer terribly from languor and hysterical affectations.

HOLMES

Shelley's refusal to adapt his mode of life to Mary's needs at Casa Magni suggests a much deeper marital discord, from which the seaside life with Edward and Jane Williams was a kind of escape. Here we begin to glimpse a little deeper into the truth of these last weeks, and the extraordinary atmosphere of brooding tension like a coming storm. Shelley gradually admitted this, to his old friends the Gisbornes in London, but kept it a secret from Mary.

SHELLEY

Italy is more and more delightful to me ... I can only feel the want of those who can feel, and understand me. Whether from proximity and the continuity of domestic intercourse, Mary does not. The necessity of concealing from her thoughts that would pain her, necessitates this, perhaps.

It is the curse of Tantalus, that a person possessing such excellent powers and so pure a mind as hers, should not excite the sympathy indispensable to their application to domestic life.

MARY

We were in wretched discomfort at first, but now we are in a kind of disorderly order, living from day to day as we can ... The Williams have taken up their abode with us, you may imagine how ill a large household agrees with my laziness, when accounts and domestic concerns come to be talked of ... baby Percy is well, and Shelley singularly so, his incessant boating does him a great deal of good. I have been very unwell for some time past, but am better now, I suppose. I have not even heard of the arrival of my new novel ...

SHELLEY   The Williams are now on a visit to us, and they are people who are very pleasing to me. But words are not the instrument of our intercourse. I like Jane more and more, and I find Williams the most amiable of companions. Jane has a taste for music, and an elegance of form and motions that compensates in some degree for the lack of literary refinement ... I listen the whole evening on our terrace to her simple melodies with excessive delight.

HOLMES   In fact it seems clear that Shelley had embarked on one more of his lifelong series of Platonic flirtations, this time with Jane Williams. He had set out to captivate her, to enchant her. She was beautiful, musical, liked bathing and boating, and emerged cheerfully from her duckings in the surf in a clinging cotton bathing-dress which revealed her 'elegance of form and motions' to Shelley's dreamy eye. Mary also had to suffer this form of magic. Shelley wrote many poems for Jane to set to music. In the manuscript of one you can read in tiny writing the words, 'Alas, I kiss you Jane.' In another Shelley cast them all as characters from

Shakespeare's last play *The Tempest*: with Jane as the wide-eyed Miranda, Williams as the noble Prince Ferdinand, and himself as Ariel – the airborne restless spirit. (Mary is not given a part.) This poem accompanied the gift of an expensive Italian guitar, especially ordered from Florence, for Jane.

*guitar, waves*

SHELLEY

Ariel to Miranda: – Take
This slave of Music, for the sake
Of him who is the slave of thee,
And teach it all the harmony
In which thou canst, and only thou,
Make the delighted Spirit glow,
Till joy denies itself again,
And, too intense, is turned to pain.
For by permission and command
Of thine own Prince Ferdinand,
Poor Ariel sends this silent token
Of more than ever can be spoken;
Your guardian spirit, Ariel, who
From life to life, must still pursue
Your happiness; – for thus alone
Can Ariel ever find his own . . .

HOLMES

The charming, flirtatious tone of this, which promises in music 'more than ever can be spoken' in words about his love for Jane, suggested to many Victorian scholars that the awful truth about the Casa Magni was simply an adulterous affair.

This is not impossible, though Jane had her own small children at Casa Magni, and was evidently very attached to Williams, for whom she had already abandoned her first marriage in India. But the truth is probably more subtle. Shelley was trying to 'enchant' *both* Jane and Williams in some more primitive, magical sense. He was trying to cast a spell over them, by transforming their normal world into a play, the magical island drama of *The Tempest*. He himself was pretending to be 'poor Ariel', but in fact he was acting the part of Prospero, the poet-magician who commands the revels. The idea of turning the Casa Magni setting into a magic island, where everything is idealized and dramatized, emerges more and more strongly in his letters and poems as the summer progresses. Other dramas are also brought to bear on the situation, so that all his actions take on symbolic meaning. One other play is Calderon's *El Magico Prodigioso*, which he had been translating from the Spanish, wherein the magician finally summons a terrifying demon out of the sea.

A third drama is Goethe's *Faust*, in which the learned doctor makes a pact with the Devil in which his soul is forfeit if he ever finds a moment and a place so beautiful that he wishes to suspend time itself. In all these dramas there is a sense of imminent crisis, in which a magic world of love and beauty will suddenly be dissolved or overwhelmed by death, by tempest, or by a demon, which has been unconsciously courted or desired.

SHELLEY

My boat is swift and beautiful, and appears quite a vessel. Williams is captain, and we drive along this delightful bay in the evening wind, under the summer moon, until earth appears another world. Jane brings her guitar, and if the past and the future could be obliterated, the present would content me so well that I could say with Faust to the passing moment, 'Remain, thou, thou art so beautiful.'

HOLMES

This is how Shelley was writing by June. It takes us a little further into the truth of those last weeks. The open invitation to death, disguised in Faust's words, was a literary allusion that only Mary might have understood.

But others at the Casa Magni sensed it in their own way. When in mid-June Trelawny arrived in the bay, sailing on Byron's much larger and more seaworthy boat the *Bolivar*, he quickly registered something peculiar in the dreamlike atmosphere of the spell-bound group of friends round Shelley. Trelawny was a runaway Cornish sailor, an adventurer with a pirate beard, a mischief-maker, a womanizer, a teller of tall stories. But even Mary liked him.

MARY

Trelawny is extravagant – *un giovane stravagante* – partly natural and partly perhaps put on, but it suits him well . . . with his Moorish face, his dark hair, his Herculean form. An air of extreme good nature pervades his whole countenance, especially when he smiles, which assures me that his heart is good, though he tells strange stories, horrific ones, so that they harrow one up . . .

HOLMES

Trelawny is always a myth-maker, and the biographer has to be aware of this when he is trying to understand the extraordinary situation developing at Casa Magni. Nothing Trelawny says is ever quite reliable, ever quite serious.

But he also has a genius for capturing the feel of a situation, the undercurrents of emotion, which he will colour-up and dramatize to bring out the human truth as he sees it. He invents dialogue, he shapes anecdotes, he exaggerates and choreographs events with raffish humour. He himself recounts the world like a series of playlets. But he is interested in the truth. From Trelawny we can learn more, if we take him with a pinch of sea-salt.

*waves, wind, shouting, laughter*

WILLIAMS     Luff up! Luff up to the wind! ... Shelley, you can't steer, you have got her in the wind's eye now ... Give me the tiller, you attend to the main sheet ... to the main sheet, Shelley ... Now ready about! helm over! let go the fore sheet ... the fore sheet, Shelley ... what a beauty, she'll spin on her heel now ... damn it Shelley, the other one ...

TRELAWNY     *(recalling)*
The main sheet was jammed, and the boat unmanageable, or as the sailors express it, in irons. When the two had cleared it, Shelley's hat was knocked overboard, and he would probably have followed it, if I had not held him. He was so uncommonly awkward that, when they had things ship-shape, Williams, somewhat scandalized by the lubberly manoeuvre, blew up the Poet for his neglect and inattention to orders ...

SHELLEY     *(against background of shouts)*
Sorry, captain ... (*laughing wildly*) main sheet, fore sheet, bed sheet ... Sword and helm, stern and helm, stern and prow ... ! 'Flitting on your prow before, / Like a living meteor' ...

TRELAWNY     *(recalling)*
Shelley was, however, so happy and in such high glee, and the nautical terms so tickled

his fancy, that he even put his beloved copy of Plato in his pocket, and gave his mind to the fun and frolic . . .

WILLIAMS     Luff up again . . . no, starboard, starboard . . .

SHELLEY     'The keen stars were twinkling . . . the guitar was tinkling.'

TRELAWNY     *(speaking to Williams)*
You will do no good with Shelley, until you heave his books and papers overboard; shear the wisps of hair that hang over his eyes in the wind; and plunge his arms up to the elbows in tar . . .

SHELLEY     My dear Tre . . . I am sure you are perfectly right . . . I am a nautical peasant . . . Neptune's farm-labourer . . . 'I see the unpastured Ocean hungering for Calm . . .'

TRELAWNY     *(recalling)*
Shelley was intent on catching images from the ever-changing sea and sky, he heeded not the boat . . .
*(aloud)*
If we had been in a squall today, with the main sheet jammed, and the tiller put starboard instead of port, we should have had to swim for it.

SHELLEY     Not I. I should have gone down with the rest of the pigs in the bottom of the boat.

HOLMES     He meant the pig-iron ballast, according to Trelawny. But was Shelley really as incompetent as Trelawny likes to make out? He had after all been sailing all his life, and navigated most of the river Arno and river Serchio in a single-handed dinghy only the previous year. Perhaps he took risks on the water, as he took risks in his poetry; perhaps he frightened Trelawny. Then again there was the time Shelley arrived late for dinner at the Casa Magni, having fallen out of the rowing boat into the surf.

*a dinner party, talk and laughter, background of sea*

TRELAWNY   (*recalling*)
Dinner was served in the central room of the Casa Magni, and they never waited for the Poet, knowing how uncertain he was . . . One of the party was saying that genius purifies; the naked statues of the Greeks are modest, the draped ones of the moderns are not. Then the talk was unexpectedly interrupted . . .

*a shriek, a crash of glass, a chair falling, laughter*

WILLIAMS   Good God, Shelley – (*amused*)

MARY   Oh, my gracious! How dare you, Shelley . . . (*outraged*)

TRELAWNY   (*recalling*)
The company were confronted by an apparition not tolerated in our chaste and refined age even in marble, even in candlelight. Shelley was just out of the sea, not in evening costume, but as naked as Adam before the fall. The brine trickled down his innocent nose, and small fragments of seaweed clung to his hair. He had been gliding noiselessly round two sides of the saloon to his room, and might possibly have succeeded un-

noticed. But now he came up to the table in the full candlelight, stopping in front of his wife, to explain the case . . .

SHELLEY      (*all innocence*) How can I help it, dear Mary? I must go to my room to get my dry clothes . . . I have not altered my hour of bathing, but you have changed yours for dining . . .

JANE      Stop dripping on me, Shelley – (*delighted*)

SHELLEY      The rowing boat has played me one of her usual tricks . . . But I have rescued my priceless Aeschylus from the wreck.

MARY      Shelley, I cannot bandy words with – (*seeing the joke*) – with a sea monster!

TRELAWNY      (*recalling*)
Having swiftly dressed, the Poet reappeared and took his place at the table, unconscious of having done anything that could offend anyone.

HOLMES      If we can believe Trelawny, then it is unlikely that Shelley was innocent in creating this little scene, walking naked out of the shadows like a ghost, to amuse Williams, to tease Jane, and undoubtedly to provoke his wife Mary. It was all part of the game or drama he was playing at the Casa Magni, creating his own world of magic events, his own *Magico Prodigioso*. Perhaps he was even enacting his own drowning, and coming back to haunt them, not with horror but with laughter.

      Yet some of the games, as Trelawny saw, became perilous and even not quite sane. There was the time he took Jane and her two children far out into the bay in the little rowing boat.

*oars in water*

SHELLEY   Now Jane, let us together solve the great mystery.

JANE   No thank you, Bysshe, not now. I should like my dinner first, and so would the children.

SHELLEY   Ah, Jane.
When the lamp is shattered
The light in the dust lies dead –
When the cloud is scattered
The rainbow's glory is shed.
When the lute is broken,
Sweet tones are remembered not;
When the lips have spoken,
Loved accents are soon forgot..

JANE   Oh look, the mist is clearing away, and there's Edward coming on shore with Trelawny, they must be famished . . .

*lapping of water, the children begin to cry*

SHELLEY   As music and splendour
Survive not the lamp and the lute,
The heart's echoes render
No song when the spirit is mute:
No song but sad dirges,
Like the wind through a ruined cell,
Or the mournful surges
That ring the dead seaman's knell.

JANE   Oh, Bysshe, that's so beautiful, so sad . . .

SHELLEY   Ah, Jane.

JANE ... It reminds me you haven't written out the words for the Indian Air for my guitar.

SHELLEY Yes, I have, long ago ...

*sound of oars as he begins rowing again*

I must write them out for you. (*laughs*) I can never read what I write down out of doors, or on the boat. I fly along too fast. You must play that Indian Air again, and I'll try to make the thing better.

*waves on the shore, the rowing boat beaches, voices of Edward Williams and Trelawny*

JANE Oh, Edward, you won't catch me in a boat again with Shelley alone!

WILLIAMS Whyever not, my dear, he rows rather well.

HOLMES Well that is how Trelawny recalls it. Shelley had threatened to drown them. Was it just another of his tall stories? Perhaps. But the suggestion that Shelley was far from happy at the Casa Magni, and that his games and flirtations hid suicidal thoughts, is not so far-fetched as it might appear. When Trelawny sailed the following day for Livorno in the *Bolivar*, he found the following letter awaiting him at the port, from Shelley.

Far from exaggerating, Trelawny may really have been very discreet in what he afterwards wrote, partly to protect Mary. Because he chose never to mention subsequently what Shelley asked him now.

SHELLEY Lerici, 18 June. My dear Trelawny ... You of course enter into society at Livorno; should you meet with any scientific person capable of preparing the *Prussic Acid*, or essential oil of bitter almonds, I should regard it as a great kindness if you could procure me a small quantity . . . I would give any price for this medicine. You remember we talked of it the other night, and we both expressed a wish to possess it. My wish was serious, and sprung from the desire of avoiding needless suffering. I need not tell you I have no intention of suicide at present, – but I confess it would be a comfort to me to hold in my possession that golden key to the chamber of perpetual rest . . . A single drop, even less, is a dose and it acts by paralysis.

HOLMES

Paralysis, suspension of time, suicide, death: again the same underlying preoccupation at the Casa Magni, running like a dark tide beneath the sunlit waters of the bay. Why should this be? The marital discord with Mary, a sense of guilt and hopelessness about his lost children, must have been a part of it. But then also he was a writer, a poet, who had not found his audience – unlike his friend Byron. His works were unread, many of his poems not even printed, and he would be thirty years old in the coming August. The causes he believed in – democratic reform in England, and if necessary revolution; wars of Independence in Spain, in Greece, in South America; all seemed to be disappearing under a great wave of political reaction across the world. The hope that had animated the writing of 'The Mask of Anarchy', and the 'Ode to the West Wind' back in 1819, seemed to have been dissipated . . .

SHELLEY

> ... Be thou, Spirit fierce,
> My spirit! Be thou me, impetuous one!
> Drive my dead thoughts over the universe
> Like withered leaves to quicken a new birth!
> And, by the incantation of this verse,
> Scatter, as from an unextinguished hearth
> Ashes and sparks, my words among mankind! ...

HOLMES

> But now that fierce spirit had become the charming, melancholy, flirtatious Ariel, playing boats, playing romance, playing life itself – or death. At times Shelley must have felt very bitter, very close to despair, on the beautiful Italian seashore.

> *waves breaking, distant voices calling and laughing*

SHELLEY

> I see the Deep's untrampled floor
> With green and purple seaweed strown;
> I see the waves upon the shore,
> Like light dissolved in star-showers thrown:
> I sit upon the sands alone, –
> The lightning of the noontime ocean
> Is flashing round me, and a tone
> Arises from its measured motion,
> How sweet! did any heart now share in my emotion.

> Alas! I have not hope nor health,
> Nor peace within nor calm around,
> Nor that content surpassing wealth
> The sage in meditation found,
> And walked with inward glory crowned –
> Nor fame, nor power, nor love, nor leisure.
> Others I see whom these surround –
> Smiling they live, and call life pleasure; –
> To me that cup has been dealt in another measure.

Yet now despair itself is mild,
Even as the winds and waters are;
I could lie down like a tired child,
And weep away the life of care
Which I have borne and yet must bear,
Till death like sleep might steal on me,
And I might feel in the warm air
My cheek grow cold, and hear the sea
Breathe o'er my dying brain its last monotony.

HOLMES  One can easily imagine Shelley reciting those haunting verses on the beach at Casa Magni. But in fact they were written four years earlier at Naples, shortly before he embarked on some of his greatest poetry, such as *Prometheus Unbound.* Such depression, such desperation, was familiar to Shelley in periods of unhappiness and unproductivity; as it is familiar to most writers. It did not necessarily mean that everything was lost, that everything was hopeless. On the contrary, it could mean that something important, something magnificent, was about to burst forth. It could mean the calm before the creative storm. As the heat of June settled sweltering over the bay, there is that sense of crisis, of almost angry impatience in Shelley. He wants to suspend time, but also transcend it. He wants to keep perfectly still, but also to sail out – fly out – beyond the horizon. He stands on the terrace of the Casa Magni looking out over the sea, as if he stood on a cliff's edge.

SHELLEY  I write little now. It is impossible to compose poetry except under the strong excitement of an assurance of finding sympathy in what you write. Imagine Demosthenes reciting a Philippic to the waves of the Atlantic! Lord Byron is in this respect fortunate. He touched a chord to which a million hearts responded, and the coarse music which he produced to please them disciplined him to the perfection to which he now approaches . . . I feel too little certainty of the future, and too little satisfaction with regard to the past, to undertake any subject seriously and deeply. I stand, as it were, upon a precipice, which I have ascended with great, and cannot descend without *greater* peril; and I am content if the heaven above me is calm for the passing moment.

HOLMES

But the fact is, whatever he said to his friends, Shelley *was* now writing hard on an entirely new poem, perhaps the greatest of his life. In these few last days he drafted over five hundred lines. Mary saw him slipping away with his papers to write, sometimes before dawn on the rocks round the bay; sometimes during the sweltering noon siesta sitting alone in the anchored boat out on the bay.

It was called, ironically, 'The Triumph of Life'. The poem is a vision, told in the *terza rima* of Dante's *Inferno*. It tells, not of the beauty of Life, but of its terror: the destruction which Life inevitably brings to every human being – the destruction of hope, of physical beauty, of love, of ambition, of spiritual identity itself. It is, philosophically, certainly the darkest thing that Shelley ever wrote. Even the great historical figures of the past – Plato, Rousseau, Napoleon – are included in its vision of doom. But it is not a poem of despair. On the contrary, it is a poem of confrontation, of courageous questioning, of demanding to know the truth of the human condition, whatever it should be.

It is the poem of a Fierce Spirit looking into the eye of a storm. This is the new Shelley, the other Shelley, that seemed to be emerging from the suspended dream world of the Casa Magni.

SHELLEY

But I, whom thoughts which must remain untold
Had kept as wakeful as the stars that gem
The cone of night, now they were laid asleep,
Stretched my faint limbs beneath the hoary stem

Which an old chestnut flung athwart the steep
Of a green Apennine; before me fled
The night; behind me rose the day; the deep

Was at my feet, and Heaven above my head –
When a strange trance over my fancy grew
Which was not slumber . . .

*out of the waves gradually grows the noise of a crowd*

SHELLEY

As in that trance of wonderous thought I lay,
This was the tenour of my waking dream:-
Methought I sat beside a public way

Thickstrewn with summer dust, and a great stream
Of People there was hurrying to and fro,
Numerous as gnats upon the evening gleam,

All hastening onward, yet none seemed to know
Whither he went, or whence he came, or why
He made one of the multitude, and so

Was borne amid the crowd, as through the sky
One of the million leaves of summer's bier.
Old age and youth, manhood and infancy,

Mixed in one mighty torrent did appear,
Some flying from the thing they feared, and some
Seeking the object of another's fear . . .

And others mournfully within the gloom
Of their own shadow walked, and called it death . . .

> *now added to the crowd, comes the noise of thunder-*
> *ous approaching waves, and storm*

SHELLEY

. . . And as I gazed, methought that in the way
The throng grew wilder, as the woods of June
When the south wind shakes the extinguished day,

And a cold glare, intenser than the noon,
But icy cold, obscured with blinding light
The sun, as he the stars. Like the young moon

When on the sunlit limits of the night
Her white shell trembles amid crimson air,
And whilst the sleeping Tempest gathers might . . .

So came a Chariot on the silent storm
Of its own rushing splendour, and a Shape
So sat within, as one whom years deform,

Beneath a dusky hood and double cape,
Crouching within the shadow of a tomb . . .

The crowd gave way, and I arose aghast,
Or seemed to rise, so mighty was the trance,
And saw, like clouds upon the thunder-blast,

The million with fierce song and maniac dance
Raging around . . .

> *at this point the poem is cut short by an agonizing*
> *scream, the voice of a woman in overwhelming*
> *pain*

MARY

On Sunday at eight in the morning I suffered
a miscarriage. I was so ill that for seven hours
I lay nearly lifeless – kept from fainting by
brandy, vinegar, eau de Cologne etc. – at
length ice was brought to our solitude – it
came before the doctor, so Claire and Jane

were afraid of using it, but Shelley overruled them and by unsparing application of it I was restored. They all thought, and so did I, at one time that I was about to die . . . My convalescence was slow, and during it strange occurrences happened to retard it . . .

SHELLEY
Mary's situation for some hours was alarming, and as she was totally destitute of medical assistance, I took the most decisive resolution, by dint of making her sit in ice, I succeeded in checking the haemorrhage and the fainting fits, so that when the physician arrived all danger was over, and he had nothing to do but applaud me for my boldness. She is now doing well, and the sea-baths will soon restore her.

HOLMES
Shelley had lost another child, and nearly succeeded in killing his wife. No medical assistance was available nearer than La Spezia, several hours by road or by sea across the bay, and Mary remained dangerously weak, lying on a couch on the terrace of Casa Magni, helplessly watching her husband sail and write on the sea below.

From this time on, in late June, life at the Casa Magni took on a surreal quality, that none of the survivors ever forgot. Shelley refused to take his family back to Pisa, but continued to mount ever more risky sailing-expeditions with Williams, and to stay up most of the night writing his visionary poem with rapt intensity, as if indeed he had become Prospero in magic control of all their destinies. When he did sleep he began to suffer from appalling nightmares, and these somehow seemed to overflow into the waking lives of the others.

The 'strange occurrences' which Mary mentions rose out of these, as if Shelley's poetic faculty was indeed beginning to swamp their real lives, or hold them within a nightmare enchantment.

WILLIAMS

21st June, Friday. Calm – the sun having excessive power. Fitted the topmasts ataunt, with these up she looks like a vessel of 50 tons.

Saturday 22nd June. Calm. Heat overpowering . . . at 7 launched our boat – with all her ballast in she floats 3 inches lighter than before. Sailmaker at work on a flying jib.

Sunday 23rd June. Calm – fit new rigging. During the night Shelley sees *spirits* and alarms the whole house. Heavy sea running in . . .

MARY

I think it was the Saturday after my illness while yet unable to walk I was confined to my bed. In the middle of the night I was awoke by hearing him scream and come running into my room. I was sure that he was asleep and tried to waken him by calling on him, but he continued to scream which inspired me with such a panic that I jumped out of bed and ran across the hall to Mr Williams's room where I fell through weakness, though I was so frightened that I got up immediately. Jane let me in and Williams went to Shelley and shook him awake . . . What had frightened him was this . . .

*sea gathering, heavy breathing, nightmare moaning*

SHELLEY

*(nightmare)*

. . . I dreamt that lying as I did in bed alone,

Edward and Jane came into me, they were in the most horrible condition, their bodies lacerated, their bones starting through their skin, their faces stained with blood. They could hardly walk, but Edward was the weakest and Jane supporting him . . .

WILLIAMS        *(nightmare)*
. . . Get up, Shelley, the sea is flooding the house and it is all coming down.

JANE        *(nightmare)*
. . . Oh, God, Shelley. Oh, God Shelley, it's all flooding.

SHELLEY        *(nightmare)*
. . . I got up, and went to my window that looks on to the terrace and the sea. And I saw the sea rushing in . . . Suddenly my vision changed, and I saw the figure of *myself* strangling Mary, so I rushed into her room, but I did not dare approach the bed . . .

MARY        All this was frightful enough, and talking it over the next morning he told me he had seen many visions lately. He had seen the figure of himself, which met him as he walked on the terrace, and said to him – 'How long do you mean to be content?'

HOLMES        'How long do you mean to be content?' Shelley had now seen his own double, his doppelgänger, challenging him about what he would do at Casa Magni. Shelley knew that in many magical and occult traditions, the meeting with one's double was an omen of imminent death. No one else at Casa Magni probably knew this, but Shelley had already written about it in *Prometheus*

*Unbound*, three years before, using the tradition of the Parsee wise man and magician Zoroaster.

SHELLEY

... Ere Babylon was dust,
The magus Zoroaster, my dead child,
Met his own image walking in the garden.
That apparition, sole of men, he saw.
For know there are two worlds of life and death:
One that which thou beholdest; but the other
Is underneath the grave, where do inhabit
The shadows of all forms that think and live
Till death unite them, and they part no more.

HOLMES

If Shelley thought of himself as Zoroaster, or Prospero, at Casa Magni, then his magical powers were getting perilously out of hand. His poetic visions were taking on a life – or death – of their own. It would be easy to explain this away, as the sensible Edward Williams did, as his 'wandering imagination' getting out of control as he worked with passionate intensity on 'The Triumph of Life'. Psychologically he may have been close to a state of nervous breakdown. But Shelley was not the only person who saw his double.

MARY

Shelley had often seen these figures when ill; but the strangest thing is that Mrs Williams also saw them. Now Jane though a woman of sensibility, has not much imagination and is not in the slightest degree nervous – neither in dream or otherwise. She was standing one day at a window that looked on to the terrace with Edward ...

JANE

It was day, and the sea was sparkling in the sunlight. I saw, as I thought, Shelley hurry by the window, as he often was then, without a coat or jacket, in his sailing clothes. Then he passed again in the same direction. Now as he passed both times the same way – and as from the side of the terrace towards which he went each time there was no way to get back, except past the window again – the wall was twenty feet from the ground – I was struck at seeing him pass twice. I was terrified. 'Good God, Edward, can Shelley have leapt from the wall?'

WILLIAMS    What do you mean, Jane? Shelley's not up here.
*(hurries out on to the terrace)*

*the sea*

WILLIAMS    Look, there he is out on the bay, writing. Look, my dear. But Jane, my darling, you're trembling all over. What is it, what is it, my darling?

JANE    Oh, Shelley. Oh, my God.

HOLMES    Shelley and Williams were now planning their most ambitious sail: a journey to see Byron and Leigh Hunt eight hours southwards down the coast to Livorno. Mary hated the idea of this voyage, but Shelley would only put it off for a few days, while new topsails were fitted to the boat, and he struggled to finish his poem before departing. The weird, dream-like atmosphere was increased by a glassy heatwave that set in over the gulf of Spezia, and the festivities of the Feast of Saint John, that the villagers of San Terenzo began to celebrate each night upon the beach.

WILLIAMS        Thursday 27 June. Employed all day about the boat. The heat increases and prayers are offered for rain. Heat so excessive that the labourers are forbidden to work in the field after 10. Strange Fiesta of St John.

MARY        Our near neighbours of San Terenzo are more like savages than any people I ever before lived among. The night they pass on the beach, singing or rather howling; the women dancing about among the waves that break at their feet, the men leaning against the rocks and joining in their loud wild chorus . . .

*sea, dancing, singing, howling, and laughter*

MARY        . . . men and women and children in different bands – the sexes always separate – they pass the whole night in dancing on the sands close to our door, running into the sea then back again, and screaming all the time one perpetual air – the most detestable in the world.

WILLIAMS        It's a damn funny business. Look at those girls, practically naked . . .

JANE        Oh, listen to the music, how strange it is.

SHELLEY        . . . The million with fierce song and maniac dance raging around . . .

HOLMES        Sitting out on the terrace under the moonlight, looking down on to this unearthly almost pagan ritual of dance and song, the little group of English exiles were carried further and further into Shelley's dream.

        For him it was a Dance of Death, a sort

of storm of sexuality and destruction, and it entered directly into his poem 'The Triumph of Life', with extraordinary prophetic metaphors of tempest and overwhelming seas. He wrote this passage perhaps in the very last days before setting sail for Livorno.

*sea, singing, dancing and approaching storm, panting breath*

SHELLEY

... Now swift, fierce and obscene,
The wild dance maddens in the van, and those
Who lead it – fleet as shadows on the green,

Outspeed the Chariot, and without repose
Mix with each other in tempestuous measure
To savage music, wilder as it grows.

They, tortured by the agonizing pleasure,
Convulsed and on the rapid whirlwinds spun
Of that fierce Spirit, whose unholy leisure

Was soothed by mischief since the world begun,
Throw back their heads and loose their streaming hair
And in their dance round her who dims the sun,

Maidens and youths fling their wild arms in air
As their feet twinkle; they recede, and now
Bending within each other's atmosphere,

Kindle invisibly – and as they glow,
Like moths attracted and repelled,
Oft to their bright destructions come and go.

Till like two clouds into one vale impelled,
That shake the mountains when their lightnings mingle
And die in rain – the fierce band which held

Their nature snaps. – While the shock still may tingle,
One falls and then another in the path
Senseless – nor is the desolation single,

Yet ere I can say *where*, the Chariot hath
Passed over them – nor other trace I find
But as of foam after the Ocean's wrath

Is spent upon the desert shore – behind,
Old men and women foully disarrayed,
Shake their grey hairs in the insulting wind,

And follow in the dance, with limbs decayed,
Seeking to reach the light which leaves them still
Farther behind and deeper in the shade.

HOLMES

By capturing this terrible vision in poetry, Shelley felt he had subdued it, and the inner tempest was coming under his control. Like Prospero, he believed that he commanded the island and the sea with his magic wand of art, and that he could look every terror in the face, including his own double which meant death. Now he was neither depressed nor suicidal, but believed with manic confidence that he only had to finish his poem and undergo a symbolic death. Forty-eight hours before setting sail he wrote with great confidence about the need for courage and truth in the affairs of men.

SHELLEY

It seems to me that things have now arrived at such a crisis as requires every man plainly to utter his sentiments on the inefficacy of the existing religions no less than political systems for restraining and guiding mankind.
Let us see the truth whatever that may be. – The destiny of man can scarcely be so degraded that he was born only to die: and if such should be the case, delusions, especially the gross and preposterous ones of the existing religion, can scarcely be supposed to exalt it. If every man said what he thought, it could not exist a day . . . I still inhabit this

divine bay, reading Spanish dramas and sailing and listening to the most enchanting music. We have some friends on a visit to us, and my only regret is that the summer must ever pass, or that Mary has not the same predilection for this place that I have, which would induce me never to shift my quarters.

HOLMES

On the 1st of July 1822, Shelley, Edward Williams and their boatboy Charles Vivian rose at 4 a.m. to prepare the topsails of the boat. They left in calm, clear weather, tacking out of the bay and then turning south to run on a broad-reach down to Livorno. People said afterwards that Shelley had never looked so happy, a tanned laughing figure with his arm held up towards the sails as they filled with wind. Mary, left on the terrace of Casa Magni with Jane and Claire, was in tears and despair.

MARY

This departure of Shelley's seemed to add insufferably to my misery. I had just begun to crawl from my bedroom to the terrace. I could not endure that he should go. I called him back two or three times and told him that if I did not see him soon I would go to Pisa with the child. I cried bitterly when he went away. They went, and Jane, Claire and I remained alone on the terrace with the children.

HOLMES

A week later, Shelley, Williams and the boatboy were drowned some ten miles out to sea while returning from Livorno. Trelawny, who had been following their course with a telescope, said that they disappeared into the black clouds of a sudden summer storm, with their sails up. Shelley had not finished his poem, 'The Triumph of Life'; but Edward

Williams had made one last entry in his Journal.

WILLIAMS      Fine. Processions of Priests and religiosi have for several days past been active in their prayers for rain – but the Gods are either angry, or Nature is too powerful.

*wind, storm and sea*

SHELLEY

The breath whose might I have invoked in Song
Descends on me: my spirit's bark is driven
Far from the shore, far from the trembling throng
Whose sails were never to the Tempest given;
The massy earth and spheréd skies are riven!
I am born darkly, fearfully afar . . .

HOLMES        Trelawny had been following them with a telescope.

TRELAWNY      It was almost dark, although only half-past six o'clock. The sea was like lead, and covered with an oily scum. There was a commotion in the air, made up of many threatening sounds coming from the sea. Fishing-craft and coasting vessels under bare poles rushed by us, seeking the shelter of the harbour. As yet the din and hubbub was that made by men, but their shrill pipings were suddenly silenced by the crashing voice of a thunder squall that burst right over our heads. When the fury of the storm, which did not last for more than twenty minutes, had abated – I looked seaward anxiously, in the hope of spying Shelley's boat, amongst the many small craft scattered about. I watched every speck that danced on the horizon. But I saw nothing more of him.

# VI

## Escapes to Paris

# INTRODUCTION

HEMINGWAY FAMOUSLY SAID that Paris was 'a moveable feast', and I have spent much of the last ten years trying to get back to that delicious table for refreshment. I think it is still possible to write in a Paris café, if you chose well, and many of my sidetracks have begun on summer mornings at the rustic Café Pomona under the canopy of chestnut trees in the Tuileries Gardens, surrounded by Maillol's bronze goddesses; or else on wet, somnolent afternoons in the backroom of the old Café Saint Paul, opposite Gautier's lycée on the boulevard Saint-Antoine, with its smell of coffee and *crocque madame* and irrepressible Gitanes Non Filtres.

Not all romantic returns are escapes though, and this is reflected in the first piece here, which traces Scott Fitzgerald's last visit to Europe with Zelda, when Gatsby's dream of 'the carnival by the sea' turned into the nightmare of bankruptcy and breakdown out of which *Tender is the Night* was written. This was the end of one kind of modern Romantic dream, though it turned Fitzgerald into a novelist of European stature, with an extraordinary prophetic sense of the great upheavals about to engulf his world.

Nevertheless, despite the haunted solitude of my earlier expeditions, the idea of happiness and the idea of Paris have now become indissolubly linked in my mind. Perhaps this was because, in the late spring of 1994, I set off with the beloved novelist Rose Tremain to spend four months in the city, looking for some literary expression of the passionate understanding which had brought us, so late and so unexpectedly, together. Officially it was, of course, a professional expedition; unofficially, an extended and secret honeymoon. After much hunting, we discovered an ancient first-floor apartment in the rue Washington, which turned out to be part of the building where Gautier's daughter, Judith, had lived for the last twenty years of her life. So the gods smiled. Judith Gautier's book of memoirs, *Le Collier des Jours* ('The Necklace of Days') set the tone for the long dreamy trail of daily walks and wanderings that followed through every arrondissement from Passy to Belleville. I agreed to write a series of 'Letters from Paris' for John Coldstream at the *Daily Telegraph* (largely to pay for our rent), but finally – and quite unexpectedly – found myself working on a detailed study of Voltaire, part of which was eventually published in the *New York Review of Books*.

The theme of all these pieces is a celebration of the city, which has enchanted so many writers, generation after generation. But it is also a practical, working account of how a biographical subject can gradually seize upon the imagination. Paris is seen from a steadily shifting angle of vision, in a simple tourist's letter home (to my sister), newspaper reportage, and finally emerging as a formal historical essay on the intellectual roots of the city's greatness. To me Voltaire, in all his struggles and adventures, his persecutions and his triumphs, his exiles and his home-comings, symbolizes much of the genius of Paris. His rational 'philosophy of happiness' is an eighteenth-century Enlightenment one, perhaps. Yet I also found in it, especially in his relationship with Madame du Châtelet, something profoundly Romantic and enduring. It is the mature happiness possible between two human beings, and the circumstances that foster or endanger it, which now confirmed itself as a central part of my biographical quest.

It was not coincidental that during this same summer in Paris, Rose began the novel that became *The Way I Found Her*, and certain places and incidents from the early part of that magical fiction can be glimpsed here in their first, mundane and tender occurrence. But do the biographer and the novelist live in the same world? – happily, I am still wondering about that. But certainly their worlds touch, and never was a Paris apartment full of so many imaginary figures demanding to pull up a creaking *faux Louis Seize* armchair and join in the endless, candlelit conversations.

# SCOTT AND ZELDA: ONE LAST TRIP

ACROSS HIS DIARY LEDGER for 1930, F. Scott Fitzgerald scrawled: 'The crash! Zelda and America'. For Fitzgerald, then thirty-four, the two catastrophes – psychological and economic – were mysteriously involved. He coined a phrase to link them: 'Emotional bankruptcy'. It meant that the party was over, the summer palaces were closing, it was time to go home.

The Fitzgeralds embarked on one last trip to Europe in the brittle spring of 1929. They docked at Genoa and took a set of rooms at Bertolinis, with a green tile bathroom suite and a big brass bedstead, where Zelda obsessively practised her ballet exercises. Scott began a story called 'The Rough Crossing' about a successful American playwright, his drunken jealous wife and a heavily symbolic mid-Atlantic tempest. 'Looking out at the night, Eva saw that there was no chance for them unless she could make atonement, propitiate the storm. It was Adrian's love that was demanded of her. Deliberately she unclasped her pearl necklace, lifted it to her lips – for she knew that with it went the freshest, fairest part of her life – and flung it out into the gale.' Such gestures still came easily to him, to everyone.

The story was rapidly published in the *Saturday Evening Post*, a popular illustrated weekly for smart East Coast families, which paid him $3,500. This was then Fitzgerald's standard fee, making him the highest-earning pure fiction writer in America with an annual income comfortably over $30,000 and still climbing.

They motored leisurely up through the Riviera in an open Renault towards Paris, turning aside as far as Villefranche in pursuit of a *salade niçoise*. To his agent back in New York, Harold Ober, Scott wrote: 'We arrive in Paris April 1st ... *The Rough Crossing* has been sent plus I've almost finished another. I hope to God the novel will be done this summer.' But it wasn't, because first of all there had to be the Crash. The Fitzgeralds' whole world had to break down with it and a new kind of writing had to emerge from the ruins, with a new kind of story to tell: not Boom, but Bust.

The strange thing was that Scott Fitzgerald seemed to see it coming from a long way off. Even before *The Great Gatsby*, in his least-remembered novel of 1922, Fitzgerald had plotted out the moral destruction of Anthony and Gloria Patch, an exemplary couple of the Jazz Age, artists by temperament but useless shimmering socialites by force of economic circumstance.

'I wish *The Beautiful and Damned* had been a maturely written book', Fitzgerald said long after, 'because it was all true. We ruined ourselves – I have never honestly thought that we ruined each other.'

Many of the forgotten newspaper interviews that he gave at the very height of his success also pointed unexpectedly to some imminent catastrophe of a more than personal nature. Ambushed once by a young reporter from *New York World* among the potted glories of the Plaza Hotel in 1927, he was congratulated on the success of *Gatsby* and politely questioned about his Hollywood script for United Artists' latest flapper girl, Constance Talmadge, rumoured to be entitled *Lipstick*. By way of reply, Fitzgerald started talking fluently about Nietzsche, Dostoyevsky and Oswald Spengler's *Decline of the West*. 'The idea that we're the greatest people in the world because we have the most money in the world is ridiculous', he announced.

'Wait until this wave of prosperity is over! Wait ten or fifteen years! Wait until the next war in the Pacific or against some European combination! . . . It is impossible for an American to have a real credo yet . . . There has never been an American tragedy. There have only been great failures.'

The reporter was genuinely puzzled, then disbelieving, then slickly amused. He confided to his readers: 'Here I was interviewing the author of *This Side of Paradise*, the voice and embodiment of the jazz age, its product and its beneficiary, a popular novelist, a movie scenarist, a dweller in the gilded palaces, a master of servants, only to find F. Scott Fitzgerald, himself, shorn of these associations, forecasting doom, death and damnation to his generation in the spirit, if not in the rhetoric, of your typical spittoon philosopher. In a pleasant corner of the Plaza tea garden he sounded like an intellectual Samson prophesying the crumbling of its marble columns.'

Yet the cracks were everywhere in the late Twenties for those who had eyes to see. It is true that Fitzgerald was not really capable of a sustained social or intellectual analysis, like his old friend from Princeton University, the critic Edmund Wilson, then at the *New Republic*. Perhaps he did make a faintly comic prophet of the cocktail hour. But as an artist, in the pale hung-over mornings of endless silent hotel rooms, he could glimpse the ominous shapes and put them down.

In the first of his post-Crash essays published for a few hundred dollars in *Scribner's Magazine*, he would write: 'By 1928 Paris had grown suffocating. With each new shipment of Americans spewed up by the Boom the quality fell off, until towards the end there was something sinister about the crazy boatloads. They were no longer the simple Ma and Pa and son and daughter, infinitely superior in their qualities of kindness and curiosity to the corresponding class in Europe, but fantastic neanderthals who believed something, something vague, that you remembered from a very cheap novel. I remember an Italian on a steamer who promenaded the deck in an American reserve officer's uniform, picking quarrels in broken English with Americans who criticized their own institutions in the bar.' The critics in the bar certainly included Fitzgerald himself; and the very cheap novel stood in for the one he could not bring himself to write until nine years after *Gatsby*.

In Paris in the summer of 1929 everyone was talking of James Joyce going blind, the undercover edition of *Lady Chatterley's Lover*, Sylvia Beach's bookshop soirées, Joan Miró's paintings and Ernest Hemingway boxing in the basement of the Club Americain and not giving his private address to the Fitzgeralds because he was drunk and she was mad.

It was the year in which the American novel made its decisive bid for serious European attention: *A Farewell to Arms*; *Look Homeward, Angel*; *The Sound and the Fury*. In 1930 it would be recognized and the Nobel Prize for Literature go to Sinclair Lewis, whom nobody had ever read outside of Minnesota and Main Street.

Hemingway's novel sold 70,000 copies inside the year, and he finally knew he had the edge on old Fitz. As for bankruptcy, he was toting his own theories. A young man should make love very seldom, said Hemingway, or he would have nothing left in middle age. The number of available orgasms was fixed at birth and could be expended too soon. As for a novel, the only thing to do with one was to finish it. 'The good parts of a novel might be something a writer was lucky enough to overhear or they might be the wreckage of his whole damned life. The artist should not worry over the loss of his early bloom. People were not peaches.' The Fitzgeralds hurried south again, to ripen off in the sun at Cannes.

Relations between Scott and Zelda were strained to breaking point. In the daytime there was their daughter Scottie and the beach; but at night it was a war of attrition. For a moment, Hemingway became Fitzgerald's confessor. He wrote: 'My latest tendency is to collapse about 11pm and, with the tears flowing from my eyes or the gin rising to their level and leaking over, tell interested friends or acquaintances that I haven't a friend in the world and likewise care for nobody, generally implying Zelda, and often implying current company – after which the current company tend to become less current and I wake up in strange rooms and strange places. The rest of the time I stay alone working or trying to work or brooding or reading detective stories.'

Loss of grip on his writing haunted Fitzgerald like a nightmare or a wasting fever. 'Your analysis of my inability to get my serious work done is too kind in that it leaves out the dissipation, but among acts of God it is possible that the five years between my leaving the army and finishing *Gatsby* (1919–1924), which included three novels, about 50 popular stories and a play and numerous articles, movies, may have taken all I had to say too early, adding that all the time we were living at top speed in the gayest worlds we could find. This *au fond* is what really worries me.'

But Fitzgerald also saw the same sickness and emptiness in those around him. He took to quizzing and questioning their rich friends, the Gerald Murphys, with a detached 'supercilious scrutiny', as if they had suddenly stopped being old acquaintances and become rare members of a dying species. 'You can't expect anyone to like or stand a *continual* feeling of analysis, and sub-analysis, and criticism – on the whole unfriendly,' wrote Sara Murphy, and stopped inviting him round.

As autumn came, hot and dusty over the corniches, and the swimming was over and 'the year's octopi had grown up in the crevices of the rocks', the Fitzgeralds moved restlessly from resort to resort. On the night of the Wall Street Crash in October they were staying at the hotel Beau Rivage in St Raphael, which had stained-glass windows to keep out the glare of the Mediterranean. 'Off there in a little village, we had such a horrible feeling of insecurity,' Fitzgerald said later. 'We had so little information from home, and we kept hearing these reports about business conditions until we didn't know but that at any moment the United States would go smash and we'd be cut adrift.' But they were far adrift already.

Letters arrived from New York, from his publisher Maxwell Perkins, from Edmund Wilson, begging them to come home. But it was not yet time. They returned to Paris and wintered miserably in a luxurious apartment at 10 rue de Boulogne. Zelda danced and danced for hours each day at Madame Egarova's unheated studio, and typed Flapper articles for *College Humor*; Scott drank at the Ritz bar with wide-eyed Princeton juniors and wrote disjointed social sketches for *The New Yorker* and *McCalls*, followed by odd communications to Harold Ober.

'*New Yorker* offer OK but uninteresting – as for Mrs Argyll (whoever she is) I will gladly modify my style and subject matter for her but she will have to give me her beautiful body first and I dare say the price is too high.' When *McCalls* turned down a piece entitled 'Girls Believe in Girls' he threatened to sue them. His fee for *Post* stories rose to $4,000. Then the cruellest month finally came round.

On 23 April, 1930, Zelda Fitzgerald, aged twenty-nine, was admitted *en cas d'urgence* to the Malmaison hospital outside Paris, suffering from nervous exhaustion and delusions. Two months later she had been moved to a large country-house asylum called Les Rives de Prangins, 12 miles outside Geneva on the shores of the lake. The initial diagnosis by Dr Otto Forel was schizophrenia, aggravated by Scott's drinking and intense mutual competitiveness. A plan to consult Carl Jung in Zurich (recommended by Edmund Wilson) was abandoned since Jung was reputed only to treat neurotic cases. Zelda was to remain at Prangins for fifteen months, sometimes skiing and basket-weaving, at other times suffering terrible relapses, hallucinations and agonizing eczema. A short story she had written 'would be incomprehensible', Scott told Maxwell Perkins, 'without a *Waste Land* footnote'. Now the Crash had really come, and Fitzgerald found himself in a new kind of Europe, chilly and alien and brooding, the world of Thomas Mann's *Magic Mountain* and T. S. Eliot's sombre poetry.

For five months Fitzgerald wrote virtually nothing except two *Post* stories. His visits to Prangins were strictly limited. He spent his time sending notes and flowers to Zelda and assembling a diagnostic dossier for Dr Forel. He lived in hotels in Lausanne, and commuted monthly to Paris, where little Scottie was staying with in-laws.

In the whole of his well-publicized career since 1920 this is the most obscure, the least-documented, the most private episode. He saw almost nobody. One of the few exceptions was a night he got drunk with Thomas Wolfe in a little Alpine village and dreamed Wolfe had reached up and fused all the power-lines and they ran away over the hill.

Edmund Wilson, who had himself recently recovered from a minor breakdown, received a brief letter in New York. 'The thought that you'd survived it helped me through some despairing moments in Zelda's case . . . She was drunk with music that seemed a crazy opiate to her, and her whole cerebral tradition was something locked in such an absolutely impregnable safe inside her, that it was months before the doctors could reach her at all. We hope to get home for Christmas.' But not yet, not yet.

Blame, responsibility, guilt – these questions were to torture what remained of the Fitzgeralds' private lives together. Clearly there had been some element of a lover's self-destructive pact. Years later Scott was to write to an American psychiatrist at Zelda's clinic in Baltimore: 'Liquor on my mouth is sweet to her; I cherish her most extravagant hallucinations.'

Equally clearly they had exploited each other – and the professional exploiter, the writer, had won, if only because his craft ultimately gave him the greater self-discipline, the greater survival power. Indeed one can sometimes believe that Zelda deliberately sacrificed herself to provide Scott with literary material. (The issue is examined in depth in a remarkable biography of Zelda by Nancy Milford, drawing on both Prangins and Baltimore clinical files.) Yet the photograph albums they kept during this whole period show a different, simpler human truth: they show Zelda's drawn, dark dissatisfaction with herself and Scott's ever-anxious, ever-hopeful, wounded kindness.

The Crash also produced a slow, painful transformation in the artist. Ultimately this destroyed Fitzgerald's marketability as popular American magazine writer (he received his first rejection slip for a decade, from the *Post* in January 1931, and thereafter his price fell steadily); but it also gave him the breakthrough into his elusive novel, *Tender is the Night*.

Some time in the autumn of 1930 in one of those lonely Swiss hotel rooms, Fitzgerald wrote a brilliant twenty-page short story entitled 'One Trip Abroad', which set out a kind of scale-map or blueprint for the full-size work he would eventually complete in America in 1934.

Nicole and Nelson Kelly are a young, moneyed, intelligent and handsome American couple who come to Europe in search of self-fulfilment. They are gifted, modest and intensely alive. What they lack is simply the toughness and self-knowledge that comes from having to work and struggle to exist. In a series of short, beautifully observed and graduated scenes, their emotions and ideas are progressively bankrupted by the aimlessness of their drifting expatriate life in search of the good life, 'the carnival by the sea'. With a new, coldly glittering authority, Fitzgerald executes in this story a miniature five-act gothic tragedy, complete with doppelgänger, lavish European backdrops and dramatic weather effects, in a tradition that belongs to the haunted moral tales of Brockden Brown, Hawthorne and Henry James, but which is also something strikingly original – the mature Fitzgerald, post-*Gatsby*, post-Crash.

The madness which becomes a central force in *Tender is the Night* ('through verdurous glooms and winding mossy ways'), as an emblem of the entire decade, here still exists only in the form of an Alpine storm. But Fitzgerald found that his experience, both as a man and an artist, had combined again into a single perception. He had found his subject once more, and now it was tragic.

This is the story of a trip abroad, and the geographical element must not be slighted. Having visited North Africa, Italy, the Riviera, Paris and points in between, it was not surprising that eventually the Kellys should go to Switzerland. Switzerland is a country where very few things begin, but many things end.

Though there was an element of choice in their other ports of call, the Kellys went to Switzerland because they had to. They had been married a little more than four years when they arrived one spring day at the lake that is the centre of Europe – a placid, smiling spot with pastoral hillsides, a backdrop of mountains and waters of postcard blue, waters that are a little sinister beneath the surface with all the misery that has dragged itself here from every corner of Europe. Weariness to recuperate and death to die. There are schools here, too, and young people splashing at the sunny plages; there is Bonivard's dungeon and Calvin's city, and the ghosts of Byron and Shelley still sail the dim shores by night; but the Lake Geneva that Nelson and Nicole came to was the dreary one of sanatoriums and rest hotels . . . Often they wondered why, of all those who sought pleasure over the face of Europe, this misfortune should have come to them.

Fitzgerald is still writing about the rich, the beautiful, idle, rich, but the context is transformed. Their glamour has faded, they are sick, used up, probably doomed. Their failure to understand their own position, their own fate, is presented with cool, almost kindly detachment. The sense of finally reaching the dead centre of the expatriate experience, the Lake of Geneva like a drainhole of wasted emotions, a prettily disguised maelstrom 'sinister beneath the surface with all the misery that has dragged itself here' is powerfully suggested.

Pearl necklaces do not have to be thrown to mark the spot. Nor are the references to Byron and Shelley merely coincidental, *renseignements touristiques*. They bid farewell to the departing shapes of an entire Romantic tradition, which Fitzgerald had once hoped to emulate in the Gatsby days, to relive and renew by combining literary imagination with commercial wealth, Art and the Good Life, the Old World and the New, in a kind of perpetual carnival, the 'many fêtes' with which he was to dedicate *Tender is the Night* to the Murphys. The Murphys were themselves to become ghostlike denizens of the Swiss sanatoriums, one of their children fatally ill and their business at home failing. The moral, if there is ever a moral, in art, was the one written a century earlier by the expatriate Shelley in Venice: 'They learn in suffering what they teach in song.' Almost as a symbol of the passing of the old order, Fitzgerald received a telegram in January 1931 that his beloved father had died in Maryland.

The stories and autobiographical pieces which Fitzgerald fitfully wrote over the next eighteen months are among the most memorable, and for the European reader the most accessible, of his entire work. They include the famous 'Babylon Revisited' (December 1930, based on a visit to Scottie in Paris); 'Echoes of the Jazz Age' (August 1931); 'Crazy Sundays' (December 1931, set in Hollywood); 'Family in the Wind' (spring 1932); and 'My Lost City' (July 1932, describing New York in a manner comparable to Baudelaire's prose poems about Paris). They point forward not only to the novel, but also to the series of confessional *Crack-up* pieces which Edmund Wilson faithfully saved and edited for his old friend, long after in 1945, when he was almost forgotten. Fitzgerald found them increasingly difficult to place in magazines, and his income after reaching the dizzy height of $37,000 in 1931 (most of it absorbed by sanatorium bills), collapsed numbingly to $16,000 in 1932. His own personal Crash was complete.

At Prangins, Zelda's temporary cure was at last announced in June 1931. They spent a brief, final holiday at Annecy, and Zelda later wrote a rambling article carefully cut and polished by Scott. 'We walked at night towards a café, blooming with Japanese lanterns, white shoes gleaming like radium in the damp darkness. It was like the good gone times when we still believed in summer hotels and the philosophies of popular songs. Another night we danced a Wiener waltz, and just simply swept around.'

Fitzgerald's new grip on 'their material' is even shown in his exacting editing. Zelda had originally written: '. . . another night we learned to Wiener waltz, and once we regimented our dreams to the imperative commands of a nostalgic orchestra floating down the formal paths of the garden of a better hotel' – but he was having none of it.

\* \* \*

In September 1931 the Fitzgeralds finally took the boat home to America, and the Depression. Even in his personal unhappiness and exhaustion, Scott was acutely aware that they were just one tiny part of some sort of mass exodus, some sort of general American retreat, and that the new decade would be hard, dangerous and uncertain. Edmund Wilson was already stumping the country, writing a set of social conscience articles which would become *The American Jitters*. Fitzgerald mailed on ahead of him a deadpan story entitled 'Between Three and Four', with a wooden plot about a businessman leaping from a skyscraper window. But the opening paragraph had an altogether different, more moving resonance:

'This happened nowadays, with everyone somewhat discouraged. A lot of less fortunate spirits cracked when money troubles came to be added to all the nervous troubles accumulated in the prosperity – neurosis being a privilege of people with a lot of extra money. And some cracked merely because it was in the air, or because they were used to the great, golden figure of plenty standing behind them, as the idea of prudence and glory stands behind the French, and the idea of "the thing to do" used to stand behind the English. Almost everyone cracked a little.'

The *Saturday Evening Post* printed it grudgingly. The magazine's policy had become happy endings, and Fitzgerald was already becoming passé. Soon they stopped putting his name on the cover.

After a brief stop-over in New York, the Fitzgeralds fled south to Alabama and settled in Montgomery, near Zelda's parents. They bought a secondhand Stutz car, a white cat called Chopin, and a dog called Trouble. It was time to begin all over again. 'Vitality', wrote Fitzgerald for his Notebooks, 'shows in not only the ability to persist but the ability to start over.' Surely Zelda would be better; surely the novel would be written; surely America would recover.

But Fitzgerald never forgot something that had happened at the moment of their return to America, after all their wanderings, 'in the dark autumn of two years later'. They had disembarked, on Manhattan Island, to discover a new, portentous shape on the glittering horizon. It was the Empire State Building, just nearing completion, a monument to something that Fitzgerald, like so many New Yorkers, could not yet define – to hope, perhaps, or hubris?

Just as it had been a tradition of mine to climb to the Plaza Room to take leave of the beautiful city, extending as far as eyes could reach, so now I went to the roof of the last and most magnificent of towers. Then I understood – everything was explained: I had discovered the crowning error of the city, its Pandora's box. Full of vaunting pride the New Yorker had climbed here and seen with dismay what he had never suspected, that the city was not the endless succession of canyons that he had supposed but that *it had limits* – from the tallest structure he saw for the first time that it faded out into the country of green and blue that alone was limitless. And with the awful realization that New York was a city after all and not a universe, the whole shining edifice that he had reared in his imagination came crashing to the ground.

The original draft of 'My Lost City' is now lodged in the Rare Manuscripts Department of Scott Fitzgerald's old university, Princeton, where the scholars come in endless pilgrimage. On the typescript, the word 'universe' has been pencilled in by Fitzgerald over a deleted phrase. The phrase was: 'a magician's palace'. After 1930, Fitzgerald knew there could be no more palaces.

# A SUMMER WITH THE NOVELIST

---

30 rue Washington
Thursday 26 May 1994

Dearest Tess –

To you the first letter from Paris. I'm at my little wooden desk
at the window, overlooking the courtyard, which an hour ago was
full of sunlight and is now shiny with rain. Opposite are five storeys
of white shutters (we are the only geranium people) and a patch
of Paris sky. Sometimes the old concierge lady, Madame Bonnel,
crosses in her flowery apron, followed faithfully by her black
poodle, her brindled cat, and her drunken, wall-eyed, but v.
charming son (aged 50) who manages the dustbins. Rose has a
slight flu – *une petite grippe Parisienne* – and has gone to bed with
orange juice and aspirins, after lunching delicately off a *tarte au
pomme* (one of those delicious, glowing, yellow pastries with a
lattice of glazed apple on top). Despite this, we are in very good
form. We divide our days between one bout of English work (writing at our separate desks) and one French event outside. The
French 'events' have so far included a monster session in PrisUnic
(the Tescos of the Champs Elysées); the flower market on the Île
de la Cité; the food market near the Bastille (four kilos of tomatoes
for 10 francs); the monumental new Arche de La Défense built
in the Paris financial district; and a fantastic supper with Rose's
publishers at a hotel near the Arc de Triomphe besieged by white
Rolls Royces. Tomorrow we are going to a concert at the Châtelet,
in cheap seats where 'you can see absolutely nothing Monsieur,
but the sound is perfect'. The rue Washington is like a village
street (you can't believe the Champs is 100 metres away), with a
*tabac* just under our drawing-room window, a butcher, a baker

(baguette-run is my first task each morning before the hot coffee and Bon Maman jam), a Felix Potin grocery, a laundry, a hairdo, a photocopy shop, a chemist, and a flower-shop full of refined blooms on exquisite stalks, white peonies, lilies, tremulous roses. In the evenings we have thirty different cinemas within ten minutes' walk, but actually have only had time for one film so far (an English, '4 Weddings and a Funeral', brilliant, Hugh Grant has a part in the film of Rose's *Restoration*). Sometimes we just go and walk in the Parc Monceau, full of lovely copper beech trees – though 'you cannot lie down on the grass, Monsieur, that is your English picnic, we respect our lawns differently'. Sometimes we sneak up to the Champs for an aperitif, where I found myself saying in a gentle haze of pastis, 'Oh look, the sun is setting over Fouquet's.' (That's one of the ultra chic old cafés in Paris.) Anyway, that gives you something of the flavour; it's all rather strange and wonderful, and we are still getting the feel of it, but it does seem ok for work, and we hope to 'impose our rhythm' further as we settle in.

# LETTERS FROM PARIS

## I

MOST VISITORS TO PARIS soon discover the daily flower market on the Île de la Cité. It's in the Place Louis Lépine, near the Palais de Justice, a sort of gypsy encampment of green potting-sheds where you can buy anything from a geranium to a 9-foot cactus. But early on Sunday mornings someone waves a wand, and like a Jacques Prévert poem all the plants sprout wings and start to chirp and trill.

The flower market becomes a bird market, with hundreds of nightingales, mynahs, parrots, finches and budgerigars, all perched in little wooden cages, waiting anxiously to be bought, bright-eyed and frantic. Their singing drifts down the Quai like confetti. Some of the Japanese nightingales are already paired, in wire boxes marked '*couples inséparables*'. I'm not sure what Jacques Prévert – the most amiable, ironic and freedom-loving of writers – would have made of it: '*un seul oiseau en cage/La liberté est en deuil*'. He himself got through two wives, and several girlfriends, as well as the screenplays of *Le Quai des Brumes* and *Les Enfants du Paradis* (which is still showing after twenty years at the same cinema in Passy). It is strange to learn that he left Paris after the war, abandoning his Montmartre flat with Boris Vian, and died in a tiny village in Brittany in 1977, the legendary Gauloise still stuck to his bottom lip.

His biography has just been published by the journalist Marc Andry (Editions de Fallois), a wonderful evocation of café life between the wars, with 'its distinctive *odeur*: a mixture of cigarette smoke, garlic, hot chocolate, cognac and water, and the Guerlain perfume called "L'Heure Bleue"'.

Prévert's book of poems, *Paroles*, with its sad love songs and surreal cityscapes, is still popular. And in the famous photograph taken at a Montparnasse café table by Robert Doisneau, where Prévert sits meditating (with battered hat, battered cigarette and battered dog) on a single brimming glass of red wine, he has become a sort of symbol of Left Bank literary Paris.

But symbols change. Few writers could now afford the price of a regular *ballon de rouge* at the Flore or the Deux Magots, and Sartre's stock is low. All the more surprising that Albert Camus's last novel, *Le Premier Homme* (Gallimard), is the hit of the season and has been at the top of the best-seller lists (170,000 copies) for weeks. The unfinished manuscript, 144 uncorrected pages, was disinterred from the wreckage of the car in which he died in January 1960, meticulously edited by his daughter Catherine, and shrewdly withheld by Gallimard for thirty-four years. Now it has caught something in the self-questioning mood of France, a crisis of identity and moral commitment, which seems familiar to everyone.

Camus planned it as a big book, his *War and Peace* he said jokingly, but what he had time to achieve emerges as a largely autobiographical sketch of his Algerian upbringing, brilliantly clear and intensely moving. The hero is a man of forty, full of doubt and tenderness, who goes in search of his roots, his lost father, his kindly school-teacher, his beloved but inexpressive mother (who like Camus's was illiterate). What he finds is his own childhood. The book includes Camus's working spiral-bound notebook entries, in an Appendix, and one is taken deep into the creative process itself, the projected story-lines, the key dialogues, the anxious meditations and slow thematic developments. 'At forty, he came to realize that he needed someone to show him the way, to give him praise or blame: a father. Authority and not power.'

Writing in the *Nouvel Observateur*, Jean Daniel remarked that few young French readers would now bother with Sartre's *Les Chemins de la Liberté* or Malraux's *L'Espoir*, but that Camus still speaks to the new generation with its profound distrust of progressive ideologies. Camus's search for identity and individual commitment has remained universal. *L'Etranger* has currently sold 7 million copies.

Several French critics have speculated on what Camus would have said about Bosnia. The Bosnian crisis has become a kind of test-case among the present generation of French 'intellos', and the young media-philosopher Bernard-Henry Lévi (known to every commentator as 'BHL') briefly entered the European elections on a 'list' or party ticket entitled 'Europe begins at Sarajevo'. His philosophic proposition was the immediate removal of the arms embargo. This created a furore among the socialists and progressives. Handsome and impassioned, a storm of long black hair over a white marble brow, he was described at press-conferences as '*le nouveau lord Byron en polo anthracite*'. This could be translated, perhaps, as 'a latter-day Robert Southey in a charcoal woolly'. BHL rather blew his credibility by resigning a few days before the elections on the 12 June. His 'list' or party eventually polled less than 2 per cent of the vote. Camus once said at an international conference in 1948: 'There is no life without dialogue. But in a large part of the world today, dialogue has been replaced by polemic. The 20th century is the age of polemic and insult. It dominates the relations between nations and individual people, just as it dominates those academic disciplines that were once held to be disinterested, and where thoughtful dialogue and exchange were once the traditional currency.'

In the middle of all this, an impressively thoughtful dialogue was taking place just across from the bird market at the Palais de Justice. Organized by the 'Paris Bar of Barristers', it was an open debate on the theme of the 'New French Family', held for a whole day in the First Court of Appeal. Attended largely by women journalists, women professors and women barristers (in their elegant black robes with white cotton cravats), it took a calm and authoritative look at the increasing divorce rates (now one marriage in three) and the high proportion of one-parent families. It concluded that whatever the toll of unhappiness in the 'black box' of modern marriage, the 'new extended family' with its generation of enlightened grandparents was coping surprisingly well with the legal rights and emotional well-being of its children.

I sat there, in a creaking jury-person's chair, entranced by this Cartesian demonstration of good hope and good humour. A professor of Theology quoted from the Biblical 'Song of Songs'; a professor of Jurisprudence sagely mocked the 'Kleenex society' with its disposable spouses; and a professor of Sociology neatly and forensically defined the two types of modern emotional commitment in the world wherein we live: '*le couple conjugal soluble et le couple parental indissoluble*'. But as I slid out at the end of the day on to the roaring boulevard, for my *bon ballon de rouge* with Rose, I was left wondering what the Paris poets, or the European philosophers, or even the Japanese nightingales might have made of it all.

## II

We close our shutters at midday, as if we were in the Midi. The tin thermometer on the wall beneath our geraniums stands at 33°. Monsieur le Concierge has stripped to the waist, and is dozing in a shimmering corner of the cobbled courtyard, wearing a yellow Tour de France cap. The cats are slumped under the Peugeots. The Champs Elysées is a molten mass of Adidas leisure-wear, Häagen Dazs ice cream, and Ambre Solaire cleavage, like a brassy Mediterranean beach. In the shops everyone is buying William Boyd's *L'Après Midi Bleu* because it sounds so cool; and Peter Mayle's *Une Anné en Provence* because it sounds so ridiculous. The cinemas are showing American B movies. Our *café-tabac* has closed. It is August in Paris.

The dreamy heat has its virtues. The *Nouvel Observateur* has cut back on book reviews, and is running an airy series on 'Les Ecrivain-Voyageurs' – Bruce Chatwin in Afghanistan, Pierre Loti in China, Joseph Conrad in the Southern Seas. The 'revelation' of the season, that the notorious *Histoire d'O* was written by the ageing mistress of the French critic and Academician Jean Paulhan ('the most ardent love-letter that any man has ever received'), has been limply applauded, as it is just too hot for erotica. No reaction from the Brigade Mondaine (the French vice squad), merely the Propriété de Paris with their bright green vans and bright green brooms hosing the streets and gutters, where fat pigeons paddle. The crowds at the Louvre are sitting ankle-deep in the fountains that triangulate Monsieur Pei's glass pyramid. And in between our sweating writing-stints, we have gone in search of the perfect, shady Paris park: a series of short summer-holidays, what Alphonse

Karr once called '*Le Voyage autour de mon Jardin*', strolling like castaways among the Tuileries, the Luxembourg, the Bagatelle, the Montsouris, the Buttes Chaumont, the Jardin des Plantes, the Monceau . . .

Every park or garden has its tutelary deity, and we have collected them into a private pantheon. In the Tuileries, for example, it is Aristide Maillol (1861–1944), the old bearded satyr-sculptor from Banyuls, whose massive bronze nymphs and graces besport themselves under the chestnut trees. One impudent Guide likens them to an English Ladies' Rugby team. But they are tender, voluptuous creatures whose huge, somnolent, gleaming limbs sink towards mineral abstraction, and clearly inspired Henry Moore. You can sit at an open-air café, dedicated to the goddess Pomona, and raise your glass with respect. Robert Doisneau once photographed one of them being manhandled into place by a solemn group of municipal workmen, a pair of gallic hands supporting each mighty breast, the whole delicate operation directed by a tiny round woman in headscarf and dark glasses who turned out to be Maillol's original model. Editions Albert Skira have just published a wonderful album of his work, and one of the glories of the autumn will be the opening of the Musée Maillol at the Hotel Bouchardon, 61 rue de Grenelle.

At the Jardin des Plantes, the home of the Paris Natural History Museum down by the Seine, you will find many marvels among the sanded walks: a tropical glasshouse, a Chinese panther, a Corsican pine dating from 1774. In the Systematic Botanical Garden we stood like children beneath the rainbow spray of a ticking automatic hose, and admired fourteen different kinds of cabbage. The great founder-figures were Buffon and Cuvier, but the presiding spirit seems to be that of Bernardin de Saint-Pierre. He is known by all French schoolchildren as the romantic author of *Paul et Virginie*, an eighteenth-century best seller of love in the New World, but his proudest achievement was as Director of the 'Jardins du Roi', when he introduced the first zoo animals. His statue gazes out cheerfully into the rue Cuvier, with Paul and Virginie at his knee; but behind him in the bushes is a large bronze lion thoughtfully devouring what looks unmistakably like a human hand. 'It is', said one of the zoo-keepers, 'a dialectic.'

Our pantheon has grown eclectic in the heat haze. At the

Montsouris (where the designer committed suicide when its lake dried up on the morning of its inauguration by Napoleon III) the genius loci seems to be Yves Montand, who popularized a louche ballad about the lovers on its benches. (It is conveniently next to the Cité Universitaire, and there is an RER train station in the middle to facilitate *les rendezvous*.) At the Buttes Chaumont, on the precipitous edge of Belleville where the unemployed workers sunbathe fearlessly on the forbidden lawns, the spirit is still that of Jacques Prévert who set anarchy in rhymes, and loved the little Greek temple at its centre which is mounted proudly on an artificial cliff composed largely of horses' bones from a nearby knacker's yard. From here you can wave mockingly at the distant white cupolas of the Sacré Coeur.

But our final choice has fallen on the parc Monceau, a small miracle of tranquillity and golden *gravillon*, hidden not five minutes away from the centrifugal roar of the Arc de Triomphe. Shaped like some magic kidney-bean, it is a masterpiece of extravagance and economy, designed of course by a Scotsman. Its subtle, curving circumference is almost exactly a thousand yards, around which executive joggers plod discreetly in the cool of the evening with Mozart on their Walkmans. Originally conceived by Baron Haussmann, perhaps in mitigation of his grandiose boulevards, it is now planted with a spectacular canopy of tulip trees, copper beech, magnolia grandiflora and giant fig. It is a haven of peace and eccentricity – containing a Corinthian colonnade, an Egyptian pyramid, a Belgian merry-go-round, an English rose-garden, and a series of *sportif* streams and waterfalls like the plot of a Tintin adventure story. One of its umbrageous alleys is dedicated to Charles Garnerin, 'the first parachutist'.

Its tutelary spirit is perhaps the most unlikely of all. For five years the young Marcel Proust lived in a sedate mansion overlooking the park at 45 rue de Courcelles, working on parts of his early and unfinished novel *Jean Santeuil* (which was eventually disinterred by André Maurois and the young Proustian scholar Bernard de Fallois, now one of Paris's leading publishers). Proust's writing-room, not yet corked, gazed across the pink pagoda of Loo et Cie (Oriental art dealers) to the Rembrandt gate into the park. According to his French biographers, a surprisingly athletic Proust used to 'refresh his hay-fever' with little daily expeditions through the Monceau, complete with gold-topped cane and lemonade-coloured chamois leather gloves.

When we returned from the Monceau the other evening, the telephone was ringing drowsily in our twilit apartment. Writers of course are always slightly ashamed at not being at their desks, especially in Paris, where they might be out – having a good time, *mon dieu*. Rose picked up the telephone crisply, and gave a proper novelist's explanation of our absence. '*Ah non, non; nous faisons le jogging avec Marcel Proust.*'

## III

IT'S AUTUMN IN PARIS, and we are miserable. *Fin de saison, fin de bonheur*: we are packing to go home. The city has never looked so beautiful. The leaves are falling in the place Furnstenburg, where a quartet is playing Vivaldi on the pavement. The shop windows of the rue Saint Honoré are full of brown and gold. At the café Washington the wicker-work chairs are pulled inside, the glass doors are closed, and people are drinking hot chocolate, brown Pelforth beer, and rum St James. The schoolchildren run to the lycée wearing bright red scarves, and the Tuileries is carpeted with gleaming conkers which we collect like so many souvenirs of *le temps perdu*.

Melancholy rises like a mist from the Seine. Brigitte Bardot has celebrated her sixtieth birthday, Françoise Sagan has published her fortieth book (*Un chagrin de passage* – a passing grief), and Jean Dutourd of the Académie Française has written a brilliant, lugubrious essay about old age, entitled – with a nod to Hemingway – *Le vieil homme et la France*. Even President Mitterrand has been on television, as pale as a ghost, talking about death like a character out of Racine. We wander about our flat like displaced spirits, folding up maps, collecting odd socks. Our extra suitcases from PrisUnic are packed with 98 kilos of books, and stand like four little tombstones in the hallway, *encore un chagrin de passage*. It's time for a little philosophy.

If one can learn to be happy anywhere, it must be in Paris. In the gardens of the Palais Royal, there is a little brass gun known as *le petit-canon*, which was invented by an eighteenth-century clock-maker to fire automatically on the stroke of midday. The ingenious mechanism works by means of a large magnifying-glass, adjusted to concentrate the rays of sunlight on a powder detonator, when the sun is exactly at the zenith. But of course it will only fire on sunny days. On cloudy days it remains silent, as if the hour had never struck. So round the plinth is this Latin inscription: *Horas Non Numero Nisi Serenas* – I only count the happy hours. It seems the beginning of wisdom. We have both put it into our Paris notebooks.

Voltaire (1694–1778), who is celebrating his 300th birthday this autumn, was perhaps the greatest philosopher of rational happiness that Europe has ever produced. He was born near the Palais de Justice and died in an elegant hotel overlooking the Pont Royal. His mischievous grinning statues can be found all over Paris, perched at some unexpected angle, bringing a sudden touch of wit and cheer to some solemn corner – high up in the façade of the Louvre, across a crowded room in the Musée Carnavalet, in the stony depth of the Pantheon's crypt (he is winking across at his old rival Rousseau), and most mockingly in a little shrubbery outside the mighty Institute.

Candide's injunction that 'we cultivate our garden' might now seem a trifle complacent; but only when one forgets all the horrors that the tender hero of that marvellous *conte moral* had actually experienced, including the terrible earthquake of Lisbon. Voltaire also wrote this wry commentary: 'people who go looking for happiness are like drunken men who cannot find their way home, but who know that they do have a home somewhere.'

It has begun to rain: a fine, light Parisian rain that makes all the umbrellas glow in perfect accordance with the Impressionist pictures now on display in the Grand Palais. We are walking through Monet and Caillebotte. We go down our little street, very soberly, saying goodbye at the boulangerie, le pressing, le fax shop, and the tiny *librairie* where Rose's new novel, *Le Royaume Interdit*, is proudly on display. At the Felix Potin grocery store, Madame Felix shakes hands thoughtfully. '*Tout a une fin*,' she says, handing over a last exquisite camembert. 'Which means,' says Rose as we head towards a certain bench in the parc Monceau, 'that it's time to begin again.'

# VOLTAIRE'S GRIN

HIS ENEMIES SAID he had the 'most hideous' smile in Europe. It was a thin, skull-like smile that sneered at everything sacred: religion, love, patriotism, censorship and the harmony of the spheres. It was a smile of mockery, cynicism and lechery. It was the sort of smile, said Coleridge, that you would find on the face of 'a French hairdresser'.

It was certainly the most famous smile in eighteenth-century Europe. But reproduced in a thousand paintings, statues, busts, caricatures, miniatures and medallions, you can now see that it was more of a tight-lipped grin. Voltaire himself rather tenderly called it the grin of 'a maimed monkey' (*un singe estropié*). And he wrote to his fellow *philosophes*, 'let us always march forward along the highway of Truth, my brothers, grinning derisively'. To understand just something of that celebrated monkey grin – which symbolizes both Voltaire's intelligence and his mischief – is to understand a great deal about the Europe he tried to change.

This last year, 1994, has been Voltaire's tricentenary. Learned foundations have been celebrating his birthday in Oxford, Geneva, Berlin, St Petersburg and Paris. He has been, especially, the toast of the French intellectuals, publishers and media men. He has appeared (by proxy) on the influential Bernard Pivot television show, 'Bouillon de Culture' ('Culture Soup'). A great exhibition of his life and times, 'Voltaire et l'Europe', has been running for two and a half months at the Hôtel de la Monnaie, Paris, organized by the Bibliothèque Nationale de France. The deputy editor of *Le Monde*, Edwy Plenel, has christened him 'the father of investigative journalism'.

The publishers did him proud. New critical studies (*Voltaire Le Conquérant*, by Pierre Lepape), new anthologies (*Le Rire de Voltaire*, by Pascal Debailly), new paperbacks (*Voltaire Ecrivain de Toujours*, by René Pomeau). *Candide* appeared as a cartoon strip by Wolinski. The Pléiade library completed the publication of his correspondence in thirteen volumes. The Voltaire Foundation (by a quirk of fate, based at Oxford) continued its monumental edition of the *Complete Works* in 150 volumes, the *Life* in five volumes, and Voltaire for the desktop on CD-ROM. The magazine *Lire* sold terracotta busts of his monkey head by mail order, price 3,500 francs plus postage on the 8-kilo package.

Although much of Voltaire's life was spent in exile (England, Holland, Switzerland and Germany), he has become a palpable presence in Paris. A street, a lycée, a métro station, a café, a bank note, and even a style of armchair (upright, for hours of reading) have been named after him. His grinning statues can be found everywhere, in unexpected corners of the city, bringing the touch of irony to some grand historic purlieus: gingerly seated in the Comédie Française; niched like a Bacchus upstairs at his old Quartier Latin haunt in the Café Procope; hovering downstairs in the musty crypt of the Pantheon; genially hosting a reception room ('La Salle des Philosophes') in the Musée Carnavalet; or peering mockingly out of a little shrubbery outside the Institut de France at the bottom of the rue de Seine.

But there is a paradox in this stately, official spread of his works and influence. Voltaire was, par excellence, the free intellectual spirit. All his life he hated organizations, systems, canonizations, state authorities and scholarly apparatus. He quarrelled continuously with the Church, the Government, the Law, and the intellectual Establishment of his time. He even quarrelled with his fellow authors of the great *Encyclopédie*, that monument to the French eighteenth-century Enlightenment, because he thought the edition was too big and too long for the ordinary reader, whom he championed.

Though Voltaire began his professional life as an author of epic poems (*La Henriade*, 1723), of vast histories (*Le Siècle de Louis XIV*, 1740–51), and mighty verse tragedies (*Oedipe*, 1718, *La Mort de César*, 1735), his true genius emerged as the master of brief forms. Speed and brevity are the hallmark of his gift and style. His great work is always scored *allegro vivace*. The short story, the pungent essay, the treatise, the 'portable' dictionary, the provoking letter, even the stinging single-sentence epigram: these now appear as the enduring and popular vehicles of his art.

Almost everything he has to say is somewhere touched on in the twenty-six *contes philosophiques* which he wrote between 1738 (*Micromégas*) and 1773 (*The White Bull*). All were the fiery distillations of age, observation and bitter experience: an *eau de vie* of literature. They are set over the entire globe, and also out of it; and many of them take the form of fantastic travellers' tales. They were frequently published anonymously (like *Candide*), and while delighting in their success Voltaire often continued to deny authorship, and mocked the whole enterprise. His modesty was perverse. He once wrote: 'I try to be very brief and slightly spicy: or else the Ministers and Madame de Pompadour and the clerks and the maidservants will all make paper-curlers of my pages.'

His *bons mots* have travelled more widely than anything else, though their precision is often difficult to translate. They give some measure of the man. 'Use a pen, start a war.' 'God is not on the side of the big battalions, but of the best shots.' 'In this country [England] it is thought a good idea to kill an admiral, from time to time, to encourage the others.' 'The superfluous, that most necessary commodity.' ('*Le superflu, chose très nécessaire.*') 'If God did not exist, it would be necessary to invent him.' 'We owe respect to the living, but to the dead we owe nothing but the truth.' 'I disapprove of what you say, but I will defend to the death your right to say it.' This often-cited dictum of free-speech is actually an attribution, and has no precise French original. It is a paraphrase of Voltaire's letter to Helvétius (on the burning of Helvétius's *De L'esprit* in 1759) first made by S. G. Tallentyre (E. Beatrice Hall) in her book *The Friends of Voltaire* (1907).

Perhaps most famous of all is Candide's wry philosophic conclusion about the lesson of his terrible adventures: 'That is well said, replied Candide, but we must cultivate our garden.' These, and many like them, have remained part of that mysterious European currency of the ironic. They are the verbal equivalents, the linguistic icons, of Voltaire's mocking grin.

Brevity, irony and a particular kind of fantastical logic were Voltaire's chosen weapons. They might appear curiously light-weight for his chosen targets: the great armies of the European night – fanaticism, intolerance, persecution, injustice, cruelty. But Voltaire was a natural-born fighter, an intellectual pugilist. He relished combat, and he committed himself absolutely to the battle of ideas. Like a later master of the ring, he 'floated' and danced like a butterfly but stung like a bee. For all his elegance, he could strike with stunning ferocity. A convinced anticleric, he could write of priests of every denomination who 'rise from an incestuous bed, manufacture a hundred versions of God, then eat and drink God, then piss and shit God'. He never pulled his punches, and he made enemies all his life, and he made them after it.

His commitment to the freedom of ideas is historically significant. The French rightly celebrate him as the first 'engaged' intellectual who attached himself to specific social and political causes. For them, Voltaire laid the foundations – in an almost architectural sense – of a unique European tradition. They see a line that runs straight as the 'Grand Axis' in Paris (that great vista from the seventeenth-century Louvre palace to the twentieth-century Arche de la Défense), from Voltaire via Hugo and Zola to Sartre and Camus. When General de Gaulle was urged to arrest Sartre for subversion during the 1960s, he replied 'one does not put Voltaire in the Bastille'.

For Voltaire, the essence of intellectual freedom was wit. Wit – which meant both intelligence and humour – was the primary birthright of man. The free play of wit brings enlightenment and also a certain kind of laughter: the laughter that distinguishes man from the beasts. But it is not a simple kind of laughter: it is also close to tears. Voltaire's symbolic grin (as we begin to examine it) contains both these elements when he surveys the human condition. Life amuses and delights him; but it also causes him pain and grief. In his *Questions sur L'Encyclopédie* (1772), he wrote this entry about 'Le Rire', an epitome of both his thought and his style.

> Anyone who has ever laughed will hardly doubt that laughter is the sign of joy, as tears are the symptom of grief. But those who seek the metaphysical causes of laughter are not foolish. Anyone who knows precisely *why* the type of joy which excites laughter should pull

the zygomatic muscle (one of the thirteen muscles in the mouth) upwards towards the ears, is clever. Animals have this muscle like us. But animals never laugh with joy, any more than they weep tears of sadness. It is true that deer excrete fluid from their eyes when they are being hunted to death. So do dogs when they are undergoing vivisection. But they never weep for their mistresses or their friends, as we do. Nor do they burst into laughter at the sight of something comic. Man is the sole animal who cries and laughs.

The simple conclusion is profoundly deceptive. The sentences gather irony even as they shorten, and the blows strike home. What is this entry really about? Is it human laughter, or human stupidity, or human cruelty? Voltaire's wit is so often double-edged like this. His tales, his essays, his epigrams cut as we smile. And nothing is sacred. Consider what he wrote about human love-making, in one of his letters:

Snails have the good fortune to be both male and female . . . They give pleasure and receive it at the same time. Their enjoyment is not just twice as much as ours, it also lasts considerably longer. They are in sexual rapture for three or four hours at a stretch. Admittedly, that is not long compared to Eternity. But it would be a long time for you and me.

This is the intellectual physiognomy, so to speak, of Voltaire's grin. But what gave it the particular historical twist, which makes it seem like the insignia of the eighteenth-century Enlightenment? Voltaire's father François Arouet (originally from Poitou) was a successful lawyer to the French aristocracy. His beautiful mother (Voltaire always travelled with her portrait) died when he was only six. The youngest surviving child, he was born in November 1694 in the heart of Paris, on the Île de la Cité.

The comfortable house stood within sight of the Palais de Justice (also the police headquarters) and the long rows of bookstalls already established along the Seine. There is something symbolic in this position. Voltaire's literary genius always contained both the lawyer's delight in argument and the poet's sense of fantasy. His wit – from childhood, swift, logical and provocative – somehow combined these two contradictory elements. (Flaubert said long afterwards, in *Madame Bovary*, that 'every lawyer carries inside him the wreckage of a poet').

Young François-Marie Arouet (le jeune) was hyperactive, almost a child prodigy – clever, mischievous and barely governable. He started as he meant to go on. He flourished under his Jesuit teachers at the Collège Louis-le-Grand, driving them to distraction with his pranks. There is a famous story of how he got the school fires lit earlier than usual one winter term. The rule was that no heating was permitted until the water froze in the stone holy-water stoop in the school chapel. Arouet accelerated this process by bringing in a large sheet of ice from the schoolyard, and slipping it unnoticed into the stoop. He was flogged when the trick was discovered, but in recompense the fires were also lit. It was a young poet-lawyer's solution: the letter of the law was observed, because the holy water did indeed freeze; but the spirit of the law was made a mockery, because Arouet had invented the ice. It was perhaps his first *conte philosophique* in action.

After graduation (rhetoric, classics, mathematics and a first brush with theology), a dangerously handsome young Arouet ran riot as a junior diplomat in Holland. When he proposed to marry his voluptuous Dutch mistress, Pimpette, he was brought home to Paris in disgrace, and promptly moved into a libertine aristo-cratic set and began publishing satires and political squibs. (He was supposed to be studying law.) He did his first stint in the Bastille prison, having offended the Court, in 1717; and emerged with his verse tragedy *Oedipe*, which made his name. Already it was *allegro vivace*.

Having made his name, he promptly changed it. By a swift transposition of letters, 'Arouet Le J' became 'Voltaire'. (The sleight of hand is rather puzzling here, but scholars explain that it was done by assuming the 'u' to be a 'V,' and the 'J' to be an 'i', which just about works, though it would not appeal to Scrabble players.) But Arouet had done something strikingly modern: he had repackaged himself under a new brand name, carrying instant associations of speed and daring: *voltige* (acrobatics on a trapeze or a horse), *volte-face* (spinning about to face your enemies), *volatile* (originally, any winged creature). It meant he was a highflyer, and everyone would know it.

\*     \*     \*

For the next decade, Voltaire soared to increasingly dizzy heights in France, writing plays, collecting gold medals and mistresses, moving in and out of royal favour with King Louis XV at Versailles. He was the supreme literary dandy about town, dining with the aristocrats as their *enfant terrible*, and 'passing his life from chateau to chateau'. His portrait was painted, his witticisms admired, and his arrogance became insupportable. The portrait in the Musée Carnavalet from this period shows him rouged and powdered in an extravagant wig, a bottle-green coat over his pink silk waistcoat, lace frothing at his wrists, and an expression of delicate self-satisfaction on his impudent, unmarked face. Much of what he wrote at this time, except for a few erotic poems ('L'Épitre à Uranie') has since been forgotten. Then in January 1726 came nemesis.

Showing off in front of his mistress Adrienne Lecouvreur, in her box at the Comédie Française, Voltaire traded insults with a particularly brutish member of the French aristocracy, the Chevalier de Rohan-Chabot. The Chevalier queried the writer's name ('Arouet? Voltaire?') The writer queried the Chevalier's lineage. The mistress – having granted favours to both chevalier and writer – even-handedly and prudently fainted between them. Scandal.

Some nights later, Voltaire was wittily dining at the Duc de Sully's *hôtel particulier* on the rue Saint Antoine. (This superb baroque building, with decorated courtyard of naked nymphs and barrel-vaulted coach-entrance, is now visitable as the Caisse Nationale des Monuments Historiques.) Called down by an urgent messenger into the cobbled street outside, Voltaire was set upon by a posse of the Chevalier's hired thugs, and beaten with clubs until he collapsed. The Chevalier, meanwhile, looked on from a closed carriage, and shouted out to his men the one remark by which history remembers him. 'Don't hit his head: something valuable might still come from that!' The beating recalls the one delivered to the British poet John Dryden in Rose Alley, London, by henchmen of the Earl of Rochester. But the consequences were somewhat different.

Voltaire staggered back up to the Duc de Sully's dining room, but was mortified to discover that neither the Duc nor his delightful friends were prepared to take his part against a fellow nobleman. Bruised and bitterly humiliated, Voltaire attempted to challenge the Chevalier to a duel with swords, but was promptly put back into the Bastille. He had learned that the intellectual must defend himself with other weapons.

One might say that if the French Enlightenment began any-where, it was on the cobblestones outside the Hôtel de Sully in 1726. A small plaque, beneath the nymphs, might not come amiss. Thenceforth Voltaire's career – he was thirty-two – followed a wholly different trajectory. He never forgot the beating, and years later Candide was to undergo a similar *batonnade* in Lisbon, at the hands of the Inquisition. 'They walked in procession, and listened to a very moving sermon, followed by a beautiful recital of plain-chant. Candide was flogged in time to the singing.'

Voltaire's travels now began. Despite brief returns to Court favour, he was not to feel really safe in Paris again until the last months of his life, fifty years later. First he fled to London, arriving 'without a penny, sick to death of a violent ague, a stranger, alone, helpless' (his own rather racy English). But being Voltaire, he was soon airborne again, and remained for two years, a decisive period of intellectual expansion. He met Pope, Congreve and Swift, who became crucial influences on his writing. (His letter of introduction to Swift is delightfully dated from 'the Whiter Perruke, Maiden Lane, Covent Garden'.) He read the works of Locke and Newton in detail, and judged them superior to Descartes (with his nonsense about 'innate ideas') and Pascal (with his gambler's view of heaven). He studied the liberal English civil code, which granted large free-doms of worship and citizenship. The British right of *habeas corpus* (as opposed to the arbitrary French *lettres de cachet*) deeply impressed him. He visited the Court, the Parliament, the lively and outspoken salons and coffeehouses, the bustling Stock Exchange. (Voltaire's brilliance as a private investor dates from this time, and he never again depended on book sales or aristocratic patrons.) He attended productions of Shakespeare's plays (then being revived), with their sublime ignorance of the three classical unities. He found 'a nation fond of liberty; learned, witty, despising life and death; a nation of philosophers'. It was an exile's idealization of course; but another *conte philosophique* as well.

Everything Voltaire saw went into his first distinctive prose work, a hymn to British liberty and eccentricity, *Les Lettres philosophiques*

(1733), also known as his *Letters Concerning the English Nation.* An anthology of essays and travel sketches, it is a compendium of free-thinking specifically designed to provoke established opinions and prejudices in France: the Quakers at worship, the Parliament in debate, Newton doing experimental science, the stockbrokers trading, or Hamlet contemplating suicide. (Hamlet's 'to be or not to be' soliloquy is exquisitely rendered into classical French alexandrines, a perfect backhanded compliment to the Bard.) Each scene is given Voltaire's special spin of irony, as in his famous sketch of the British doing business, from the Sixth Letter.

> Go into the London Exchange, a place more dignified than many a royal court. There you will find representatives of every nation quietly assembled to promote human welfare. There the Jew, the Mahometan and the Christian deal with each other as though they were all of the same religion. They call no man Infidel unless he be bankrupt. There the Presbyterian trusts the Anabaptist, and the Anglican accepts the Quaker's bond ... If there were only one religion in England, there would be a risk of despotism: if there were only two, they would cut each other's throats; as it is, there are at least thirty, and they live happily and at peace.

Voltaire's return to France was uneasy. He was no longer the darling of Paris, he was increasingly suspected of liberal and unpatriotic ideas, and his attempt at a sparkling satire of French cultural dullness, *Le Temple de Gout* (1733) – inspired by Alexander Pope's *Dunciad* – produced not dinner invitations but denunciations. He skulked in an aged comtesse's apartment in the Palais Royal (no plaque), and indulged his lifelong love of amateur theatricals, while preparing for his next débâcle with the authorities. When the *Lettres philosophiques* was published, a warrant was immediately issued for his arrest.

But Voltaire was dancing again. He had met the remarkable woman who was to shape the whole middle period of his career. The Marquise du Châtelet was a handsome, headstrong eccentric of twenty-seven, with a passion for geometry and jewellery. A portrait shows her at her desk, in a tender flutter of blue silk ribbons, one milky elbow on a pile of books, an astrolabe at her shoulder, and a pair of gold dividers held thoughtfully, yet rather erotically, between her fingertips. She was married to a bluff and kindly career soldier, who was always away at some European front. Having borne him two children, the Marquise was ready to take a lover of greater finesse, and she already had the mathematician Maupertuis in tow. She met Voltaire at a party in Saint-Germain, and they talked about Newton and fell in love. Voltaire said she had green eyes and could translate both Euclid and Virgil, and make him grin. It was an Enlightenment love match.

When the warrant for his arrest was issued, Voltaire decamped for Madame du Châtelet's charming chateau at Cirey, far away in the misty borderlands of Lorraine. Here they made a new life together over the next decade, redecorating the rambling apartments, establishing a garden, writing for ten or twelve hours a day, receiving inquisitive visitors, and occasionally playing host to the Marquis on his return from a dull military campaign. One of the first things they did together was to submit prize essays, without consulting each other's findings, on the subject of 'The Propagation of Fire', for an award offered by the French Academy of Sciences. They were suitably outraged to find that both had lost.

There are many accounts of their stormy, and highly productive, ménage a trois. Nancy Mitford once wrote a diverting book about it, *Voltaire in Love* (1957), which she described as less of a biography and more 'a Kinsey report on his romps with Mme du Châtelet'. Both sexually and intellectually, it was a time of high stimulation. Encouraged by Madame du Châtelet, Voltaire turned away from pure literature, and began to publish a stream of histories and popular science, most notably his *Eléments de la philosophie de Newton* (1737). This contained the famous story of Newton and the falling apple, which 'demonstrated' the universal law of gravity. At their long suppers (the only meal their guests could rely on), they argued everything from physics to theology, and Voltaire did ludicrous imitations of their enemies. There were poetry readings, picnics, laboratory experiments and financial investments. There were letters from all over Europe. And there was endless, enchanting talk, punctuated by the occasional amorous row. André Maurois once described Madame du Châtelet's main interests as 'books, diamonds, algebra, astronomy and underwear'. Voltaire shared them all.

Once, driving back to Cirey one freezing winter's night, their coach overturned and help had to be sent for. The servants were amazed to find them peacefully curled up together in a pile of rugs and cushions, deep in a snow drift, carefully identifying the outlines of the lesser constellations.

It was with Madame du Châtelet that Voltaire, complaining perpetually of ill-health and middle age (he was now in his forties), began to concentrate on the problem of happiness. He viewed it not as a domestic matter, but as a profound philosophical conundrum in a world of ignorance, injustice and fanaticism. His inquiries went into the short stories he began to write: the first of which was *Micromégas* ('Mini-Mighty'), begun at Cirey about 1738.

His initial target was the philosopher Leibniz, whose sturdy complacence had produced an immensely sophisticated argument to prove that, in accordance with the inevitability of Divine Providence, everyone lived 'in the best of all possible worlds'. All local suffering was part of a greater system of good. Curiously, this was a view highly fashionable among Enlightenment intellectuals, and had been popularized by Pope in his *Essay on Man*:

> All discord, harmony not understood;
> All partial evil, universal good;
> And, spite of pride, in erring reason's spite,
> One truth is clear: Whatever is, is right.

Voltaire attacked this absurdity with what was in effect 'An Essay on Space Monsters', one of the earliest pieces of science fiction. Micromégas is approximately twenty miles high in his stockings, and comes from a deeply civilized planet near Sirius. He surfs through outer space on comets, making notes on everything he sees, because he, too, is a philosopher. Arriving on Earth (with a five-mile dwarf from Saturn as his companion), he believes it is uninhabited until he spots a whale in the Baltic, using his pocket microscope with a two-thousand-foot lens.

At last, Micromégas discovers a scientific expedition sailing back from the Arctic Circle, and questions the 'mite-sized philosophers' on the nature of human existence (he uses an improvised hearing trumpet made from a fingernail paring). They wisely quote Aristotle, Descartes and Leibniz, which cuts no ice with Micromégas at all. Only a follower of Locke, who affirms that 'there are more things possible than people think', makes any sense to the Space Giants.

Finally, a Thomist theologian, in full academic regalia, steps forward. He tells them that everything – the stars, the planets, the sun and they themselves – is created by God uniquely for man's benefit. 'On hearing this, our two Travellers fell about, choking with that irrepressible laughter which, according to Homer, is the portion of the gods.' The philosophers' tiny ship is nearly engulfed, but the shaken survivors are sent home to report to the Paris Academy of Sciences.

Voltaire withheld the publication of *Micromégas* for several years. Meanwhile, on the strength of his growing reputation as a historian, he sought to place himself back at the centre of political power in Europe. It was the time of the 'Enlightened Despots', and Voltaire flirted with them. He began a mutually flattering correspondence with Frederick the Great of Prussia, and much to Madame du Châtelet's consternation (she was not invited), Voltaire visited his court. He was then in turn invited back to Versailles, where he was appointed Royal Historiographer to Louis XV in 1745, and elected to the Académie Française in 1746. Again, Madame du Châtelet was largely excluded from this glory, and doubts and recriminations began on both sides.

Voltaire now wrote his second great *conte philosophique*, entitled *Zadig* (1748). This time he used the conventions of the oriental tale, with its thousand and one twists, to show the absurdities of the supposedly benevolent workings of Providence. The young Zadig, 'an affectionate young man who did not always wish to be right', pursues his fortune (he is briefly Prime Minister of Babylon) and the beautiful Astarte through a series of wildly improbable adventures, accompanied by talking parrots and other portents. The story is notable for its two, alternative endings. One is happy: 'Zadig glorified heaven.' The other is hopeless: 'But where shall I go? In Egypt they'll make me a slave. In Arabia they'll probably have me burned to death. In Babylon they'll strangle me. But somehow I must find out what has become of Astarte. Let us depart, and see what my sorry destiny still has in store for me.'

The second ending was nearer the truth, for Voltaire. In his absence from Cirey, Madame du Châtelet took a lover, became pregnant, and died in childbirth in September 1749. Voltaire was half-mad with grief and regret. At Cirey he fell down the stairs. In Paris he roamed through the streets at night, weeping, and believing his happiness was lost for ever. He quarrelled with the French king, and unwisely accepted an official post at Frederick's court in Berlin. (The huge pink-and-blue marble working desk that Frederick gave him, presumably as a form of paperweight, has now somehow found its way to the Café Procope.) Voltaire remained for three unhappy years, finally fleeing in 1753, to be imprisoned briefly on Frederick's instructions at Frankfurt. The Enlightened Despots of Europe were finished with Voltaire.

But Voltaire, as it turned out, was also finished with them. With his amazing powers of resilience, he again chose independence. He moved to Geneva in 1754, rented an estate at Les Délices, and finding the intellectual air (and the banking) to his liking, finally settled just inside the French border (so he could slip easily into exile) at Ferney in 1758. This would be his home until the final months of his life. Immediately, he began to write his masterpiece, *Candide, or Optimism,* which became the epitome of all his adventures.

Voltaire was not alone at Ferney. He had taken a new lover: a fat, blonde, domestically-minded young woman known to history as Madame Denis. It is said that she dressed like a Watteau, but looked like a Rubens. Madame Denis also happened to be Voltaire's niece, his sister's daughter. This mildly incestuous arrangement seemed to work admirably. Voltaire's enemies said she was little more than a coarse housekeeper and crude bed-warmer. But she proved a skilled secretary and administrator, she obviously adored her capricious uncle, and Voltaire's erotic letters to her (he was now in his late fifties) are hymns of autumnal concupiscence.

He wrote from Germany, while they were still apart, in 1753: 'My heart is pierced by everything you do. None of my tragedies contains a heroine like you. How can you say I don't love you! My child, I shall love you until the grave. I get more jealous as I get older . . . I want to be the only man who has the joy of fucking you . . . I have an erection as I write this, and I kiss your beautiful nipples and your lovely bottom a thousand times. Now then, tell me that I don't love you!'

With Madame Denis at Ferney, Voltaire reconstructed the lost happiness of Cirey on a grander basis. His investments had made him rich, and he could create a little enlightened kingdom of his own. He spread himself *en grand seigneur*, developing a model farm, building a theatre and a chapel ('erected for God by Voltaire' over the lintel), employing some sixty servants and even starting a silk farm for the manufacture of fine stockings to the gentry. Not only letters but visitors now came from all over Europe, including the young James Boswell, who questioned him on the immortality of the soul ('desirable, but not probable,' thought Voltaire) and excessively admired his buxom Swiss serving girls. Voltaire's grin seemed genial to Boswell. Voltaire told him: 'There is evidently a sun, and there is evidently a God. So let us have a religion too. Then all men will be brothers under the sun.' Voltaire, like Candide, had decided to cultivate his garden.

But *Candide* is not a treatise on gardening, or even on happiness. It is more like a treatise on misery. From his stronghold at Ferney, Voltaire looked round the world and saw squalor, injustice, disease, ignorance, cruelty and fanaticism. The figure of Candide, the young man from Westphalia 'whose soul was written upon his countenance', is a sort of brilliant animation or personification of that all-seeing Voltairian gaze. Candide travels the earth – Germany, Portugal, England, Eldorado, Surinam, Constantinople, Italy, France – and witnesses and suffers the absurdities and horrors of existence. It is a *catalogue raisonné* of historical disasters: the Lisbon earthquake, the Spanish Inquisition, the German wars, the South American Jesuits, even the English executing a heroic admiral on his own quarterdeck.

The clear glassy fire of the narrative is unique. *Candide* has been described as *The Thousand and One Nights*, condensed by Swift, and translated by Montaigne. Yet its speed and wit and counterpoint are wholly Voltairian. Journeying on with his faithful companions – Pangloss the Optimist, Martin the Pessimist, Cunégonde the fat Princess – Candide plays out a constant dialogue between hope and despair, innocence and disenchantment.

> 'But for what purpose was this world created, then?' asked Candide.
>
> 'To drive us all mad,' replied Martin.
>
> 'But don't you find it absolutely amazing,' continued

Candide, 'the way those two girls I told you about – the ones who lived in the land of Lobeiros – loved those two monkeys?'

The question is pure Candide; but it is Candide's reply that is pure Voltaire. Moreover Voltaire's world of rational absurdities is not safely fixed in the eighteenth century. Again and again, it flashes up towards our own. Fundamentalism, genocide, civil war, ideological persecution, environmental disaster: all are foreseen. Uneasy shadows stir at the edge of each bright page.

After the good Dr Pangloss has been temporarily mislaid from the narrative in Germany (these sudden disappearances of the faithful companions are a favourite device), he turns up again in Bulgaria: gaunt, racked with coughs, and half his nose rotted away. The cause, he tells the appalled Candide, is love.

> You remember Paquette, that pretty lady's maid to our noble Baroness. Well, in her arms I tasted the delights of paradise, and in turn they have led me to these torments of hell. She had the Foul Disease, and may have died of it by now. Paquette was made a gift of it by a learned Franciscan, who had traced it back to its source. For he had got it from an old Countess, who had contracted it from a Captain in the Cavalry, who owed it to a Marchioness, who had it from a page-boy, who caught it from a Jesuit, who – during his novitiate – inherited it in a direct line from one of Christopher Columbus's shipmates. For my part, I shall bequeath it to nobody, because I'm dying of it.

Needless to say, Dr Pangloss, being an optimist, survives. But he only lives to insist that his lethal infection was 'a necessary ingredient' in the best of all possible worlds. Without it, how could Columbus have discovered America, or the cafés of Europe have served delicious hot chocolate drinks?

Voltaire denied authorship of *Candide*, and called it *'une coionnerie'* (in effect, 'a load of old balls'). But it immediately bounced right across Europe, first published in Geneva, and then instantly pirated in Paris, Amsterdam, London and Brussels. It was the greatest international best-seller of its time. In its first year it sold over thirty thousand copies, an astonishing figure for a work of fiction in the mid-eighteenth century, over three times the sales of Swift's *Gulliver's Travels* (1726) in a similar period.

With *Candide* – 'my diabolical little book' – Voltaire had broken through to a new international, middle-class readership, and created the voice that all Europe recognized. For the remaining nineteen years of his life at Ferney, stories, satires, squibs and treatises poured from his pen. Largely ignoring the kings, the despots, the courts and the academies, Voltaire wrote and published directly for a new liberal intelligentsia: a Fourth Estate who began to believe that the world could be changed through the battle of ideas. His first edition of *The Portable Philosophic Dictionary* was published in 1764, with 118 alphabetical entries, a true 'pocket' book. (Subsequent editions enlarged it to 600 entries.) Its compact declarations – some less than a page – on Love, Laughter, Fanaticism, Equality, Liberty, Torture, Tolerance, War, Dogma, Virtue and Beauty, went round the world. Voltaire launched his fighting motto: '*Ecrasez l'infame*' – a vivid but almost untranslatable rallying cry to the liberal conscience everywhere. One version would be: 'Crush bigotry and superstition (the infamous thing).' Another, more spirited version, might run: 'Make war on the fanatics.'

Voltaire now engaged with the authorities in a new and daring way. He began to take up specific causes, particularly cases of injustice or malpractice, and fight them through the press. The first and most famous was that of Jean Calas in 1762.

Monsieur Calas was an ordinary, middle-class citizen of Toulouse, in south-west France. He owned a successful cloth shop in the rue des Filatiers, and lived above the premises with his English wife Rose, and their grown-up children. Monsieur Calas and his wife were Protestants, in a city that was overwhelmingly Catholic and had a long history of persecutions dating back to the Albigensian wars. Their eldest son, Marc-Antoine Calas, who was twenty-eight, had converted to Catholicism. One evening in October 1761, Marc-Antoine's body was found hanging from a rafter in the lower part of the shop. Jean Calas was arrested, tortured, tried for murder, broken on a wheel, and after a two-hour respite for 'confession' (which was not obtained), executed by strangulation. The Toulouse law court pronounced that Monsieur Calas's motive for murdering his son was Marc-Antoine's conversion to Catholicism.

When news of the case reached Ferney, Voltaire's lawyer's instinct was aroused. After extensive investigations and a long, searching interview with Calas's younger son, Voltaire took up the case in April 1762. He was convinced that there had been a grave miscarriage of justice, born out of fanatical religious prejudice in Toulouse.

His grounds for appeal rested on two salient points. First, Jean Calas was not in the least anti-Catholic. His family servant of many years was Catholic, and one of his other sons, after also converting to Catholicism, had continuing financial support from Calas. So there was no convincing motive for murder. Second, the twenty-eight-year-old Marc-Antoine had been the one misfit in the family. He had been an endless source of worry to his parents: moody, immature, theatrical. He had failed to marry, failed to become a lawyer, and failed to pay large gambling debts. He had dined with the Calas family on the very evening of his death, and left early, 'feeling unwell'. Almost certainly he had committed suicide in a fit of depression. So there had been no murder anyway.

Voltaire pursued justice on several fronts, with all his customary energy (he was now nearly seventy). He contacted government ministers in Paris, and drew Madame de Pompadour to his cause. He wrote letters to all the contributors to the *Encyclopédie*. He publicized the case in the English newspapers. Most important of all, he published his classic *Treatise on Toleration* (1762). It begins with a brilliant (and indeed thrilling) forensic analysis of the Calas case, and ends with a moving declaration of the principle of universal tolerance.

> Let all men remember that they are brothers! Let them hold in horror the tyranny that is exercised over men's souls ... If the curse of war is still inevitable, let us not hasten to destroy each other where we have civil peace. From Siam to California, in a thousand different tongues, let us each use the brief moment of our existence, to bless God's goodness which has given us this precious gift.

In June 1764 the judgement against Jean Calas was annulled by the Supreme Paris court. Legal compensation for the family was never obtained, but the King was shamed into providing a large grant in aid. Voltaire had achieved a small legal victory, but a great moral one. He took up several similar cases over the next decade, and the authorities trembled whenever he moved. (The most terrible concerned a young man in Abbeville, twenty-year-old La Barre, who was convicted of singing blasphemous songs, urinating on a tomb, and possessing Voltaire's *Dictionary*. He had his tongue pulled out, his right arm chopped off, and was executed by burning. For years Voltaire supported his family and friends, seeking compensation. But La Barre was a chevalier.)

Voltaire had established what were to become the crucial weapons of the 'engaged intellectual' over the next two hundred years: investigation, exposure, dispassionate argument, ridicule and 'the oxygen of publicity'. Above all he had established the fighting power of plain truth, 'the facts of the case', the small stubborn foot soldiers of veracity, which can rout the greatest armies of church or state by using 'the best shots'. He had become what Pierre Lepape calls 'Voltaire the Conqueror'.

Voltaire's *Treatise on Toleration* contains one vital exception to the universal principle. Philosophically this has profound implications for those who have inherited it, from the French Revolutionaries and the American Founding Fathers down to our present governors. Chapter 18 is entitled 'The One Case in which Intolerance is a Human Right'. In it, Voltaire grasps the nettle that stings all liberals. How can we tolerate those groups in society who are themselves intolerant, and thereby threaten the principle itself?

Voltaire's answer is succinct: we cannot. For the individual, toleration is an absolute right and an absolute duty. But for society and its legislators, toleration has a limit. Where intolerance becomes criminal, the laws of the liberal state cannot tolerate it. And the fanatical intolerance of any social group, where it is sufficient to 'trouble society' at large, is always to be condemned as criminal. This is Voltaire's 'one case'.

Here is the vital passage. 'For any Government to abrogate its right to punish the misdeeds of citizens, it is necessary that these misdeeds should not class as crimes. They only class as crimes when they trouble society at large. And they trouble society at large, the moment that they inspire fanaticism. Consequently, if men are to deserve tolerance, they must begin by not being fanatics.'

The most problematic issue raised by Voltaire's 'one exception' to tolerance is painfully illustrated by his own attitude to the Jews. How exactly do we measure the supposed 'fanaticism' of another social or religious group, who may merely hold strong beliefs and separate traditions, without falling into 'fanaticism' ourselves? Voltaire's weird, anti-Jewish prejudice runs like a barbed thread throughout his work; over thirty of the entries in the *Philosophical Dictionary* contain anti-Jewish statements; and the article on Toleration itself refers to the Jews as historically 'the most intolerant and cruel of all the peoples of Antiquity'.

It has been argued that Voltaire's position was essentially anti-Biblical and satirical – part of his general attack on the ludicrous extremes of Old Testament Christianity – rather than anti-Semitic in any modern sense. Certainly the persecution of the Jews by the Inquisition appalled him.

As Prince Hamlet says, 'Aye, there's the rub.' Voltaire had not shown how the battle could be won. But he had defined the field of combat. For him, 'fanaticism' is expressed essentially by religious or racial persecution, the two great curses of civilization. Two hundred years on, one might think he was still right. Wherever there are pogroms, lethal fatwas, book burnings, race riots, ethnic cleansing, apartheids, his spirit looks down grinning with pain. But out of that grin is born the notion of Human Rights, a term he specifically uses.

The British philosopher A. J. Ayer once observed that Voltaire's concept of toleration was based on one of the most noble dreams of the eighteenth-century Enlightenment. All religions and racial codes prepared us for the emergence of one universal, rational morality which would gradually come to be accepted over the entire globe.

'Voltaire . . . wishes to maintain that there is a law of morality that holds universally, like Newton's law of gravitation.' The good action, the proper decision, the right thing to do, should be as obvious as the fall of an apple.

Voltaire lived on at his beloved Ferney until he was over eighty. There are many accounts of his kindly, eccentric household, and sheet after sheet of brilliant caricatures made by Jean Huber, a local Swiss artist, whom Voltaire allowed to make mocking sketches of his most intimate moments. (When Voltaire got irritated with his intrusions, Huber merely quoted from Voltaire on Toleration.) One of Huber's best paintings is of Voltaire in his bedroom, standing on one foot, pulling on his knickerbockers, and dictating a letter. Voltaire seems to have lived permanently in a series of brilliantly coloured dressing gowns, with silk slippers that were always falling off his feet.

He never stopped writing, and guests record that he was often at his desk for fifteen hours a day. In the 1770s he wrote or dictated over five hundred letters a year. In 1770 he began a series of philosophic essays, *Questions on the Encyclopaedia*, which eventually extended to nine volumes. He continued to add to his *contes philosophiques*, still usually published anonymously, slipped into newspapers or surreptitiously circulated in pamphlets purporting to be printed in Brussels or Amsterdam. Notable among these are *The Ingenue* (1767), a sly attack on Rousseau's theories of education; *The Princess of Babylon* (1768), an interesting excursion into sexual politics; and *The White Bull* (1773).

*The White Bull* was written when Voltaire was seventy-nine, and has the feeling of a will and testament. As in many of the later stories, it conjures a fantastic world where bigots rule, innocents travel, and animals speak the truth. In this case the beautiful Princess Amasida (who has read Locke's *On Understanding*) has fallen tenderly in love with a large white bull (who is really the young King Nebuchadnezzar). She is trying to save both him and herself from execution by the religious authorities, who fanatically disapprove. Amasida succeeds, and the last chapter is entitled, 'How the Princess Married her Ox'.

The story is unusual in that it contains a mocking self-portrait of Voltaire as the Princess's faithful companion, the philosopher Mambres, 'a former magus and eunuch to the Pharaohs', who is 'about thirteen hundred years old'. Mambres gives exquisite dinners ('carp's tongue tart, liver of turbot and pike, chicken with pistachios') and dispenses wisdom. In his ironic, absent-minded fashion, Mambres succeeds in averting various catastrophes for the Princess and her Bull, and finally sees that the monstrous creature gets changed back into the handsome young king. 'This latest metamorphosis astonished everybody, apart from the meditative Mambres . . . who returned to his Palace to think things over.' To his great satisfaction he hears the people shouting, 'Long live our great King, who is no longer dumb!'

It would be too much to expect Voltaire to die quietly and meditatively at Ferney. Instead, he decided on one last assault on Paris. He succeeded in taking his native city by storm, not once, but twice. Once, while he was dying; the second time when he was dead. In 1778, in the spring of his eighty-fourth year, he attended a performance of his last tragedy, *Irène*, at the Comédie Française, and sat in on a session of the Académie. Both occasions were a personal triumph. Over three hundred distinguished visitors called on him, where he was staying at the Marquise de Villette's *hôtel*, now 27 quai Voltaire (on the corner of the rue de Beaune, with the restaurant Voltaire serving 'Candide cocktails' on the ground floor).

But amid this public glory, Voltaire was exhausted, and in the privacy of his bedroom spitting blood. He died in much pain on May 30, 1778. He had received a Jesuit priest in his dying hours, whom he seems to have teased, as in the old days: on being urged to renounce the devil, Voltaire gently replied, 'This is no time for making new enemies.' But to the relief of Enlightenment Europe, he refused to renounce any of his works. His body was smuggled out to a secret burying place in the Champagne region.

Thirteen years later, in July 1791, Voltaire came storming back posthumously. He was reburied as a hero of the Revolution in the crypt of the Paris Pantheon: and there (unlike many of his temporary cohabitants) his monument has always remained. The modern inscription – probably written by André Malraux – describes him as one of 'the spiritual fathers' of France, and as 'the immortal symbol of the Age of Enlightenment'. His marble statue, with a quill in one hand, and a sword beneath his foot, grins at that too.

Far above him, in the nave of the Pantheon, a curious law of physics is at work. The stonework of the great eighteenth-century vault has become unstable, and chunks of masonry are imploding on to the hallowed floors beneath. Safety nets have been set up, and the public are warned to keep clear. The authorities announce that they are making investigations. But they do not yet know the cause of this disturbance in the great structure. Perhaps it is a *conte philosophique*.

# VII

## Homage to the Godfather

# INTRODUCTION

*FELIX QUI POTUIT rerum cognoscere causas.* These words from Lucretius were inscribed above the gateway of my College in Cambridge. 'Happy the man who knows the causes (the origins) of things.' It was the motto for a scientific community – Churchill College was a modern foundation, which contained by statute a minimum of 70 per cent science undergraduates, and its culture was open-minded, democratic, iconoclastic to a degree. As one of its few arts undergraduates, vigorously defended by the nuclear energy of Professor George Steiner, I breathed in a pioneering atmosphere of excitement and questioning.

Here I first looked at the blue mountains of the moon through an enormous reflector telescope, saw molecules of human body tissue on the glowing screen of an electron microscope, and heard the passionate arguments about Heisenberg's Uncertainty Principle. All life could be seen as exploration, an endless search for cause, shape and meaning. And I now think that Lucretius's motto would do very well for biographers, who are dedicated to the search for the human *causas* after their own fashion. But that, of course, is an incorrigibly Romantic view.

I often wish I had met James Boswell in a tutorial, as you will see in my last piece. Any attempt to explain the origins and workings of English biography must eventually lead back to him. Boswell's *Life of Samuel Johnson LL.D.* is our foundation text, our *Principia* or Old Testament; and he is our prophet. His great book is in fact astonishingly unorthodox: a mighty chronicle which is also an intimate conversation in a back parlour, an eighteenth-century Grand Tour of the Johnsonian landscape which is simultaneously a profound Romantic study in friendship. There are few experimental techniques that Boswell has not already tried. His subtle layerings of autobiography upon biography, dramatized dialogues upon sober documentation, reverence upon mockery, are still an instruction and exhilaration to behold. Perhaps it is only the youthful Johnson, the uncertain young man in the dark city, long before Boswell had encountered him as the bear-like sage in Davies' bookshop in Covent Garden, that somehow slips through his capacious net. It was this shadowy time that I tried to recapture myself in *Dr Johnson & Mr Savage*, a further investigation of the strange byways of biography and friendship.

But to do Boswell himself justice was another matter. What proper form could be found to salute the master? I have tried many times, and here at the last I offer just three versions, each in its own way provisional and unsatisfactory. The first is a formal celebration of the bicentenary of his great *Life*, which attempts to trace the immediate impact of his work, and then follow something of its repercussions down to our own day. It is also a modest defence of biography itself, a claim that the genre Boswell founded, the multifarious family that he godfathered is – despite all doubts and objections – more than ever alive and kicking.

The second, 'Boswell Among the Tulips' might be described as a floral tribute. Here is a glimpse of Boswell in his salad days, romping through the flatlands of Holland, solitary and yet gregarious, melancholy and yet madcap, learning his métier. His discovery of biography is also a discovery of his own heart, and if he does not quite fall in love with the clever, contradictory Zélide, she teaches him something of self-knowledge without which there can be no human understanding, no true empathy, at all. His tall cathedral tower still stands in Utrecht, and looking down you can still see the roads and tracks and canals stretching far away into the mist, as if they might go on for ever in every direction, busy with life and movement, glinting and then gone.

And what shall I say of 'Dr Johnson's First Cat'? Nothing, except that it was written for the radio, when I was asked if a biographer had ever been known to tell the truth.

# BOSWELL'S BICENTENARY

BIOGRAPHY, LIKE LOVE, begins in passionate curiosity. Where it ends – or should end – has become a matter of some dispute, in the current bookshop boom of sales and advances. In fact the British, with their bristling sense of privacy, have long been a nation of biographers; and if there really is a boom in the form, it began exactly 200 years ago with the publication of James Boswell's *Life of Samuel Johnson LL.D* on 16 May 1791. The two enormous quarto volumes sold out in eighteen months, and earned its author spectacular profits of £1,555 18s 2d, bringing praise and condemnation with equal extravagance.

Boswell is the godfather of English biography, in both the literary and the mafia sense. He championed the art, and he launched the business. No one before him had reconstructed another life on such an epic scale (modern editions run to 1,500 pages), or with such relentless, brilliant intimacy. He spent nearly twenty years on the research (unveiling his project to Johnson by degrees in 1782), and six years in the writing up of materials after Johnson's death in 1784. He persisted obsessively through periods of extreme depression, alcoholism (and worse, teetotalism), and the death of his beloved wife Margaret. He wrote up thousands of pages of conversations recorded in his private Journals; collected hundreds of letters; interviewed bishops, actresses, philosophers, booksellers, blue-stockings, childhood friends and household servants. (Johnson's black servant Francis Barber was sent a detailed Questionnaire; while Johnson's confidante Mrs Desmoulins was carefully cross-questioned about cuddling-sessions in Hampstead.) Boswell deftly explored Johnson's lifelong melancholia, delving deep in his private *Diaries, Prayers and Annals*. He minutely observed the Great Cham's nervous tics and religious terrors, his Rabelaisian eating habits, his fondness for cats.

Finally he wrote proudly in his Preface: 'I will venture to say that he will be seen in this work more completely than any man who has ever yet lived. And he will be seen as he really was; for I profess to write not his panegyrick, which must be all praise, but his Life.' This, in effect, was the manifesto of modern biography.

In one of his moments of manic optimism, Boswell even considered applying for a royal endorsement, 'By Appointment to His Majesty, Biographer of Samuel Johnson', for the 2nd edition title-page, as if his work was a pot of successful marmalade on the breakfast tables of *le tout monde*.

In fact reactions to his labours were divided in a way now familiar to modern biographers. Dr Charles Burney, the distinguished musicologist, considered he had achieved a noble work of memorial art, as Xenophon had done for Socrates. While Mrs Barbauld, the novelist, reckoned he had produced a fascinating but cheap piece of popular gossip: 'It is like going to Ranelagh pleasure-gardens; you meet all your acquaintance: but it is a base and mean thing to bring thus every idle word into judgement.'

Modern doubts about biography – particularly raised by the peculiar form of anti-hagiography, as in recent 'celebrity lives' of Picasso, John Lennon and Nancy Reagan (polemics as unreliable as panegyricks) – run much along these lines. The biographer is seen as a type of predator, grave-snatcher, or gossip driven by commercial instincts; the stock-in-trade is betrayal, invasion of privacy and superficial scandal; the biographical method is shallow, and can say little about the deep springs of character, or the profoundly inward process of the creation of a work of art; and biography, so flourishing in Britain, is at best a productive part of the heritage industry, a pungent but malodorous mushroom of the nostalgia culture. In short, the 'boom' is a hollow, passing drum, beaten by industrious clowns.

Well, maybe some of it is. But the bicentenary of Boswell's masterpiece – which has remained one of the most widely read and reprinted books in the English language – should give us pause for reflection. Why *is* biography so popular? Why does it, at best, seem to fulfil Dr Johnson's own epitome of fine literature, that balances entertainment with instruction, and helps us the better to enjoy life or to endure it? And indeed why did Johnson himself, no literary lightweight, consistently say that biography was the part of literature that he 'loved best'?

Boswell seems to me to have bequeathed to us not a technique of exploitation, but an idea – even an *ideal* – of truth-telling. Conceived within a calm, noble culture of Augustan Enlightenment – 'the proper study of mankind, is man' – it has burnt ever more brightly in the dark *sturm und drang* that has followed. In our own age of scepticism, discredited ideologies and disabling self-doubt, the possibility and the desirability of knowing our fellow man and woman – how we 'really are' (beyond the masks of fame, 'success', obscurity, or even ordinariness), the worst and the best – has remained extraordinarily constant. And biography has gradually become a prime instrument, a major artistic form, of that essentially humane, courageous and curiously cheering epistemology.

It has certainly been a gradual arrival. Boswell did not, with rare exceptions, convert the Victorians, even though his book was almost canonized by Macaulay and Carlyle in famous essays. Instead, the protectionism of the 'authorized' biographer, like Dickens's friend John Forster or Arnold's one-time pupil A. P. Stanley, drew a cloak of respectability and family pieties around the eminent subject. It hardened, as Edmund Gosse (significantly, an inspired autobiographer) observed, into the marbled monuments of multi-volumed 'Life and Letters', massive, shapeless, stainless and sepulchrally concealing. Forster, for example, only once mentions in his thousand pages the name of Ellen Ternan, Dickens's intimate companion for over a decade, now herself the subject of a wonderfully revealing, tender biography by Claire Tomalin, *The Invisible Woman*. Indeed, Victorian biography, in the hands of Sir Leslie Stephen, ended by erecting a Great Wall of China, the DNB, around the outposts of public truth-telling: thus far and no further may civil knowledge go.

Of course there were exceptions – notably Mrs Gaskell's vividly empathetic *Life of Charlotte Brontë* (one novelist upon another); or Froude's grimly honest exposé of – ironically – Carlyle's own marriage. And Victorian biography is at last beginning to receive study, in the work of A. O. J. Cockshut, or the recent Clark Lectures of Christopher Ricks. One can now see how its very restrictions have, paradoxically, given modern biographers something to work *against*; in William St Clair's striking analogy, like huge archaeological sites to be patiently re-dug and redefined, down through layer upon layer of silted deceptions.

But perhaps Boswell's first true heir was Lytton Strachey, whose *Eminent Victorians* (1918) – four short lives of Cardinal Manning, Florence Nightingale, Dr Arnold and General Gordon, each elegantly pierced and mocked – breached the Great Wall of respectability for ever. It was the end of Empire in several ways. Strachey was perhaps less of a truth-teller, than a destroyer of illusions and a liberator of forms. What he released was a generation of brilliant experimenters in biographical narrative, who at last began to ask *how* can lives be genuinely reconstructed: what is memory, what is time, what is character, what is 'evidence' in a human story?

Thus Virginia Woolf (daughter of Stephen, or 'rebellious daughter of DNB', as Julia Briggs called her) wondered how to describe the *twenty* or so personalities a single life may contain. She produced a fictional biography of her friend Vita Sackville-West, covering several centuries and a change of sex, in *Orlando*; and presented the Browning household through the biography of Elizabeth Barrett's dog, *Flush*.

A. J. A. Symons made the biographical chase itself the subject of his eccentric, dandified *The Quest for Corvo*. Harold Nicolson described his early intimates – from an infuriated governess to an unflappable Lord Curzon – in the manner of Chekhovian short stories, in *Some People*; he demystified the lordly Poet Laureate in *Tennyson*; and wrote one of the pioneering studies of the whole form in *The Development of English Biography*, in which Boswell is praised as a cinematographer. Maurice Baring invented 'lost' letters and diaries in his *Unreliable Histories*, and suggested intriguing versions of 'alternative lives', including Shelley retiring as Tory MP for Horsham, and Coleridge completing his 'epic Kubla Khan' in fifteen volumes at the age of eighty.

Many other writers, such as the ex-actor Hesketh Pearson, contributed to this flexing and exercising of Boswell's grand ideal. What it meant was that the monumental form lost its rigidity, and was recognized at last as a subtle, responsive art, as various as the lives it contained.

Our own generation has seen literary biography especially, freed of Victorian inhibitions, rise to power as a virtually new genre.

Its early landmarks are now clear: Richard Ellmann's *James Joyce*, Michael Holroyd's *Lytton Strachey*, Robert Gittings' *John Keats*, George Painter's *Proust*, Hilary Spurling's *Ivy Compton Burnett*, among others. They are the work of scholar-artists, totally committed to both painstaking research and polished story-telling, often over many years.

One enters these great biographies, as into entire worlds of historical re-creation, having the human density of large novels peopled by many characters, and yet focused upon the single, minutely documented experience of an actual life. They contain extraordinary richness and conviction; they shimmer with innumerable points of living light. At their heart often lie mysterious, contradictory tragi-comedies – perhaps of all modes, the most modern, the most immediate, the most true to our perceptions of *how things are*. And in this range, touch and tonality, they most clearly and directly rival Boswell, the first master.

The appeal of such a genre, to a wide public, has also become more evident than perhaps it was to Boswell's startled contemporaries. The partial collapse of the large, naturalistic novel – precisely the form invented by Boswell's peers like Fielding and Richardson, and continued from Dickens to Lawrence – has left an immense hunger for the large, naturalistic biography, with its solid, architectural colonnade of beginning, middle, end. (Peter Ackroyd has remarked that his highly successful *Dickens* was originally conceived in the exact form of such a Victorian *novel*.) A similar collapse of academic literary criticism into the dry ruins of deconstructionism, has left the old, humane Arnoldian form of commentary at the disposal of biographers and their readers. Jon Stallworthy, both academic and biographer, superbly deployed this critical tradition in his *Wilfred Owen*, a matchless account of the war poet; and recently observed that the finest *critical* work on Joyce remains Ellmann's *Life*.

At another level, much modern biography has something of the inescapable tension, and steady unfolding, of the classical detective story: with the psychological promise of some sort of 'revelation' (not of a crime solved, but of a human mystery – at least partially – resolved). The resolution often appears not in narrative, but in figurative form, which a skilled biographer can sometimes give with almost poetic force. Boswell had already divined this art, and central to his revelation of Johnson's inner-most struggles, is not a conversational exchange, but an embattled image.

> His mind resembled the vast amphitheatre, the Colis-seum at Rome. In the centre stood his judgement, which, like a mighty gladiator, combated those appre-hensions that, like the wild beasts of the Arena, were all around in cells, ready to be let out upon him. After a conflict, he drove them back into their dens; but not killing them, they were still assailing him.

This image has such power that it resonates through the entire biography, representative not simply of Johnson's moral struggles, but of a whole Augustan culture soon to be beset by the wild beasts of Romanticism, of Rousseau and his hirsute crew.

It may also suggest how biography offers a shapely doorway back into history, seen on a human scale. Carlyle called history the sum of innumerable biographies; a view profoundly opposed to the current statistical sweepings of economic history and sociology. But if one wants to understand, say, the impact of the French Revolution on English society, what better way than to read William St Clair's *The Godwins and the Shelleys*? This is a precise, but enthralling account (written incidentally by a senior member of HM Treasury) of the wild entanglements of two families of radical writers, between the 1760s and 1820s, who engaged with Conti-nental enthusiasms at every level, from philosophical treason to efficient birth-control.

Even the most recherché fields can be illuminated by light from this human doorway: the complex development of Romantic music in David Cairns's rumbustious *Berlioz*, or the arcanae of early-twentieth-century philosophy and logic in Ray Monk's patient, limpid *Ludwig Wittgenstein*. It does tell us something cru-cial about the delphic, regimented and numbered propositions of Wittgenstein's *Tractatus*, to discover it being drafted in the forward observation post of the Austrian artillery on the Russian Front in summer 1916, under heavy fire.

But above all, modern biography continues the Boswellian inquiry into the quiddity of human nature: what motivates us, what forms or splinters character, what gives self-identity, what brings intimacy. At a recent Biography Conference at Oxford, I was asked by a marriage-counsellor how well the biographer could ever discover the truth about married couples – when she herself often wondered, after extensive confidential interviews, if two partners were really living with the same spouses, so different were their accounts of each other.

This provoked animated discussion, which Margaret Boswell and Tetty Johnson would have enjoyed. But the short answer was to read something like Nigel Nicolson's account of his parents in *Portrait of a Marriage*, followed by Victoria Glendinning's generous, all-embracing life of *Victoria Sackville-West*. Such biographies, with the comprehending perspective of time, and the multiple intelligence of diaries, letters, memoirs, autobiographical fiction from both sides (and from outside), move far beyond banal bedroom truths about a relationship. The biographer may simply be in the position to know more, and more variously. In this subtlety, and this relativity, biography is post-Freud and post-Einstein.

Indeed, biography can provide a kind of ethical mirror, in which we can see ourselves and our lives from new angles, with sudden force. Such 'mirrors' can have great influence over current movements: it is impossible to imagine the development of Feminism over the last twenty-five years, without the rediscovery and reinterpretation of such exemplary existences as those of Mary Wollstonecraft, Aphra Behn, Dorothy Wordsworth, Zelda Fitzgerald, or indeed Vita.

Nor is the biographic form itself static. Boswell had already tried many narrative modes to bring Johnson to vivid, complex, front-of-stage life. His dramatized conversations drew on the conventions of the Restoration comedy-of-manners (often using himself as foil and butt); his handling of Johnson's correspondence is partly inspired by Richardson's epistolary novels; his use of the *Diaries and Prayers* establish a Johnsonian inner voice from the Protestant tradition of solemn meditation.

Similarly, modern biographers experiment with the modes and conventions of truth-telling. Andrew Motion used the Forsythian interplay of a family saga to present three generations of *The Lamberts*. Ian Hamilton explored the limits of investigative journalism, and legal confrontation, when actually blocked by his own subject, in the sardonic, self-questioning, cautionary tale, *In Search of J. D. Salinger.* Peter Parker sensitively used a minor, tangential life of J. R. Ackerley to illuminate a whole literary period (and also another dog's life). Marina Warner re-examined a celebrated historical figure in terms of the legends and archetypes, transforming her through centuries, in *Joan of Arc.* Alan Judd brought his skills as a novelist to bear on the enormous series of displaced, fictional autobiographies that made up the apparently impenetrable, shape-shifting, comic epic of the life – or lives – of *Ford Madox Ford.* My own *Footsteps* is an attempt to explore the vertiginous experience of biographical research itself, through perilous time-warps of self-projection, solitary travel and the peculiar infatuations of the wandering scholar.

It is finally an unmistakable sign of the times, that modern novelists have themselves begun to respond to this challenge of the biographer invading new territories, so close to their fictional heartlands. They are decidedly *en garde.* The 'biographer' has indeed become a recognizable fictional type, often rapacious or self-deluded, but treading close upon the heels of the novelist in the search for shy, retreating, human truth.

In Julian Barnes's *Flaubert's Parrot,* in Penelope Lively's *According to Mark,* in William Golding's *The Paper Man,* or in A. S. Byatt's aptly named *Possession,* fictional biographers pant along the trail of fleeing authors – physically breathless and metaphysically out-manoeuvred – but memorably alive and relentless. Some even have fast cars. Here parody and polemic are surely a form of grudging tribute: the biographer has come of age, and demands the keys to the house of literature.

And that age, in my view, is still a golden one. It is still largely unhampered by critical theory, still flourishing outside the groves of academe, still maverick and impassioned, still genially in touch with a general readership. The godsons and goddaughters of Boswell have reason to be modestly rampant. Boswell once announced, in another of his delirious moments (he was in Cornwall, under heavy rain), that he preferred to be known as plain 'Mr B the biographer', than as 'Sir James B the High Court Judge' (which indeed, he never was). A delusion of grandeur, no doubt. But in celebrating his bicentenary, many readers may indulgently agree with him.

# BOSWELL AMONG THE TULIPS

When young James Boswell arrived in Holland in August 1763 at the age of twenty-two, his first impulse was to commit suicide. When he departed ten months later something much more alarming had occurred: he had fallen in love – or half in love – with a Dutch girl more intelligent than he.

After a respectable education at Edinburgh University, studying under David Hume, Boswell had run riot for a year in London, fathering an illegitimate child and flirting with deism, gambling and dreams of military glory. His redoubtable father, Lord Auchinleck, had called an abrupt halt to this dangerous libertinage and, recalling his own youthful sojourn at Utrecht (the Boswells had distinguished Dutch relatives in their Scottish ancestry), he despatched his prodigal son for a period of moral improvement among the Calvinist worthies, burghers and professors of the United Provinces. He was to acquire tone and intellectual rigour at the famous Law School in the cloisters of the huge, shadowy cathedral of Utrecht.

Arriving in the Hague from Harwich, Boswell embarked alone on a sluggish canal boat drawn by lumbering carthorses for the nine-hour journey to Utrecht, suddenly overcome by his 'own dismal imaginations'. His whole life seemed to grind to a gloomy halt amid these intolerable, green, empty flatlands. In Utrecht, at the Castle of Antwerp Inn, he was given an attic bedroom packed with ancient, dark wood furniture. There he was served a dry meal on a polished tray.

> At every hour the bells of the great [cathedral] tower
> played a dreary psalm tune. A deep melancholy seized

> upon me. I groaned with the idea of living all winter
> in so shocking a place. I thought myself old and
> wretched and forlorn ... All the horrid ideas you can
> imagine, recurred upon me. I was quite unemployed
> and had not a soul to speak to but the clerk of the
> English [Presbyterian] meeting ... I thought I should
> go mad ... I went out into the streets, and even in
> public could not refrain from groaning and weeping
> bitterly ... I took general speculative views of things; all
> seemed full of darkness and woe.

Such was Boswell's introduction to the improving delights of Holland.

He thought desperately of going to Berlin, Geneva or Paris, 'but above all of returning to London and my dear calm retreat in the Inner Temple'. Escape seemed the only alternative to madness. He seized upon an American doctor he found in the doorway of the inn and accompanied him on a rapid tour of Gouda, Amsterdam and Haarlem. On returning to Utrecht he was again overcome by horror and fled to Rotterdam half-determined to re-embark for home. He wrote to his old friend George Dempster (a Scots lawyer and Member of Parliament eight years his senior) who was in Paris, and, 'irresolute and fickle every hour', begged him to rendezvous immediately at Brussels. Answering this *cri-de-coeur*, Dempster flung himself into the next mail coach and covered the 186 miles from Paris in thirty hours, only to find that Boswell, overcome by guilt, had returned to Rotterdam, having finally resolved 'to go up to Utrecht for a week, and force myself to study six hours a day during that time'. If that failed to steady his nerve – well, he would try Leiden.

Dempster sent him a gentle letter of advice, based on his own superior experiences. To start with, he must accept that the glooms of British academia would be a 'a joke to Utrecht'. He must crack the conundrum of Dutch money and Dutch language. He must resign himself to the inspiring company of 'Dutch professors in tartan nightgowns with long pipes'. Like a good Christian, he must consider Utrecht as a vale of tears which would lead eventually 'to a better life in another country'. He must regard Holland as 'the dark watery passage which leads to an enchanted and brilliant grotto. For such is a French academy ...' Meanwhile, to ward off Calvinistic gloom: 'I should think you might amuse yourself in acquiring the French, keeping a journal and writing to your friends, and debauching a Dutch girl.' He must grow immune to silence, smoking, dullness and stinking cheese, and 'try to Dutchify your immortal soul'.

Boswell duly survived his first week in Utrecht, taking lodgings in the north-east corner of the cathedral square in Keizershof buildings, and hiring a Swiss manservant, François Mazarac, who was a paragon of punctuality – 'I am quite ready to lay a bet on him against all the clocks in the country.' By the end of September he had established a proper Dutch routine of severest virtue, combining classical French and legal studies with a little billiards and fencing by way of recreation. He was up at six-thirty a.m., read Ovid until nine, Tacitus till eleven and attended Professor Trotz's lectures on Civil Law at midday. In the afternoons he walked briskly round the tree-lined boulevard of the Utrecht Mall, bowing to the academical worthies, did a two-hour French conversation class and dined with the Reverend Robert Brown, an English pastor, and his family, practising Dutch. In the evenings he wrote a one-page essay in French or Dutch, a ten-line verse stanza, and composed entries in his daily journal and letters to his friends, who were properly amazed at this transformation.

There were one or two suspicious anomalies in this spartan perfection: he slipped out to a Dutch tailor and ordered two dazzling suits, 'of sea-green and lace, and scarlet with gold' for future parties; and his fencing-master turned out to be ninety-four years old. His early rising produced curious effects:

> As soon as I am awake, I remember my duty, and like
> a brisk mariner I give the lash to indolence and bounce
> up with as much vivacity as if a pretty girl, amorous and
> willing, were waiting for me.

(Early rising was always a delicate subject with Boswell, and he once considered patenting a device for tilting his bed into a vertical position, so that he slid out painlessly from under the blankets on to the floor.)

Lord Auchinleck wrote to congratulate his son on his resolutions and advised him to study the management of cattle and the Dutch 'contrivance for making their dung in no way offensive to them', and also to cultivate the society of Count Nassau, a prime mover in the Utrecht beau monde.

By October, Boswell was so spiritually well-regulated that he drew up at immense length a philosophical resolution about his future life, grandly entitled 'The Inviolable Plan', in which he determined to forswear all excesses and mould himself into a 'Christian gentleman', distinguished lawyer and Scottish paterfamilias. He promised himself to consult this document frequently and stick faithfully to all its commandments. Dempster now recommended the exemplum of Dutch society: 'Examine their industry, their commerce, the effects of frugality, freedom and good laws.'

Boswell had studied the English travel literature about Holland, notably the *Observations on the United Provinces* by the seventeenth-century British ambassador to the Hague, Sir William Temple; and the popular volume on the Netherlands in Thomas Nugent's *The Grand Tour* (1749). A vivid stereotype of Dutch virtues emerges from these works: stolid, hard-working, earthbound, egalitarian, commercially-minded, hygienic and irremediably dull. Temple summed it all up in a diplomat's measured and crafty formula, carefully dispensing praise with one hand and withdrawing it with the other.

> Holland is a country, where the earth is better than the air, and profit more in request than honour; where there is more sense than wit; more good nature than good humour; and more wealth than pleasure; where a man would choose rather to travel than to live; shall find more things to observe than desire; and more persons to esteem than to love.

But it was Thomas Nugent's comments on Dutch domestic life which particularly intrigued Boswell, whose Inviolable Plan included the search for a virtuous wife:

> The women have the whole care and management of their domestic affairs, and generally live in good fame; a certain sort of chastity being hereditary and habitual to them. They are more valued for their beauty, than their genteel carriage. A great many of them under-

stand trafick [trade] as well as the men; and it may be
said, that most of them wear the breeches.

They were, in short, the opposite of French women (who haunted
Boswell's wilder dreams), and allowing for the breeches clause,
were tantalizingly marriageable. This solemn thought gradually
came to occupy Boswell, the reformed rake and earnest student,
a good deal.

In mid-October the Utrecht social season opened, and Count
Nassau held the first of his grand soirées. A certain shift in moral
priorities now emerged in Boswell's outlook.

> Dress in scarlet and gold, fine swiss, white silk stockings,
> handsome pumps, and have silver-and-silk sword-knot,
> Barcelona handkerchief, and elegant toothpick-case
> which you had in present from a lady. Be quite the man
> of fashion and keep up your dignity.

But he still urged himself to be sober and serious. 'Don't think
it idle time, for while abroad being in good company is your great
scheme and is really improving.' These exhortations now become
a regular chorus in his memoranda for the journal, summarized
by the repeated word *retenue* – prudence and restraint.

> Always try to attain tranquillity ... Learn *retenue.* Pray
> do. Don't forget The Plan ... The more and oftener
> restraints, the better. Be steady.

It was in this mood that James Boswell met the first of his Tulips,
the colourful Dutch ladies who would hover entrancingly before
him, blooms to be plucked – as he thought – for the greater
improvement and decoration of the Boswellian pasture. Here, as
he hoped, was the true meaning of his Dutch cultivation. Here
the traveller would become a truly European gentleman.

She was the Count's younger sister-in-law, la Comtesse Nassau,
a glamorous and elegant lady married to a septuagenarian husband and renowned for her charm, her boredom and her love
affairs. The inflammation greatly improved Boswell's French and
his self-esteem. He was soon crowing in his letters:

> Our noblesse are come to town and all is alive. We have
> card-assemblies twice a week, which I do assure you, are

very brilliant, and private parties almost every evening. Madame la Comtesse de Nassau Beverweerd has taken me under her protection. She is a lady that, with all your serenity, would make you fall on your knees and utter love speeches in the style of Lord Shaftesbury's *Philosophical Rhapsody*, and that would please her exceedingly, for she delights in Shaftesbury's benevolent system. I really trembled at the transition which I made last week. But I have stood firm . . .

During the next few weeks Boswell danced attendance on the thirty-year-old Comtesse, his dry academic days alternating with glittering candle-lit evenings. He encouraged himself with ethical instructions: 'La Comtesse is charming, delicate, and sentimental. Adore her with easy affability, yet with polite distance, and acquire real habits of composure.' But he began to suspect that Thomas Nugent had not entirely understood the intriguing charms of Dutch women. He steadied himself by writing essays on the 'horrible fogs and excessive cold' of the climate; he tested himself by refusing to have a fire in his rooms until November, 'studying three or four hours on end shivering like an Italian greyhound'; and he sobered himself writing notes on the eccentricities of Professor Trotz – his fund of historical anecdotes and his memories of Friesland that made Utrecht sound like the centre of world civilization and 'the seat of felicity'.

The airy gallantry of the Comtesse did not however solidify into a flirtation. Unknown to Boswell she was involved elsewhere and duly produced an illegitimate child the following year. Though he upbraided himself – 'no love; you are to marry' – he also admitted that he was 'sorry somehow' that his virtue was 'not to be put to the trial'. The Comtesse did on the other hand rapidly introduce him to Utrecht society and even drew up a list of eligible ladies for Boswell's edification. From November onwards the names of two other Tulips began to sprout regularly in Boswell's memoranda: Madame Geelvinck and Mademoiselle de Zuylen. One of his earliest memories of the latter was of her playing an expert game of shuttlecock.

Catherina Elisabeth Geelvinck was a Dutch merry widow. The charming, spoilt daughter of an exceedingly rich local family of merchants, she married at eighteen, produced a child at nineteen and was fortuitously widowed at twenty. Now twenty-four, exceedingly beautiful and with a large private income, she laid waste the drawing-rooms of Utrecht with broken-hearted suitors. Students sang about her, and foreign visitors (especially the minor German nobility) got drunk in her honour. She was known universally and somewhat breathlessly as *la Veuve*. Low-voiced, cool and coquettish, she spent vast sums on the latest Paris fashions to show off her splendid, milky charms. Her large brown eyes had a slight cast, and transfixed Boswell with their hint of sexual naughtiness. In reality Madame Geelvinck had a calculating heart, poured all her emotions into her only son and comported herself with enough care to achieve two more marriages and an even larger income. But for Boswell she was an immediate challenge.

Isabelle van Tuyl van Serooskerken, the expert shuttlecock player, was the eldest daughter of the aristocratic family of van Tuyl, with their ancestral castle at Zuylen, just outside Utrecht. Very different from the languid Madame Geelvinck, she was a young woman of the new age: essentially restless, inquiring, forever dissatisfied with the world about her. She was the same age as Boswell and the very opposite of all his assumptions about Dutch women. Tall, fun-loving, brilliantly quick and clever, she had a fine open face with a high intellectual forehead and carelessly brushed back auburn hair which seemed to flame above her head. From the start she both fascinated and frightened Boswell; she was capable of wrong-footing him at every turn. His very first entry about her says he had put on 'foolish airs of passion for Miss de Zuylen'; his second that he had been deeply shocked by her 'unlimited vivacity'.

Isabelle was highly educated: encouraged as a child to read and write by a clever Swiss governess, she had pursued her studies in classics, mathematics and philosophy, not always regarded as the most ladylike of subjects. While her younger sister married, Isabelle retained her own apartment at Zuylen (overlooking the gatehouse where she could observe the comings and goings of the world) and read Plutarch, Newton and Voltaire late into the night. In her late teens she began to write a stream of stories, essays, poems and letters in French, and patronized the Utrecht bookseller for the latest titles. She became expert in algebra and conic sections, the harpsichord, shuttlecock and witty repartee. She grew mocking about decorous behaviour, dull marriages, Calvinist religion, even money and the weather.

At twenty, Isabelle met a Swiss army officer at the Hague named Constant d'Hermenches, an aristocratic rake twice her age. They began a clandestine correspondence (via the Utrecht bookseller) which was to last over a decade. The correspondence sealed Isabelle's reputation in Utrecht for eccentricity and unladylike behaviour. In fact the letters are exercises in style and self-analysis, rather than romance; they give a matchless picture of daily life at Zuylen and Utrecht and contrast Isabelle's free-thinking views on marriage with d'Hermenches's worldly cynicism.

At the time of Boswell's arrival in Holland, Isabelle had completed a satirical short story, 'Le Noble', telling of a romantic elopement from an ancestral Dutch castle surrounded by a moat, with an unmistakable resemblance to Zuylen. In a scene that shocked Utrecht society, the heroine, Julie, hurls down from her bedroom window a series of oil-paintings of her illustrious forebears, in order to form a bridge by which she can escape over the moat into her lover's arms. The story was signed 'Zélide', and it was by this literary pseudonym that Boswell came to refer to her.

While Boswell's social life began to flourish, his private existence in his solitary lodgings at the Keizershof was less easy. He was dogged by depressions and the old longing for dissipation. He admonished himself: 'Fight out the winter here, and learn as much as you can. Pray, pray be *retenue*.' Cheerful and amusing in company, he relapsed into the deepest gloom in his lodgings, where the huge cathedral tower cast its shadow over his windows, always standing between himself and the watery winter sunlight. He worried about his future and mused on Calvinist questions of predestination and damnation. He was a young man discovering a contradiction in his own nature – his own national characteristic, perhaps – and slowly finding that the only palliative was what had begun as a light-hearted hobby: his obsessive, self-analytical journal-keeping. Boswell was discovering the controlling element of his literary genius: the impulse towards an astonishingly candid autobiographical form. Describing himself through others, he would end by describing others through himself, with unparalleled intimacy, sensitivity and wit. It was a pleasure that grew out of pain; a sociable form that grew out of extreme solitude; a strategy of survival learned by a traveller in a foreign land.

At the same time as his launch into the drawing-rooms of Utrecht, Boswell almost committed an unpardonable *faux pas* in the streets by getting involved with a drunken group of students, rashly revealing his rakish propensities. He entered this memorandum for the night of 23 November.

> At night you truly had an adventure. You saw an entertainment of Dutch students; a concert; all keen on meat and drink; then marching like schoolboys with *Kapitein* and frightening the street. Then home; then saw the masks, and one like a woman; then house again, conditionless, drank roaring – songs. King George [the toast Boswell proposed amidst the mêlée]. Compliments paid you etc. Mark all in Journal.

The following day, in penitential sobriety, he anxiously recorded this close shave with his private, uncivilized self, and issued a stern warning.

> Yesterday you recovered well after your riot with the Dutch students. But remember how near you was to getting drunk and exposing yourself, for if you had gone on a little longer, you could not have stopped. You have important secrets to keep ... always shun drinking, and guard lips ...

Boswell's public reputation survived this lapse, and in December he set off for the Hague to celebrate Christmas, look up his distant Dutch relatives, make contact with the British ambassador and take stock of his position. For there was now a delicate question forming in his mind, as he later explained to his friend Temple in the bluffest manner he could command.

> There are two ladies here, a young, handsome, amiable widow (Madame Geelvinck) with £4,000 a year; and Mademoiselle de Zuylen, who has only a fortune of £20,000. She is a charming creature. But she is a *savante* and a *bel esprit*, and has published some things. She is much my superior. One does not like that. One does not like a widow, neither. You won't allow me to yoke

myself here? You *will* have me married to an English woman?

Boswell found out a good deal about his Tulips at the Hague, much of it through dinner-party gossip. He found the Dutch habit of intimate gossip fascinating – everyone seemed to know everyone else's secrets, rather on the same principle that Dutch parlours never had their curtains drawn against the onlookers' gaze. He learned to provoke the gossip with innocent questions, and practised recording the dialogue in his journal.

He passed 'three weeks in the most brilliant gaiety' at the Hague, pleasantly surprised by a style of living that was 'much in the manner of Paris'. He was presented to the Prince of Orange and all the foreign ambassadors and cut a fine figure in his alternating suits of scarlet and Leiden green. He noted 'formerly such a change of life used to unhinge me quite', but he felt in control of himself and returned calmly to Utrecht – now 'the seat of the Dutch muses' – in mid-January 1764 to resume his studious regularity 'with much satisfaction'. But the real reason for his equanimity was less the philosophic pleasure of Professor Trotz's lectures than the tantalizing delights of the Utrecht salons, where his Tulips were now blooming again before his eyes.

By the end of January he was engaged in an intricate social minuet with the three ladies. The Comtesse tended to be jealous, the widow to be flirtatious, the *bel esprit* to be satirical. It was all very good for his education. A typical evening of this amorous dance occurred on 28 January, which Boswell recorded with the greatest satisfaction.

> At Assembly you was easy with *la Comtesse*, but saw her piqued. You must make up this by easy complaisance, as she can do you more service than Zélide. You played cards with Madame Geelvinck – charming indeed. You said to Zélide 'I love Sue' etc. But the contrary is true with you and me.

The 'I love Sue' was a mocking reference to a popular song about falling in love with a girl before the lover had even met her. Boswell was implying that he felt like that about Madame Geelvinck, but not about Mademoiselle de Zuylen, alas. Zélide was quite up to this teasing, and replied with ironic regret: 'Oh, *I* was prepossessed in *your* favour.' This hit its mark, and afterwards Boswell feared he had been 'too severe' with Zélide.

By February it was clear that Madame Geelvinck, with her huge brown eyes and generous inviting figure, was winning ascendancy in Boswell's heart. The Comtesse began to concentrate on beating Boswell at cards, but Zélide – who was less flattered than amused by Boswell – adopted a more subtle strategy to hold his attention. Alone among the ladies at Utrecht, Zélide had penetrated the introspective side of Boswell's character; she already suspected that he kept an intimate journal (this was one of the 'secrets' that Boswell always feared he would let slip) and guessed at his literary leanings. She saw that he played and experimented with human nature – his own and everyone else's. She saw that he loved drama, complication, self-revelation: the comedy of human identity and exchange. Indeed in this, as in his depressions and solitude, he was much like herself. She therefore teasingly announced that she had written 'Character Portraits' of many of her friends – including the Comtesse and Madame Geelvinck – and also of herself, and that if he continued to amuse her Boswell might eventually see them. This was to prove an intellectual seduction quite as powerful, in the long run, as Madame Geelvinck's promising *décolletage*.

As Boswell plunged towards that delicious object, Zélide's subtler influence continued to make itself felt, although not enough to spoil the would-be lover's self-importance.

> At Assembly you appeared in sea-green and silver and was really brilliant – much taken notice of and like an ambassador. You begin to be much at your ease and to take a true foreign polish. Madame Geelvinck was charming. You told her you expected to see her 'Character' by Zélide. She said, 'It is not interesting.' You said, 'Oh, do not say that to me' . . . You played whist well. After it you felt, for the first time in Holland, delicious love. *O la belle Veuve!* She talked low to you and close, perhaps to feel breath. All the *Heeren* looked blue. You took her to the coach, and your frame thrilled . . .

Throughout February this tantalizing courtship among the cards and candles continued, with Madame Geelvinck whispering in her low voice, 'looking all elegance and sweetness', patting Boswell's hand and 'correcting his French delightfully'. 'You are much in love,' he wrote. 'She perhaps wishes to marry rationally. But have a care.'

Meanwhile a very different sort of friendship was developing with Zélide. Boswell was introduced to her family at their Utrecht house and became a particular favourite with her father. He was also much liked by her brothers, sharing tales of field sports and the army. Zélide could speak fluent French and English, and also helped him with Dutch. She could still sometimes be 'nervish' and too boisterous for his taste, making fun of anything conventional – even religion and marriage – but on the whole she played gently with Boswell, and talked seriously about his studies.

> You drank tea at Monsieur de Zuylen's. He shook you cordially by the hand. All was *en famille* and fine. You talked of your [plan for a] Dutch Dictionary.

Just occasionally she played the *bel esprit* and delivered one of her shafts of ironic knowledge, so that he winced.

> You supped elegant at Mademoiselle de Zuylen's with [her uncle] the General etc. She said, 'You write everything down.' Have a care. Never speak on that subject.

But now, almost without Boswell being aware of it, Zélide had set up an emotional triangle in which the lines of power and affection played continually against each other in his heart. While he was officially 'in love' with Madame Geelvinck, he was 'in confidence' with Zélide: he courted one woman, but confided in the other.

This pattern is steadily revealed in his memoranda.

> Yesterday you sent note to Madame Geelvinck, quite young man of fashion . . . At Assembly you was quite at ease. You begin really to have the foreign usage. You said to Zélide, 'Come, I will make a pact of frankness with you for the whole winter, and you with me.' You talked freely to her of prudence. But you talked too much. They all stared.

Madame Geelvinck perhaps understood what was happening better than Boswell. When he declared his love for her openly on

19 February, she responded with the greatest tranquillity. Boswell was a little put out, as he records.

> *Boswell:* But did you not know that I was in love with you?
> *Mme Geelvinck:* No, really. I thought it was with Mademoiselle de Zuylen; and I said nothing about it.

In other conversations (Boswell was now revelling in his dialogue-writing) Zélide's name keeps cropping up at the very point where Boswell is trying to be most intimate with his glamorous widow; she is summoned up at the exact moment that should be most private. It must have been very tiresome for Madame Geelvinck to be flirting through the invisible presence of this third party:

> *Boswell:* Madame, I am discreet. I would that my heart were plucked out for you to see.
> *Mme Geelvinck:* Are you good-natured?
> *Boswell:* On my honour. I am a very honest man with a very generous heart. But I am a little capricious, though I shall cure that. It was only a year ago that I was the slave of imagination and talked like Mademoiselle de Zuylen. But I am making great advances in prudence.
> *Mme Geelvinck:* Have you good principles?
> *Boswell:* Yes. When I say, 'That is a duty', then I do it. Mademoiselle de Zuylen says that I am never bored, but I do get bored, though I never show it.

The widow had many other admirers, but Boswell joyfully kept up his siege, reporting back to Zélide on his manoeuvres: he cornered *la Veuve* at card parties, whispered to her behind the potted plants at the Assembly and even got himself invited to her little son's birthday party – a notable *coup* – tactfully informing her that the boy was like 'a spark from the sun in heaven'. However, at the end of the month Madame Geelvinck announced that she was leaving for the Hague, and though she promised to write, Boswell knew he was now doomed to play the much less satisfactory role of abandoned suitor. On the day of her departure, after a restless night, he rose before dawn, slipped a flask of gin in his pocket and hurried over to the St Catherine's Gate to watch her coach leave Utrecht. It was freezing, but deploying his new-found Dutch he talked his way into the sentry's guard-post and, huddled in the doorway, he watched her pass. 'She looked angelic, and that glimpse was ravishing. You then treated the sentinel with Geneva (gin). You stood on the ramparts and saw her disappear. You was quite torn with love.'

Boswell then marched manfully off to his fencing lesson, but was miserable – 'very bad all day' – and had an awful premonition that his depression was about to return. He managed to keep up a good front at the Comtesse's evening reception, but fell into gloomiest reflections back at his lodgings. He now had only one Tulip left, and the next morning he tried to take comfort from that.

> Love has now fairly left you, and behold in how dreary
> a state you was in. At night you was listless and distressed
> and obliged to go drawling to bed. This day study hard;
> get firm tone; go on. Mademoiselle [de Zuylen] will be
> your friend.

He had need of her. In March the dreaded Utrecht depression returned. The weather became damp and foggy – although not cold enough for skating – and he caught a severe head-cold which lasted for nearly six weeks. He then received news from friends that his illegitimate son Charles had died. The regular Assemblies closed down for the season. He felt horribly marooned. There was only one source of light.

> You was fine with Mademoiselle de Zuylen. She was
> amiable. She said you might see her at home at least
> once a week . . . She said *la Veuve* had no passion, and
> often ill humour. This girl trusts you; like her . . . Shun
> marriage. Today, honey for cold.

Boswell's battle with gloom, ill-health and homesickness was to last until April, and Zélide gradually became his main ally in the fight.

She gave him her 'Character Portraits' to read and also probably her satirical story 'Le Noble'. She began to share confidences with him, describing her claustrophobic situation at the castle at Zuylen and hinting at her clandestine correspondence with Constant d'Hermenches. But Boswell was never quite sure how to respond, how far to trust her; she was so changeable, so clever. He never quite admitted his guilty secret about Charles to her.

> You told her you was distressed for the death of a friend, and begged to see if she could be company to the distressed. She said yes, but she soon showed her eternal laughing . . . You told her she never had a better friend. She said, 'I believe it.' This day *retenue*, be firm and only silent. What a world is this!

When he was impatient with her, he considered writing a comedy about the absurdities of her life, her blue-stocking intrigues and her stolid Dutch family (of which, in reality, he was very fond). It was to be entitled *The Female Scribbler*, with a good range of character parts, and himself as the 'sensible' foreign hero. It would contain 'old, surly squire; weak, ignorant mother; light, trifling lover whom she does not care for; foolish maid; heavy, covetous bookseller; generous, sensible lover etc.' In this mood he also vented his spleen on the Comtesse, by the more direct method of trouncing her at cards.

> *La Comtesse* was truly chagrined. But you knocked a pair of ducats out of her pocket at cards. This turned up her Dutch nose . . . After dinner you said imprudently you had so bad a view of life that you could do almost anything.

By now Boswell was again swinging through terrible extremes. On one day he rose 'dreary as a dromedary'; on the next he was valiantly determined to 'sustain the character of a country gentleman'. He received a 'sweet and elegant letter' from Madame Geelvinck in the Hague, and momentarily thought her 'the finest prize in the Provinces'; but then found – 'alas! it did not elevate your gloomy soul.' He tried eating at a raffish hotel in the Oudkerkhof, but then came home in misery.

> You dined at Kloster's – blackguards. You was direfully melancholy and had the last and most dreadful thoughts. You came home and prayed. You read Greek, and Voltaire on the English.

He tried to drown himself in study: Xenophon, Plato, Civil Law, his idea for a Dutch dictionary; but ended up discussing predestination with the Reverend Brown.

Assailed by thoughts of suicide, Boswell turned his mind to his warlike Scottish ancestors and went out one winter's dawn into the deserted meadows beyond Utrecht Cathedral where he performed a curious ritual with a dress sword.

> You went out into the fields, and in view of the [cathedral] tower, drew your sword glittering in the sun, and on your knees swore that if there is a Fatality, then that was also ordained: but if you had free will, as you believed, you swore and called the Great God to witness that, although you're melancholy, you'll stand it, and for the time before you go to Hague, now own it.

Then he went grimly off to Professor Trotz's lecture.

Later in the day he returned to the cathedral, climbed the narrow stone steps to the top of the tower, over 350 feet high, and stood silently looking down on Utrecht, and far out across the stretching misty expanse of Holland, pierced with innumerable spires, towards his Scottish homeland far in the north. Then he hurried off and took tea with Zélide.

Zélide's highly iconoclastic views on marriage gradually came to fascinate Boswell, providing not merely a diversion to his melancholy, but something of a solace. He found a new role: no longer the desperate, lovelorn traveller, he became the wise, amusing, philosophic friend.

Her autobiographical 'Character', which he kept among his papers with a series of sheets headed 'Portrait of Zélide', provided him with much material for reflection. In many ways she seemed strikingly like himself (though he would never admit this), and her situation was one that he instinctively understood. Certain passages went straight to his heart. Zélide had written of herself:

> Realising that she is too sensitive to be happy, she has almost ceased to hope for happiness. She flees from remorse and pursues diversion. Her pleasures are rare, but they are lively. She snatches them, she relishes them eagerly. Aware of the futility of planning and the uncertainty of the future, she seeks above all to make the passing moment happy. Can you not guess her secret? Zélide is something of a sensualist. Too lively and too powerful feelings; too much inner activity with no satisfactory outlet: there is the source of all her misfortunes.

Boswell could identify with that restlessness, that secret 'sensuality', that excessive 'inner activity', only too well. It was exactly these things that he was trying to curb in himself. So he set out to curb them in Zélide instead. He would not so much court this Tulip as cultivate her, guide her and if necessary defend her in the little daily duels of Dutch gossip. He would become her adviser and her champion. It was understood that she was wittier, cleverer perhaps, than he; but in exchange it was also to be understood that he was wiser, more morally sound, than she. That is the role that Boswell now assigned to himself, and which, with touching vanity, he assumed that Zélide (not to mention her parents) would gratefully accept from a young Scottish gentleman of parts. It was one way, after all, of avoiding suicide. And psychologically it also represented a subtle shift from the autobiographical to the biographical mode.

Boswell was determined to stay on in Utrecht – to 'stick to his post' – until the end of the academic year in June. But it was Zélide, not Madame Geelvinck, who now held him. He wrote long letters to his friends Dempster and Temple, and even to his father, explaining his depression and also his determination.

> It is certain that I am subject to melancholy. It is the
> distemper of our family. I am equally subject to excess-
> ive high spirits. Such is my constitution. Let me study
> it, and let me maintain an equality of mind.

They all wrote back encouragingly, Lord Auchinleck with the greatest feelings of sympathy, having experienced similar emotions in youth. He bracingly quoted Virgil:

> You are not therefore to despond or despair; on the
> contrary, you must arm yourself doubly against them,
> as the poet directs: '*Tu ne cede malis, sed contra audentior
> ito.*' [Thou shall not give way to misfortune but strive
> against it with greater daring.]

And he warned gently against his son's amatory flights: 'Your Dutch wit and Dutch widow are not so easily caught as our Scots lasses.'

As part of his philosophic strategy, Boswell now told Zélide that he was busy finding her an ideal husband in England who would greatly improve her moral outlook. This was an ingenious form of displaced courtship. Temple was chosen for this delightful task, and he responded enthusiastically to this new double intrigue of his wayward friend.

> So the Countess turns out to be a jilt. I am already in love with Mademoiselle de Zuylen. Charming creature! young and handsome, *une savante et bel esprit.* Tell her an Englishman adores her and would think it the greatest happiness of his life to have it in his power to prostrate himself at her feet. You shall have the widow. Don't be angry.

Boswell might have been angry, or at least a little put out, had he known in what spirit of mischievous fun Zélide received these confidences and observed all his grand, philosophic man-oeuvrings. Her own side of the story can easily be traced through the letters she was sending almost daily to Constant d'Her-menches. She first mentioned Boswell in March. 'When I go to the Assembly, I chat and play with a young Scotsman, full of good sense, wit, and *naiveté*.' The emphasis was undoubtedly, for Zélide, on that *naiveté*. By May, she was relishing his plan to make her 'more rational, more prudent, and more reserved' through the curious mechanism of marriage to a Scotsman: 'I am greatly amused.' She was running rings round him; it was this fact which gave her such a genuine pleasure in his company.

Boswell was now in the liveliest state of confusion about his own feelings. While speaking to Zélide of reason and prudence, he was secretly planning a thoroughly imprudent visit to the red-light district in Amsterdam, as a way of treating his depression and completing his Dutch education. While singing Zélide's praises to Temple, he was simultaneously writing in extreme exasperation in his journal.

> Yesterday you continued in a kind of delirium. You wrote all day. At night you was at Monsieur de Zuylen's . . . Zélide was *nervish*. You saw she would make a sad wife and propagate wretches. You reflected when you came home that you have not made enough use of your time. You have not been active enough, learned enough Dutch, enough of manners.

Yet when Zélide was criticized by a Dutch naval captain, Petre

Reynst, he again leapt faithfully to her defence. Reynst had remarked cuttingly that Zélide had been brought up in Geneva, and there was 'unlimited wit among the ladies' but a total lack of 'good principles'. She sacrificed 'probity to wit', like a typical blue-stocking.

Boswell answered with a gallant broadside. 'I fought like her champion. I said, "That young lady makes me feel very humble, when I find her so much above me in wit, in knowledge, in good sense."'

Reynst politely demurred. 'She lacks good sense and consequently she goes wrong; and a man who has not half her wit and knowledge may still be above her.'

Boswell pretended to disagree, but did not know exactly what to reply, for it was secretly just what he thought himself. Boswell believed that it was the male sex who must always command, out of a natural God-given superiority. Zélide directly challenged this notion. It was a profound clash of cultural assumptions, in its own way a clash between Enlightenment and the advance shock-wave of Romanticism. If Boswell aspired to be an Enlightenment *philosophe*, Zélide was already acting like a Romantic rebel. Boswell added a comment that is one of the most acute things ever observed about Isabelle de Zuylen.

> I thought [Reynst's criticism] very true, and I thought it a good thing. For were it not for that lack [of good sense], Zélide would have an absolute power. She would have unlimited dominion over men, and would overthrow the dignity of the male sex.

At the end of May, Boswell took the canal boat to Amsterdam, in an ecstasy of nerves and expectation, to assert the God-given superiority of man in a Dutch bawdy-house. At the same time he had accepted an invitation from 'dear Zélide' to visit her for the first time at her family castle. The two expeditions, which took place within twenty-four hours of each other, reveal his divided self with a comedy worthy of Diderot.

Boswell chose a Saturday night for his Amsterdam expedition. Having spent all Friday night awake on the canal boat 'among ragamuffins', he arrived 'restless and fretful', put up at Grubb's English Hotel and spent the morning paying courtesy calls on a series of Scottish clergymen. He then dined with an English merchant, drinking a good deal. These psychological preparations were somewhat marred by the realization that he had no condom to protect himself against venereal disease, and he did not know where to purchase one in Amsterdam. (The eighteenth-century condom was usually made of animal-bladder, and referred to as a 'sheath' or 'armour'; it was expensive and therefore considered to be reusable in an emergency.)

Trusting to luck, Boswell blundered off to a bawdy-house at five o'clock. 'I was shown upstairs, and had a bottle of claret and a *juffrouw*.' But on closer inspection Boswell concluded that the girl had more need of a doctor than a customer and excused himself. 'I had no armour, so did not fight. It was truly ludicrous to talk in Dutch to a whore. This scene was to me a rarity as great as peas in February.' He suddenly felt ashamed of himself, wondering what he was doing in 'the sinks of gross debauchery', and he fled in deepest gloom. Back in the streets he then upbraided himself for moral cowardice: 'so sickly was my brain that I had the low scruples of an Edinburgh divine.'

But the comedy was not over. Boswell rushed off to another Scottish clergyman, James Blinshall (there seemed to be an endless supply of these hospitable reverends in Amsterdam), and sat talking of 'religious melancholy like a good sound fellow' until nine in the evening. This revived his spirits, and he then went drinking at a Scottish tavern called Farquhar's 'among blackguards', and supped with an Irish peruke-maker. It was, he thought hazily, turning into a 'queer evening' altogether. By eleven he was back on the streets looking for a *speelhuis*, the Dutch equivalent of a dance-hall. But he had no guide (and still no 'armour').

> I therefore very madly sought for one myself and strolled up and down the Amsterdam streets, which by all accounts are very dangerous at night. I began to be frightened and to think of Belgic *knives*.

But weaving through the narrow alleys, he persisted until he heard music, found the *speelhuis* and 'entered boldly'.

One can just about reconstruct the scene from his by now rather confused notes. A band was playing in one corner; the place was packed with sailors and whores; everyone was dancing and drunk. Boswell lurched to the bar, obtained a drink and a pipe and launched himself into the mêlée, talking wildly in Dutch to anyone he bumped into. 'I had near quarrelled with one of the musicians. But I was told to take care, which I wisely did.' He was transfixed by the extraordinary fancy dress worn by all the girls. Finally he found one got up in 'riding-clothes', with a mass of lace frou-frou, and cheerfully danced with her 'a true blackguard minuet'. For a little while he forgot everything in this strange, erotic *pas de deux*. 'I had my pipe in my mouth and performed like any common sailor.' Then he was suddenly tired and drunk and hopeless. 'I spoke plenty of Dutch but could find no girl that elicited my inclinations. I was disgusted with this low confusion.' Boswell staggered out, miraculously found his way back to Grubb's Hotel, and 'slept sound'.

He played out the final act of his great Amsterdam expedition, which he realized had turned into low farce, on Sunday morning. He went meekly off to the English Ambassador's chapel, heard a 'good sermon', dined and then returned to hear James Blinshall preach. He was overwhelmed by 'all the old Scots gloomy ideas', and determined on one last sortie before the return to Utrecht.

> I then strolled through mean brothels in dirty lanes. I was quite splenetic. I still wanted amour. I drank tea with Blinshall. At eight I got into the *roef* of the Utrecht boat. I had with me an Italian fiddler, a German officer, his wife and child.

So his wild weekend finished penitently, on a subdued domestic note. Boswell did not know whether to be more ashamed by what he had attempted to do in Amsterdam, or by what he had failed to do. Back at Utrecht he was 'changeful and uneasy' all day. There was nothing for the philosopher to be proud of, either way.

His expedition to Zuylen was such an absolute contrast that even Boswell was somewhat bewildered by his own capacity for extremes. In response to Zélide's invitation, he and the Reverend Brown walked the five miles to the ancestral castle on the Vecht, and were instantly captivated by the old moated building with its four pointed turrets reflected in the still waters. Gazing round at the ancient brick gatehouse, the cobbled paths, the formal gardens and the stretching vistas of beech trees opening out on to placid water meadows dotted with windmills, Boswell had a new vision of Zélide's existence. She became for him the daughter of a magic domain, a princess in an enchanted tower, imprisoned perhaps by her own brilliant perversities, which the wandering young philosopher must waken with a kiss. Or the spiritual equivalent of a kiss. This image of Zélide, like a figure out of a Dutch fairy tale, would never quite leave Boswell. And her enigmatic quality, her refusal ever wholly to yield her mysterious independence of soul, became for him a symbol of Holland itself.

They returned that evening to Utrecht, and dined with the assembled van Tuyl clan. Boswell at once set about charming Zélide, summoning up all his Scottish sagacity, teasing, reasoning, playing his philosophic part to the full. She was highly responsive, and together in that elegant company, they danced a very different kind of minuet, each wondering who was in love with whom.

> Zélide was too vivacious, abused system, and laughed at reason, saying that she was guided by a *sentiment intérieur*. I was lively in defence of wisdom and showed her how wrong she was, for if she had no settled system one could never count on her. One could not say what she would do. I said to her also, 'You must show a little decorum. You are among rational beings, who boast of their reason, and who do not like to hear it flouted.' Old De Zuylen and all fifteen friends were delighted with me.

After dinner Boswell and Zélide slipped away and walked together outside in the fine spring evening, wandering into 'a sweet pretty wood'. It was the moment for romantic declarations, but Boswell carefully changed tack, and deployed his double intrigue.

> I delivered to Zélide the fine compliments which my friend Temple had charged me to deliver; that is to say, the warm sentiments of adoration. She was much pleased. I talked to her seriously and bid her marry a *bon baron* of good sense and amiable manners who would be her superior in common life, while he admired her fine genius and all that.

Zélide gazed at Boswell with amusement. 'She said she would marry such a man if she ever saw him. But still she would fain have something finer.' They turned to go back into the house, and Boswell risked a final shift of direction.

'I said she should never have a man of much sensibility. For instance, "I would not marry you if you would make me King of the Seven Provinces." '

Zélide burst out laughing and later reported the whole conversation to d'Hermenches. 'He told me the other day that although I was a charming creature, he would not marry me if I had the Seven United Provinces for my dowry; I agreed heartily.' So the princess and the philosopher dallied, and in 'fine, gay, free conversation did the minutes fly'.

There was not enough time left for Boswell to resolve his own paradoxes, or those of Zélide. His Dutch sojourn was drawing to its close. In early June, Lord Marischal, an old friend of Lord Auchinleck's, arrived at the Hague and announced that he had come to take Boswell on the next stage of his European journey. He promised to take him into Germany on a visit to the Prussian Court of Frederick the Great. Boswell's thoughts swung rapidly from love to glory, and he began to pack his law books, while ordering 'a genteel flowered-silk suit'.

Boswell's last days were spent in a flurry of visits to Zélide in her enchanted castle and a series of extended farewells. He swung between passion and relief. Peter Reynst informed him that Zélide was 'really in love' with Boswell. 'I believed it. But I was mild and *retenue*.' On 10 June, he rushed up to Zuylen in a splendid hired chaise and his mood was very different.

> I was in solid spirits in the old chateau, but rather too odd was I; for I talked of my pride, and wishing to be kind. Zélide and I were left alone. She owned that she was hypochondriac [melancholy], and that she had no religion other than that of the adoration of one God. In short, she discovered an unhinged mind; yet I loved her.

He saw her again on the eleventh, when she was in 'a fever of spirits', as was he. On the twelfth he met her at her music master's, where she played delightfully and then took him for a walk. 'I was touched with regret at the thought of parting with her. Yet she rattled on so much that she really vexed me.' It was all very confusing to Boswell.

On 14 June, he again leapt into his chaise to take his final farewell at Zuylen. Once more the talk was of husbands: of Boswell's ideals of deference and Zélide's notions of freedom. Their conversation was inconclusive. 'I owned to her that I was very sorry to leave her. She gave me many a tender look. We took a kind farewell, as did all the family.' They had agreed to write secretly to each other, and that evening Zélide began a long letter to pursue him into Germany. 'I find you odd and lovable,' she wrote succinctly. Meanwhile back at Utrecht the Scottish chaplain observed: 'It is lucky that you are no longer together; for you would learn her nonsense, and she would learn yours.' Boswell manfully agreed.

On the eve of Boswell's departure from Utrecht, old Lord Marischal, who had evidently heard a great deal of Zélide, mischievously announced that he would be fascinated to visit Zuylen himself. Accordingly Boswell found himself one last time at the castle. With curious Dutch formality, they all sat round drinking tea in the open air, while the swallows spun round the moat and along the darkening colonnades of beech. Boswell drew Zélide aside, and she whispered, 'Are you back again? We made a touching adieu.' Then she gave him the letter, which he was told not to read until he was actually and really going.

> Zélide seemed much agitated, said she had never been in love, but said that *one* might meet with *un homme amiable*, etc. etc. etc. for whom *one* might feel a strong affection, which would probably be lasting, *but* this amiable man might not have the same affection for *one*. In short she spoke too plain to leave me in doubt that she *really* loved me. But then she went with her wild fancy, saying she thought only of the present moment.

All was confusion and Boswell told himself she was 'a frantic libertine'. In the circumstances, it was a conclusion of the most perfect irony.

It was dusk when they rose to leave. Zélide gave Boswell her hand, and in the half-light of that Dutch still life, he thought he could glimpse a painterly luminescence: 'The tender tear stood crystal in her eye. Poor Zélide!' Or rather, poor Boswell.

The next day he left for Germany.

Boswell and Zélide never met again, although they corresponded in a desultory fashion over the subsequent four years. Boswell did finally propose marriage, and Zélide, inevitably, turned him down.

# DR JOHNSON'S FIRST CAT

IN THOSE DAYS, I often used to hold conversations with Mr Boswell about the great Doctor. We would lounge in the little pannelled backroom of the Mitre tavern on Fleet Street, and warm our porter by the sea-coal fire. Mr Boswell was then in his biographical pre-eminence, and sported extravagant silver buckles on his shoes. He was much inclined to reminisce about his long-departed friend, and took much pleasure in what he called a *two-bottle talk*, when he would hang his wig upon the bench-end and refer to it with his eye, very quick and bright and mischievous.

I was then a mere law-student at the Inner Temple, with a shabby cupboard above the great clock. But young and bookish as I was, Mr Boswell was kind enough to call me *one of the ancient fraternity of night*. Indeed he seemed to relish company in those after-hours, and treated my half-sovereigns in his fine, free clubbable manner. 'Let us *lucubrate* upon the unaccountable laws of human nature,' he would say.

One of his most curious revelations concerned Johnson's cats. They were creatures upon which the great Lexicographer, as is notorious, doted with uncommon tenderness. But Mr Boswell was always very uneasy in their presence, since – as he said – they had an air of contemptuous knowledge. If they chose to tell us what they knew of mankind, we should all be confounded. Besides, they were very lascivious creatures and would fawn upon Johnson's great bulk with an unbecoming intimacy.

The most celebrated of these feline companions was one Hodge, a large uxorious tabby-cat, for whom Johnson would purchase oysters in Houndsditch market. Mr Boswell has dedicated a famous passage in his *Life of Johnson* to this familiar, which he once recited to me with a nice turn of Scotch emphasis. 'I frequently suffered a good deal from the presence of this same Hodge. I recollect him one day scrambling up Dr Johnson's breast, apparently with much satisfaction, while my friend smiling and half-whistling, rubbed down his back, and pulled him by the tail; and when I observed he was a fine cat, saying, "why yes Sir, *but I have had cats whom I liked better than this*;" and then as if perceiving Hodge to be out of countenance, adding, "but he is a very fine cat, a very fine cat indeed." '

Mr Boswell ended this recitation with a kind of speculative *hum*, which was peculiar to him, half humorous and half doubting, as if there might be more to be said on the matter. His quick eye referred to the wig hanging between us, and the empty goblet at his side. I made the necessary adjustments, while he leaned forwards and very delicately prodded the fire with the iron poker, as I was afterwards pleased to think, like a man dipping his quill into the embers of memory that were still hot. 'Yes,' he murmured into the glowing coals, '*there were other cats whom he liked better.*'

There followed, over several evenings, a strange *testament* (if I may so term it), which I piece and plot together as best I can, being wholly without Mr Boswell's biographical arts. Sometimes we sat at our accustomed fireside, and sometimes we sauntered about the courts and alleys off Fleet Street and the Strand, where Johnson himself had so often roamed in the night and where, as Mr Boswell said, we might yet accompany him in his earliest solitude.

For we had to go back, said he, to the time when Johnson first arrived in the great city: a solitary, friendless young man of twenty-seven years, without profession and without resource, a mere schoolmaster from the provinces, whose literary powers lay undiscovered and unsuspected. 'To be sure,' said Mr Boswell, 'he was a married man; and yet' – here with great emphasis – 'he was not a man who had found his Muse. I mean, Sir,' he added with his quick bright candid glance, 'he had not found the English Language which he loved.'

I was to recall too, he continued, that Johnson was a fearsome figure to behold. Tall, bony, scarred by scrofula on his neck, half blind in one eye, and subject to convulsive twitchings of his face, he was divorced from all the elegant departments of life. The schoolchildren mocked him behind his back, the ladies retreated twittering behind their fans, the very dogs barked at him in the street. (Here the *hum* sounded briefly.) Johnson's was a life *radically miserable*, and subject to a religious melancholy that no human tenderness had relieved. The hand had not reached him, the touch of nature had not found him, that might release him into life.

I was surprised by Mr Boswell's strength of feeling at this juncture, and how his voice echoed round a darkened courtyard off Fetter Lane. A passing nightwatchman raised his lantern at us, and the bars of light and shadow swung across us like a dungeon grid in Newgate. We saluted the old man with his cudgel, and pursued our way in gloomy silence towards Fleet Ditch.

But you cannot mean, I asked at length, that it was the friendship of a cat which saved the great Johnson for the world? The speculative *hum* again sounded at my side, followed by something like a sigh. 'Ah,' said Mr Boswell after a long interval, 'it was fair Esther *and* the cat. I have read his private memorial on the matter, and you perhaps might peruse his *Dictionary*. For that, after all, is the truest memorial of all.' But no more did he say that night, and for many nights after he drank his porter and talked of other things.

I had learnt from Mr Boswell that in matters of the heart, a merest hint might contain a whole history; a *precedent* worthy of all Blackstone's *Laws*. Accordingly I rummaged through the great leather folio of Dr Johnson's *English Dictionary*, and was again astounded by the felicity of his definitions, the scope of his learning and the charm of his illustrations. 'Lexicographer', he records in a famous entry: 'a writer of dictionaries, a harmless drudge, that busies himself in tracing the original, and detailing the signification of words.'

Yet I found little to my biographical purpose, except a growing sense of wonder that the task had been achieved at all. Indeed, it was a monument of intellect, a survey of the expressive world entire! How Johnson ever assembled that great compendium in his attic at Gough Square, forty thousand words brought sparkling into the light new-minted, struck me as both a miracle and a mystery renewed. It was the labour of five long and lonely years. And the cant phrase echoed in my mind, it was a labour of love.

Of course, in my probings and peerings, I turned upon the

word 'cat'. Johnson records it with noble gravity, 'a domestick animal that catches mice, commonly reckoned of the leonine species'. So a creature with the heart of a lion. And he adds an illustration from the naturalist Peach: 'A cat, as she beholds the light, draws the ball of her eye small and long, being covered over with a green lense; and she dilates it at pleasure.'

'You must comprehend', said Mr Boswell suddenly one night, 'that Esther was blind.' It was a wintry evening, and the rain beat against the casements of the Mitre and rattled the panes in their lead. Outside the dung-cart men swore and sang with uncommon energy. We trembled upon the lip of a third bottle, and Mr Boswell's buckles winked and shone as he stretched his legs towards the fire. 'It was her blindness that let her see him; and let her hear him. And she it was that first touched the spring.'

He pulled from his waistcoat a tiny pocket book, with a silver clasp. 'These are his own memorials, from his earliest days in London. They record his first lodgings, up one pair of stairs, near Covent Garden, indeed an incommodious address. It was the house of one Norris, a fellow country man, a Lichfield man.' Then he read gravely, as one who reads the Scriptures. 'Norris the staymaker – fair Esther with the cat – a guinea at the stairs – Esther died.' He closed the little book, and sat gazing at me with the *hum* much in evidence, his eye very bright and inquisitive. 'Fair Esther with the cat, you see? And she died. But the cat,' and here he shook his head with a kind of impatience, 'the cat did not die, you comprehend?'

I did not see, I did not comprehend, and for a while there was a long silence between us, and Shakespeare's phrase came to me: 'like the poor cat i' the adage.' At length I observed to Mr Boswell that this matter of Esther and the cat was not in his great *Life of Johnson*, and I wondered at the omission. He laughed, and replied that there was much in any Life that was omitted, and there indeed lay a curious *common-law* of biographical truth. 'What we do not know, we may yet feel; what we leave in shadow, may one day shine out upon us yet. I was uneasy at my suspicions, I did not think them worthy of him. But come now, you must judge for yourself.'

Then he told all he guessed of that strange history. He told me how Johnson in his loneliness had conceived a great tenderness for fair Esther; and how she, being blind, had not feared to caress and console him. She did not *see* the poor monster, she *heard* only the marvellous man. It was with her that his wondrous powers of speech, his marvellous generosities of language, were first unfolded and displayed. It was from this time that his essays, his poetry, began to pour forth upon the press. 'He was, Sir, like a man released from his dungeon, a man who has found himself in the light, and who begins to walk abroad with his natural gait, and see the world around him, and find it answerable to his words and thoughts.'

And then came Esther's death from a fever, swift as an arrow from heaven, and the darkness closed upon him again. He buried her in the little graveyard of St John's Clerkenwell, hard by Albion Place, where you may find it still, beneath a flowering almond tree. And so he was left with nothing but her little cat, the sole companion and confidante of all those precious hours, who still touched his breast and gazed upon him in the dark with pleasure. 'And what that cat meant to him,' said Mr Boswell in a low voice, 'who can tell? Perhaps only the others that came after it.'

It was, to be sure, a strange history, and I have told it with some haste and confusion, for on that night the third bottle was well upon us, and if I mistake not, a fourth too. Mr Boswell was talking like a man who dreams, and nodding at his wig, as if to say, 'You hear me Sir, you hear me all the while.'

We ventured out at last into the street. He took my arm, and we progressed with solemn ceremony down towards old St Paul's, and then with a sudden fanciful digression into the shadows of Bolt Court. 'Quite like old times,' he hummed, leading the way forward over the accumulated rubbish of the day. We reached Gough Square, and stood respectfully upon the gleaming cobbles, gazing up. The windows of Johnson's erstwhile attic were quite dark.

But is this story never to be told? I inquired of Mr Boswell through the wind and rain. Is Esther to have no monument? 'She has it, far better than I could contrive, far better than any wild biographical surmise of mine. She has it in his great *Dictionary*. Every word brought into the light is her monument. Every word is the great Johnson's act of love for her, shining in the dark.' We stood steadily for a moment in this solemn reflection and the wind whipped and pawed at our coat-tails.

I could not forbear one further question of the wise biographer. 'And the cat, Sir, what of the cat?' Then Mr Boswell said the most curious thing of all. 'If I know anything of the English race, Sir, and their infinite respect for their literary authors, a cat, Sir, a very fine cat indeed will have a monument in bronze, a statuette in bronze, eternally eating oysters upon this very place.' Then he hummed, a very long Scotch hum, that seemed to spread far into the London night. 'But, Sir, it will not be the right cat, all the same.'

*

*A bronze statue of Samuel Johnson's cat Hodge was erected in Gough Square in 1997.*

# Acknowledgements

## I A Romantic Premonition

Thomas Chatterton: first published in *Cornhill Magazine*, 1970

## II Lost in France

Monsieur Nadar: first published in *The Times*, 1974
Gautier in London: first published in *The Times*, 14 June 1975
Poor Pierrot: first published in *The Times*, 10 January 1976
Inside the Tower: first transmitted on BBC Radio Three,
    31 October 1977

## III Five Gothic Shadows

The Singular Affair of the Reverend Mr Barham: first published
    in *The Times*, 22 December 1978
The Reverend Maturin and Mr Melmoth: first published in *The
    Times*, 7 February 1981
M. R. James and Others: first published in *The Times*, 1974
John Stuart Mill: first published in *The Times*, 28 July 1979
Lord Lisle and the Tudor Nixon Tapes: first published in
    *Harper's* magazine, New York, August 1982

## IV A Philosophical Love Story

The Feminist and the Philosopher: a condensed version first
    published as Introduction to *A Short Residence in Sweden,
    Norway and Denmark/Memoirs of the Author of 'The Rights of
    Woman'*, Penguin Books, 1987. This expanded version was
    translated into Dutch and published as *De feministe en de
    filosoof*, Contact, 1988.

## V Shelley's Ghost

Scrope's Last Throw: first published in *Harper's* magazine, New York, April 1977

To the Tempest Given: recorded on 27–28 August 1992 and first broadcast on BBC Radio Four on 10 September 1992


## VI Escapes to Paris

Scott and Zelda: One Last Trip: first published in *The Times*, 22 March 1980 (with acknowledgement to Frances Scott Fitzgerald Smith, Mary Hemingway and Charles Scribner's Sons for quotations from copyright material, and thanks to Jean Preston, Curator of Manuscripts, Princeton University Library

A Summer with the Novelist: taken from a selection of pieces first published in the *Daily Telegraph* during summer 1994

Voltaire's Grin: first published in *New York Review of Books*, 30 November 1995


## VII Homage to the Godfather

Boswell's Bicentenary: first published in *The Times*, 11 May 1991

Boswell Among the Tulips: first published in *Granta* (1992) Extracts from Boswell's journal are reprinted by kind permission of Edinburgh University Press

Dr Johnson's First Cat: first broadcast on BBC Radio Four, Book at Bedtime, March 1999

# Index

# INDEX

Bisson *frères*, 58
Blackwood, Algernon, 164
*Blackwood's*, 140, 145
Blake, William, 200
Blanche, Emile, 92, 100, 118–19,
121–2, 127
Blanche, Esprit, 100
Blinshall, James, 396, 397
Blood, Fanny, 210, 221–3, 224
Blunt, W.S., 9
Boissard (painter), 104–5
Bolden, Sarah, 143–4
Boleyn, Anne, 184, 185, 187, 191
Bond, Fanny (*née* Barham), 142–3,
145, 148
Bosnian crisis, 337
Boswell, Charles, (son of JB), 377,
390, 391
Boswell, James: in Amsterdam, 394,
395–7; as biographer, 367–8,
369–71, 393; dress, 379, 381, 386,
399; relationship with Dutch ladies,
380–4, 385–95, 397–401;
education, 377, 381, 391–2; at the
Hague, 385–6; in Holland, 368,
377–401; Inviolable Plan, 380; visit
to Voltaire, 358; at Zuylen, 397–8,
399, 400
Boswell, Margaret, 369, 375
Boyd, William, 338
Breton, André, 157
Briggs, Julia, 372
Brissot, Jean-Pierre, 258
Bristol: Chatterton in, 10–12, 28–9,
38; Coleridge and Southey in, 38;
St Mary Redcliff church, 11,
13–14, 16, 19, 29–30
Brown, Robert, 379, 397
Brown, Thomas, 262
Browne, Brockden, 327
Browning, Oscar, 165
Brummell, Beau, 280
Brunel, Marc Isambard, 69
Brussels Exhibition (1856), 63
Buffon, Comte de, 339
Bunyan, John, 237
Burke, Edmund, 214, 259
Burnet, Timothy, 277, 279
Burney, Charles, 370
Burney, Fanny, 45
Bute, John Stuart, 3rd Earl of, 31
Byatt, A.S., 376

Byrne, Muriel St Clare, 185–6, 190,
192–3
Byron, Allegra, 288
Byron, George Gordon, Lord:
bankers, 273; Drury Lane Theatre
Committee, 154; Fitzgerald on,
328; in Greece, 236; manuscripts,
275–6; publisher, 274; royalties
scheme, 155; friendship with
Scrope Davies, 271–2, 275–81;
Shelley's visit, 310; works, 151

Cairns, David, 374
Calais, 183–4, 185, 186–7, 190–1
Calas, Jean, 358–9
Calas, Marc-Antoine, 360–1
Calderon de la Barca, Pedro, 292
Cambridge: Churchill College, 367;
King's College, 161–3, 165–7, 171
Cameron, Julia Margaret, 58
Camus, Albert, 336–7, 346
Canterbury, Barham in, 139–40, 147
Canynges, William, 13–14, 20
Carlyle, Thomas, 173, 175, 178, 179,
371, 374
Carne, Marcel, 86
Cary, Thomas, 15, 35, 37
Casa Magni, 283, 284–93, 296–7,
299–300, 302, 306, 308–9
Catcott, Alexander, 38–9, 45
Catcott, George, 19, 21–2, 25, 35–7
cats, 168–9, 368, 403–8
Champfleury (Jules Fleury-Husson),
60, 63, 81, 87
Channel Tunnel, 69, 73
*Charivari*, 61
Châtelet, Marquise du, 320, 351–5
Chatterton, Thomas: appearance,
38–9, 46; apprenticeship, 19, 23,
24–5; birth, 10; in Bristol, 21–5,
29; character, 11–12, 34–5;
childhood, 11–14; death, 5, 25–6,
45–6; drug taking, 5, 25, 40, 45;
education, 15–16, 17–18, 32;
father, 11; friends, 18, 34–5;
letters, 34, 39, 42–4; in London,
25–6, 42–8; reading, 32–3;
reputation, 6–10, 26–34; Rowley,
14–17, 19, 29, 35, 38–9, 43–4,
48–50; venereal disease, 45; works,
5–6, 26; writing, 19–25; 'Ælla',
21, 25, 30–1; 'African Eclogues',

*412*